The Language of
Business Communication

The Language of Business Communication

M. Lily Kretchman
Co-ordinator, Business Studies
Peel Board of Education

Dorinne L. Wagner
Vice-Principal
West Credit Secondary School

Peter J. Lowens
Department of English
J.A. Turner Secondary School

John Wiley & Sons

Toronto   New York   Chichester   Brisbane   Singapore

Copyright © 1988 by John Wiley & Sons Canada Limited.
All rights reserved.

No part of this publication may be reproduced by any means, stored in a retrieval system, or transmitted in any form or by any means, electronic, mechanical, photocopying, recording or otherwise, without the prior written permission of the publisher.

Care has been taken to trace ownership of copyright material contained in this text. The publisher will gladly receive any information that will enable them to rectify any reference or credit line in subsequent editions.

Canadian Cataloguing in Publication Data

Kretchman, M. Lily, 1932-
    The language of business communication

Includes index.
ISBN 0-471-79677-8

1. Communication in management. 2. English language - Business English. I. Wagner, Dorinne, 1948-   . II. Lowens, Peter, 1950-   . III. Title.

HF5718.K74 1987   651.7   C87-094678-1

ILLUSTRATION: Peter Grau
DESIGN: Brant Cowie/Artplus Limited
TYPE OUTPUT: Tony Gordon Limited

Printed and bound in Canada by John Deyell Company
10 9 8 7 6 5 4 3 2

Dedication

For my husband, Alex, and my daughters, Julie, and Janice - L.K.
For my husband, George - D.W.
For my wife, Allison, and in memory of my mother - P.L.

Acknowledgements

We are very grateful to Susan Howlett, for her commitment to this project and her help in bringing it to completion, and to Lenore Wilson, for her patience and time in providing photographs.

In addition, we would like to thank the following reviewers who helped evaluate this book:

Roy Ingram, Bayside Secondary School
Mary Olscamp, Holland College
Margaret Procter, Erindale College
Shelley Smith, TV Ontario
Lois Tarnai, Carleton Board of Education

We acknowledge with gratitude the teachers and students of J.A. Turner Secondary School and Central Peel Secondary School for testing the material in this textbook in the classroom.

Table of Contents

PART ONE: COMMUNICATION IN SCHOOL AND EVERYDAY LIFE

Chapter 1 Communication *3*

Introduction 5; The Communication Process 6; Precision in Communication 11; Communication and Self-Awareness 16; Kinds of Communication 19; Barriers to Communication 22; Safeguards for Effective Communication 23; Chapter Summary 24; Making It Work 25.

Chapter 2 Listening *27*

Introduction 29; Hearing and Listening 29; The Process of Listening 30; Listening and Good Communication 30; Barriers to Effective Listening 32; Improving Your Listening 36; Levels of Listening 40; Chapter Summary 44; Making It Work 46.

Chapter 3 Teamwork and Group Interaction *49*

Introduction 51; Effective Group Interaction 52; The Members of a Group 55; Primary Roles of Group Members 56; Positive and Negative Roles of Group Members 59; Chapter Summary 62; Making It Work 62.

Chapter 4 Speaking *65*

Introduction 67; Introductions 67; Conversations 71; Instructions/Directions 73; Speaking Before A Group 74; Characteristics of Effective Speaking 79; Chapter Summary 84; Making It Work 85.

Chapter 5 Reading and Viewing *89*

Introduction 91; Reading Effectively 91; Reading Rate 92; Reading Styles 93; Steps to Effective Reading 97; Viewing Effectively 100; Discriminating Viewing 101; Steps to Effective Viewing 104; Making a Summary 105; Chapter Summary 107; Making It Work 108.

Chapter 6 Writing: The Prewriting and Drafting Stages *111*

Introduction 113; Writing and Speaking 113; The Writing Process 116; Prewriting 116; Drafting 120; Chapter Summary 121; Making It Work 121.

Chapter 7 Writing: Editing and Publication *125*

Introduction 127; Editing 127; Language and Writing Units 128; Words 128; Sentences 133; Paragraphs 139; Making Changes to Your Draft 141; Publication 142; Chapter Summary 144; Making It Work 144.

PART TWO: COMMUNICATION IN BUSINESS

Chapter 8 Business Communication *151*

Introduction 154; Problem Solving 154; Lines of Communication 158; Levels of Business Communication 160; Forms of Business Communication 163; Barriers to Effective Business Communication 165; Safeguards for Effective Business Communication 166; Chapter Summary 168; Making It Work 169.

Chapter 9 Speaking and Listening in Business *173*

Introduction 176; As a Prospective Employee 176; As an Employee 181; As a Peer 191; As a Supervisor 192; Chapter Summary 194; Making It Work 195.

Chapter 10 Speaking Skills in Making Presentations *199*

Introduction 201; Types of Presentations 201; Planning before the Research 205; Researching the Topic 206; Preparing the Outline 210; Audio and Visual Aids 213; Preparing a Model 215; Delivery Techniques 216; Chapter Summary 217; Making It Work 217.

Chapter 11 Reading and Viewing in the Workplace *221*

Introduction 223; Researching a Business or Industry 223; Becoming an Assertive Reader or Viewer 229; Day-to Day Reading in Business 230; Chapter Summary 234; Making It Work 234.

Chapter 12 Writing Business Documents *237*

Introduction 240; Characteristics of Effective Writing 240; Information Letters and Memos 247; Favourable Letters and Memos 252; Unfavourable Letters and Memos 254; Persuasive Letters and Memos 256; News Releases 258; Chapter Summary 261; Making It Work 262.

Chapter 13 Business Report and Technical Writing *265*

Introduction 266; Styles and Types of Reports 267; Steps in Writing a Report 268; Visual Aids 273; Parts of a Report 278; Chapter Summary 284; Making It Work 285.

PART THREE: SUCCESS IN BUSINESS AND INDUSTRY

Chapter 14 Teamwork in Business and Industry *291*

Introduction 293; Productive Team Members 294; Non-Productive Team Members 296; Business Work Groups 299; Effective Teamwork in Business and Industry 301; Kinds of Business Meetings 302; Robert's Rules of Order 305; How to Make a Meeting a Success 306; Chapter Summary 310; Making It Work 312.

Chapter 15 Job Search *315*

Introduction 317; Job Search 318; Your Résumé 322; Letters of Application 328; The Interview 330; Starting out at Your Job 336; Job Performance Evaluation 336; Changing Jobs 337; Chapter Summary 338; Making It Work 339.

Appendix A English Usage *343*

Appendix B Letter and Memorandum Formats *359*

Appendix C Business Forms *371*

Appendix D Glossary *377*

Index *383*

To the Student

Times have changed. Once, the disciplines of business studies and English were quite distinct. Now, you have an opportunity to study these two areas at the same time in a Business English course. We believe you will enjoy this process.

The Language of Business Communication will outline the skills of clear thinking, problem solving, and, above all, effective communication. You will learn to relate these skills to your daily life at home, at school, and in the business world. You will learn to develop your listening and speaking skills. You will find out how to read effectively, whether it be a newspaper for information, a novel for inspiration, or a business form you encounter at work. You will discover how teamwork and group dynamics can help you solve problems in daily life as well as on the job. You will learn about the writing process, and how it will help you in a wide range of situations that you will meet now at school and later in the workplace.

The Language of Business Communication has been written with you, the student, in mind. We have attempted to show you the connections between the skills you learn now in the classroom and the skills you will need later in the workplace. By acquiring these skills now, you will find the world of work a more familiar place. Good luck, now, and in the future!

The Authors

Text Features

- *The Language of Business Communication* is structured around three parts. It teaches communication skills first through familiar situations at home and at school, then in the workplace, and then brings these situations together by discussing teamwork on the job and skills needed to enter the world of work.

- *Chapter Goals:* This section states the key ideas and concepts that a student will know about after studying each chapter.

- *Vocabulary Building:* Important words that will be introduced in each chapter are highlighted here. If they are unfamiliar, students may wish to take a moment to look them up in the glossary.

- *Viewpoints:* The scene is set in each chapter with a dialogue which introduces the communication skills dealt with in the chapter from the viewpoints of young people. Questions that follow can be answered by students in a group, and can lead to discussion of the key concepts of the chapter. Students may want to answer these questions again when they have absorbed the content of the chapter to see how their answers have changed.

- *Applications:* These follow each section of text and give students the chance to practise the skills discussed. To help in working through them, a short summary or checklist appears in the margin with points to remember when answering the questions.

- *Chapter Summary:* These help students review and remember material covered in each chapter.

- *Making It Work:* These activities come at the end of each chapter. They enable students to apply the skills they have learned to the business world. Students will answer these questions by researching their business community, by meeting the people who use business skills on a daily basis, and by talking with these people about the way their skills have helped them become successful. In this way, each piece of theory is related to actual business or industry situations.

    The last part of *Making It Work* often consists of case studies. These provide opportunities to analyze situations and apply to them the principles of effective communication. Through analyzing real-life situations in which these principles apply, students are better prepared to meet a variety of on-the-job challenges.

- Vocabulary which appears in the *Vocabulary Building* section and in the *Glossary* is boldfaced when it first appears in the text. It is defined by a paraphrase the first time it is used.

- *Appendices:* Three appendices at the end of the book provide information on English usage, the format of business letters, and business forms.

PART · ONE

COMMUNICATION IN SCHOOL AND EVERYDAY LIFE

Chapter 1   Communication
Chapter 2   Listening
Chapter 3   Teamwork and Group Interaction
Chapter 4   Speaking
Chapter 5   Reading and Viewing
Chapter 6   Writing: The Prewriting and Drafting Stages
Chapter 7   Writing: Editing and Publication

CHAPTER 1

Communication

GOALS

At the end of this chapter you should be able to
1. *identify the basic parts of the communication process;*
2. *list the factors that affect communication;*
3. *recognize the importance of effective communication; and*
4. *apply the rules of effective communication.*

VOCABULARY BUILDING

message
sender
medium
receiver
communication
communication environment
feedback
ambiguity
encode
decode
denotation
connotation
empathy
verbal communication

VIEWPOINTS

Communication makes interaction with other people possible. We learn from one another, we co-operate with one another, and we share our thoughts and feelings with one another. We spend much of our time communicating, yet we still need to acquire the skills to make our communication more effective.

In the dialogue that follows, Jorg, one of the speakers, is unsure of how to communicate the feelings and information he wants someone else to understand. Try to put yourself in his position as you read it.

Jorg and his older sister Erica are sitting down to breakfast. Jorg appears preoccupied.

ERICA: Well, you must be happy. After today you're into Spring Break. I've got to wait until summer for a holiday.

JORG: I guess today is the last day.

ERICA: You certainly don't seem excited about it.

JORG: I've got things on my mind.

ERICA: A problem?

JORG: Maybe. I guess it wouldn't be for some people, but for me it is.

ERICA: What is?

JORG: I've got to tell Mr. Mercer tonight that I'm not going to be working for him after next week because I've taken a job at Deluxe Pizza.

ERICA: How long have you worked at Mr. Mercer's cycle shop — two years?

JORG: Almost two and a half.

ERICA: I know you've learned a lot.

JORG: Yes, and Mr. Mercer has been really nice to me and fair. I don't want him to think that I don't appreciate what he's done for me.

ERICA: So you need to let him know how you feel about leaving. Do you think it might help if I pretend to be Mr. Mercer?

JORG: Maybe.

ERICA: Okay, let's try. What do you want to tell me?

JORG: That I'm quitting my job.

ERICA: (taking role of Mr. Mercer) I'm sorry to lose you, Jorg. You have been a good worker and I've enjoyed your company.

JORG: I've enjoyed working here too and you've taught me a lot.

ERICA: Do you have another job you're going to?

JORG: Yes, I'm going to be working at Deluxe Pizza, taking orders and delivering pizzas. In the spring I'll be working in the kitchen too.

ERICA: That sounds like good experience. What made you decide to change jobs?

JORG: I plan to go to college next fall and I need to save as much money as possible. At Deluxe Pizza I can work more hours. Also if they like me I'll be able to transfer to the branch store close to the college next year.

ERICA: Well, I can see why you want to make the change. When do you plan to leave here?

JORG: My new job starts in two weeks, so if it's all right with you, a week this Saturday will be my last day.

ERICA: That's fine, Jorg. I hope you enjoy your new job. (back to being herself) What do you think? Is it still going to be difficult?

JORG: I guess not too bad. I just wasn't sure what I should say.

ERICA: Tell me tonight how you make out.

QUESTIONS

1. Why do you think Jorg was worried about talking to Mr. Mercer?
2. Erica thought that putting herself in the position of Mr. Mercer would help Jorg. Do you agree? What other method would you have used in the situation?
3. Would writing a letter of resignation be a better way to handle the problem? Explain your answer.

Figure 1-1
We are involved in communication every day, when we read, write, and speak.

INTRODUCTION

Communication is the exchange of information, ideas, or feelings among people. It takes place when you are giving the answer to a math problem, as the student on the right in Figure 1-1 is doing. Communication also takes place when you are suggesting ideas for raising money for charity, or telling a friend how you feel about something distressing you heard on the news.

Sometimes, like Jorg in the section *Viewpoints*, you may have something to communicate but you are unsure how best to do it. You may have mixed feelings and may be confused as to how to express them. Or you may be concerned about how the other person will react to what you have to say. Communication may seem difficult under these circumstances. At times communication may lead to misunderstanding instead of understanding. By practising the skills you will learn in this book, it should be possible for you to increase understanding in your communication.

Communication is not limited to speech. We also communicate through letters, newspaper articles, books, movies, plays, TV, radio, and by the expressions on our faces, shrugs of our shoulders, nods, or gestures. Figure 1-2 illustrates some specialized forms of communication that you may have encountered before. Can you think of other forms? You will be learning about several forms of communication later on in this chapter and in other chapters of this book.

First let us examine the mechanics of communication. What are the parts of the communication process and what is involved when we communicate?

COMMUNICATION

Figure 1-2
Various forms of communication: The semiphore, Morse code, and hand signs all spell the word "language."

THE COMMUNICATION PROCESS

In a science lab you may dissect a preserved animal. In so doing, you will be able to see the different parts that enable the animal to function. Likewise, by dissecting the process of communication, you can examine its parts and learn how they work together to make communication possible.

In order to communicate, you need to know the four parts of the process: (1) a **message**, or what is communicated, (2) a **sender**, or the person who wishes to send the message, (3) a **medium**, or the way in which the message is sent, and (4) a **receiver**, or the person to whom the message is sent.

Will the communication process be complete with these four parts? If the receiver does not hear the message because someone is speaking at the same time as the sender, will communication have taken place? The answer is no. The sender will have failed to communicate the message because the receiver is not able to hear it.

There is another important point to consider. Suppose the sender uses the English language for the message, but the receiver does not understand English. The sender will have failed to communicate the message too. For communication to take place, the message must be received, interpreted, and recreated in the mind of the receiver. That is, the receiver's mind must be able to process the message.

The word **communication** may then be defined as the act of sending a message that is received and processed by the receiver.

What then is *effective communication*? Based on our definition of communication, we may say that it is the act of sending a clear message that is received and fully understood by the receiver.

Sometimes messages are not received because there are distractions that prevent the receiver from hearing or concentrating. The **communication environment**, that is, the physical space or conditions

PART ONE: COMMUNICATION IN SCHOOL AND EVERYDAY LIFE

through which the message is sent, has interfered with the reception of the message. Loud or sudden noises, the appearance of another person, or an uncomfortable air temperature are a few examples of environmental interference.

We can add one more part to the communication process. The receiver must let the sender know that the message has been heard and is understood. The receiver's confirmation is called **feedback**.

Figure 1-3 shows the parts of the communication process we have covered so far.

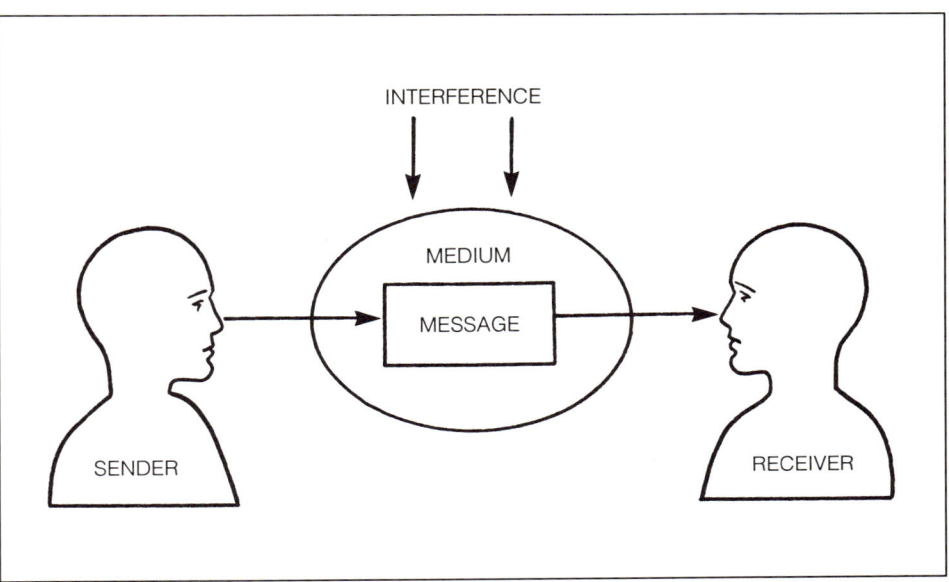

Figure 1-3
The Communication Process

Although communication may seem simple, you need to be skilful in each part of the process if you wish to communicate well.

The Sender

The sender should have a clear idea of what is to be communicated, otherwise the message will be vague and not understandable.

It is also important that the sender uses words that will convey the intended meaning. The level of language should be tuned to the receiver. Using words which are unfamiliar to the receiver will greatly reduce understanding. A good working vocabulary will help to make this task easier.

Selecting the medium of communication will be the decision of the sender. Can the message be best handled by a meeting, memo, letter, or telephone call? If a lot of data are contained in the message, spoken language may not be the most efficient medium. A chart may be a better way to communicate the information. Selecting the appropriate medium for your message determines whether or not it is positively received. If a job advertisement states that applicants should reply in writing and you telephone instead, your application may be rejected.

COMMUNICATION

Figure 1-4 *Steps to Effective Communication*

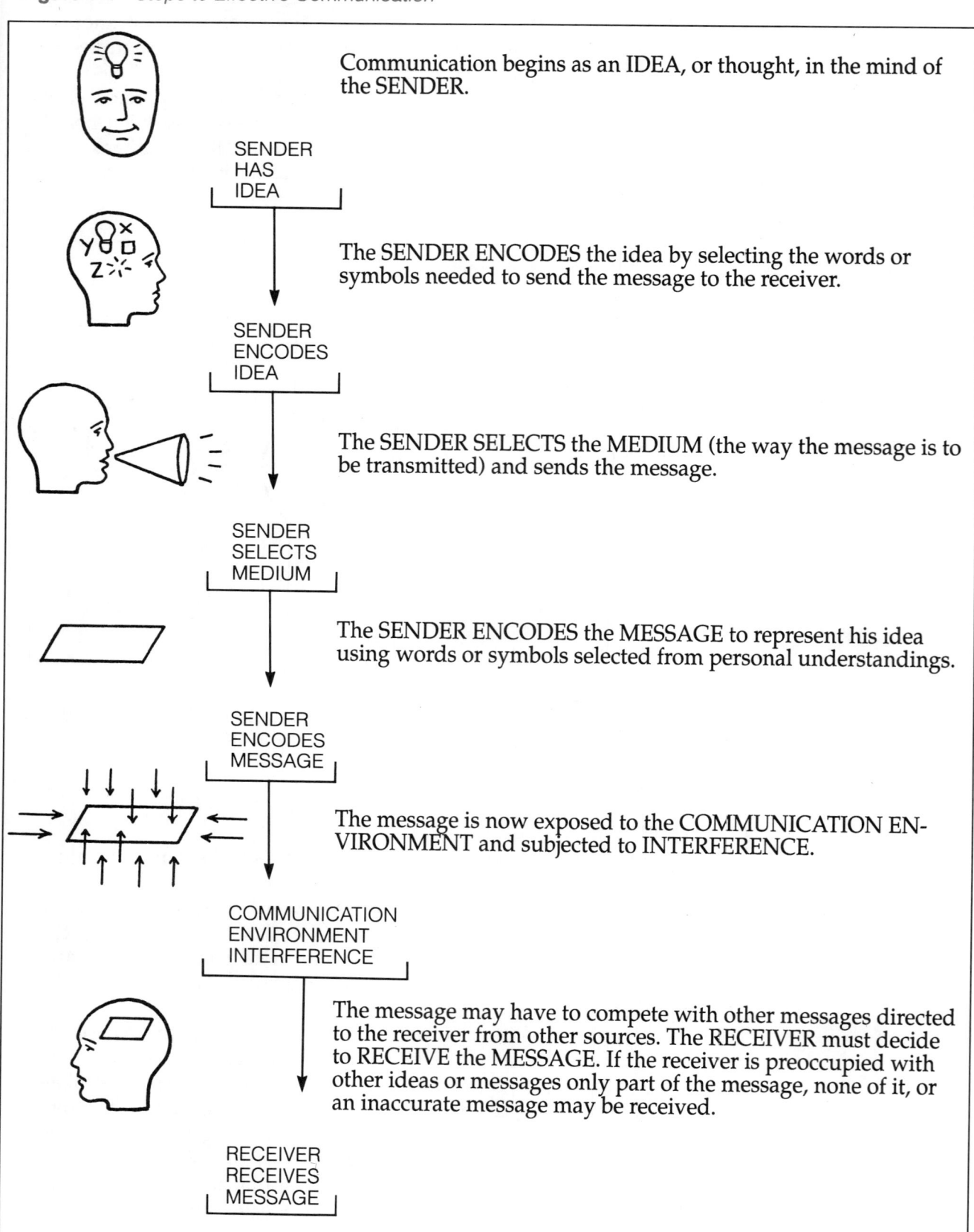

PART ONE: COMMUNICATION IN SCHOOL AND EVERYDAY LIFE

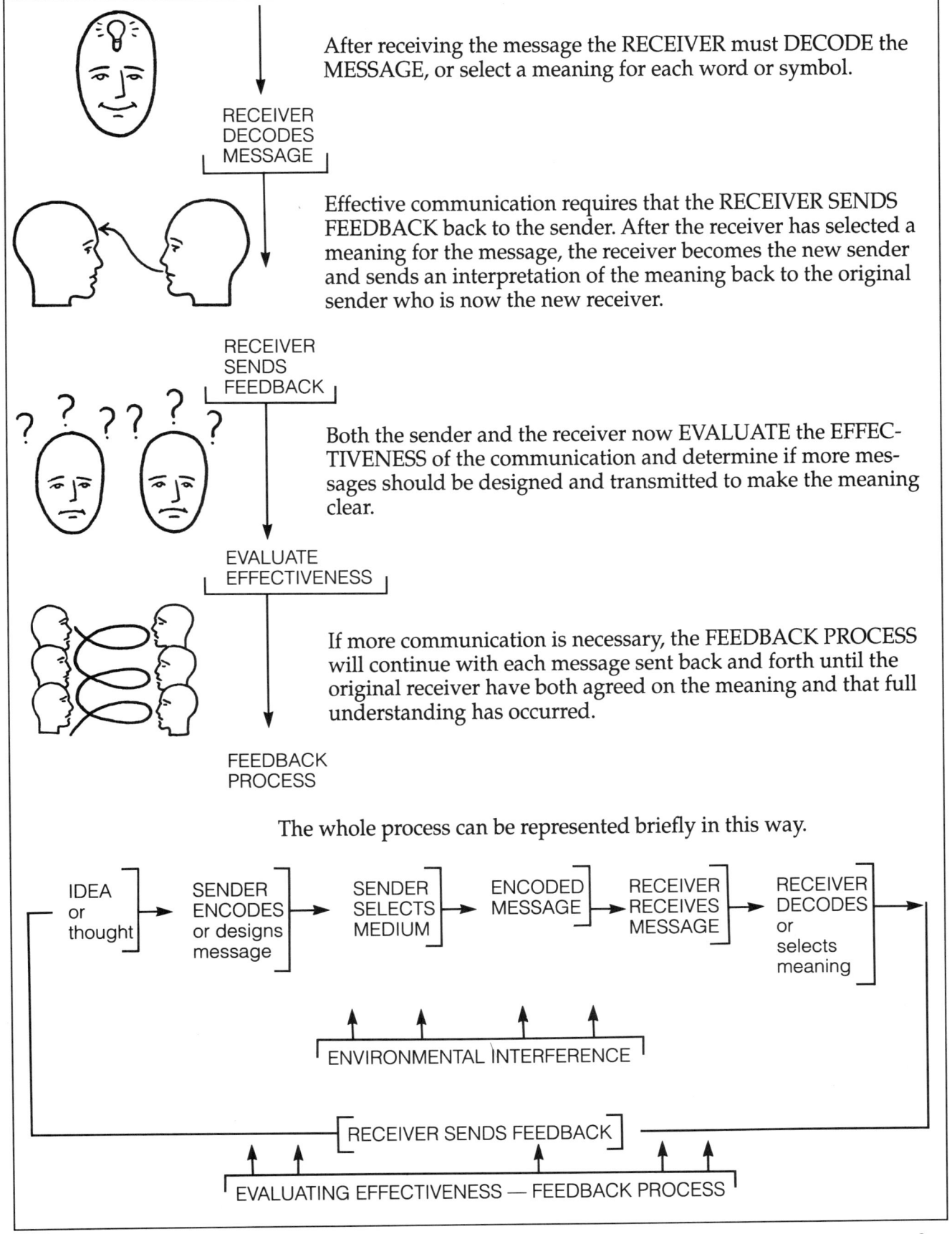

The Message

The message can be information, ideas, or feelings. Usually the messages you send contain elements of information or ideas in combination with elements of your feelings about the subject.

To send a *clear* message, the language used must be precise. Any **ambiguity**, or lack of clarity, could result in misunderstanding. Can you think of any recent mix-ups in which you or another person failed to give a clear message? Often people arrange to meet in busy locations but do not find each other right away because they are waiting at different entrances, or one is inside and the other is outside the building. The next time they arrange to meet, they will make the message clear and precise.

The process of transforming, or changing, your thoughts into appropriate words is called **encoding**. The level of language must be selected as the message is encoded. If the person who is receiving the message is a child, it will be necessary to use words that the child can understand. If the person is an employer, the words may include technical terms understood by both of you. If the person is a close friend, you may use a few slang terms that are mutually acceptable and understood.

The encoded message is then **decoded** by the receiver, that is, transformed from the words received into thoughts.

The Receiver

The receiver's role in communication is first to select the message to listen to, in the event that more than one person is speaking, then to listen carefully to the selected message. An inattentive listener will not receive a full or accurate message from the sender.

The receiver will then decode the message, interpreting its meaning. Next, the receiver will confirm that the message has been received and indicate if it has been understood. The receiver's reaction to the message is termed "feedback." If the feedback indicates that the receiver has understood the sender's message, the sender may proceed with the communication, or end it if all the information has been relayed. If the receiver stares blankly, frowns, or in some other manner lets the sender know the message is not understandable, then it will be necessary for the sender to adjust the message. The sender must be able to interpret the feedback accurately in order to complete the communication process.

In *Viewpoints*, Erica paraphrases Jorg's words when she asks, "A problem?" Her feedback indicates that she is listening, but that she needs more information to understand. Gradually, with the feedback she provides, she draws Jorg out, getting him to talk about what is on his mind.

Figure 1-4 summarizes the steps that are followed for effective communication.

The sender selects
1. *the receiver*
2. *the medium*
3. *the appropriate level of language*
4. *the organization of information*
5. *the encoding*
6. *the environment through which the message will travel.*

The receiver selects
1. *the message to receive*
2. *meanings to apply to the words in the message*
3. *the feedback to give to the sender.*

APPLICATIONS

1. In class, identify the different media that could be used to apply for a job and to resign from one.
2. Will the medium chosen by the sender usually suit the receiver? Discuss.
3. Find a photograph in the newspaper or in a magazine of a number of people in conversation. Try to identify what each person is communicating by means of expression and posture.
4. Draw your own model of the communication process, adding any details that you think will help to explain it.

PRECISION IN COMMUNICATION

Organizing Ideas and Information

We do not usually blurt out whatever comes into our mind. To some degree, we organize our thoughts before we speak. A person listening to you would become very confused if you should give instructions or directions without organizing them into a logical pattern. Communicating in an organized manner requires some forethought, or planning, but it results in better understanding.

Too Many Links in the Chain

Messages invariably become distorted when they are passed on by several people. All of the people involved apply their own meanings to the words of the message and pass the message along with a slightly different interpretation. At each link in the chain the message may be interfered with and information may be lost.

Have you ever played the game "Telephone" or "Gossip"? The message at the end of the chain often bears little resemblance to the message given to the first person in the chain. Figure 1-5 illustrates how a message can be distorted.

Encoding and Decoding

In encoding a message, it is important for the sender to select words that most accurately convey the meaning intended. In decoding the message, it is the receiver's job to get as close as possible to the sender's intended message. The more skilled a sender and receiver are at encoding and decoding, the more precise and effective their communication.

Sometimes you may have trouble finding appropriate words to express your ideas precisely. Building a good working vocabulary will reduce the number of times this will happen.

COMMUNICATION

Figure 1-5
During the First World War, messages were passed from one soldier to another, much in the way they are when people play "Gossip." It is said that on one occasion, the message "Send reinforcements — we're going to advance" became "Send three or four cents — we're going to a dance."

Denotation and Connotation

Precision in communication is achieved by choosing the words that best express your thoughts. At the same time you should make sure that your listener shares the same meanings of those words.

Words often have more than one meaning as shown in Figure 1-6. They have **denotations**, or dictionary meanings, and **connotations**, or several shades of meaning, which are more emotional or implied. For example, the word "bat" denotes a quadruped with a mouse-shaped body and membranous wings that flies at night. However, for some people a bat connotes an animal associated with evil and witches. Confusion can easily result if the sender and receiver attach different meanings to the words used. Feedback is one way of making sure your meaning has been understood.

Workers in different professions often have connotations for words that apply to their particular line of work as you can see in Figure 1-7. Musicians, athletes, computer technologists, doctors, and dentists, for example, have special meanings for certain words. In the dictionary the word "chip" is defined as a splinter or broken-off fragment. For someone in the computer industry, the meaning is quite different. Among musicians the word "patch" refers to a choice of electronically produced sound rather than to a piece of cloth applied to a hole in a garment. Specialized dictionaries for many professions are available. They contain the technical terms and connotations familiar to people in those professions. Connotations that become recognized by wider areas of society may eventually find their way into the standard dictionaries.

Figure 1-6
Sometimes, the different meanings that sender and receiver attach to words can have startling results.

For effective communication
1. *organize your ideas*
2. *communicate directly with the intended receiver*
3. *choose the most appropriate word.*

People in English-speaking countries around the world attach different meanings to certain words. George Bernard Shaw, a famous British writer, once said that the Americans and the British were two great peoples divided only by their common language. Canadians too differ from both the Americans and the British in their use of some words. In Britain the "hood" and "trunk" of a car are the "bonnet" and "boot". We walk on the "sidewalk" whereas the British walk on "pavement" and we take an "elevator" while the British take a "lift". If a Canadian talks of wanting a "chesterfield", an American is likely to think of a "cigarette". The Canadian connotation of chesterfield relates to "davenport" or "sofa" in the United States. The British equivalent is a "settee" or "couch".

Precise communication is especially important in the work environment. It plays an important role in the success of an operation and in the building of good relationships among co-workers. Imprecise communication can sometimes lead to costly errors and serious misunderstandings. If you are aware of different connotations that words can have when you are encoding and decoding, you may be able to avoid confusion. Make sure the other person attaches the same meanings to the words as you do. The following exercises will test your ability to communicate precisely.

COMMUNICATION

COUPLE: A couple is not two railway workers.
　To couple is to join two railway cars together with an automatic device. The device, naturally, is called a coupling.
　So there.

BREAK A KNUCKLE: This isn't an injury common to train workers.
　It also doesn't hurt.
　If you break a knuckle, it means you are breaking a coupling, and you know what that is.

BABBITT: Babbitt is the thin layer of metal that lines part of a journal box, the mechanism that houses the wheel bearing. An overheated journal box is believed to be the cause of the Mississauga derailment, and the babbitt is one of the first parts that usually melts in such heat.
　Babbitt is often a silvery color.
　Thus the old railway expression: "Every journal box has a silver lining."

VAN ON THE MOVE: Once they get going, trains are pretty fast.
　The thing is, though, it takes a train a while to get going in the first place. The engineman starts up the engines, and sure enough, the front of the train moves.
　But it can take two or three minutes, in a 100-car train, for the rear of the train to get into motion, too. When it does, the conductor sitting in the caboose, or van, gleefully shouts into his radio: "Van on the move!"

MILE BOARDS: Mile boards are just what they should be — boards that appear a mile before each station.
　Conveniently the station's name is on the board, just in case the crew is lost.

TIMETABLE: Self-explanatory, this one, you say?
　Not so.
　We all know that for passenger trains, a timetable is the schedule they are always running behind.

But for freight trains, it gets ridiculous.
　If the timetable has a freight train scheduled to leave at 2 p.m., all it means is that the train can't leave before 2 p.m. (God forbid it should arrive early.). It can leave just about any time afterwards.
　You figure it out.

SUPERIOR TRAIN: This is not a high-class train.
　Neither is it a train with high-class passengers, or anything of the sort.
　A superior train is simply a train that has precedence over other trains — i.e., a passenger train is given higher priority than a livestock train, which is in turn more important than a fourth-class freight train.

HIGHBALL: This is not a popular railway cocktail.
　But it's almost as much fun.
　After a train passes the mileboard (you know what that is), it's given a running inspection by its crew and, if everything is all clear, the conductor gets to yell in his radio:
　"Highball, Toronto!" Or wherever else the train is going.
　No wonder everyone in the railway business wants to be a conductor.

BAD ORDER: This isn't a poor directive from a dumb boss.
　One doesn't get a bad order, one bad-orders a car. It means that a rail car with a defect so serious it's unsafe to move is given a "bad-order" card, requiring that it be fixed before being moved again.
　Okay, now let's try and put some of the words together, as in a sentence.
　For instance: "If we don't break a knuckle or have to bad-order a car, and as long as the couplings hold, we can highball Toronto.
　You get the picture.

Figure 1-7
The railway industry has its own jargon, as this article shows.

APPLICATIONS

5. Humpty Dumpty in *Through the Looking Glass* said: "When I use a word ... it means just what I choose it to mean — neither more nor less."
　List five words you can think of that have more than one meaning. Write one sentence using two different meanings of each word to show what Humpty Dumpty meant.

6. In order to see how Canadian, British, and American connotations are different, try the following survey of Canadian English. When you have completed the survey, compare your responses with those of your classmates.

PART ONE: COMMUNICATION IN SCHOOL AND EVERYDAY LIFE

Figure 1-8
What does the language you use reveal about where you live?

> **Survey of Canadian English**
> 1. What do you call the chair a baby travels in?
> 2. What is the dug-out area under your house called?
> 3. What is the last letter of the alphabet, spelt as you would pronounce it?
> 4. What do you call the main living area of your house?
> 5. What do you call a public vehicle which travels on tracks on the street?
> 6. What is the area behind your house called?
> 7. What do you place on your lap when you eat?
> 8. What do you call a small river in which you might have fished when younger?
> 9. Do you eat the main meal of the day in the middle of the day or the evening?
> 10. And what do you call that meal?

7. In groups of two or three, select an area of music or a particular sport. Using the area of music or sport that you selected, list as many words as you can that have come to mean something a little different from their denotation, or dictionary meaning. Give the connoted meaning for each one. For example, in football you might start your list with: *bomb* - a long successful pass; or in baseball: *taking a pitcher downtown* - hitting a homerun. In music a couple of examples might be: *licks* - short, usually difficult sections often played by one musician; and *chops* - the ability to perform well (e.g., He has the chops for that part.).
Compare your list with those of other groups and, wherever possible, add their words and connotations to yours.

8. In a class discussion, evaluate the importance of clear meaning in everyday communication.

9. Have five or six students leave the room, and the rest of the class write up a short incident that might be part of a police investigation. Use descriptive details such as colours, time of day or year, directions (right or left; north, south, east, or west), noises present, and other observations such as doors and windows opened or closed.
Bring one student back into the room and read the account of the incident. Have the first student call the next student back into the room and repeat the incident. The second student tells it to the third and so on. The last student to be told repeats the incident to the class.
Record any distortions or omissions that have occurred with each repetition and discuss them at the end of the exercise. How and why did they occur?

10. Three or four volunteers take turns describing objects or shapes drawn on a piece of paper by the teacher or another volunteer. The rest of the class are seated with their backs to the speaker

COMMUNICATION

and draw a picture of the shape or object as the description is given.

Compare the class pictures with the original after each session and discuss ways in which the descriptions might have been more precise. Were some pictures fairly accurate? Why?

COMMUNICATION AND SELF-AWARENESS

In the section *The Communication Process* we briefly mentioned that interference from the environment can hinder communication. Our feelings and attitudes toward ourselves and others influence and sometimes interfere with communication. Some of these attitudes and their possible effects on communication are described below.

Emotions

Your emotions can put up a barrier to effective communication if you are not thinking clearly. When you are angry, for example, you may not be capable of organizing your thoughts in a way that is understandable. Your anger may prevent you from listening attentively too. Anger is an emotion that also hampers communication in the workplace. Often, the best course of action is to delay the conversation until the anger subsides and you can think clearly.

Worry can also act in a similar way. It prevents you from expressing and listening effectively, and, consequently, interferes with communication. You may recall from the dialogue earlier in this chapter that Jorg was worried about how to tell Mr. Mercer he was leaving his job. Having Jorg rehearse the conversation with Erica, who pretended to be Mr. Mercer, in an unemotional environment helped clarify Jorg's thoughts. At the time of the real conversation, Jorg would not be so worried because he would already know what to say.

Value Systems

A value system is a combination of the attitudes, hopes, and beliefs that a person or a society considers to be important. During your lifetime you develop your own value system. Usually it reflects the cultural and social environment of your home and community.

Values are the basis for making decisions and setting personal goals. Consequently, they have a considerable impact on your relationships and communication with other people. If your values strongly conflict with someone else's, you may experience difficulty in communicating effectively with that person. When you feel that a principle or value that you hold strongly to is being attacked, it will be necessary to listen as carefully and objectively as possible in order to understand the other person's point of view.

Sincerity

Sincerity is appreciated by everyone, and sincere messages will usually be listened to. If your message lacks sincerity, the receiver will probably detect the insincerity and discount or ignore what you are saying.

As a listener, sincerity is also important. Sincere feedback will be noted and appreciated by the sender.

Empathy

Empathy is entering into another person's feelings or emotions. It takes some effort to detach yourself from your own feelings and ideas and to see things through another's eyes. The results, however, are usually well worth it. Your communication will be more relevant and therefore much more effective.

The next time you are involved in an argument, try backing off for a moment and looking at the matter from the other person's point of view. Understanding the other person's feelings or motives may help you to resolve an argument.

Self-Perception

Look at Figure 1-9 and decide how these people see themselves. Which ones do you think are confident and at ease? How you see yourself affects how you communicate with others. If you consider your own opinions to be of little value, your communication will reflect that feeling and the receiver will also place little value on them. Your lack of conviction and enthusiasm will have been communicated. It is important to develop a good self-image. This will improve your self-confidence and in turn strengthen your communication skills.

Role Perception

Knowing what your role is will help you to define when and how to send your messages, and when to listen. When you are chairing a meeting, for example, you are responsible for keeping people on the subject until an issue is resolved. Being aware of your role should help you know what to say and when to say it.

Feelings and attitudes affect understanding. Listen carefully and objectively in order to understand the sender's point of view.

Figure 1-9
We reveal our self-image when we have to perform before an audience at such times as graduation. Which of these students do you think are confident and at ease?

APPLICATIONS

11. Give an example of a negative emotion such as fear, anger, or worry acting as a barrier to communication. Describe how you might handle the situation to improve communication.

12. Look through a daily newspaper, listen to a commentary on the radio, look at a film, or watch a television report on a current issue. List examples of misunderstandings or poor communication that might have resulted from a lack of appreciation of a particular cultural or social value.

13. Think of a situation in which a positive emotion such as joy, enthusiasm, or love might hamper communication. Write briefly about such a situation.

14. How do you think having a set of values similar to another person's might influence your communication with that person?

PART ONE: COMMUNICATION IN SCHOOL AND EVERYDAY LIFE

KINDS OF COMMUNICATION

Verbal Communication

Verbal communication is the sending and receiving of information, ideas, or feelings by means of words — spoken or written. In our daily business and social activities, verbal communication plays a vital role. Chapters 4, 8, 9, and 10 will deal with aspects of verbal communication in greater detail.

Non-Verbal Communication

As the term implies, non-verbal communication does not make use of words. Non-verbal messages are conveyed by such means as visual art forms, music, tone of voice, and body language.

At a rock concert, non-verbal communication between performers and audience is usually dynamic. The message is the feelings imparted by the music. Both the music and the accompanying body language, including facial expressions and gestures, send a message of feelings to the audience. The lyrics are probably of secondary importance in expressing the feelings of the performers. The response of the audience may rely heavily on body language as well — laughter, tears, and applause. Look at Figure 1-10. The performers will have no doubt in their minds that they have delivered their message effectively and have the audience on their side. They will know this from the feedback.

Visual Messages

Surprising someone you care about with a specially prepared meal is another example of non-verbal communication. The time and thought involved in preparing the meal will be apparent to the receiver and your message of appreciation will be clear. The message is the meal. If your message is packaged in an exciting way, it will have more impact. Advertising is based on this kind of thinking.

In business, graphs and charts are a useful non-verbal way of communicating complex information. The receiver can absorb complicated data, for example, more readily in visual rather than verbal form. Used effectively, graphs and charts convey more understanding and in a more interesting way. Chapter 13 of this book will examine the effective use of graphs, charts, and tables and discuss how they are prepared.

Figure 1-10
The feedback the audience is offering the performers here is very clear.

Body Language

Another non-verbal way of communicating, mentioned briefly in the rock concert example, is through body language. Gestures, facial expressions, eye contact, posture, dress and grooming, and personal spacing are all ways of communicating our feelings by means of the body.

Often body language is more eloquent than words in communicating our emotions. It can also be more accurate since it mirrors our feelings whereas words often do not. The expression "words fail me" is often used to indicate the difficulty we have in putting our feelings into words.

Sometimes body language is difficult to interpret. Crying, for instance, can express several quite different emotions: anger, joy, sadness, despair, frustration, or pain. A smile can be friendly and open, shy and hopeful, or sarcastic and contemptuous. Downcast eyes can indicate anxiety, lack of interest, or, in some cultures, respect. Body language varies from individual to individual and from culture to culture. The similarities among us, however, seem to outnumber the differences to a great degree.

Mixed Messages

Sometimes the verbal message you send is inconsistent with the body language you use. Such a message is therefore unclear. Can you think of any examples? Which message do you think the listener will believe, the words or the body language? Why?

Much of the time non-verbal messages are sent and received without your being aware of them. Your mind assigns meaning to them without your knowing it. According to some research, when body language conflicts with the verbal message, people will believe the body language, even though they are not conscious of having observed it.

If someone denies knowledge of a crime and at the same time avoids eye contact, what will your conclusion be? Have you ever blushed and betrayed your true feelings after claiming different feelings?

Desmond Morris, a specialist in animal behaviour and author of several popular books on human behaviour, has written a thorough and fascinating book on body language entitled, *Manwatching*. This book is worth reading if you wish to learn more about the subject.

Gestures, facial expressions, eye contact, posture, dress, grooming, and personal space often say more than words in the communication process.

APPLICATIONS

15. Find a public place where you can observe a number of people of all ages and, if possible, of different cultures. List the types of body language they use and the feelings you think are being expressed. Discuss your findings with the class.

16. Discuss how heavily impersonation, or dramatic imitation, relies on body language.

17. The teacher will assign to each student a feeling to express in body language. Work in pairs guessing the meaning of the body language and discussing the clues that prompted your conclusions.

18. Discuss with the class how body language can be misread and how we can improve our awareness and understanding of the body language we use and observe.

19. Ahmad was hoping to be selected for the lead role in a play his school was presenting in the spring. After the audition his friends were waiting for him outside. As soon as Ahmad appeared at the door they could tell he had not been given the role. How? How could they know if he had been successful at the audition?

20. The handshake may have originated as a gesture of peace, the open and empty right hand demonstrating the lack of a weapon. Many messages can be sent by moving the hand or arm. List as many as you can together with their meaning.

BARRIERS TO COMMUNICATION

Often communication is less than precise and satisfactory and it is necessary to determine how the process fails. You have already encountered some factors that can influence communication in a negative way. They are difficulties in organizing ideas and information; too many people passing the message along; problems in encoding or decoding or with different word connotations; emotions; differing values; lack of sincerity or empathy; negative self-image; and faulty role perception. All of these factors can act as barriers to successful communication.

As well, you have seen that the physical space within which you communicate, that is, the communication environment, can interfere with sending and receiving messages. Extremes of noise or temperature, strong odours, distracting movements, or lighting can inhibit your ability to send a clear message and hinder your listener's ability to receive and process it.

Figure 1-11 illustrates the potential barriers that are present when we communicate.

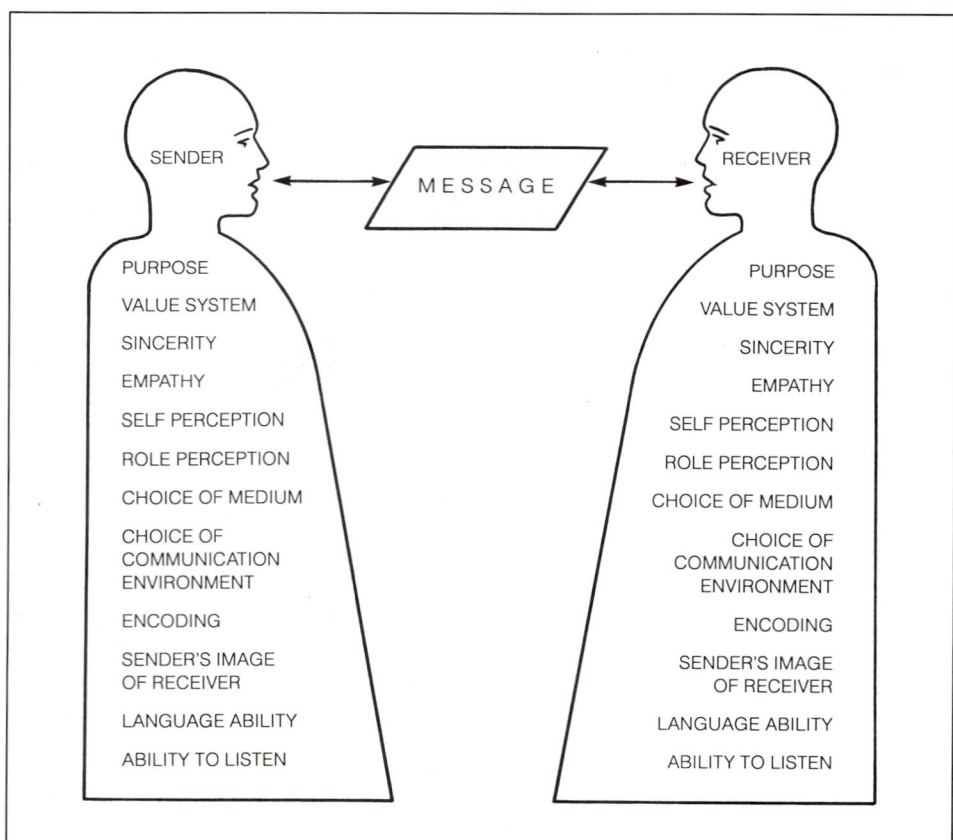

Figure 1-11
Potential Barriers to Effective Communication

Be aware of potential barriers in your communications.

In Chapter 2 you will be exploring the barriers in greater detail from the listener's point of view.

22 PART ONE: COMMUNICATION IN SCHOOL AND EVERYDAY LIFE

APPLICATIONS

21. Name five barriers to communication that you have personally experienced.
22. How did each of the barriers you named in Question 21 affect your communication?
23. Can glancing at a clock interfere with communication? Explain how it may affect sender and receiver.

SAFEGUARDS FOR EFFECTIVE COMMUNICATION

There are several ways to ensure that the communication process is working for you. The following chapters will detail specific reading, writing, listening, speaking, and thinking skills to help you to develop and refine your communication skills.

In almost every communication activity, there are four steps you can take to break down the barriers to effective communication. These steps will also help to minimize the negative effect of any interference that may be present.

1. Be sensitive to the presence of barriers such as differing values or physical distractions as outlined in this chapter.
   - Being aware of potential barriers is the first step toward overcoming them or avoiding them.

2. Work continually at improving your communication skills.
   - Think about what you read, write, speak, see, or hear everyday. Plan your communication with the receiver in mind. When you are the receiver, think about what the other person may have meant as you interpret the message. Work at expanding your ability to use language effectively. Add new words to your vocabulary and use them often.

3. Use feedback effectively.
   - Both senders and receivers should constantly seek and provide feedback throughout the communication process. Continue to listen, redraft, and resend messages until you are sure that they have been understood.

4. Evaluate for understanding.
   - As frequently as necessary, stop, think, assess the communication process, correct any interference, and then continue with the communication. The following questions can act as guides:
   (a) Is the communication progressing as it should?
   (b) Is the receiver listening or reading with understanding?
   (c) Is the environment supporting effective communication?

1. Be sensitive to differing values or physical distractions.
2. Plan your communications carefully.
3. Use feedback effectively.
4. Evaluate the communication process and make necessary adjustments.

APPLICATIONS

24. Find an example of a conversation in literature. (Your teacher may suggest a conversation to use.) Analyze the conversation using the information you have learned.
    (a) Write down any barriers to effective communication that you notice.
    (b) Suggest safeguards that you feel would have led to more effective communication in this case.

25. Recall a conversation you recently had at home or at school that was not effectively communicated.
    (a) In pairs, role-play this situation.
    (b) Read over the safeguards for effective communication and role-play the situation again, this time making the conversation more effective and positive.

26. In small groups discuss the following topics until agreement has been reached:
    (a) Does a statement have to be received to be a message? Explain.
    (b) If the sender and the receiver have interpreted a message differently, has communication occurred? Why or why not?
    (c) Can the absence of outside noise or activity be a barrier to effective communication? Explain.
    Have one person from your group present your opinions orally to the class.

27. In the next 24 hours, make note of at least ten types of non-verbal communication you have not considered previously. List them and be prepared to discuss them in class.

28. Identify a variety of communication skills used in a play, television drama, or movie that you have seen recently. Try to include examples of verbal and non-verbal communication in your response.

CHAPTER SUMMARY

The communication process involves

A Sender who
- encodes the message
- selects the medium
- sends the message

A Message that
- travels through a communication environment
- is affected by the environment

A Receiver who
- selects the message
- decodes the message
- provides feedback to the sender

Feedback is necessary to help the sender determine whether or not to redesign the message and send it again.

Both the sender and the receiver are involved in the evaluation process to determine if the true meaning of the message has been communicated.

Barriers to effective communication
- emotions
- differing value systems
- lack of sincerity
- lack of empathy
- poor self-perception
- poor role perception
- inappropriate choice of medium
- poor encoding/decoding abilities
- weak language skills
- hostile communication environment

Safeguards for effective communication
- be sensitive to barriers
- practise communication skills to improve them
- use feedback to establish understanding
- evaluate frequently and, if necessary, redraft or redesign the message

Good verbal communication skills are the key to understanding. The more effective you are in communication, the more successful you will be in all areas of your life, both at work and leisure.

MAKING IT WORK

1. Assume that you are teaching a Business English course to a grade 8 class. From the description of the communication process in this chapter, prepare a definition that grade 8 students would understand. Also name and describe the various parts of the process.

2. If you have a part-time job, ask your supervisor what special communication skills are needed in that particular kind of work. If you are not working, speak to a friend or a member of your family who employs students on a part-time basis. Make a list of the necessary communication skills and discuss your findings with the class.

3. Prepare a collage from newspaper clippings of a variety of ways in which people are communicating. Examples are a political debate, a judge's address to the jury, an interview, or a police report. Identify the factors that may affect communication in each example and determine the appropriate safeguards to ensure effective communication.

4. Invite a local business person to talk to your class about how communication skills can affect that business.

5. Prepare a display of pictures that portrays people in various types of clothing or hairstyles in business situations. Identify the non-verbal message that each person is communicating through appearance.

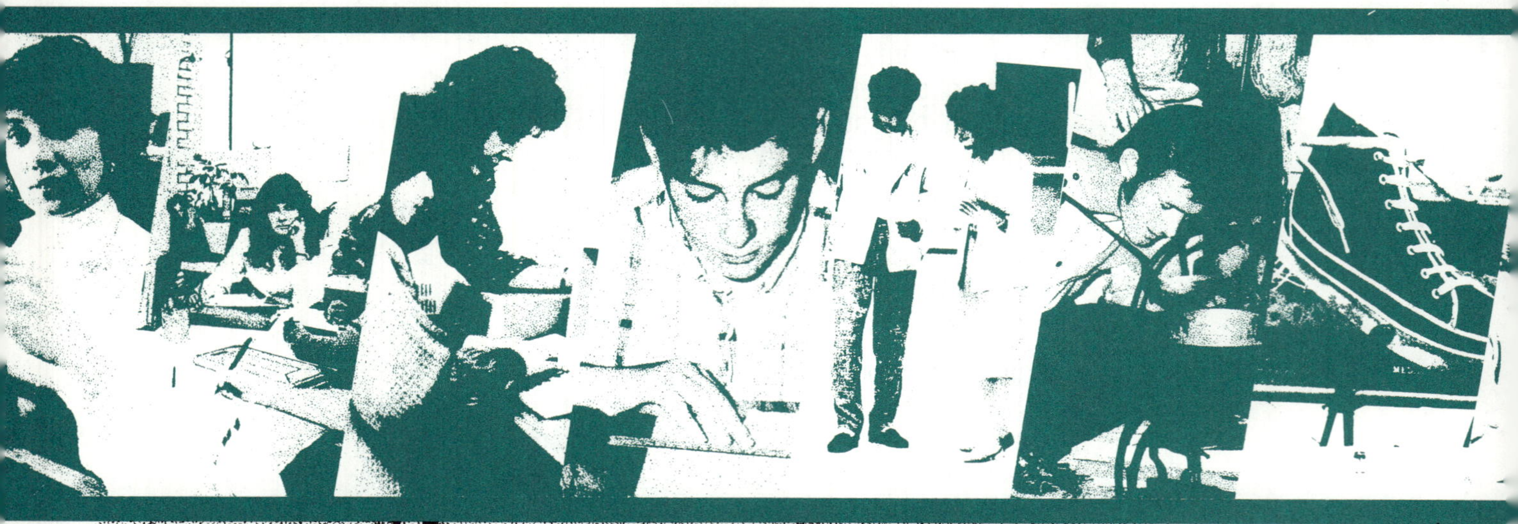
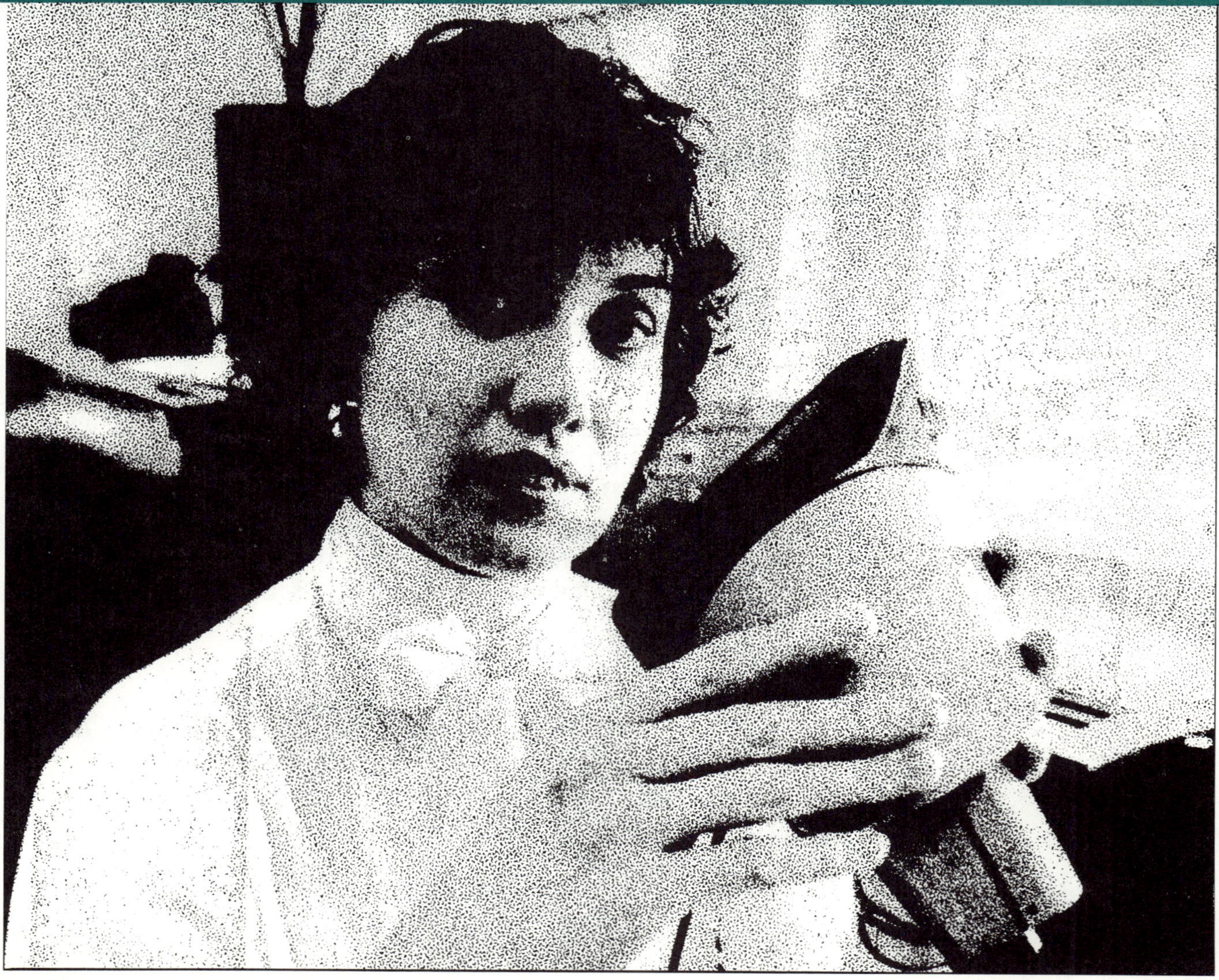

CHAPTER 2

Listening

GOALS

At the end of this chapter you should be able to
1. *differentiate between listening and hearing;*
2. *identify the barriers to effective listening;*
3. *overcome the barriers to effective listening and improve your listening skills; and*
4. *identify the five levels of listening.*

VOCABULARY BUILDING

facet
impaired
intact
nuances
biases
salient
inflection

VIEWPOINTS

You learned about the important **facets**, or aspects, of the communication process in Chapter 1. We will concentrate on two of them, listening and providing feedback, in this chapter. As you read the following dialogue, keep in mind the role of the listener in communication.

Sandy Hoffman is working at Speedway Garage as part of the cooperative education program, and is responsible for writing out work orders for each car brought in for servicing. By questioning the customer, Sandy finds out what needs to be done or checked. A customer is approaching the counter.

SANDY: Good morning, sir. What can I do for you?

CUSTOMER: Good morning. I'm Toni Cardarelli. I phoned yesterday about bringing my car in for servicing.

SANDY: Yes, Mr. Cardarelli, and what do you want done?

CUSTOMER: A general tune-up and I think the brakes need adjustment.

SANDY: (writing) So that's change oil filter and oil, check spark plugs, grease job, check brakes. Anything else?

CUSTOMER: Well, I'd like you to check the noise it makes when it's running over 60 km/h.

SANDY: What kind of noise does it make?

CUSTOMER: A grinding sound. It has me baffled. But if you find

27

something that's going to be expensive to repair, please let me know before you go ahead.

SANDY: All right. And where can we reach you if we need to?

CUSTOMER: 746-5834 for most of the day.

SANDY: (writing) And if we can't reach you there, is there another number we could try?

CUSTOMER: You could try 659-4838 and leave a message.

SANDY: Sorry, I didn't catch that. (Goes and closes garage door) What was that number again?

CUSTOMER: 659-4838.

SANDY: Thanks. Unless we find something major, your car will be ready around 4 o'clock.

CUSTOMER: Thanks. Goodbye.

QUESTIONS

1. How would you rate Sandy's listening skills?
2. What role did feedback play in this conversation?
3. Should Sandy have asked any more questions? Were there any ambiguities?
4. What factors in the environment might have hindered effective communication?

Figure 2-1
When we listen, we concentrate all our attention on the speaker. Do you think the person on the left is listening or just hearing?

INTRODUCTION

Listening carefully to customers is important in Sandy's job. Have you, or someone you know, ever taken a car in for servicing and returned to find that part of the work has not been done? A garage can lose business this way, or possibly be sued if an accident happens as a result of the incomplete job. Employees with poor listening skills can cost a company a great deal of money and time. If you do not listen when your friends want your attention, you can cause them to feel frustrated and neglected. In the sections that follow, you will learn that hearing and listening are not necessarily the same (see Figure 2-1), and that listening is a skill that can be improved with practice.

HEARING AND LISTENING

In the communication process shown in Chapter 1 (Figure 1-3), listening played a major role. Without a listener, no communication can take place. Many people, however, consider listening to be a passive function and equate it with hearing. If you think of the expression "in one ear and out the other," the distinction between hearing and listening is easily made. Hearing is a passive process. It takes place when the sound waves enter the receiver's ear. It is different from listening, which is an active mental process. The receiver pays attention to the message and understands what has been communicated.

Among your friends are there some you would rather talk to more than others? When you are in a group, is there one person everyone talks to? What is the special quality in this person that encourages others to talk? Probably it is the person's ability to listen when people talk — not just hear, but listen to them.

A good listener listens to the entire message. Do you recall from Chapter 1 that messages usually contain more than just information or ideas? They also contain the sender's feelings about the subject. In some cases the sender's feelings are the most important part of the message. You have probably heard friends say things like: "I don't care if I have to miss the party," or "This weather is really getting me down." In both cases, if you are listening for the underlying feelings, you will respond to the real messages. In the first example, your friend probably cares very deeply about missing the party. In the second example, it is likely that much more than the weather is affecting the speaker's mood.

Learning to listen to the feelings contained in messages will improve your listening skills. We will be discussing this subject in greater depth later in the chapter.

In business and in your daily life, listening is a valuable skill. It can prevent costly errors from occurring and can help establish good communication with co-workers. Listening is similar to other skills in that it can be improved with training and practice. This chapter will provide you with some guidelines for sharpening your listening skills.

THE PROCESS OF LISTENING

Throughout the day, unless your hearing is **impaired**, or reduced, your ears are bombarded with sounds. Because your brain filters out a great deal of the noise you hear, many of these sounds make no impression on your conscious mind. When you do your homework with the radio playing, you probably listen to very little of what the announcer is saying. However, an announcement that free tickets are being given away to a concert by your favourite pop group may make an impression and cause you to listen. In other words, you have been hearing the radio, but listening to it only when something comes on that interests you. Some sounds (such as the motor of a refrigerator) are noticeable only when they start or stop.

From the many sounds that you hear, you select those to which you will pay attention. This is called *attending*. Once you have paid attention to a particular sound, such as someone speaking, you will automatically *interpret* its meaning.

The next step in the listening process is *evaluation*. How do you feel about what you have just heard? Do you agree with it? Does it call for a *response*?

The steps in the listening process are shown in the diagram below:

Listen for the total message — information, ideas, and feelings.

Message filters **Attention Interpretation Evaluation Response**

Optimum listening = attending + interpreting + evaluating + responding

A final step is remembering the message or sound and the circumstances surrounding it.

APPLICATIONS

1. Working in small groups, develop a skit to demonstrate the importance of attending, interpreting, evaluating, and responding in the listening process.
2. Which has the greater impact — the way you speak to a person or the way you listen to the person? Support your answer.

LISTENING AND GOOD COMMUNICATION

Good communication requires a good listener. Each step of the listening process described in the previous section requires effort and skill if you want to be a good listener.

Attending

Paying attention to the sender and to the message is obviously necessary if you want to understand and respond to the message. It takes conscious effort to pay attention (Figure 2-2). Have you ever thought that you were listening to someone, but when the person finished you realized that you did not know what had been said? Your lack of attention was probably not intentional. You were probably distracted by other thoughts. Whatever the reason, your attention was not focussed on the speaker. Only when the listener is paying attention to the sender can the **intact**, or entire, message be received — the main idea, the supporting details, and the **nuances**, or shades of meaning.

Figure 2-2
Attending to a speaker requires constant attention.

Observing

Another important aspect of listening is observing the speaker and paying attention to non-verbal messages, such as a hesitation during a message; an **inflection**, or a change in the tone of voice; the loudness or softness of the voice; and body language, including gestures, facial expressions, posture, and personal spacing. All these things contribute to the message being sent. As a listener, your eyes and ears work together in helping you to interpret, understand, and evaluate the message.

Providing Feedback

Once the receiver has listened to, interpreted, and evaluated the message, a response or feedback is necessary. Feedback lets the sender

LISTENING

know that the message has been received, and whether or not it has been understood. It may be just a nod, a smile, or a single word such as "yes" to encourage the sender to continue. The feedback may be a request to clarify what has been said, or a paraphrase to check for understanding, such as, "What I understand you to be saying is ...."

When feedback makes the sender feel uncomfortable or threatened, the communication will probably be discontinued. Interrupting, offering unwanted advice, and passing judgement are a few examples of feedback that indicate a lack of respect for the sender. This could have negative results on the communication. Even if you disagree totally with the sender, you can still phrase your opinion in a way that will convey respect. Instead of passing judgement and saying "That's ridiculous," you can just as easily say something like "I think you may not have considered . . ."

Are You a Good Listener?
- Do you look at the person who is speaking to you?
- Do you pay attention and not fidget?
- Do you let the speaker finish and not interrupt or change the subject?
- Do you let the person take whatever time is necessary to complete the message?
- Do you give the speaker a nod, a smile, a frown?
- Do you ask questions if you need to clarify what you do not understand?

A good listener
1. *focusses on the speaker*
2. *is alert to non-verbal messages*
3. *provides appropriate feedback.*

APPLICATIONS

3. Working in groups of six to ten, each person assumes a new name. Introduce yourself to the group using your new name. After all the introductions have been made, try to repeat the new names of all the other people in the group.

4. We are quickly aware of whether or not the listener is paying attention to us. What observations lead us to that conclusion? When you are a listener, what ways can you use to let a sender know that you are listening?

5. Collect articles, cartoons, lines from songs, commercials, or quotations that call attention to ineffective listening. Assemble your material in a report.

BARRIERS TO EFFECTIVE LISTENING

Even when you make the decision to listen to someone, you may find it difficult to concentrate on the speaker's message. There are several barriers that can interfere with listening. These barriers fall into two groups, external and internal.

External Barriers

External barriers are those outside the listener's immediate control. They include such things as
- physical distractions — uncomfortable surroundings, competing noises, hunger, fatigue;
- negative attributes of the speaker — appearance, voice, mannerisms; and
- difficulty with the material or vocabulary — highly technical material, unfamiliar words.

Physical Distractions

Physical distractions often prevent effective listening. Have you ever found a nearby conversation competing for your attention while you are listening to someone? Usually, however, physical distractions are less of an impediment to listening if the subject matter is interesting or important to the listener. Workers being taught to handle potentially dangerous materials will undoubtedly listen carefully to instructions despite the fact that it is almost lunchtime and the room is uncomfortably warm. They will manage to screen out other noises, or if that is not possible they will request another location for the instruction session.

Negative Attributes of the Speaker

Sometimes a particular aspect of the speaker can be a formidable barrier to listening. When someone is talking, have you ever found yourself concentrating on the appearance, mannerisms, or a style of speech (e.g., tone, pitch, enunciation, pronunciation)? To overcome this barrier, it is necessary to concentrate on the content of the message.

Difficulty with the Material or Vocabulary

Sometimes you may have difficulty with your listening because of technical content or unfamiliar terms. The concepts that you are introduced to may be hard to grasp. Sometimes you may feel like the character in the cartoon in Figure 2-3. At times like this, it is easy to say to yourself, "I don't understand" and tune it out. Whenever possible, take the time to read about the subject beforehand. This enables you to be familiar with the vocabulary and helps you to understand better. Listening will then be less difficult.

Figure 2-3
What is the barrier to effective communication in this case?

Reprinted by permission: Tribune Company Syndicate, Inc.

Internal Barriers

Internal barriers to communication are those that can be controlled more readily by the listener. They include the following:
- posture
- bias
- wandering attention
- lack of interest
- planning a response
- concentration on details
- self-consciousness

Posture
Slouching is a behaviour that often accompanies a slack mind. Sitting or standing up straight and focussing your attention on the speaker will help you to listen more carefully.

Bias
Our past experiences — what we have read, heard, and seen — all contribute to the way we think and feel about issues. Sometimes our opinions are based on faulty or incomplete information. When these are strong opinions, that is, when we will not consider new information that conflicts with the old, they are termed **biases**.

Personal bias may lead you to dismiss the opinions of the speaker as being uninformed, too conservative, too liberal, or out of touch with the times. You may even become upset listening to a speaker who expresses a viewpoint that strongly conflicts with your own. Your emotional response may make it difficult for you to listen carefully to the rest of the message. In Figure 2-4, the listener is obviously upset and is not listening closely to what the speaker is saying.

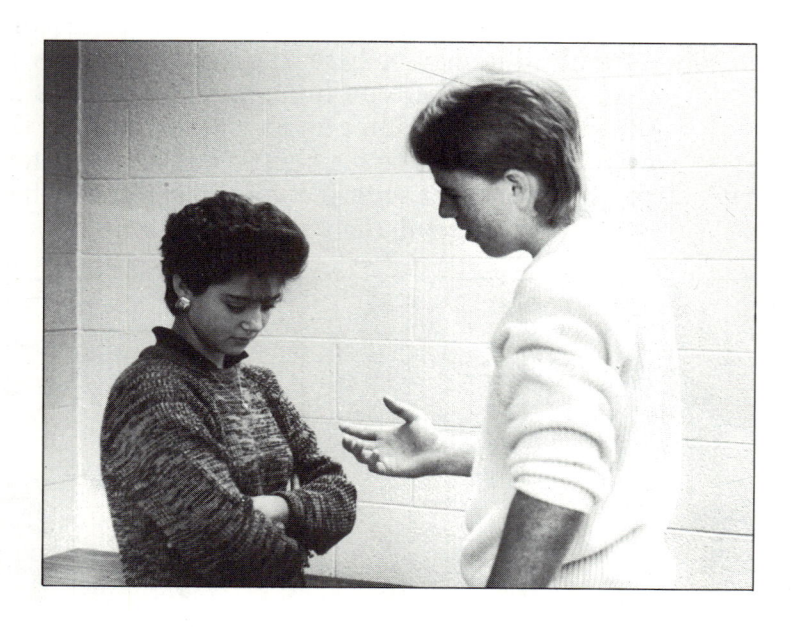

Figure 2-4
If you are angry or not responsive, it is hard to concentrate on what the speaker is saying.

It is always more comfortable to listen to those who reinforce our views or support what we say. However, when we encounter other viewpoints, we should at least try to understand what is expressed. Sometimes the views expressed are sound and if we listen to them objectively, we may end up modifying our own opinion.

Wandering attention
Have you ever thought that you were listening to someone and then suddenly realized that you did not know what the person had said? Your lack of attention was probably not intentional. You might have been distracted by a noise or upset by something. Whatever the reason, your attention was not focussed on the speaker.

Wandering attention occurs more frequently in situations where you are unlikely to be called upon to respond verbally, such as in a group. Once concentration is broken and your mind wanders, you will not receive the message intact, and you may miss some of the important points as well as the nuances.

Lack of interest
If you are not interested in the subject matter, you will not be inclined to listen to the speaker. In business, if you do not want to consider a wide range of ideas and information, you may not make progress.

Planning a response
Some people like to talk so much that they are planning what to say next as soon as they have finished speaking. Planning a response before the speaker is finished prevents you from listening carefully and reduces the usefulness of your response.

Concentration on details
Concentrating on details can cause you to miss the more important points the speaker is making, or even the overall theme. Focussing on the main ideas and then on the facts that support them will lead you to a better understanding of what the speaker is trying to communicate.

Self-consciousness
Being self-conscious, or preoccupied with your appearance or the impression you are making, will interfere with listening and reduce understanding.

Be aware of external and internal barriers to effective listening.

APPLICATIONS

6. Comment in writing on the statement, "There is no such thing as an uninteresting subject; there are only uninterested people."

7. You have decided to have a family room built onto your present house. The contractor has arrived to describe a possible plan to you. As the contractor is talking, you begin to write down all the important facts to help you make your decisions. After the contractor leaves, you realize that you do not know what the room will look like. Your notes are as follows:

LISTENING

6 wall outlets, 2 ceiling outlets, 24 sheets of drywall, 16 bundles of shingles.
   (a) Which barrier to listening has caused your lack of understanding?
   (b) Imagine that you are a contractor. Write a description of a room that has these features.
   (c) Working in small groups, have one person read the description written in (b) while the others make notes of the important facts. Have one of the listeners describe aloud the room from the notes taken.

8. In groups of two, role-play the situation of someone being interviewed for a job. Afterwards, write down
   (a) the mannerisms that you were conscious of in your own behaviour
   (b) your partner's mannerisms which you found distracting.
   Compare lists to see if you were conscious of mannerisms your partner found distracting, and vice versa.

IMPROVING YOUR LISTENING

After reading the previous section you may wonder how it is possible to overcome so many barriers to listening. Below are some steps you can take to become a better listener:
- Motivate yourself to become a better listener.
- Prepare yourself physically and mentally to listen.
- Empathize with the speaker.
- Be objective in your evaluation of the speaker's message.
- Provide feedback to the speaker.
- Take notes when appropriate.

Motivate Yourself

Being motivated to become a better listener is the first step toward reducing the barriers to listening. If you want to become a better listener and you approach this goal with a positive attitude, your listening skills are sure to improve.

You have probably found from past experience that changing your attitude toward a task will influence the results. A negative attitude usually produces negative results, while a positive attitude is likely to produce positive results. For many athletes their training program includes visualizing themselves performing their best and winning. Studies indicate that such visualization exercises do improve performance significantly.

Prepare Yourself

Preparing yourself to become a better listener can mean reading about the subject beforehand to become familiar with the concepts and terms, or having paper and pen ready for making notes. When you have a choice, place yourself in a comfortable location where you are least likely to be distracted. Listening selectively, that is, only to the speaker; focussing on the message; and maintaining an alert posture and eye contact with the speaker are also steps that will help you to listen effectively. Since effective listening requires energy, proper rest and nutrition are also important.

Empathize

Empathizing with the speaker is listening with sensitivity to the feelings of the speaker, not just to the factual information that is being communicated. There are many situations in business where the ability to empathize will pave the way for efficient problem solving and smooth the rough edges that occur in relationships with your co-workers, bosses, and employees. Being able to put yourself in the other person's shoes strengthens interpersonal communication immeasurably.

Be Objective

Objectivity in listening means setting aside prejudgements, biases, or negative feelings about the speaker and concentrating on the speaker's message. Make judgements after you have heard the complete message. Listening to someone who holds a different view may provide you with new insights.

While listening, keep the central theme in mind. What are the main points? Evaluate the evidence given to support main points and try to answer the questions how, what, where, when, and who.

Provide Feedback

Feedback, your response to the speaker's message, can convey not only that you are listening but also that you are willing to understand. The speaker will appreciate your willingness to understand. It indicates respect.

The kind of feedback you provide will, of course, depend on the situation. A one-to-one conversation with a friend will require much more feedback than a lecture with fifty people in the audience. In the latter case, the only feedback required may be an alert expression on your face.

There are verbal and non-verbal forms of feedback. Often your response will be a combination of the two. Think of a conversation that you had with a friend recently. As you talked, your friend's body language undoubtedly gave clues of the effect of your message. Your friend might have shown disbelief, interest, boredom, sympathy, amusement, impatience, or anger. If the clues you observed indicated negative feelings, such as boredom, would you have chosen to discontinue or modify your conversation? Have you ever tried to communicate with someone who keeps glancing at a clock? How does it make you feel? Do you feel like continuing with the conversation?

As a listener, what body language do you usually use to demonstrate your interest and understanding? Eye contact, straight posture, smiling (if appropriate), and gestures such as nodding are a few. In Figure 2-5, the girl on the left is giving feedback as she listens. What kind of feedback can you identify from her expression?

Figure 2-5
In listening, you should provide feedback to the speaker.

Verbal feedback can include saying "I see" or "yes" to encourage the speaker to continue, or mirroring the speaker's words to clarify the message, such as, "It seems to me you're saying the accounting routines are no longer suitable now that the business has expanded. What does this mean in terms of my responsibilities?" If your interpretation of the message is inaccurate the speaker can correct it. Your question indicates to the speaker that you are applying the message to yourself and are interested in continuing.

If you don't understand the message, let the speaker know that you have a problem with it rather than show a blank expression. Your blank look might otherwise be interpreted as lack of interest.

Take Notes

Note-taking, when appropriate, is helpful if you need to recall and act on the information later, or if you need help in focussing on the main points. It will also help you to pay close attention to the speaker and resist daydreaming.

Reading relevant material in advance will familiarize you with the subject. The speaker will then be reinforcing points you have already covered and you can pay more attention to difficult points. Listen for cues such as "first," "next," "consider," and "finally." These words will help you to know when the speaker is about to present important facts.

Another way to anticipate important facts is to recognize the pattern used by the speaker in organizing the material. A chronological organization of ideas may be used, in which case your notes will be based on a time sequence. If an analytical approach is taken, the material may be organized under the headings what, where, when, who, why, and how. Order of importance, comparison and contrast, and problem and solution are other organizational patterns used by speakers. These are discussed in more detail in Chapter 6.

It is important that you do not become so involved in writing long notes about one point that you stop listening to other points. On the other hand, notes that are too brief may not be of any use when you refer to them later. Because main ideas are essential to your comprehension of the material, you may wish to write them out in full. Supporting details can be noted in short phrases or single words to be filled out later when you review your notes. Often in a lecture situation the speaker will repeat the **salient**, or most important, points when summarizing the material. You will then be able to check that you have not missed anything that should be noted. During pauses, mentally review the main ideas to reinforce them and to help you identify any points that need clarification. If there is a question and answer period, you will be ready with your questions.

It helps to review your notes while the speaker's remarks are still fresh in your memory. Then you can expand on material written in point form and this will help you to understand your notes at a later date. Verify that material you did not comprehend previously is now understood.

Help yourself to become a better listener.

APPLICATIONS

9. Does Sandy, in the section *Viewpoints*, require note-taking skills? Support your answer.

10. Briefly describe three situations that require note-taking skills in a part-time job or in a full-time job that you like.

11. Working in pairs, ask permission for your pair to attend a meeting in school and to take notes. Record what you believe to be the most important aspects of the meeting and from your notes prepare a report. Compare your report with your partner's.

LISTENING

Discuss with the chairperson of the meeting, or with your teacher, how effectively each of you captured the essence of the meeting.

LEVELS OF LISTENING

You may use different levels of listening depending on the identity of the sender and the content of the message. Your listening skills will be adapted to each particular level. The levels are as follows:
- appreciative
- discriminative
- comprehensive
- critical
- therapeutic

Appreciative

Appreciative listening is listening for enjoyment to such things as music, the sounds of nature, or drama. Listening skills are not necessary for appreciative listening but the ability to focus and minimize distractions may improve the experience.

For many people music is a medium of self-expression and it gives enjoyment to the listener. The beat, the mood created, and the musical phrasing can be appreciated in many types of music — classical, jazz, rock, or heavy metal. Listening to music with earphones for the first time can be a startling experience. It is then that we realize how much of the sound is missed through environmental interference and lack of concentration.

Some people can captivate audiences with their speeches and provide an enjoyable listening experience. Sir Winston Churchill, Martin Luther King, and John F. Kennedy were three speakers whose presentations were compelling. They combined a dynamic style with strong, emotionally charged content. John F. Kennedy's 1961 inaugural address will be long remembered: "And so, my fellow Americans: Ask not what your country can do for you — ask what you can do for your country. My fellow citizens of the world: ask not what America will do for you, but what together we can do for the freedom of man."

Oral renditions of literary works can bring the printed words to life. Poetry, prose, and plays are often more easily appreciated when presented orally than when read.

Discriminative

Discriminative listening is listening to distinguish certain sounds from others. People who work with machinery know whether it is operating properly by the sounds it makes. They are able to distinguish between normal operating sounds and sounds that might signal a malfunction.

In conversations we use discriminative listening to detect **inflections**, or changes in the pitch of a person's voice. The word "yes" may indicate mild agreement, emphatic agreement, boredom, indecision, or enquiry, depending on the inflection in the speaker's voice.

We can also distinguish to some extent the accents of national and regional groups. By listening to someone speaking, can you determine which country that person comes from? And from which region in that country?

Comprehensive

Comprehensive listening is making an effort to understand a message, such as following operating instructions on a piece of equipment, or listening to a description of your job responsibilities. This type of listening requires you to focus your mind and often to memorize the information. Many of the listening skills described in the above section will apply to comprehensive listening.

Critical

Critical listening goes one step beyond comprehensive listening. In addition to understanding the message, you evaluate it and decide whether or not to accept it. At a staff meeting, for instance, the president of the company may propose various solutions to the same problem and ask the employees to decide which one will work best from their point of view. It will be necessary for you as an employee firstly, to understand each solution and secondly, to weigh the merits of each one before arriving at a decision.

A person interviewing job applicants, such as the interviewer in Figure 2-6, must listen critically to decide who the best person is for the job. She is constantly evaluating what the applicants are saying and trying to determine from their remarks how each person would perform and fit into the position that is open.

Radio and television advertising requires critical listening as well. Advertising tries to show how a product or service can benefit a buyer. To back up the benefits, the advertiser shows the product's features. The listener must firstly assess the benefits to see if the product or service is needed and, secondly, examine the features to see if they support the claims.

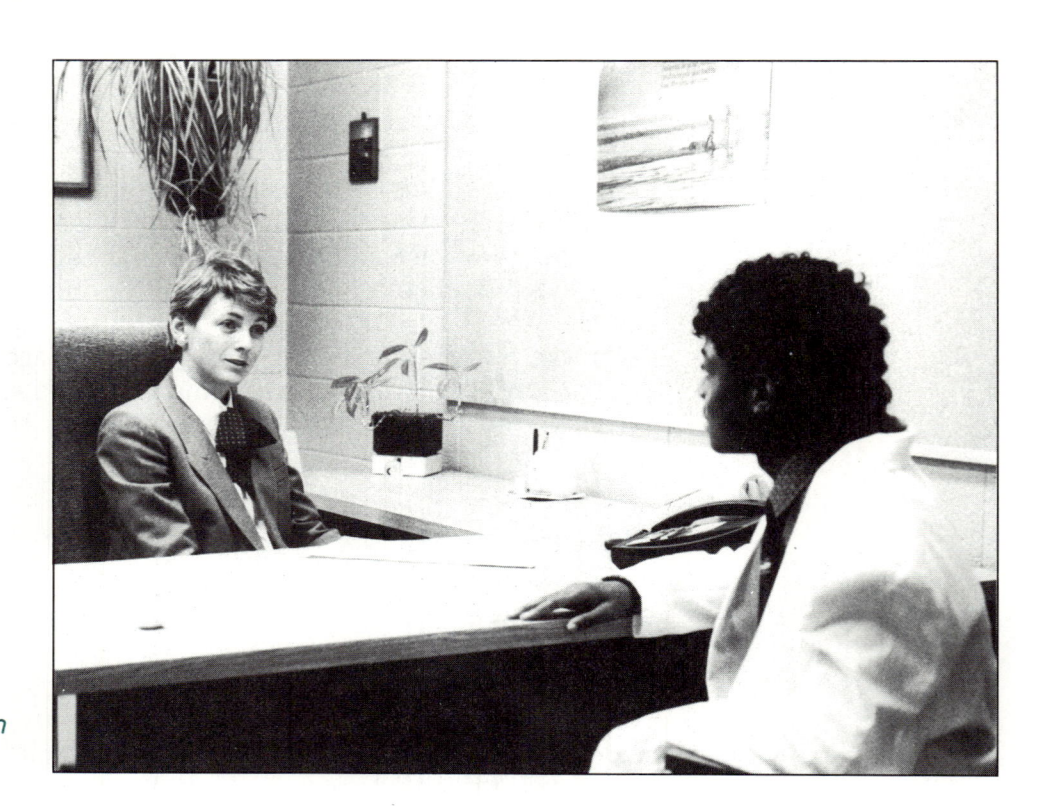

Figure 2-6
Skilled interviewers listen critically.

Therapeutic

In therapeutic listening, the listener becomes a sounding board for the speaker. Skills such as empathizing and providing feedback will be important for this kind of listening. Try to listen patiently and objectively, offering encouragement where necessary and allowing the speaker to finish. Avoid offering advice or solutions when not asked for. The speaker is often able to come up with an acceptable solution without intervention on your part. Your role is simply to offer support.

You do not expect others to solve your problems, but it often helps to talk about them with a trusted friend who will listen. Sometimes the act of talking about the problem will help you to see things more clearly and to find a solution yourself. It is much easier to accept and act on a solution that comes from yourself.

The following poem describes the sensitive techniques of therapeutic listening.

> *We listen with our hearts.*
> *When I listen with the heart*
> *I stop playing the game of non-listening.*
> *In other words,*
> *I step inside the other's skin;*
> *I walk in his shoes;*
> *I attempt to see things from his point-of-view;*
> *I establish eye contact;*
> *I give him conscious attention;*

PART ONE: COMMUNICATION IN SCHOOL AND EVERYDAY LIFE

The five levels of listening are
1. *appreciative*
2. *discriminative*
3. *comprehensive*
4. *critical*
5. *therapeutic.*

I reflect my understanding of his words;
I question;
I attempt to clarify.
Gently,
I draw the other out
as his lips stumble over words,
as his face becomes flushed,
as he turns his face aside.
I make the other feel that
I understand that he is important,
that I am grateful that he trusts me enough
to share deep, personal feelings with me.
I grant him worth.

Courtesy Loretta Girzaitis, *Listening: A Response Ability* (Winona, Minnesota: St. Mary's Press, 1972), p. 42. Reprinted with permission.

APPLICATIONS

12. From the poem, "We listen with our hearts," identify the different levels of listening the speaker uses.

13. The poem, "We listen with our hearts," tells us that listening is very important. In your own words state how listening will make you become a more effective person and help you to understand more.

14. Move into small groups. Each person in a group should take his or her turn and say "yes" in a different way to express a different meaning. Make a note of what you think each "yes" was meant to suggest, including your own, and compare the responses.

15. Referring to Question 14, discuss how inflection affects the meaning of a word.

16. Write a brief essay of about 200 words outlining a recent occasion when you used one of the five levels of listening. Include in your essay how you demonstrated attention, interpretation, evaluation, and response.

17. Keep a journal for a week, making entries to describe your use of different levels of listening.

18. Use a record or tape in your library of a speech, soliloquy, or reading and listen to a section of it. Speculate on the speaker, audience, and occasion. Describe your response to the material. Using no more than the first two sentences of the work, complete the material in your own words.

CHAPTER SUMMARY

The components of optimum listening
- attending
- interpreting
- evaluating
- responding

The external and internal barriers to effective listening
- distractions
- negative attributes of the speaker
- difficult material or vocabulary
- posture
- bias
- wandering attention
- lack of interest
- planning a response
- concentration on details
- self-consciousness

Help yourself to become a better listener
- be motivated
- be prepared
- empathize
- be objective
- provide feedback
- take notes where appropriate

When note-taking is required, follow these steps
- do any necessary preparatory reading
- listen for verbal cues
- determine the organizational pattern
- listen for a summary
- write only as much as you need to
- mentally review the main ideas during speaker pauses
- review your notes as soon as possible

The five levels of listening
- appreciative
- discriminative
- comprehensive
- critical
- therapeutic

Figure 2-7
Court reporters record the proceedings of court cases. It is important that they work accurately and quickly. This article describes the technology they use, and will help you answer Questions 4, 5, and 6.

A CAT to speed up court records

By Tom Spears Toronto Star

It's been 66 years since a little machine that took shorthand revolutionized the way courts keep records. Now the stenotype machine has joined the computer age.

When a witness, judge, or lawyer talks, it's crucial that everybody in court be able to get a written copy of what's said.

The job of writing it all down is left to Ontario's 750 court reporters, who either repeat everything they hear into a microphone inside a sound-proof facemask or take it down in shorthand.

Either way, their notes or tape recordings end up as neatly typed transcripts that lawyers and judges must rely on as gospel.

The trouble has always been speed. A court reporter in Ontario has to be able to take down 200 spoken words a minute, but it takes considerably longer to do the meticulous job of transcribing from tapes or shorthand symbols into plain English.

Enter the CAT (computer-aided transcription) machine from Texas Instruments and Stenograph Corp.

Computer Screen

The court reporter sits in the usual spot in court, tucked in front of the judge's bench, typing away on the lap-level keyboard that looks like a regular stenotype machine, reporter Ray Cuthbert says.

This machine is the stenotype's descendant, a $4,000 data writer that will make a cassette storing electronic impulses encoding every shorthand symbol the reporter types.

Technology

The information on the cassette can be transferred to a floppy disc, which then shows the words — in plain English — on a computer screen for editing. For good measure, the shorthand symbols can be called to the screen as well, enabling the reporter to iron out any oddities the machine hasn't yet been programmed to handle.

Speed crucial

District Court reporter Bill Nicholls says he hasn't heard of any move among his own colleagues to computers. In some District Courts, though not in Metro, reporters use stenomasks — masks with microphones that connect to tape recorders.

Paul Christie, a Provincial Court reporter who uses the stenomask, considers his machine — developed about 20 years ago — a modern implement.

"Some areas haven't accepted us yet," he said, referring to the Supreme Court's refusal to allow the use of stenomasks. "A lot of people think of us as the new kids on the block."

The computers, meanwhile, are breaking into the Canadian market very slowly.

"The government still won't buy the computers for them" as basic office equipment, Cuthbert said.

One reason may be that so many reporters, especially in Provincial Court, use stenomasks, and therefore wouldn't benefit from the computerized stenotypes, he said.

It takes "two full years of intensive study" to master the intricacies of the stenotype keyboard, and it might not pay off to spend all that time learning it if new technology soon makes it unnecessary, he said.

"The latest information is that in about five years there will be a machine to transcribe (tape recordings made on) stenomasks — what they call a voice printer. The Japanese are working on it."

For all the new computer technique, James hasn't heard much reaction from judges and lawyers.

"When they are in court and they ask for a transcript by 9 o'clock the same night, I don't think it really occurs to them where it comes from," she said.

Parliamentary use?

The other institution with a demand for fast transcripts is Parliament, where debates must be printed in *Hansard* within hours.

Traditionally, in the House of Commons and Senate, as well as in provincial legislatures, relay teams of shorthand reporters take 10-minute shifts in the House and then dictate to a typist in a back room.

But now even the Senate is taking a close look at the newfangled gadgetry. George Baker, a Senate official charged with looking at the role of computers in publishing *Hansard*, came to Toronto recently to see computers in action.

"We're interested to the point where we've had a demonstration," said Baker. "Eventually I think the idea is to go with it. But it's at least a year away, and even then it will just be on an experimental basis."

MAKING IT WORK

1. From the dialogue at the beginning of the chapter, state the levels of listening used by Sandy at Speedway Garage. Give an example of each level to support your answer.
2. Read the following situations. For each situation state whether listening or hearing has occurred. Support your answer.
   (a) Kitty has an interview after school for a part-time job. At the moment, she is sitting in a science class, and her teacher is explaining the procedures to be followed during today's experiment. Then the teacher tells the class to begin the experiment. Kitty looks around, wondering what it is she is supposed to do.
   (b) During the interview, Kitty is asked whether she has ever worked in a shoe store before. Kitty replies that she hasn't; however, she has worked in a clothing store and so is used to helping people. Kitty is then asked if she is available for evening work on Wednesday and Thursday in addition to the days and times mentioned in the advertisement. Kitty replies that she cannot work on Wednesday evenings but Thursday evenings are fine.
   (c) Kitty is hired for the part-time job. During the first evening on the job, the store supervisor notices that Kitty frequently brings out from the stockroom either the wrong size or style of shoe for the customer.
3. Obtain permission from a company to tape a radio advertisement of its product and play it for the class. Determine the benefits and features of the product. Explain why you would either accept or reject the need for this product and the product itself.
4. Discuss how the barriers to listening can affect a court reporter.
5. Do you think you would like to be a court reporter? Give reasons to support your answer.
6. Suggest other means of recording testimony in a court room. Why do you think these other means are not used?
7. Invite a court reporter to your classroom or take a field trip to a courthouse and have the court reporter demonstrate the recording equipment used in the court room. Prepare two questions to ask the reporter.
8. Listening and note-taking are important skills for a police officer to have. Working in groups of three, select one person to be the police officer. The other two are to think out a traffic accident without the "officer" hearing. The officer then questions the two "involved in the accident" and writes notes covering all the important details. The notes should be evaluated for accuracy and completeness by the other two. Change roles until all three have had a turn to be the police officer.

Figure 2-8
Court reporter Bob Silk sits in front of a computer-aided transcription system (known as CAT) which is used to record court proceedings. Why do you think it is important that a court reporter record what is said in court accurately?

Figure 2-9
Colleen Cleveland shows her soundproof stenomask which is connected to a tape-recorder. This is a device used by many court reporters to cut down on background noise.

9. Ask a secretary from the office to discuss with the class the value of accurate note-taking.

10. Ask the Principal, Vice-Principal, or someone from the community to discuss the role of note-taking in an administrative position.

11. If some of your classmates are in a co-operative education program, ask them to interview someone at their place of employment and report back to the class. For this assignment, the class as a whole should prepare a series of questions to be asked. When the interview is completed, the class should discuss the value of the questions asked and the effectiveness of the note-taking procedure.

LISTENING

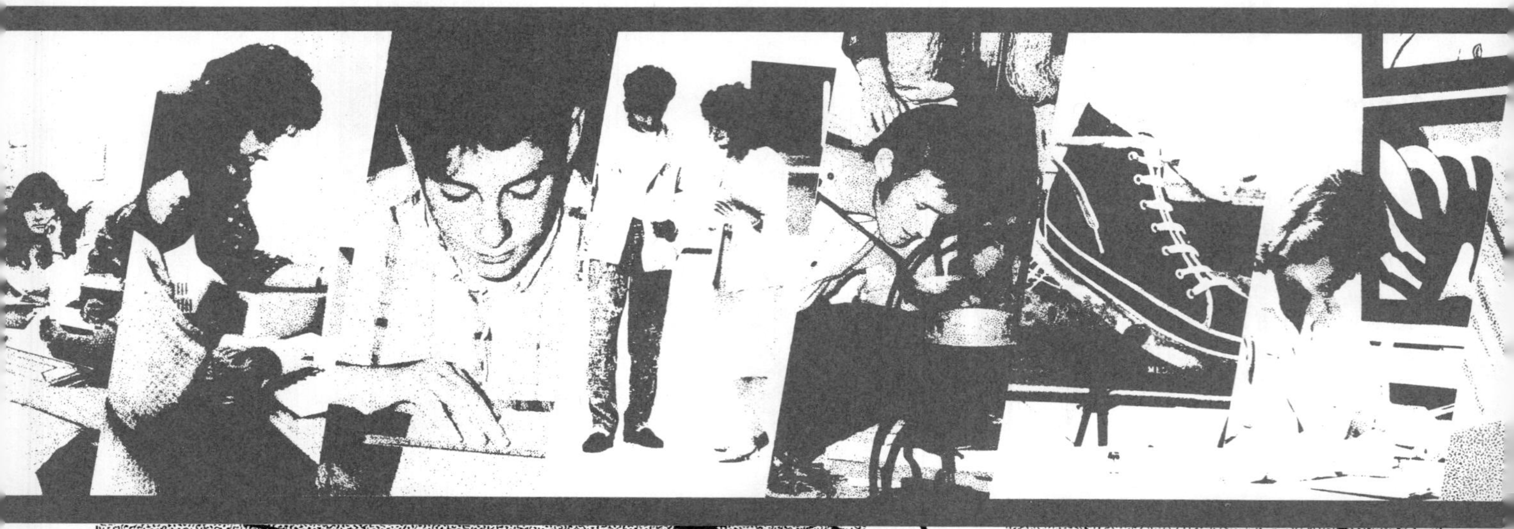

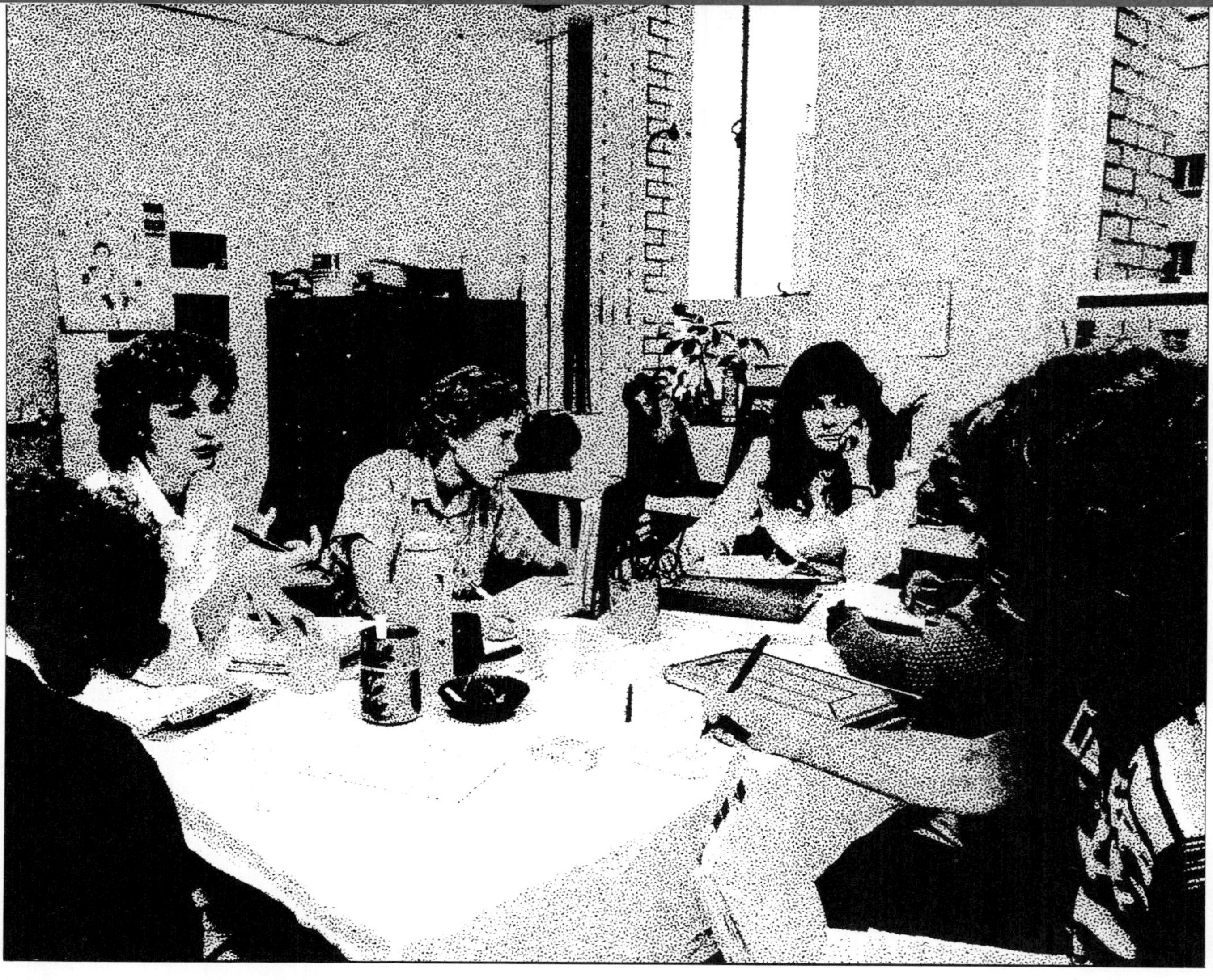

CHAPTER 3

Teamwork and Group Interaction

GOALS

At the end of this chapter you should be able to
1. describe the elements of effective group communication;
2. identify the roles of group participants;
3. identify the characteristics of effective team or group members;
4. recognize and compare different leadership styles;
5. identify effective group attitudes.

VOCABULARY BUILDING

group dynamics
internal
interpersonal
mediated
evaluate
norms
agenda
roles
chairperson

VIEWPOINTS

The following dialogue shows how important co-operation and participation are in making group decisions. Some members of the group in this dialogue are not given a chance to share their ideas and creativity. When all members of a group cannot participate fully, the **group dynamics**, or interaction of the group, fails to produce satisfactory results.

Sol, the waterfront director at Camp Wabikon, storms into the camp counsellors' lounge. Striding across the floor, he kicks a footstool out of the way and stops to glare out the window at the beach.

Anik, the assistant camp director, looks up from her magazine in surprise.

ANIK: Sol, what's the matter?

SOL: Nothing much.

ANIK: You don't usually kick furniture out of your way. Could the regatta have something to do with it?

SOL: I wouldn't call it a regatta. I'd call it a disaster, and one that everyone will think I'm responsible for even though I didn't know about it until this morning.

ANIK: What do you mean? You're the waterfront director and part of the camp program staff. You're supposed to be organizing all the waterfront activities and taking responsibility for them.

SOL: Well, how about telling your counselling staff that?

ANIK: I can understand you would be upset over how the regatta went. No one seemed to know what was happening, the kids or the counsellors. I don't understand though why you didn't know about it until this morning or why you're angry with the counsellors.

SOL: All right, I'll fill you in. Yesterday was my day off. When I got back last night, I checked in at the office, had a coffee with Nick and Cass, and then I went to bed. This morning after breakfast I arrived at the beach to find the whole camp setting up for a regatta. Some of the counsellors were strapping life jackets on the kids for a canoe race and others were lining kids up for a relay swim. No one, including the waterfront staff, seemed to know what was happening then, or what the events would be. The kids thought I could clear up the mess but since I didn't know what was happening either, I ended up looking like an idiot.

ANIK: But why didn't you know about it?

SOL: Yesterday, while I was away, the counsellors called a program meeting and decided something needed to be done to make the camp program more exciting. Someone suggested a regatta and the decision was to hold it this morning. No one bothered to ask me or the waterfront staff first whether it would be all right or how it should be organized. You saw the results. Now, unless I kick up a fuss, everyone will think the mess was my fault. The counsellors won't tell anyone that they were the organizers. And if I do make a stink about it, everyone will think I'm a jerk.

ANIK: I didn't know that the counsellors were holding meetings on their own. They're encouraged to suggest programs for the campers, but not to develop and carry them out. That's the responsibility of the program staff.

QUESTIONS

1. Do you agree that the counsellors displayed poor communication skills? Give reasons for your answer.
2. Do you think Anik should take some responsibility for the poor communications at the camp? Find examples of Anik not being a successful part of the communication process at the camp.
3. Summarize all of the problems that occurred during the regatta and the causes that led to these problems. By analyzing your list, you will see many areas of concern and some repeated problems. As a group discuss why some problems seem to occur more often than others.

Figure 3-1
Groups meet formally and informally, around tables or just in hallways. When they meet for a purpose, teamwork is essential to get results.

INTRODUCTION

Effective teamwork and group interaction are important to the success of business, school, and personal activities.

In Chapters 1 and 2, you learned about the skills involved in the communication process. You learned the importance of expressing yourself clearly and listening actively. In this chapter we will discuss how those same skills are applied to group situations, such as the one in *Viewpoints* or in the photograph in Figure 3-1. We will examine how communication skills contribute to effective group dynamics.

In addition to communication, group decision making requires each group member to co-operate and to take risks. We will explore how co-operation and risk-taking affect group dynamics. Participating in creative and problem-solving activities with a group can be exciting and satisfying. Suggestions for group activities are included in this chapter to enable you to experience group dynamics.

EFFECTIVE GROUP INTERACTION

Much of your life is spent working, learning, and enjoying leisure activities with other people in a group setting. You belong to a variety of groups — family, neighbourhood, school, industry, business, etc. Probably you have belonged to, or you now belong to special interest groups such as clubs, teams, volunteer groups, or work-related organizations. Society as a whole is still another kind of group to which you belong. A common feature of all these groups is the need for effective communication among their members.

Once you are part of the business community, you will find that decisions are mostly made by people meeting in groups. In fact, some research indicates that on average, business people spend half their working time in meetings. It follows that the better you are at communicating in a group situation, the better your chances will be of contributing meaningfully to group decision making. Being an important part of the decision-making process can be personally rewarding and it can also improve your chances of success within an organization.

There are three forms of communication you use when you participate in a group. They are **internal**, **interpersonal** (inter = between), and **mediated** communication.

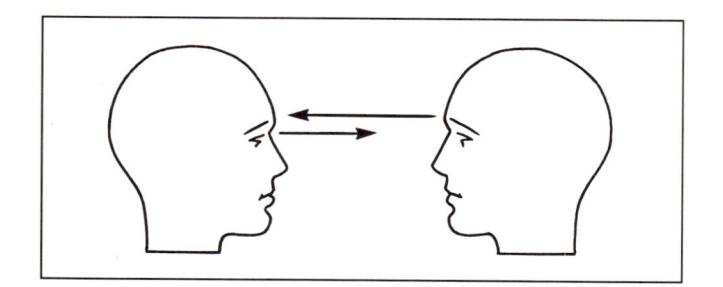

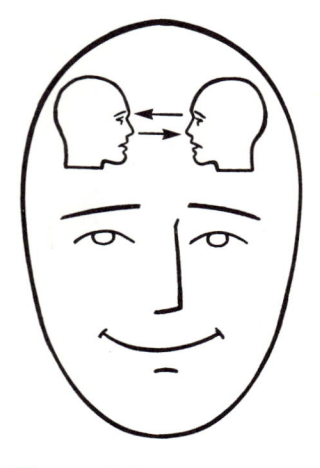

Internal Communication

Internal communication is simply what happens when you think. In thinking, you act as both sender and receiver. You create, receive, and process messages within yourself. Internal communication is the way that you become in touch with yourself. In your mind, you **evaluate**, or judge, make choices, and re-evaluate, and you learn how to deal with your environment. Each day through internal communication you decide what you will do, wear, and eat, and who you will talk to and share time with. Figure 3-2 is a diagram of internal communication.

Figure 3-2
Internal communication

Interpersonal Communication

Interpersonal communication takes place when two or more people talk face to face, as shown in Figure 3-3. Conversations, dialogues, and small group discussions are examples of interpersonal communication.

Figure 3-3
Interpersonal communication

PART ONE: COMMUNICATION IN SCHOOL AND EVERYDAY LIFE

During interpersonal communication, each person is also communicating internally, as shown in Figure 3-4. If you and your friends are trying to decide what to do on a Saturday afternoon, each of you may first be communicating internally, that is, you may be wondering if going to a movie is a good idea and your friends may be wondering about going to a baseball game, or organizing a trip to visit a friend who has moved out of town. The interpersonal communication will be the verbal exchange among the group members as you work toward an agreement of what to do on Saturday.

Figure 3-4
Internal and interpersonal communication

When you communicate with others, it is important to express feelings in a constructive way, especially with negative feelings such as anger. Most of the time, it is a good idea to postpone a discussion until the strong negative emotions have a chance to cool down. After some time has elapsed, the issue can be approached more objectively and rationally. If you state your position politely, but firmly, and choose your words carefully to avoid casting blame, you will earn the respect of others. A calm approach, rather than an emotional approach, will go a lot further in resolving issues.

Sol in the section *Viewpoints* is very angry and hurt by his exclusion from the regatta planning. However, he will have to face the counsellors eventually to tell them how he feels and to restore his authority so that another incident of this sort can be prevented. If he were to communicate with them in his present state, he would probably be

TEAMWORK AND GROUP INTERACTION

unable to focus on the real problems. Instead, he might lash out with unfocussed anger and cause an even greater breakdown in the camp's communication process.

Interpersonal communication relies heavily on feedback to be effective. In Chapters 1 and 2, we discussed the need for feedback, and the ways of providing feedback and interpreting it. As a sender, it is possible to improve the quality and quantity of feedback by asking questions along with your messages, such as:
- Which one of my suggestions do you like best?
- What do you think about what I have just said?
- What do you like or dislike about these solutions?
- Would anyone care to expand on that idea?

By asking appropriate questions, it is possible to draw out those who are listening to you. Quite likely, communication will be improved by the greater flow of ideas and opinions.

Mediated Communication

Mediated communication, the third type of communication, requires an inanimate medium to pass along the message. A sports broadcast of a baseball game is an example of mediated communication. Mediated communication is often transmitted or received by mechanical or electronic devices such as radio, television, teletype, and communication satellites. Letters, cards, books, reports, printed forms, and billboards are also used to transmit mediated messages.

As a member of a group, you may be called upon to produce a report, write up the minutes of a meeting, circulate a summary of a meeting, or take charge of advertising a group activity.

In mediated communication, immediate non-verbal feedback is not possible. If you cannot see the faces of those with whom you are communicating, you cannot interpret the non-verbal component of their feedback. Unless you happen to have a telephone with closed-circuit TV, you must rely on verbal feedback.

With mediated communication directed at the public, feedback is often delayed. The feedback in advertising is the response of the public to the advertisement. If attendance or sales increased following an advertising campaign, you would conclude that the public received the message favourably and responded positively to it. Similarly, audience reaction to radio and television shows is watched closely and evaluated.

We communicate
1. *in our own minds, through internal communication*
2. *with others, directly, through inter-personal communication*
3. *with others, by means of a mechanical medium, through mediated communication.*

APPLICATIONS

1. In small groups, list some of the ways that Sol could deal with his anger and hurt feelings.

2. In groups of three or four, identify a particular group situation where, due to poor communication or a complete lack of communication, one member in the group (or team) had feelings similar to Sol's.

3. State specific reasons for the feelings identified in Question 2 and share your findings with the class.

4. What other questions, besides those listed on page 54, can you think of that would improve and clarify communication? Make up at least five questions.

THE MEMBERS OF A GROUP

People are brought together in groups at bus stops, in banks, and in supermarkets, but we will not be talking about such groups when we discuss group interaction and communication. In this chapter, when we talk of a group, we are talking about several people who have chosen to come together for a common purpose.

The members of a group meet for a purpose and expect results. Sometimes the meeting is held simply to give or share information. At other times, the meeting is held to make decisions or plan strategies.

To function smoothly, groups adopt **norms**, or procedures, which are rules that govern how the members will operate and behave. For formal meetings an **agenda** will be drawn up, that is, an outline of the issues that will be covered in the meeting. The group will also establish the time, location, and length of the meetings. There may be a code of behaviour and dress as well.

The leader is usually in charge of seeing that the norms are observed. For instance, if one member continually arrives late for meetings, the leader must speak to that person. If norms are not followed, the structure of the group will be weakened.

Within a group, certain patterns of interaction will develop — some people will do most of the talking and most of the remarks will be addressed to only a few group members. The patterns may be a result of the relationship of the people in the group. The patterns may also be determined by the seating arrangement in a meeting, or the personalities of the members. Some people are willing to speak up whether they have something to contribute or not, whereas others are embarrassed about speaking to a group and will keep valuable ideas to themselves. Some members will do most of the talking, and their opinions may dominate. It is important that the patterns of interaction within the group do not become fixed, or certain members will be excluded from contributing.

Having the skills of effective interpersonal communication is obviously important if you want to be an effective member of a group. Being aware of how people interact within groups is also important. In the next section we will discuss the **roles**, or expected patterns of behaviour, of members of a group as they interact and contribute to the group.

Groups meet for a purpose, expect results, have norms, and develop patterns of interaction.

TEAMWORK AND GROUP INTERACTION

APPLICATIONS

5. What characteristics distinguish a group that comes together by chance from the kind of group we are examining in this chapter?
6. List some of the norms of a group you belong to or have belonged to.

PRIMARY ROLES OF GROUP MEMBERS

In most group activities, each member of the group assumes or is assigned at least one role. The roles and responsibilities of everyone in the group should be known and understood by all members. The three primary group roles are participant, recorder, and leader.

Participant

All members of a group should function as participants, contributing their experience, knowledge, skills, and insight when appropriate. Everyone in a group has something to contribute. Those who do not choose to speak up for one reason or another are letting the group down. Sometimes members are hesitant because they are afraid of ridicule or rejection. However, they will be encouraged to make their opinions and ideas known if other group members respond to messages in a positive and constructive way.

Participants should take an active part in determining how the group will function. They must identify issues and problems, contribute to problem solving, and evaluate results.

Many of you must have played a team sport. You will know that there can be good players and good team players, and the two are not necessarily the same thing. A player who decides to try for a goal even though another team-mate is in a better position to score is not considered a good team player, even if a goal has been scored. Most coaches would rather have good team players, those who play for the glory of the team and not for their own personal glory.

Similarly, group participants are expected to help promote the work of the group rather than promote themselves. When you listen with sensitivity to what others in the group are saying and show respect for their opinions, then offer your ideas when it is appropriate to do so, you will be furthering the work of the group.

If the group decides on a course of action that differs from the one you have been promoting, give in gracefully. The group process requires that members respect and accept group action.

For effective group dynamics, team or group participants should:
- know and be committed to the goals of the team or group;
- play a part in determining how each goal should be accomplished;
- be open and give freely and willingly of thoughts, ideas, and actions to help accomplish the goals of the group;

- act as part of the team rather than independently;
- respect the skills and expertise of other members of the group; and
- share the glory (or the failures) with everyone else in the group.

Recorder

Someone in the group is usually responsible for keeping a record of all the issues raised, decisions reached, and tasks assigned.

Ideally, the record should be written up in the form of a summary and distributed to members of the group. In this way, there is no confusion as to what was discussed, what was decided, and who was given assignments. The summary should also contain information on when and where the meeting was held, and how long the meeting went on; which members were present; who the **chairperson**, or leader of the discussion, was; and the time and place of the next meeting.

Notes and note-taking for a variety of listening and viewing activities were discussed in detail in Chapter 2.

Leader

The group leader, or, in formal groups, the chairperson, is responsible for running the meetings smoothly. This means ensuring that all members observe the norms, that the business of the meeting is conducted in an orderly fashion, and that members of the group participate in the decision making and share in the responsibilities assigned.

Having an agenda and observing it will help to ensure that the members of the group co-operate to accomplish the goals they have set themselves. Whenever the discussion strays away from the items on the agenda or it becomes repetitive, the leader must put the group on track and keep the discussion moving.

Leaders need to create a positive atmosphere for the exchange of views so that all members will be encouraged to discuss issues and contribute ideas. This can be accomplished by providing and promoting constructive feedback and asking for opinions from those who are not participating. It may be necessary to discourage any members who try to take over the meeting or who obstruct decision making.

Being aware of and respecting the value systems, attitudes, and customs of others will help in creating an atmosphere in which free discussion is possible and emotional conflicts are minimized.

Disagreement in a group is inevitable. Not everyone will have the same opinions. However, to be productive, the discussion should focus on issues, not personalities.

There are three basic kinds of leaders: authoritarian, democratic, and permissive leaders.

Authoritarian leaders like to dictate the process used to establish rules and procedures. They prefer to assign tasks and responsibilities without consulting the other members of the group, and they try to push their decisions through regardless of what the group thinks.

Democratic leaders share responsibility for determining priorities, actions, and procedures. They use group decision making to decide on tasks, assign responsibilities, and evaluate results.

Permissive leaders do not interfere in the decision-making process. Instead they supply information or ideas only when asked. They do not join in the group to set rules, establish procedures, assign tasks or responsibilities, or evaluate results.

A permissive leader works well in groups whose members have shown they work well together with little outside direction.

Three key roles in a group are participant, recorder, and leader.

APPLICATIONS

7. Think of a recent group or team activity in which you were a participant. With reference to the six rules for effective group dynamics on pages 56-57, how would you rate your participation? Use the following scoring chart: 3 for each rule you followed perfectly, 2 if you partially followed it, 1 if you only slightly followed it, and 0 if not at all. Explain why you assigned yourself those scores.

8. All three leadership styles - authoritarian, democratic, and permissive — have some positive and some negative qualities. List as many of these positive and negative qualities as you can for each leadership style.

9. In groups of three or four, compare your answers to Question 8, adding qualities that other group members listed and you did not. Resolve any disagreements over these qualities. Make notes on how you resolved your differences and what leadership styles were used in your group.

10. With reference to the dialogue in *Viewpoints*, what was Anik's leadership style? Support your answer with evidence taken from the dialogue.

11. In small groups, decide which leadership style is best suited to each of the situations described below:
    - the selection of a group to play at the next school dance
    - the selection of a football team captain, cheerleading squad, or class rep
    - the assigning of various household chores such as putting out the garbage, mowing the lawn, removing snow, house cleaning, cooking, babysitting
    - the selection of the employee who gets first choice of hours at a part-time job
    - the election of a government

12. In groups of four, organize a logical system of communication that could be created in Camp Wabikon mentioned in *Viewpoints* so that everyone would contribute to the program and all areas of camp life would function more effectively.

POSITIVE AND NEGATIVE ROLES OF GROUP MEMBERS

In addition to the primary roles of participant, recorder, and leader, there are other roles that people play in groups. Some of these roles are positive and hence productive, but other roles are negative and hinder the work of the group.

Following are some of the different roles that can be played by members of a group, including the leader. Perhaps you can identify some of these roles in the photograph in Figure 3-5.

A Positive Group Member:

Initiates	suggests new or different ideas and approaches for discussion and problem solving
Gives Opinions	offers pertinent opinions on an issue and makes suggestions
Elaborates	elaborates or builds on suggestions made by others
Relieves Tension	uses humour at appropriate times to reduce negative feelings, and calls for a break when needed
Compromises	does not stick stubbornly to a point of view that is unpopular or irrational, yields for the purpose of group progress
Clarifies	presses for meaning and understanding of any problems by offering relevant examples and rationales, and by restating problems
Tests	raises questions to test whether the group is ready to come to a decision
Summarizes	brings together points of the preceding discussions for review
Harmonizes	mediates differences of opinions and reconciles points of view
Encourages	praises and supports others for their contributions, is friendly and encouraging, and creates opportunities for others to contribute

A Negative Group Member:

Acts Aggressively	deflates the status of others in the group, aggressively disagrees with members, and openly criticizes them
Blocks	objects to any proposed solution, stubbornly disagrees with and rejects other members' views, states unrelated personal experiences, and returns to topics already discussed

TEAMWORK AND GROUP INTERACTION

Withdraws	does not participate, often carries on private conversations with other members, usually abstains from voting
Seeks Recognition	tries to show self-importance by boasting and excessive talking, is overconscious of own status
Changes the Topic	continually changes the topic of discussion
Dominates	tries to take over the meeting, asserts authority, manipulates the group
Is Uncommitted	uses the group's time to show off or tell funny stories, acts with nonchalance or cynicism
Plays the Devil's Advocate	always takes the opposing point of view to promote a disagreement

Figure 3-5
In this group, which person would you say is the leader? Who is the withdrawer? Who is acting as the recorder?

For a group to operate effectively, the overall attitude of members should be positive. This means that members need to have a positive attitude toward themselves, their fellow group members, and the activities of the group. Look at Figure 3-1 and Figure 3-5. Which participants in these groups appear to have a negative attitude to the group?

Sometimes a positive attitude can be overdone and the results can be negative. For example, it is important that we take pride in our achievements, but if the pride combines with conceit and boastfulness, the result can be a loss of friends and respect. In terms of

Members of a group can play positive, productive roles or they can play negative, obstructive roles.

group participation, the vain and boastful person fits into the negative role of the recognition seeker or the dominator. Self-confidence is another attitude that can turn negative if it is excessive. Someone who is too self-confident may become arrogant. That person will probably not play a positive role in a group either.

APPLICATIONS

13. What attitudes are demonstrated by Anik, Sol, and the counsellors in *Viewpoints*?

14. Copy the chart below and evaluate the attitudes you showed during a recent group activity or assignment. Place a check mark on the line between each pair of attitudes, closer to the positive side if your attitude was positive and closer to the negative side if it was negative.

Positive Attitudes	Negative Attitudes
enthusiasm	cynicism
concern	disregard
humility	boastfulness
co-operation	obstruction
determination	indecision
tolerance	prejudice
trust	distrust
self-confidence	insecurity
honesty	dishonesty
friendliness	hostility
curiosity	apathy

15. In small groups, assign a different group role to each member and role-play one of the following decision-making situations:
    - What are the ways to raise money for the next class field trip out of town?
    - What kind of special event should the school host to raise money for new team uniforms?
    - Should tobacco companies be allowed to advertise on television or in the printed media?
    - Should individuals be required to take a drug test when they apply for a job?

CHAPTER SUMMARY

Groups meet to solve problems, and effective communication is necessary for these meetings to be successful. Communication in these situations is of three kinds:
- Internal communication (within a person's mind)
- Interpersonal communication (between people)
- Mediated communication (between people through a mechanical medium)

Groups adopt procedures or norms in order that they function smoothly. Sometimes an agenda, or outline of issues to be discussed, is drawn up.

Primary roles of group members
- a leader or chairperson
- a recorder, or note-taker
- participants

The role of participants in groups can be positive and constructive, or negative and destructive. They may help the group to reach its goals, or may stand in its way.

MAKING IT WORK

1. In groups of two or three, interview managers of various businesses in your local business community. Ask them to describe the interpersonal communication skills and attitudes needed to fit into their organization. Prepare an oral or visual report to present to the rest of the class.

2. Read the following case, then answer the questions that follow.

   Maria has a part-time job working in a fast-food outlet after school. Every two weeks, the manager meets with the part-time staff in a group to communicate information and solve problems. Maria is embarrassed about talking in front of other people and never speaks at these meetings. Recently she overheard the manager telling her assistant manager that Maria did not seem to care about her job.
   (a) How do you think Maria felt about this evaluation of herself?
   (b) What do you think she could do to overcome her shyness at meetings?

3. Read the following case, then answer the questions that follow.

   Joe wants to be an actor when he leaves school, and in preparation joins an after-school drama club. He hopes to get as much experience in acting as he can to prepare himself for his career. To his frustration, the other people in the group do not take the club's activities as seriously. They use drama club meetings to make jokes and show off. Joe wants to leave the drama group, but wants to give it one last try.

(a) Look at the list of negative group roles on pages 59-60, and identify the roles of the others in the club.
(b) Look at the list of positive group roles on page 59 and see if there are any roles that Joe could assume to make the group meetings more successful.
(c) What advice would you give Joe to help him make the drama club meetings more constructive?

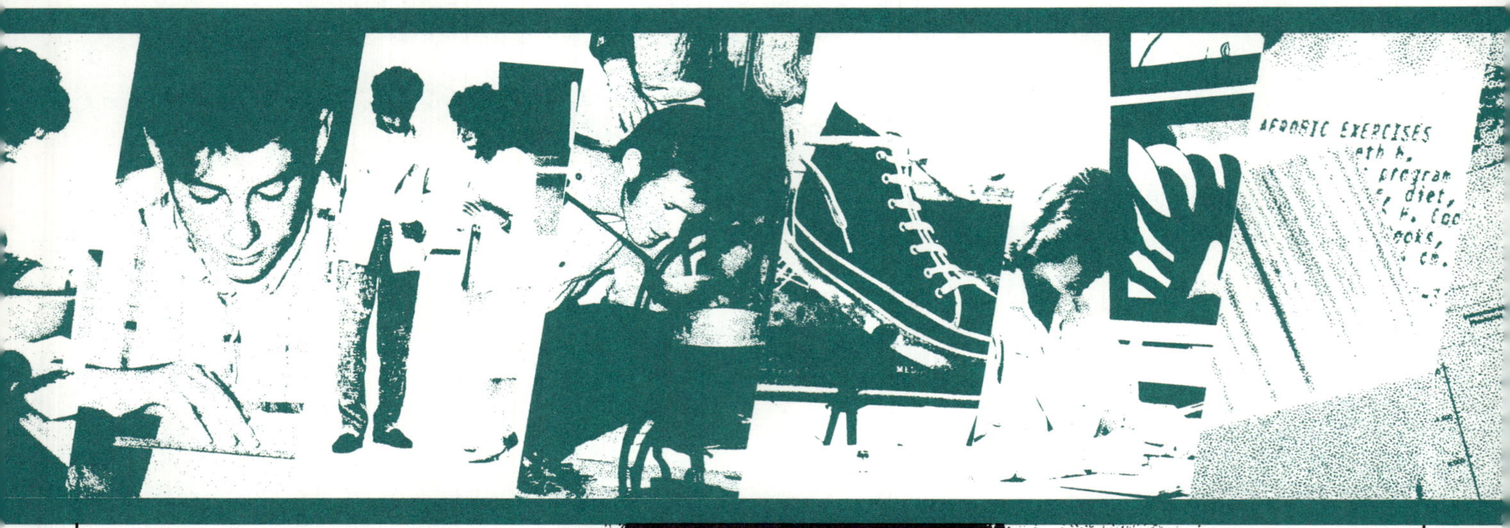

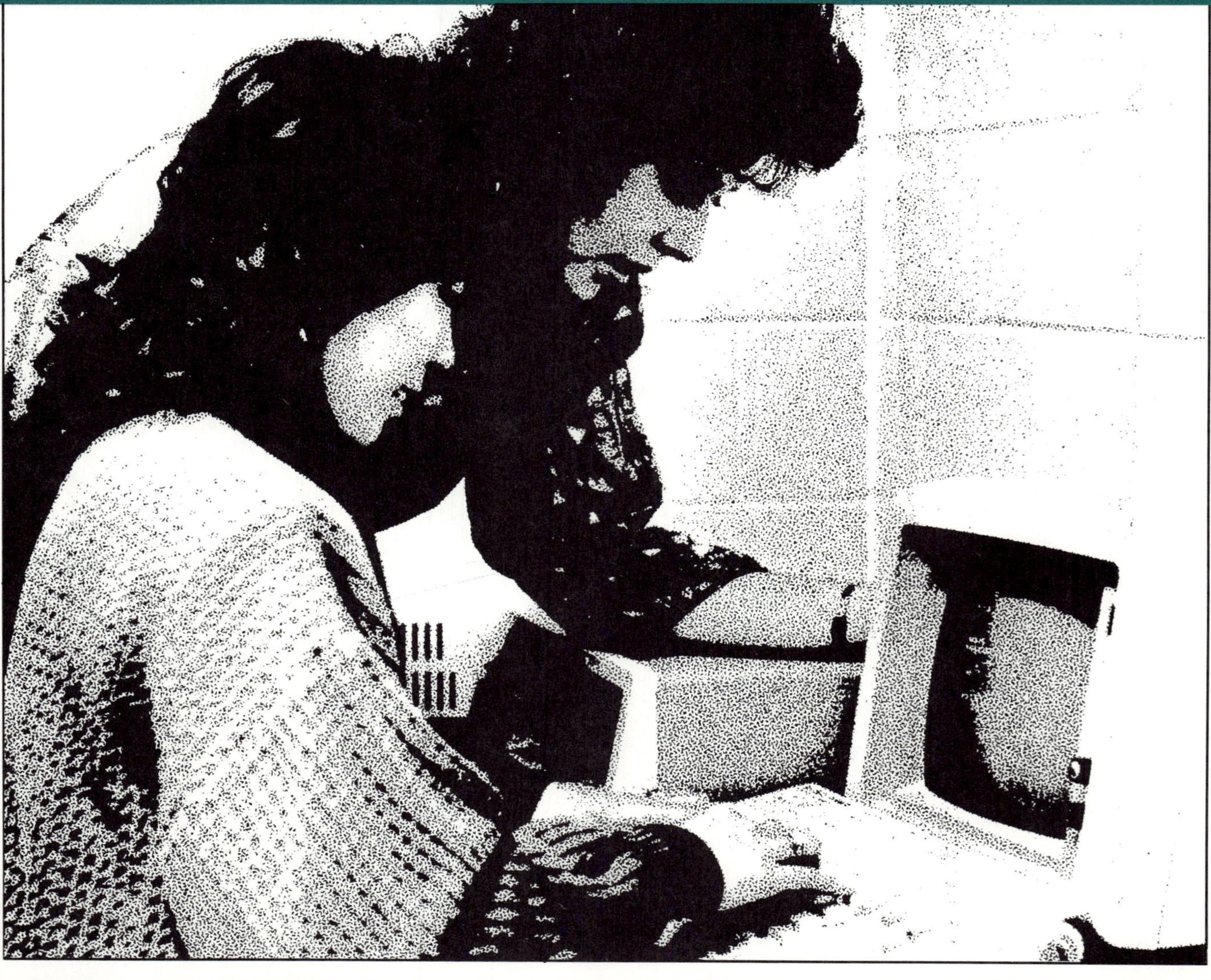

CHAPTER 4

GOALS

At the end of this chapter you should be able to
1. make introductions and respond to introductions with confidence;
2. begin, continue, and end conversations skilfully and smoothly;
3. give instructions or directions in a clear manner;
4. deliver impromptu, extemporaneous and written speeches;
5. introduce and thank speakers in an effective way; and
6. identify the characteristics of good voice quality and good speech, and the importance of body language.

VOCABULARY BUILDING

gauge
sequential
extemporaneous
constitute
simulate
incorporate
monotone
dialect
carriage

Speaking

VIEWPOINTS

In this dialogue a new student is informally introduced by a classmate. Try to empathize with the new student. Decide whether the introduction helps the new student to know the other two students.

Diane and Marcel are eating lunch together and discussing an upcoming accounting test. Sergio, another friend and classmate approaches with Mai, a new student at Northern.

SERGIO: Hi, I guess we're a bit late. This is Mai Wong. She just started here today. Mai, I'd like you to meet my friends Diane Baker and Marcel Durand.

DIANE: Hello Mai, have you got some lunch with you? Good. Come and sit down. We're just thrashing out accounting principles for the test on Friday.

MARCEL: Hello Mai. Welcome to Northern.

MAI: Thank you, Diane and Marcel. Is that right? I've met so many people this morning I'm not sure I'll remember any names.

SERGIO: I'd say you're doing very well. Whenever I'm introduced to someone, my hearing seems to shut down just as the person's name is given.

DIANE: I hear the name, but five minutes later I've forgotten. It's been embarrassing sometimes.

MAI: Well, I've done so much moving around that I've started to use little tricks to remember the names of people I meet. I repeat the name in my mind as I hear it and then say the person's name aloud when it's my turn to speak. The system works quite well as long as there aren't too many new names to remember at one time.

MARCEL: That sounds like a good system. I'm going to try it next time I get a chance.

DIANE: Me too. I guess it's not so much of a trick as just making a conscious effort to remember a name. And speaking of efforts, are you taking accounting with us, Mai?

MAI: Yes, but I haven't taken accounting before so I'm going to be hopeless until I catch up on the half term I've missed.

MARCEL: Well, I for one would be glad to help you after school a couple of days a week. It would help me to review the material at the same time.

SERGIO: I could help too.

DIANE: Let's work out a schedule.

QUESTIONS

1. In your opinion, how did Sergio's introduction make Mai feel about speaking to Diane and Marcel?
2. Was there awkwardness on anyone's part during the introduction? Why do people often feel awkward at introducing someone or at being introduced?
3. Which role do you feel more comfortable with, as the one making the introduction or as the one who is introduced? Why?
4. Can you think of other ways that would help to remember new names in an introduction?

Figure 4-1
Groups meet to solve problems. The skills you learn in this chapter will help you develop your ability to speak in such groups.

PART ONE: COMMUNICATION IN SCHOOL AND EVERYDAY LIFE

INTRODUCTION

In this chapter we will build upon the communication skills learned from the previous three chapters and apply those skills to different situations. We will describe various techniques that will help you to speak comfortably within a group and to a group, whether you are discussing accounting principles, as the students in the dialogue are doing, or the sales figures of the company which employs you.

First we shall start with the more familiar speaking situations — introducing people and being introduced, starting and continuing conversations, and giving instructions or directions.

INTRODUCTIONS

A gathering of friends at home, a wedding, a school committee meeting, a meeting in a bank manager's office, an interview in a human resources office for a part-time job — these are a few settings in which you may be called upon to introduce someone or in which you may be the one to be introduced.

Think of occasions when you have introduced someone or someone has introduced you. Perhaps you can recall introducing a new neighbour to your friends, or a girlfriend or boyfriend to your family. You may remember introducing yourself to the parents of a child when you went to baby-sit, or your boss taking you around to introduce you to your co-workers when you started a new job. Do you recall your reactions to the introductions? Did you feel relaxed and confident, nervous and awkward? Did you feel that you handled the situations well?

Many people find introductions difficult. They are unsure whose name to mention first or they become embarrassed over mispronouncing or forgetting a name. Then there is the hurdle of what to talk about after the introduction has been made. Introductions do not have to be a difficult experience for you, however, if you follow a few accepted guidelines.

The first step in introducing someone is knowing whose name to say first. Here are two rules to follow:
1. Present the person of lower rank to the one of higher rank.
2. Mention the name of the person of higher rank first.

For example, if you were going through the receiving line at your graduation formal, you would need to introduce your date to the principal. The introduction might go something like this: "Mrs. Pearson, I'd like to introduce my friend, Jocelyn Cartier. Jocelyn, this is Mrs. Pearson, the principal of Laurier." Other phrases that are just as acceptable are "May I present," "May I introduce," "This is," and "I'd like you to meet."

Figure 4-2
One of these people is obviously of higher rank. How can you tell from the body language they use?

There are times when you will be introducing someone to a group of people. Rather than making individual introductions, it is easier and quite acceptable to say, "I'd like all of you to meet Iria Lefebre, who is new to the school. Iria, this is Kim Stewart, Jim Gordon, and Nelia Galvao." The introductions should start with the person nearest to you and proceed in a clockwise direction. By giving some information about the person being introduced, in this case the fact that Iria is new to the school, you give the others a basis on which to begin the conversation. Figures 4-3(a) and 4-3(b) show how a person is introduced to a group.

Figure 4-3(a)
When introducing someone to a receiving line, present your guest to the first person in the line first.

Figure 4-3(b)
When introducing someone to a group, introduce your guest to the nearest person first, then to the others in a clockwise direction.

SPEAKING

If the person being introduced has a title that would mean something to the other person, then include it in the introduction. Your introduction would then be, "Mr. Lamb, I'd like you meet Karl Borg, the new manager of public relations."

When you are the person being introduced, respond with "How do you do." Adding the other person's name, for example, "How do you do, Mario," shows that you are paying attention and it will have a positive effect. Saying the name also provides an opportunity for the person to correct you if you have not heard it distinctly and have made a mistake. If you know something about the person that would be appropriate for beginning the conversation, add it to your response: "How do you do, Mario. I understand you were one of the people who started this group two years ago."

Sometimes there will not be a person to introduce you and it is necessary for you to introduce yourself. In this case, state clearly and in a friendly tone who you are and why you are there. "Hello, I'm Neil Szabo. I just started working in the stockroom this week." This is usually sufficient to draw an introduction from the other person and begin the conversation.

Introductions can be formal or informal depending on the circumstances. In a business meeting where a client is being introduced, for example, the introduction will need to be formal. Starting off, "Hi, folks. This is Daphne Gold," or replying "Hi, Daphne" would be inappropriate. In other cases, such as the cafeteria scene in *Viewpoints*, an informal introduction is called for. It is necessary to **gauge**, or judge, the level of formality needed for the particular occasion.

When making introductions
1. *present the person of lower rank to the person of higher rank*
2. *mention the name of the person of higher rank first.*

APPLICATIONS

1. Five students form a receiving line and three others act as guests. All eight students assume fictitious names. Each person in the receiving line introduces each guest to the next person in the receiving line.

2. In groups of six, devise situations such as the ones that follow and take turns making introductions.
   (a) A new employee is introduced to a group of other employees.
   (b) A couple of visiting relatives are introduced to your friends.
   (c) A new friend is introduced to an old friend.
   (d) You are introducing yourself to a special interest group that you have just joined and where no one knows you.

3. Literature provides us with many examples of characters revealing their personalities by the way they speak. Look at the meeting between the school board members and Mr. Digby in *Who Has Seen the Wind* by W.O. Mitchell. Read over this passage and in class discuss the emotions, beliefs, and positions of the characters as revealed by their speech and body language.

4. Role-play the scene described in Question 3 and have the audience make notes of the phrases used by the characters that reveal their positions.

CONVERSATIONS

Much of your time on an average day is probably spent in conversation: walking to school with friends, having lunch with classmates, working at a part-time job after school, dining with your family, or phoning a friend in the evening. Most likely, in these kinds of conversations, you feel fairly comfortable because you know the people to whom you are speaking. Yet you are constantly meeting new people and need to be able to carry on conversations with them. When you meet people for the first time, their body language can make it difficult to approach them, as you can see in Figures 4-4(a) and 4-4(b). Striking up a conversation with someone you have just met requires an effort. With practice, however, the task will be less demanding.

Figure 4-4(a) and (b)
The body language of this student communicates two different attitudes in these two photographs. Which pose do you think is the more approachable?

If you are told something about the person during an introduction, use that information to start the conversation. Even if you are not given any information when you are introduced, you can try asking the person about their interests or their opinions about an event, a movie, or another topic. Asking questions can help you find shared interests such as sports, films, or hobbies. Once you have found one topic of mutual interest, the conversation will probably flow naturally to other topics. It may help you to keep in mind that the other person is probably wondering how to make conversation too. Your friendly efforts will usually be appreciated.

SPEAKING

The trick to asking questions is to phrase them so that they elicit more than a simple yes or no. For example, instead of asking, "Did you enjoy the movie?" ask "What did you think of the plot?" Asking a series of questions that require yes or no answers may sound more like an interrogation than an attempt at friendly conversation.

As the conversation moves to other topics, you may find that you do not agree with the other person's point of view. Do not be afraid to say so. Mild disagreements can add spark to a conversation. However, remember that you will never convince everyone of your point of view. At some point, even though you may both disagree, you should move on to another topic. A tactful change of subject will also be necessary if your conversation develops into an argument.

Conversations require give and take. One person talks while the other listens and then the roles are reversed. As we stressed in Chapter 2, the listener's role is just as important as the speaker's.

The listening skills you learned in Chapter 2 apply to conversations. Remember to take an interest in what the other person is saying and to show interest through verbal and non-verbal feedback. By doing these two things, you will go a long way toward making the conversation interesting and enjoyable.

To show your interest, look at the person speaking and indicate by your posture that you are attentive. Listen carefully, avoiding the temptation to work out your response in your mind while the person is talking. Also avoid interrupting the speaker. Instead, wait for a natural break in the conversation before you respond.

When ending a conversation, take the time to let the person know that you have enjoyed the conversation. Using the person's name will show that you care enough to remember it and will leave a good impression.

Some conversational tips are
1. *be interested in the other person*
2. *ask questions*
3. *respond with more than a yes or no*
4. *encourage different points of view.*

APPLICATIONS

5. (a) Working in groups of four, have one person begin a conversation by sharing some information about a part-time job, vacation, or hobby. The others in the group react or add to the first person's comments. At the end of two minutes, each group member answers the following questions in writing: Did I listen to the other members or was I busy trying to think of something to say? Did I participate? How did I participate?

   (b) Using your answers from (a), describe in writing how you can improve your conversation skills.

6. Develop a list of five questions or statements you could use to start a conversation. Combine your list with another student's and, if necessary, develop additional items so that you have a list of ten. Share your list with the class.

INSTRUCTIONS/DIRECTIONS

How well do you give instructions or directions? Have you ever been asked to give a demonstration in one of your classes? Were your instructions clear and logically ordered? When asked for directions to your house, are you able to give directions that are precise and easy to follow?

Giving instructions or directions is important when another person is in an unfamiliar situation. In Figure 4-5, for instance, the person in the foreground is receiving instructions in the operation of a piece of equipment. In a case like this, it is important to plan what you will say so that you remember to include all the necessary information as well as to provide information that is **sequential**, or logically ordered.

Figure 4-5
Learning to operate a new piece of equipment is easier when someone helps you.

SPEAKING

Listening and watching for feedback will help you to determine whether your instructions or directions are understood. If the receiver looks puzzled, it will be necessary to repeat or reword what you have said.

Often instructions or directions are clearer if presented visually. A hand-drawn map of a route, for instance, will be more helpful than a series of verbal directions. Pointing to equipment parts as you describe their use will help the listener to visualize how they operate. Seeing reinforces hearing.

The following are some general rules to follow, if you are called upon to give directions or instructions in a school or business setting.

1. Organize any materials or equipment before you begin.
2. Position the listener(s) for ease of viewing and listening.
3. Describe what you are about to do, for example, "I am going to instruct you on the use of the 35 mm reflex camera."
4. State the instructions or directions in sequential order.
5. Maintain eye contact as much as possible in order to keep your listeners' attention and to determine their level of understanding.
6. Use verbal as well as non-verbal communication.
7. At the end, summarize what you have said.
8. If applicable, distribute handouts after the demonstration.

When writing instructions
1. *describe what you are going to say*
2. *state the instructions in sequential order.*

When demonstrating
1. *organize materials before you start*
2. *maintain eye contact*
3. *position yourself close to your audience*
4. *use verbal and non-verbal communication.*

APPLICATIONS

7. Prepare instructions on how to perform a familiar procedure, for example, tying a tie or shoelaces, or making a paper airplane. Working in pairs, instruct the other student in the procedure. If there are any difficulties in following the instructions, stop the exercise and alter the instructions as required. Then begin again.

8. Demonstrate the operation of a piece of equipment to the class and provide verbal directions at the same time.

SPEAKING BEFORE A GROUP

Not all speaking is done with one person or a small group. If you continue with your education, if you become involved in community groups, or if you choose to work in a business, then you will probably find it necessary from time to time to speak before a group.

In Chapter 10, we will be examining the steps and methods involved in different kinds of presentations. For now, we shall describe the types of delivery that can be used when speaking to a group and how to introduce or thank a speaker.

Types of Delivery

Speeches can be delivered in three different ways: impromptu, extemporaneous, and read or given from a prepared script.

Impromptu

A speaker is not given prior warning when asked to give an impromptu speech. Consequently, there will be no notes or visual aids and the organization and content must be developed in the speaker's mind as the speech progresses.

Impromptu speeches tend to be informal and it is expected that the topic will be related to the occasion, to the audience, or to a previous speech. Often the occasion for an impromptu speech will be a wedding or a social function and someone will be called upon to "say a few words."

Extemporaneous

Although an **extemporaneous** speech is planned in advance, the speaker uses only abbreviated notes consisting of key words or phrases. It is therefore necessary to be thoroughly familiar with the subject.

Since the speaker is using very few notes, the speech can be conversational in tone. Gestures and other forms of body language will be appropriate. The speaker is also able to look at the audience and gauge their reaction. The speech can then be modified if need be.

An extemporaneous speech requires as much preparation as one that is to be read. Research may be required if the speaker is unfamiliar with the subject. Usually, however, a speaker asked to give an extemporaneous speech will already be knowledgeable about the subject. Once the material is organized, the speaker will decide which key words or phrases will **constitute**, or make up, the notes.

To deliver an extemporaneous speech effectively requires practice. Carefully organize your material and then decide which words or phrases will best represent the main themes and important points.

Simulate, or imitate, the conditions in which your speech will be given as closely as possible. If you will be standing behind a lectern or using audio-visual equipment, rehearse your speech with those props in place. As you rehearse, practise gestures, volume, pacing, and eye contact as if this were the real situation. If you are not sure how your voice sounds, tape-record your speech. When you feel comfortable with your presentation, invite your friends to listen. Ask them what you are doing well and what needs improvement.

Extemporaneous speeches usually have the advantage of being entertaining and some of the most successful addresses given by valedictorians are extemporaneous speeches. Can you think of any disadvantages of an extemporaneous speech?

Read from a Prepared Script

Speeches that require careful phrasing or precise wording are often read. In Parliament, the Speech from the Throne and budget speeches are read because of the technical nature of the material and the necessity for accuracy.

It is difficult to bring life to a speech that is read because it is necessary to concentrate on the written words. There will be little eye contact with the audience and inflections will be limited.

Figure 4-6
Do you think a valedictorian who uses a prepared speech is as effective as a valedictorian who speaks extemporaneously?

Speakers who do not choose to read their speech may choose to have the entire manuscript with them to refer to if necessary. If the speech is well prepared and rehearsed, the speaker can maintain frequent eye contact with the audience and they will not have the feeling that the speech is being read.

Double space the typing of the manuscript and highlight the main points in colour. This will help the speaker to follow the material more easily.

Introducing a Speaker

Quite likely you will be a member of the audience more often than a speaker. You could be asked, however, on behalf of the audience to introduce or thank a speaker.

Usually the introduction of a speaker requires about a minute. In that one minute you should try to make the speaker feel welcome, make the audience receptive to the speaker, and interest the audience in the topic of the speech.

If you were a famous author called Margaret Lee, how would you feel about speaking to a group after the following introduction?

> This is the first of our series of lecturers for this winter. The last series, as you all know, was not a success. In fact, we lost money on our series last year. So this year we are starting a new line and bringing in cheaper talent. May I present Margaret Lee.

How receptive do you think the audience might be after that introduction?

When preparing an introduction, gather all your facts. What is the speaker's name? What are the speaker's qualifications for speaking on the topic? What is the title of the presentation? After you have this information, write it down in an organized manner.

Organizing the Introduction
1. Indicate the title of the speaker's talk.
2. Briefly outline why this topic will be of interest to the group.
3. State those of the speaker's qualifications that are relevant to this particular presentation.
4. Give the speaker's name, making sure you pronounce it correctly.

Tips for Delivering the Introduction
1. An extemporaneous delivery is best. If you were to read the introduction, you would have to look down at your notes and the audience might not be able to hear you.
2. Look at the audience when you give the speaker's name, then turn to the speaker. If you turn as you say the speaker's name, the audience may miss it.
3. "May I present" or "I present" are preferable to overworked expressions such as "It gives me great pleasure" or "It is a great privilege to introduce to you." The latter two expressions, because they have been used too much, may sound insincere.

Thanking a Speaker

Sometimes you are asked ahead of time to thank a speaker after a delivery. You can do some research into the speaker's background. In addition, as you are listening to the speech, jot down some of the main points. A good thank you speech **incorporates**, or includes, material from the speech that has special significance for the audience.

Organization and Content
1. Say that you welcome the opportunity to thank the speaker.
2. Refer to the most significant point you have jotted down.
3. If appropriate, mention some attribute, such as the speaker's sense of humour or extensive knowledge of the subject, that made the presentation enjoyable or effective. If the speaker travelled a long way for the occasion and this was not mentioned in the introduction, you may want to include it at this point.
4. Say thank you on behalf of the group and if there is a gift for the speaker, present it at this time.

Until now in this chapter we have been concentrating on the speaker. Of course, in each of the situations we have dealt with, listening skills are just as important. As a review, copy out this chart on Listening Behaviour Profile and try rating your listening skills.

SPEAKING

Listening Behaviour   **Rating**

1. Do I seat myself where I can see and hear the speaker?   _____
2. Do I listen for the tone of voice and not just to the words?   _____
3. Do I listen to and follow accurately instructions and directions?   _____
4. Do I pay careful attention to what others are saying?   _____
5. If I do not understand what is said, do I ask questions to clarify the meaning?   _____
6. When someone is introduced to me, do I mentally practise saying and spelling the name in order to remember it?   _____
7. During and after an introduction, do I use the new name in conversation with that person or with others to help me remember the name?   _____
8. Do I make a mental note of oral messages I need to remember?   _____

Rate yourself according to the following scale:
1 = always   2 = sometimes   3 = seldom   4 = never

Speeches can be
1. impromptu
2. extemporaneous
3. read or given from a manuscript.

APPLICATIONS

When introducing a speaker, mention the title of the talk, why the topic is of interest, and the speaker's qualifications. Pronounce the speaker's name correctly.

When thanking a speaker, refer to the content of the speech and praise some aspects of it. Thank the speaker on behalf of the group.

9. Each student chooses a topic, then stands in front of the class and makes a statement about that topic. The rest of the class then asks the student questions about the topic. After two minutes change speakers.

10. Each student writes a one-word topic on a piece of paper. The suggestions are collected. Each student draws a topic and then goes to the front and speaks for 30 seconds on that topic.

11. Role-play a student asking the principal to speak on the significance of public speaking to the role of principal. Choose a student to actually invite the principal to speak to the class.

12. Divide the class into small groups. Each group prepares an introduction to be used when the principal speaks to the class and presents it to the class. The class picks the introduction that will be used.

13. After the principal's speech, each student is to write notes for an extemporaneous thank you speech. Choose one student to thank the principal. In small groups, each student delivers a thank you speech.

14. Work in groups of three for this exercise. Read William Faulkner's Nobel Prize acceptance speech, Dr. King's "I Have a Dream," or a speech of your choice. Your librarian will be able to assist you in

locating material. One student researches the background of the speaker and prepares an appropriate introduction. Another student delivers the speech to the class, using one of the delivery techniques discussed in this chapter. The third student thanks the speaker, making specific reference to the content of the speech.

CHARACTERISTICS OF EFFECTIVE SPEAKING

Characteristics of Good Voice Quality

The quality of your voice is a key element to be considered in speaking before a group. The components that contribute to voice quality are pitch, rate, volume, and tone. None of these components should remain static, or the same all the time. They should be varied if you want your voice to be pleasant, audible, and interesting.

Pitch

Pitch refers to how high or low the tones of a voice are. A loud high-pitched voice is shrill and therefore unpleasant. A soft, very low-pitched voice may be difficult to hear. While speaking, we vary the pitch of our voices to emphasize key elements and in doing so, add meaning and interest to our voices. A **monotone** voice lacks inflection and is monotonous to listen to. The meaning of a message delivered in a monotone will be obscured by the lack of stress on important words and ideas.

How would you read the following sentence, as a statement, a question, and an exclamation?

There are snakes in this box.

Rate

Rate is the speed at which you speak. The rate should be fast enough to keep your audience interested, but slow enough to allow understanding. Varying the rate can help emphasize key words or ideas. For instance, important points can be stressed by pausing before or afterwards. A brief silence can also be used effectively to attract the listeners' attention. At which points in the section *Viewpoints* do you think the speakers might have varied their rate of speaking?

Volume

Volume refers to the loudness or softness of your voice. You will naturally vary the volume according to the cirumstances under which you are speaking. When you speak to a group, your volume will be greater than when you are engaged in conversation with one person. Variations in volume can also give emphasis and meaning to words or ideas.

SPEAKING

Tone

Tone is the combination of pitch and volume that allows your voice to express emotion. When you say hello to someone, your tone can indicate uncertainty, happiness, friendliness, surliness, or boredom. A friendly, pleasant tone will win more listeners than a sullen, bored, or sarcastic tone.

Characteristics of Good Speech

Equally important in speaking are the characteristics of good speech: fluency, enunciation, pronunciation, and word choice.

Fluency

Fluency is the ability to speak smoothly and easily. A fluent speaker does not pause to find the right word or to organize the thoughts.

A non-fluent person speaks in a disjointed fashion and is difficult to follow and to understand. The use of "eh," "like," "uh," "um," "er," and "OK" when searching for the next thought or word tends to produce a disjointed effect that distracts the listener.

The use of "eh" is an example of **dialect**, the regional variation of English used in Canada.

Enunciation

When you enunciate well, you say words distinctly. Slurring, mumbling, running words together, leaving sounds out of words, or adding sounds to words are common errors in enunciation. Saying "bringin" rather than "bringing," or "I'm gonna" instead of "I'm going to" are two examples. Poor enunciation makes it difficult for others to hear the words and can lead to misunderstanding. Listeners must concentrate much harder to catch the meaning of poorly enunciated speech, and may not bother to make the effort.

Can you say the following sentences clearly and correctly?
- She sold sea shells by the seashore.
- Yes, Mrs. Slater is going to the Board of Directors meeting. (Did you say going or goin?)
- February is a short month. (Did you enunciate both r's in February?)
- We saw a boring film yesterday. (Did you say film or filum?)

Pronunciation

Pronunciation is saying words correctly. If you are unsure of the pronunciation of a word, check with a dictionary. Usually the pronunciation appears in parentheses before a word is defined. The syllable to be stressed and how each syllable is to be sounded will be given. If you do not know how to interpret the dictionary pronunciation, study the pronunciation key or guide in the front of the dictionary.

Mispronouncing words when you are speaking to a group can have a jarring effect on the audience and will detract from your presentation.

Word Choice

Your choice of words can determine whether what you say is dull and flat or vibrant and exciting. The words you use can also impart ambiguity or clarity to your message. Taking the trouble to build a good working vocabulary will certainly pay off if you want people to understand you and take an interest in what you have to say.

Slang should never be used in formal speech; however, it is acceptable in casual conversation if the other person is familiar with it and has no objection to it. In *Viewpoints*, the slang term "thrashing out" was used. If Mai Wong were a new arrival in Canada, she might have been perplexed by the expression.

The Importance of Body Language

When we are speaking, not only our voice, but also our body conveys the message. The message we send with our body must therefore be the same as the one we put into words. If they are different, confusion will result.

Body language includes mannerisms, facial expressions, and posture and carriage.

Figure 4-7
What can you tell about each of the people in the foreground of this photograph?

Mannerisms

We may have habits that are distracting to others. We may be unconsciously tapping our feet, drumming our fingers, whistling tunelessly, twisting a ring, biting our lips, or frequently pushing hair or glasses into place. Our listener is aware, however. In fact, the listener can become preoccupied with our mannerisms and miss the message we are sending.

SPEAKING

How can you know if you have any distracting mannerisms? Sometimes your friends will tell you, especially if you ask them. The mannerisms may surface only when you are under stress, for example, when you are delivering a speech or making a presentation. Observing and making a list of other people's mannerisms may make you more aware of your own. Once you are aware of your own mannerisms, you can take steps to correct them.

Facial Expression

Look around you at the expressions on other students' and teachers' faces. What can you tell about their mood? Your face also gives out messages about you — whether you are approachable, happy, shy, bored, or angry. A warm smile and a pleasant expression will always make people feel comfortable around you and make them more inclined to listen to you.

When speaking to a group, direct your gaze at each section of the audience in turn. Remember to hold your head up so that they will be able to see your expression.

Posture and Carriage

Your expression sends a message about how you are feeling. So do your posture and **carriage**, or the manner in which you carry your head and body.

When speaking to a group, demonstrate good posture as you take your place at the front, during your presentation, and as you leave. Good posture and carriage will make you feel and appear more self-confident.

While addressing the group, stand in one place with your weight balanced evenly. Rocking back and forth, pacing or leaning on the lectern will make you appear ill at ease and will distract your audience from what you are saying.

When sitting in front of a group, keep your knees together and your back straight in order to appear composed and attentive.

Pitch, rate, volume, and tone determine good voice quality.

Good speech is determined by fluency, enunciation, pronunciation, and word choice.

Your mannerisms, facial expressions, and posture are important when you are speaking.

APPLICATIONS

15. Using a tape-recorder, read the section on extemporaneous delivery in this chapter. Play back the tape. Copy out the Voice Analysis Chart in Figure 4-8 and evaluate your voice characteristics.

16. After completing Question 15, record the same passage again. Evaluate your voice characteristics one more time. Write a report on areas in which you show improvement and on areas in which you must continue working.

17. Work in groups of three. Assign one person to be the speaker, one to be the listener, and one to be the observer. The speaker begins by describing in detail what he or she has done that day since getting up in the morning. The listener asks the speaker to clarify or expand on any statements. The observer listens to both

the speaker and the listener. When either of the two uses a verbal filler such as er, um, like, etc., the observer points it out and the person must begin the sentence again. Rotate the roles so that everyone has a chance to be speaker.

18. List five slang expressions. Write a brief explanation of the meaning of each expression and give a synonym (not slang) for it.
19. Discuss how television, radio, film, and stage require different speaking skills from the performers.
20. Choose a poem or a soliloquy to record. Your selection must allow for voice expression. If you have difficulty finding a selection, you may want to use Cyrano's description of his nose from *Cyrano de Bergerac* by Edmond Rostand. Afterwards, decide how appropriate your reading style was to the material, using evidence from your reading.
21. Speak to the class on a topic of your choice such as your part-time job or your career plans. The class evaluates your voice, using the chart in Figure 4-8.
22. Develop a pantomime routine to accompany a musical recording or mouth the words of a song by a vocal artist. In both cases use gestures and facial expressions appropriate to the musical phrasing and emotional content of the music.

Figure 4-8
Use this chart to rate your speaking skills.

Voice Analysis Chart			
Voice Characteristics	*Very Effective*	*About Average*	*Could Use Improvement*
Pleasing tone, not shrill or nasal			
Variation in pitch			
Rate was varied appropriately			
Voice was easily heard			
Tone was appropriate for the material			
Material was delivered smoothly, no hesitation between words			
Words spoken clearly			
Words pronounced correctly			

CHAPTER SUMMARY

Steps to follow when making introductions
- present the person of lower rank to the person of higher rank
- mention the name of the person of higher rank first
- use expressions such as "This is," "I'd like you to meet," or "May I introduce"

Tips for conversation
- be interested in the other person(s)
- ask questions that require more than a yes or no answer
- respond to questions with more than a yes or no
- encourage different points of view

Tips for giving instructions
- describe clearly
- state the instructions sequentially

Tips for giving a demonstration
- organize the materials before you start
- maintain eye contact
- position yourself close to your audience
- use verbal and non-verbal communication

The three ways of delivering a speech
- impromptu
- extemporaneous
- read or given from a manuscript

Things to know when introducing a speaker
- the title of the speaker's talk
- why the topic is appropriate
- the speaker's name and the correct pronunciation

Things to say when thanking a speaker
- state that it is a pleasant responsibility
- refer to a significant point made by the speaker
- refer to a positive attribute of the speaker that contributed to making the presentation particularly enjoyable or informative

Elements that determine good voice quality
- pitch
- rate
- volume
- tone

Elements that determine good speech
- fluency
- enunciation

- pronunciation
- word choice

Important aspects of body language when speaking
- mannerisms
- facial expressions
- posture and carriage

MAKING IT WORK

1. Read the following case, then answer the questions that follow.

    Vince is the new manager at a fast food restaurant that has just employed four students. At the end of his first week, Vince is contemplating firing one of the students. Three days before, Vince spent fifteen minutes with the student, explaining the kitchen duties. The student, however, is not performing satisfactorily, and in fact, seems not to know what the duties are.
    (a) If you were Vince, would you fire this employee? Why?
    (b) What would you do in the future to prevent this problem?

2. Read the following case, then answer the questions that follow.

    Melanie, an accountant employed by MacGyver and Hewitt Chartered Accountants, is responsible for supervising the college students who work there as part of their college work experience program. Roy, one of the students, is serious about his work and realizes the importance of accuracy in accounting. For this reason he immediately checks with Melanie whenever he is unsure of how to proceed with an entry or a calculation.

    Just a while ago, when Roy went to ask Melanie a question, he sensed some irritation on her part. Back at his desk Roy wonders what he might have done wrong and how he should proceed in the future.
    (a) Why do you think Melanie is irritated?
    (b) What can Roy do to correct the situation?

3. Listening and speaking skills are important in every job. Those involved in sales must use these skills daily, as they are continually meeting new clients.

    The following is an interview with Carol McMurray, a real estate agent. Read the interview, and then answer the questions that follow.

    Question: Carol, what are some of the personal qualities that help to make you successful?
    Carol: *Empathy.* I find that I can put myself in other people's shoes, whether they are wealthy buyers or first-time buyers. Also, the ability to read between the lines and listen carefully. *Patience.* I do not get exasperated easily. I have a high tolerance for other people's decision-making process. Another would be *stability.* I am a stable person in a business that is not stable. *Honesty.* If I make

SPEAKING

a mistake, I admit it. If I had to rank the top three, they would be honesty, empathy, and patience.

Question: What do you mean by "the ability to read between the lines?"

Carol: You listen to the words, but you watch the people. You watch the interaction between them. One person may be talking and the other person is glaring at the speaker. The speaker does not realize the reaction in the companion because he or she is busy talking and is not looking at the other person. If I sense that there is a difference, I get that straightened out first so that they are both on the same wavelength.

Question: You are constantly meeting new people, and you have to get to know them fairly quickly. How do you put people at ease?

Carol: Most importantly, I am prepared to like people and to enjoy working with them. I really like what I do, and it is so interesting because I do not know what the next day is going to bring. I also feel confident about my appearance. I cannot concentrate on other people if I am worried about my hair, nails, or clothing. No matter what, you have to really listen at the outset to catch the people's names and why they are there. In order to allow yourself to do that, you have to come into the meeting not being self-conscious about your appearance. Something else I do is read the newspaper from first to last page and listen to the radio. Current events can keep a conversation going, and if you know of something that has happened in the client's area, talking about it puts the client more at ease.

(a) Would you say that Carol understands the difference between listening and hearing? Support your answer.
(b) In what part of the interview does Carol show that she notices the body language that people use in conversations?
(c) List the ways that Carol makes people she meets feel at ease.

Figure 4-9
"If I had to rank the top three qualities, they would be honesty, empathy, and patience."

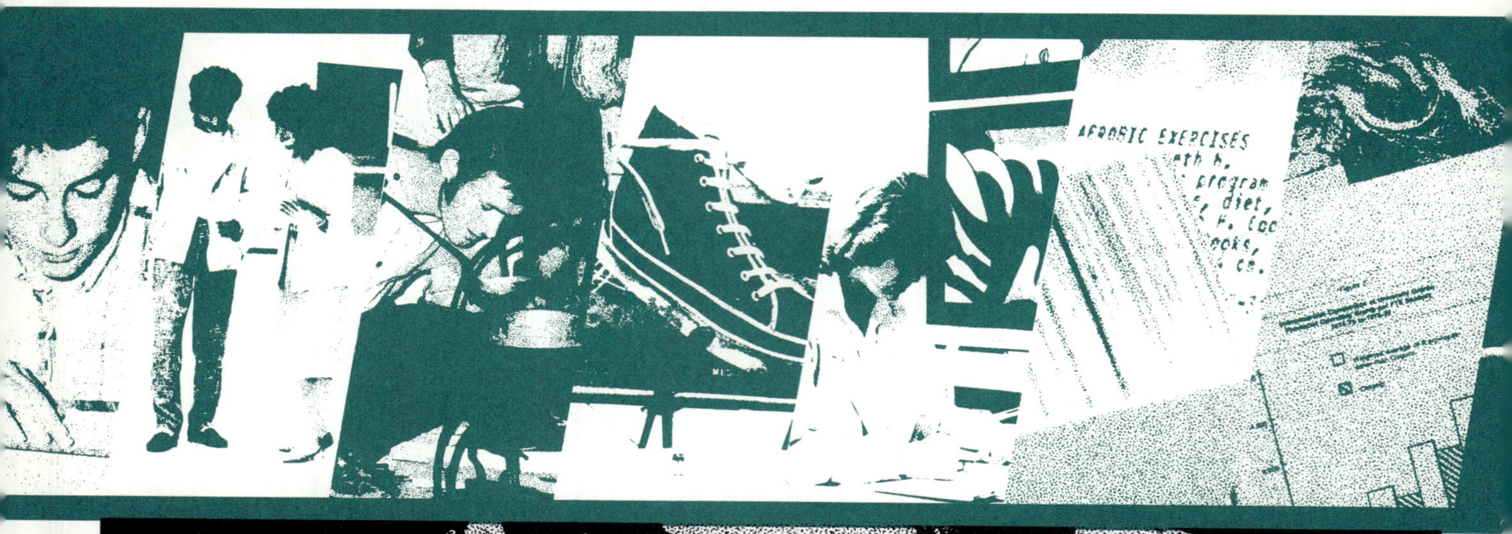
AEROBIC EXERCISES

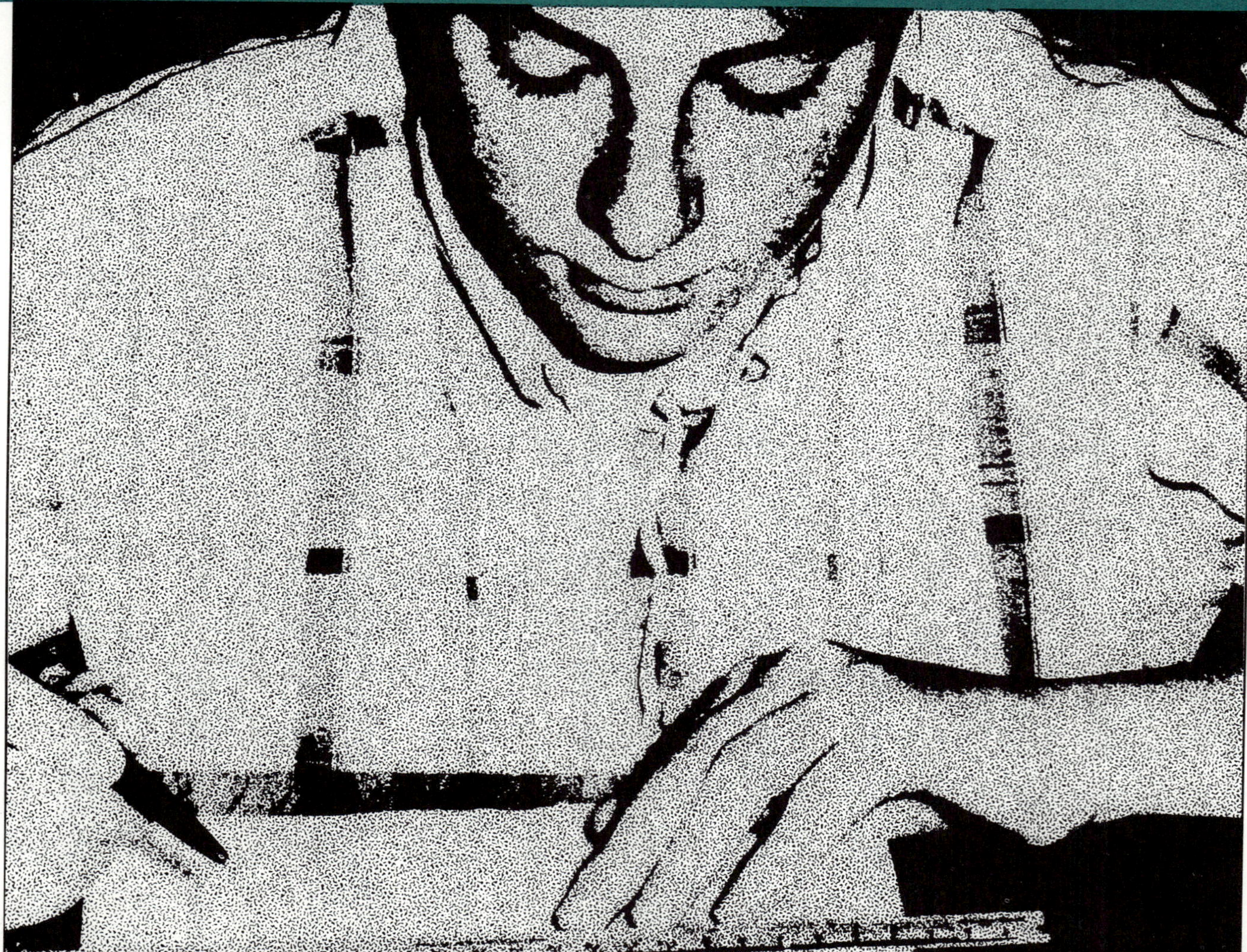

CHAPTER 5

Reading and Viewing

GOALS

At the end of this chapter you should be able to
1. vary your reading rate to suit the material and your reason for reading it;
2. choose a reading style to suit particular reading requirements;
3. practise the procedures for effective reading and viewing; and
4. prepare effective summaries.

VOCABULARY BUILDING

aesthetic
inference
discriminating
headline (advertising)
copy (advertising)

VIEWPOINTS

This dialogue examines how reading can be adapted to particular purposes. Two students, one of whom, Sol, you met in Chapter 3, are beginning to plan a trip to Greece next summer. They have just been to the travel agent and to the library and have with them a stack of pamphlets and books on Greece.

SOL: That travel agent was really helpful. The trip seems more real now. (Puts down a stack of books and a large envelope full of pamphlets) I guess we've got enough material for a start.

KYLE: For a start! I'll be lucky if I can get through half of this material before it's time to go.

SOL: Well, you don't have to read it all through.

KYLE: What's the use of getting it then?

SOL: What I mean is, these books can be skimmed to pick out information that we'll need. We don't have to read them all word for word.

KYLE: You mean skim them the way you read a newspaper?

SOL: That's right, except with books you can scan the Table of Contents and the index to see what's in the book and what you want to read. Then you can skim those passages to find what you're interested in.

KYLE: I tried doing that when I had to write a report on recycling last term, but I kept getting bogged down with details and I ran out of time.

SOL: I know, it's easy for that to happen, especially if what you're reading is technical. Then it's hard to skim and you have to read it slowly to understand.

KYLE: That's what happened. I ended up reading a lot of material that I couldn't use because I was concentrating on the meaning and not on what I needed for the report.

SOL: If you keep in mind the particular information you're looking for as you skim, then maybe you won't get too involved. I'm getting better at it now but I used to find myself drawn in and reading every word before.

KYLE: Well, I'll practise on this travel material. Then maybe my next report won't be such a disaster.

SOL: Okay. I'll deal with the material on customs, food, and geography. You take history, archeology, and art. Does that sound fair? (Kyle nods yes.) Then we can get together with our information and plan what places we want to see.

KYLE: The travel agent suggested that we write to the Canadian Youth Hostel Association to find out about hostels. I'll do that since I've got a typewriter.

SOL: And I'll ask the Greek Consulate to send whatever tourist information they have. Do you think three weeks is enough time to go through this reading material?

KYLE: I think so. Then we can get together and compare notes. The seven months until we go is beginning to seem shorter.

SOL: Good thing we're starting to plan now.

QUESTIONS

1. How do you think Kyle should have organized his reading on the subject of recycling for his report?
2. Make a list of reading materials on Greece or any other country that you find in your school library that would be suitable reading if you were planning a trip there.
3. What methods did you use in preparing the list in Question 2?
4. Can you think of any films Sol or Kyle could view to help them plan their trip? Write down their names.

Figure 5-1
When we read, we gain new insights into the world around us.

INTRODUCTION

Much of the communicating we do takes the form of written or visual material — instruction manuals, magazines, reports, newspapers, letters, signs, advertisements, films and videos, and books on any number of subjects. When dealing with these materials, we talk of *reading* when the subject is presented in print (Figure 5-1), and of *viewing* when the subject is presented through other visual means, such as film. We use many of the same techniques when we view and when we read, and we will discuss in this chapter how these techniques can help us make the most of our reading and viewing time. Let's start by looking at the purposes and methods of reading.

READING EFFECTIVELY

Do you know the old saying "travel is broadening"? Reading is broadening too. When you read, you enter into the world of the writer and see things through the writer's eyes. Good readers are able to appreciate fully what they are reading, whether they are reading for pleasure, guidance, inspiration, or information. They extract and incorporate information and ideas, and evaluate the importance or relevance of a variety of reading materials.

READING RATE

You vary the rate at which you read depending on two main factors:
- your ability to comprehend the material and the difficulty of vocabulary
- the nature of the reading material and your reason for reading it

The difficulty of the material and the vocabulary will have a great deal to do with how quickly you can comprehend it and consequently how fast you will read it. A light novel or magazine article that makes use of familiar vocabulary and simple grammatical structures can be read very quickly. A technical article or book may employ a vocabulary that is specialized and unfamiliar and use long, complicated sentences. Such material will require slower and more careful reading to be understood. It may also require that you consult a dictionary for the meanings of certain words.

The speed at which you read various materials will depend also on what you want to get out of them. You read advertisements, magazine articles, newspaper articles, and light fiction quickly because you do not particularly wish to remember details. You may also skip the parts that you already know or that are not of interest. Other material may be instructional or educational and will need to be read slowly, with great concentration. You may wish to understand the author's point of view, or the material may contain information that you want to commit to memory. Poetry, if you wish to share in the poet's feelings and savour the sounds of the words, is read slowly.

Your reading speed depends on
1. *the difficulty of the material*
2. *your vocabulary*
3. *your purpose in reading it.*

APPLICATIONS

1. Read a poem that you like, or one chosen for you by your teacher. First read it quickly. Then read it slowly to yourself two or three times, looking up any words that you do not know in a dictionary.
   (a) Which method of reading is more appropriate to the reading of the poem?
   (b) Write a short summary of what the poet is saying, based on your second reading of the poem.

2. Sometimes, reading quickly is an appropriate way of gathering information. Look rapidly through the yellow pages of a telephone directory to find the addresses of
   - a dentist
   - a plumber
   - a hardware store

3. As a class, list a variety of print materials read by students. In small groups determine an estimated number of hours spent per week on each reading activity.

4. As a class, rearrange the list in Question 3 in order of student priority.

5. Prepare a questionnaire to determine the following kinds of information:
   - age, sex, and special interests of students to be sampled
   - regular reading habits such as reading textbooks, magazines, daily newspapers, etc.
   - reasons for reading each kind of reading material
   - amount of time spent weekly on these reading activities

   Survey a sampling of your school student population and present a summary of your findings in a chart.

READING STYLES

People read different materials for a variety of reasons. We already mentioned a few: pleasure, guidance, inspiration, stimulation, and information. The way, or style in which you read, will depend on why you wish to read the material.

Careful Reading

Material that is read for understanding and retention is read carefully and at a slower rate. In this way the reader is able to concentrate on specific details and points of interest.

Careful reading is commonly used to:
- follow directions;
- gain maximum understanding of an issue or topic;
- distinguish the known from the unknown;
- evaluate style and content;
- appreciate the **aesthetic**, or beautiful, experience offered; and
- proofread and check for accuracy.

Careful reading is particularly important when we read our own or another person's work to check for errors as the person in Figure 5-2 is doing. In this activity, the reader concentrates completely on the material to be checked. Running a ruler underneath the material to be checked line by line, and even reading the material from right to left instead of left to right are methods of ensuring that attention is fully concentrated on the particular words and phrases being proofread. It is particularly important to use a dictionary (or software that checks spelling) when reading for errors.

Figure 5-2
Special care and accuracy are important when we proofread, or check for errors.

Rapid Reading

Light pleasure reading lends itself to a rapid reading style. With this style you can absorb chunks of material at a time while still appreciating the essence of what is being said.

Rapid reading is commonly used to
- read magazine and newspaper articles of general interest, as the person is doing in Figure 5-3;
- read light fiction or easily absorbed non-fiction; and
- read materials found in waiting rooms that are meant to pass time quickly.

Skimming

Skimming through written material requires an even faster rate than rapid reading. Probably you read much of the newspaper by skimming and stop to read the article more carefully only when a headline strikes you.

Skimming is used effectively to
- preview and select reading material;

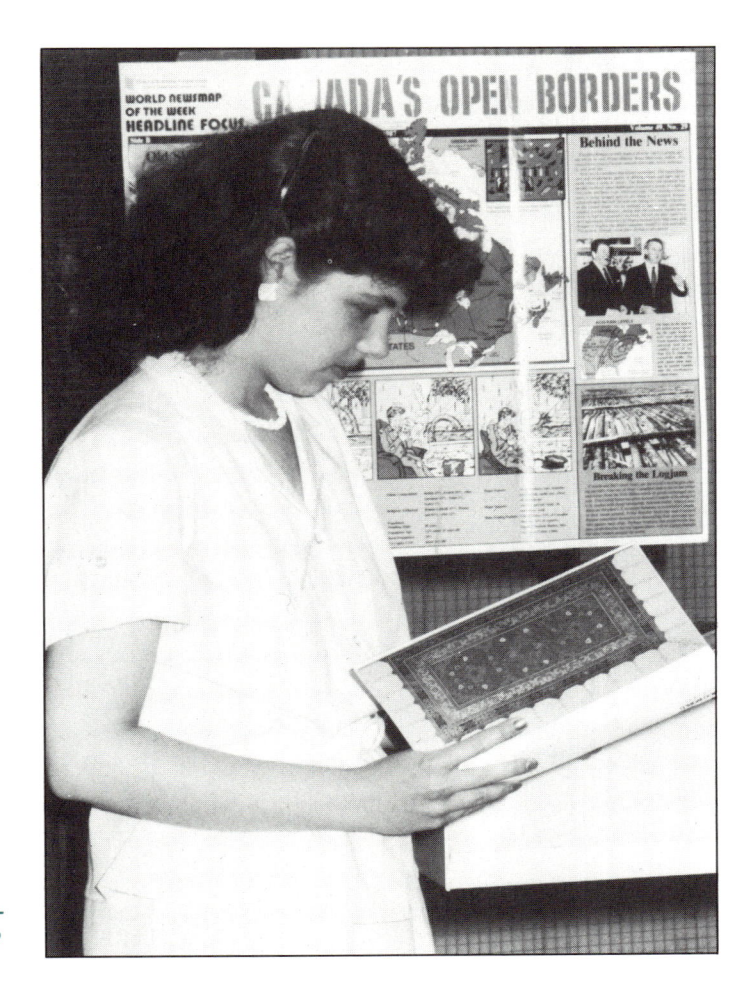

Figure 5-3
How many times in one day do you use the techniques of rapid reading?

- extract the main idea of an article;
- obtain an overview of the material;
- predict the outcome; and
- identify questions that need answers from other sources.

Scanning

Scanning is still more rapid than skimming. It is used for quickly moving through printed materials to find a particular item that you want.

Scanning is used to
- locate a certain section or body of text; and
- find a particular piece of information in a directory, index, or reference book.

One element of effective reading is adapting your reading style to suit your purpose for reading.

READING AND VIEWING

Figure 5-4
An index, such as the one pictured here, requires rapid reading to find the material you need.

INDEX

Note: Pages listed in boldface indicate a definition or, in the case of scientists' names, an illustration.

A

Aberration
  chromatic 346, 347
  in mirrors 323
Absolute zero 173
  and force and mass 97-100
  and Newton's Second law 101
  due to gravity 76, 77, 84-86
  uniform 65-89
Accelerator, particle 166, 602
Accelerometer 90
Accommodation (of the eye) 367
Acoustics 298-301
Action force 105, 106, 107
Adaptor 471
Additive colour mixing 387,
  Colour Plate 2
Adhesion 204
Air columns 285-289
Air reed instruments 289
Airplane wings 219
Alchemists 556
Alhazen 335, 346, 347
Alpha decay 543, 556
  tracks 546
Alternate energy sources — see
  Energy or Renewable energy
  resources
Alternating current (AC) 471
  motors, 509, 510
Altimeter 191
Ammeter 449
Ampere 448, 507, 613
Ampère, André-Marie 448
Amplitude
  of a pendulum 225
  of a wave 234, 235
Anechoic chamber 300
Aneroid barometer 191

Angle
  critical 340
  of declination 494
  of deviation 385
  of emergence 336, 337
  of incidence 315, 336, 337
  of inclination 494
  of reflection 315
  of refraction 336, 337
Annular eclipse 310
Antimatter 602
Antinode 245, 286, 287
Antiparticles 602
Aperture 364
Applied physics 14
Arabic language 9
Archimedes 8, 186
Archimedes' principle 200
Area of graphs 48-50
Aristotle 8
Armature 509
Astigmatism 370
Astronomical telescope 374
Athabaska Tar Sands 158
Atmosphere, as a source of heat 164
Atmospheric pressure 189, 190, 191
Atomic mass 553
Atomic mass number 553
Atomic mass unit 553
Atomic number 415, 552
Atomic theory 414-416
Atomists 8
Atoms 8, 414
  and radioactivity 536-570
  models of 416, 417, 548-551
Attack of a sound 298
Attitude (of image) 317
Attraction
  electric 413
  magnetic 489

Audible range 249, 263
Aurora 495
  Australis 495
  borealis 495, Colour Plate 5

B

Balanced forces 44
Barometer 191
Barrier, sound 265
Baryons 602, 603
Base unit 19, 612
Baseball curve 220
Bathyscaphe 209
Battery 443
Bearing 113
Beats 256, 257
Becquerel, Henri 542, 546, 556
Bed of nails 188
Bel 276
Bell, Alexander Graham 276, 277
Bell timer — see Recording timer
Bernoulli, Daniel 218
Bernoulli's principle 218-221
Beta decay 543
  tracks 546
Bimetallic strip 176
Binoculars 342, 343
Bioluminescent materials 307
Biomagnetism 494
Biomass (energy) 163
Bitumen 158
Blood pressure 193, 194
Body waves 247
Bohr, Niels 550
Bohr's atomic model 550
Boiling water reactor 585
Boldt, Arnold 136
Brass instruments 290
Breeder reactor, 587, 588, 592

PART ONE: COMMUNICATION IN SCHOOL AND EVERYDAY LIFE

APPLICATIONS

6. Divide your class into four groups. Members of each group should bring copies of daily newspapers. Each group will use the newspapers to complete the tasks as assigned below:
   (a) Students in Group A act as advisers to the Prime Minister. They should skim through the newspapers and compile articles and information on topics that the Prime Minister should read in detail.
   (b) Students in Group B assume they are radio talk-show moderators. They should identify the people in the news they wish to interview, the topics to be addressed during the interview, and the specific questions that should be asked.
   (c) Students in Group C assume that they are members of a television newsroom. They should choose news stories of importance together with supporting facts and information for inclusion in a fifteen-minute news report.
   (d) Students in Group D assume that they are comedy writers for a comedian who does a nightly five-minute monologue on topical subjects. They should find material that might be used for the monologue.
7. Each of the four groups prepares a list of the reading styles that were used to complete the tasks in Question 6 and the reasons why that particular style was effective.
8. As a class, discuss how different reading styles are suited to difficult reading requirements.

STEPS TO EFFECTIVE READING

Remember Sol and Kyle in the dialogue? They hoped to get more out of their trip to Greece by planning ahead of time. Reading is much the same. You will get more out of reading if you prepare for reading before you start. The following steps will make the time you spend on reading more productive.

1. Identify your purpose.
   Ask yourself these questions:
   - Why am I reading this material?
   - What do I hope to get out of it?
   - How will I use the information or ideas I gain from it?

2. Provide the right reading environment.
   If you are reading for pleasure, look for a comfortable spot. If you are reading for retention, look for a place where distractions and interruptions are minimized. Lounging on a couch in a room where a television is on and people are talking and moving around is not the best place to study for an exam. Proper lighting is also necessary in a good reading environment to prevent eye strain.

Figure 5-5(a) and (b)
Different reading materials require different environments.

3. Skim through the material.

    Skimming helps you to get a feeling for the content and how it is arranged before you read the material in depth. Looking at the Table of Contents and the headings will provide an overview and the scope of the material to be presented. Familiarize yourself with any key words you come across.

    Taking these steps, you will be better able to identify and concentrate on the main ideas and important information when you read it in detail. Just keep in mind that you are skimming and why, otherwise you might be drawn into reading the material in a piecemeal fashion and not gain maximum benefit from your time.

4. Read the material carefully.

    When you are reading material that requires your undivided attention, try to control both the internal and the external distractions. Block out any thoughts that are interfering with your concentration and any external distractions that are preventing understanding.

    You will likely find that reading the material carefully is easier after the first three steps have been followed. It should also take less time to understand than it would have without the preparation.

    When you come across words that you do not understand, take the time to look them up in a dictionary and establish the correct connotation from the context in which they are found.

5. Evaluate what you read.

    As you read, try to draw **inferences**, conclusions made by evidence and reason; make judgements; note and test concepts; interpret emotions; predict outcomes; and resolve ambiguities. Contrast new information with what you already know. Be alert to bias, or unfair opinions, that are stated without adequate reason.

    If you are reading material that is detailed or complicated and you need to remember it, make notes.

Read effectively by
1. *determining your purpose*
2. *providing a conducive environment*
3. *skimming the material first*
4. *reading carefully afterward*
5. *evaluating as you are reading.*

Figure 5-6(a) and (b)
These two articles present different viewpoints on the use of lie-detectors, or polygraphs. Reading them will help you answer Question 9.

Don't entirely rule out worker polygraph tests

The government's Bill 68, a law that would ban the use of so-called lie detectors in industrial personnel administration, is sailing through the Ontario Legislature with all flags flying.

Nobody is opposing it, and hardly any questions are being asked about Labor Minister Russ Ramsay's legislation, except by a body called the Ontario Association of Polygraph and Audiostress Analysts, who represent the lie-detector industry and therefore understandably feel they are being shafted.

Maybe they are. Certainly when this bill goes through they will be put out of business in Ontario, except as police agents. That raises the first question about what the government is trying to do.

The government's (and the opposition's) case against lie detectors as an employment screening procedure rests on two main points: First that it is an invasion of personal privacy, and second that it is an inaccurate measure of an employee's honesty.

If so, why are the police going to go on being permitted to use this investigative device? If it is an invasion of privacy, then the police shouldn't be allowed to use it on a suspect who by law is presumed innocent. If it is unreliable, then the police shouldn't even be guided by it in their investigations of a crime.

The principle is the same, whether it is a matter of the police trying to narrow the range of suspects, or an employer trying to assess the integrity of potential employees.

Honesty vindicated

The odd thing is that, despite the hostility of the political establishment, a lot of people seem to welcome the polygraph test as a vindication of their own honesty.

Appearing before the Legislature committee studying the bill, lawyer Peter Fallis cited the case of a young woman employee of a large Canadian hardware chain who had been fired on suspicion of raiding the till. She wanted to sue for wrongful dismissal. Fallis' law partner, who was handling the case, suggested a lie detector examination. The woman agreed, was cleared by it, and on the evidence the company came to a wrongful-dismissal settlement.

In another case, a cashier in a fast-food chain was under suspicion by police. She, too, went through a lie detector test and was cleared.

The point is not whether lie detector tests should be categorically banned from all employment situations, but whether their use can be controlled in a way that is, on balance, useful to society.

There are alternatives, of course. Instead of a polygraph test, a job-seeker can have his job application form investigated point by point, reference by reference. It takes times and the results are not necessarily happy all round.

Personal experience

Some years ago I was appointed to a federal government position that conditionally involved a security investigation by the RCMP. That involved (among other things, I suppose) a door-to-door check among my neighbors in Toronto about the habits of the Duffy family, myself in particular.

I was suitably cleared in due course, but not without some curious glances from neighbors who had been questioned.

The hilarious aspect of it all was that the Mountie who was doing the check ended up on my own doorstep, evidently having got his addresses mixed up. He was greeted by my wife, who said "Oh sure. Come on in. I'll tell you all about him."

Personal investigations are, by definition, unpleasant and disagreeable. But they have to be done, one way or another, because there really are a lot of crooks and ripoff artists around.

The polygraph test is no more absolute than the usual interview as a means of assessing a job applicant or his performance on the job. But it is a device that shouldn't be simply dismissed out of hand. On the whole, I think I would have preferred a lie detector test to the neighborhood survey carried out by the Mountie.

Lie-detector ban makes sense

Imagine you work in a restaurant where a number of people have access to the cash register. Suddenly, daily calculations reveal that somebody is stealing money from the till.

In order to find the guilty party, the boss demands that everyone with access to the till take a lie-detector test. Three people fail the test and all of them are fired.

Yet it's entirely possible that none of the three who failed the test was in fact guilty. Since the lie-detector machines — called polygraphs — measure stress, heart rate and the electrical conductivity of the skin, failure to pass the test may indeed be indicative of guilt. It may also be indicative of fear of losing one's job.

To prevent this kind of unfairness and intimidation, the Ontario government quite properly proposes to ban the use of lie-detectors by employers. The machines are increasingly being used in Ontario not just to check workers' honesty but to screen prospective employees. The appropriate amendment to the Employment Standards Act is being debated by the all-party Justice Committee of the Legislature.

The Ontario Association of Polygraph and Voice Stress Analysts appeared before the committee this week to object to the ban. That's not surprising; their business will be adversely affected.

But the lie-detector operators didn't stop there. They turned the concept of civil rights on its head by insisting that employers should have the right to demand lie-detector tests because workers have the right to prove their innocence.

In our society everyone — even a known criminal accused of new offence — is deemed innocent until proven guilty in a court of law. To suggest that a worker should have to prove innocence in the workplace is to deny that fundamental principle.

And surely lie-detectors aren't needed to screen prospective employees even though, as one objector told the committee, people do lie on their job application forms. The time-honoured methods of interviewing applicants and checking their references worked before polygraphs were invented and are still suitable. And preferable.

When Labor Minister Russel Ramsay introduced his bill last June he said of lie-detectors: "Not only are they scientifically invalid and inaccurate, but (they) also constitute an invasion of privacy and engender a sense of fear in the workplace."

Precisely. The government has introduced an enlightened piece of labor legislation. Its enactment shouldn't be put off by the polygraph operators' misguided opposition and their threat to challenge it in the courts.

APPLICATIONS

9. The question of whether to allow the use of a polygraph (lie detector) test in business is of concern to all people in the workforce. Divide the class into two groups, A and B. Students should read and prepare notes on either of the following articles:
   A. "Don't entirely rule out worker polygraph tests."
   B. "Lie detector ban makes sense."
   In a class discussion, each group should present statements to support the conclusions made in the article they were assigned to read. They should then prepare an evaluation or assessment of the accuracy and persuasiveness of the statements made in their assigned reading.

10. Assess your personal reading habits by preparing answers to the following questions. When your answers are ready, move into groups of three or four to discuss them.
    (a) What is the one component of the reading process that you need to improve?
    (b) Do you think about why you are reading a particular piece of reading material?
    (c) Do you identify questions you wish answered from the reading that you do?
    (d) Do you skim through the material to familiarize yourself with the content and organization?
    (e) Do you make sure that you understand key words found in skimming before you begin a careful reading of the material?
    (f) Do you attempt to understand new words or difficult terms from their context?
    (g) What steps do you take to minimize disturbances and distractions?

VIEWING EFFECTIVELY

What do we mean by viewing? When we watch material that is presented on a television or movie screen, we are using viewing techniques. But we use our viewing skills every day, in less obvious ways, as well — when we interpret body language at a meeting or a school assembly; when we absorb the advertisements that appear on billboards or in magazines; and when we "read" the signs, pictures, and designs that appear around us.

In all these activities, our eyes take in a visual message in much the same way as they do when we read print. We know almost automatically when we are driving that a yellow triangle means we should yield the right of way, and, in a restaurant, that a red circle with the picture of a cigarette inside it and a bar through it means that smoking is forbidden.

In these examples, where we viewed or read the visual messages to yield or not to smoke, we used the same techniques that we use for scanning reading matter. And so it is with other material we view — some viewing activities require much more attention than others, just as some reading activities require more attention than others. For example, when you watch television, you will probably vary your viewing habits in much the same way as you vary your reading habits. If a sports broadcast is shown on television at the same time as a rock video show, you may be able to flick from one channel to another, just as you do when you skim-read through a magazine or newspaper. A drama or a documentary, however, will probably demand all your attention, as material which you should read carefully does.

DISCRIMINATING VIEWING

Changes in technology in the twentieth century have made it important that we use **discriminating**, or selective viewing. We are bombarded by images every day, often trying to sell us a product or an idea. It is important that we be selective and sort out which images apply to us individually and which do not. We need to look at the purpose behind the portrayal of the material, and who the intended audience is. We often do this automatically, and we often automatically disregard material that does not apply to us.

The technology of the twentieth century makes it easier for us to view more carefully. Video-cassette recording attachments provide us opportunities to view selectively. We can watch a pre-recorded program, carefully concentrating on every detail, or scan quickly to a part of the program that we want to spend more time examining.

Advertising

Businesses offer a vast array of goods and services for sale. To influence the purchase of their products or services, businesses advertise in print, on radio, or on television. The purpose, audience, and AIDA formula are blended together to produce effective ads.

Purpose

There are many reasons for advertising. Some of these reasons are described in this section. Advertising can be used to increase the demand for a product or service. Car manufacturers often promote sales by offering reduced loan rates. Companies specializing in the preparation of income tax returns advertise heavily during the months before the deadline for submitting returns.

Another purpose might be to increase the number of users of a product. When computers were first manufactured, producers concentrated their sales efforts on large businesses. As that market became saturated, computer manufacturers looked to other groups.

Smaller computers were built with the advertising focussed on small businesses and individuals.

Promoting goodwill, providing a public service, and benefiting an entire industry are other reasons for advertising. For example, pulp and paper companies advertise their reforestation projects to offset the concerns raised by environmental groups regarding the cutting down of large tracts of forests. Various levels of government use advertising to inform people about their services. The egg and milk marketing boards advertise their products to increase the total demand for the benefit of all the producers.

Audience

Advertisements are designed to appeal to groups of people according to factors such as age, income, or interest. Having determined the target group, appropriate vocabulary and illustrations are chosen, keeping in mind the purpose and AIDA formula as well as the group.

AIDA Formula

The psychology of advertising is summed up as the AIDA formula. Because of the number of advertisements seen and heard each day, it is necessary to gain the *attention* of the consumer. This must be followed by appealing to the consumer's *interest*; for example, a sport, career, or hobby. Next, the ad must create a *desire*. This is accomplished by appealing to a psychological need. The final step is to convince the consumer to take *action*. The AIDA formula then is attention, interest, desire, and action.

Parts of a Print Advertisement

This section briefly outlines the basic parts of an advertisement. It provides a simple overview of this topic. Professionals who design advertisements spend years studying and practising their skills to create effective ads.

Headline
The **headline** refers to the word(s) in large type. This might be the product or company name, a command such as "BUY TODAY!", a question such as "WHO OFFERS YOU MORE FOR LESS?", a superlative such as "THE BIGGEST SALE ANYWHERE!", or an advantage such as "SAVE TIME." The purpose of the headline is to grab the readers' *attention* so that they will focus on that ad rather than pass it over and read another one.

Illustration
The illustration may be a photograph, cartoon, or artist's rendition of the product. Depending upon the desired effect and cost, colour or

black and white is used. The purpose of the illustration is to create an *interest* in the reader to read the ad.

Copy
The **copy** is the written part of the advertisement. As the choice of words creates the *desire* to buy, the writer needs to be aware of the connotative meaning of the words. Also, the words must match the audience towards whom the ad is directed.

Signature
The signature may be a company name, trademark, slogan, or brand name. The purpose of the signature is to tell the reader either where the product can be purchased or what company manufactures the product so that the consumer may take the *action* of buying the product.

When we view, we read visual images. We can discriminate our viewing by sorting out the purpose of an image and by identifying the intended audience.

APPLICATIONS

11. Find three examples of material that you have seen recently, such as a television program, a sign in a public place, and an advertisement in a magazine. For each example, identify the purpose and the audience for which the image is intended.

12. Look at Figure 5-7 and see if you can write out on paper the six stages involved in removing an old cassette of typewriter ribbon and loading a new one.

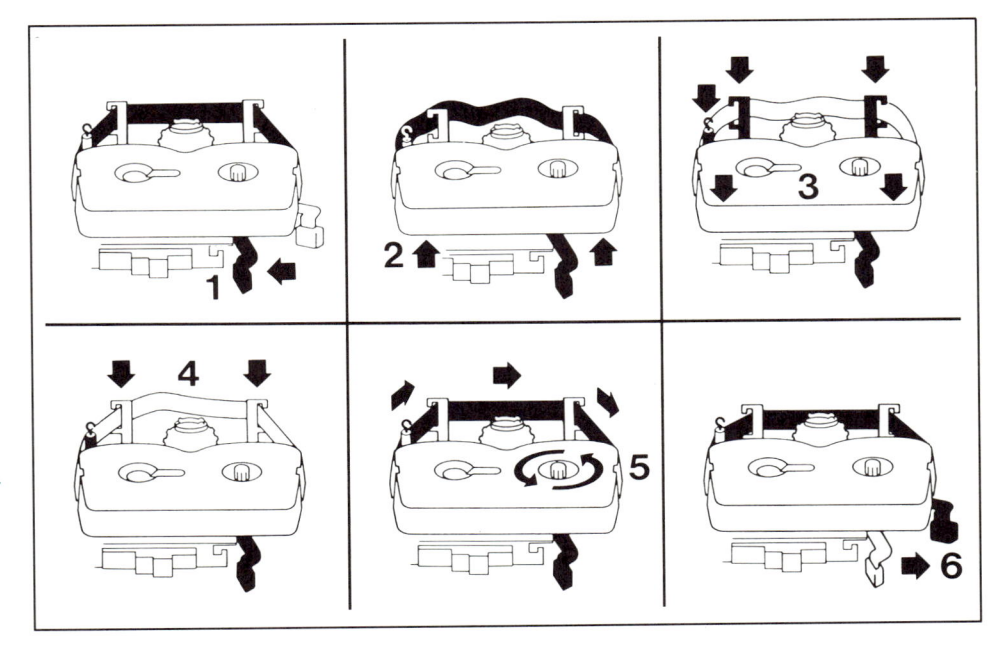

Figure 5-7
These pictorial directions tell you how to unload an old cartridge of typewriter ribbon and load a fresh one. Pictorial directions are often clearer than instructions given in words.

13. Divide into two groups. In one group view a film clip of a speech, a debate, or an advertisement. In the other group listen only to the sound track of the same film clip. At the end of this exercise, compare the two groups' understanding of the presenter's attitude

READING AND VIEWING

When writing an advertisement, consider
1. the purpose
2. the audience
3. the AIDA formula.

The parts of an advertisement are
1. the headline
2. the illustration
3. the copy
4. the signature.

towards the message. Is the presenter serious or entertaining? Does the presenter convey emotions or demand an intellectual response?

14. Determine the techniques used to clarify the message when the film clip in Question 13 is viewed as well as heard.

15. Ask for and receive permission to record a variety of TV advertisements. View these in class and identify the audience they address. List the techniques used to convey the message to sell the product in each case.

16. Using a variety of magazines, find two different advertisements for the same product. Write a brief summary of the differences and similarities between the ads, suggesting reasons for each.

17. Cut two advertisements from newspapers or magazines. Name the purpose and audience for each advertisement. Analyze the effectiveness of each advertisement making reference to the headline, illustration, copy, and signature.

18. Working in groups of three or four, pick a new product you would like to introduce; for example, a perfume, toothpaste, or cleanser. Determine the audience for the product. Prepare an advertisement for your product.

STEPS TO EFFECTIVE VIEWING

Just as with reading, you can apply the same kind of steps to effective viewing.

1. Identify your purpose.
   Ask yourself these questions:
   - Why am I viewing this program?
   - What do I hope to get out of it?
   - How will I use the information or ideas I gain from it?

2. Provide the right viewing environment.
   If you are viewing for pleasure, find a comfortable spot. If you are viewing for retention, make a point of getting rid of all possible distractions and interruptions before you begin.

3. Preview or review.
   If you have pre-recorded a television program, you can watch it several times and zero in on important parts of it wherever necessary. If you are watching a film or a television program, you might want to read a description of the film (or program) first to know what kind of information to look for as you watch.

4. Concentrate on what you view.
   When you are viewing something that requires your undivided attention, make an effort to block out any thoughts that might interfere with your concentration. Keep a pencil and paper handy and jot down important facts or ideas as they are presented.

Steps to effective viewing
1. Identify your purpose.
2. Provide the right viewing environment.
3. Preview or review the material.
4. Concentrate.
5. Evaluate.

5. Evaluate what you view.
   As you watch, try to draw inferences, make comparisons, draw conclusions, ask questions, test concepts, predict outcomes, and resolve ambiguities. Contrast new information with what you already know. Watch for bias and determine where it comes from.

APPLICATIONS

19. Assess your personal viewing habits by preparing answers to the following questions. When your answers are ready, move back into groups of three or four to discuss them.
    (a) How much time do you spend viewing as opposed to reading or listening?
    (b) What materials do you spend most of your time viewing? Why?
    (c) What changes would you like to make in your viewing habits? Why?

20. Using half-hour time blocks, draw up a weekly schedule of your viewing habits. On a scale of 1 to 10, determine the degree of enjoyment or satisfaction you achieve for each time block.

21. Prepare a viewing improvement program for yourself and in small groups explain your reasons for designing the program and how you will go about implementing it.

MAKING A SUMMARY

In addition to knowing how to gather and remember important information from what we read or view and, as we learned in Chapter 2, how to prepare helpful notes, we need to know how to summarize material.

These days, many readers are overwhelmed by the amount of material that is available for them to absorb. Some readers would rather read summaries than read the original, longer material. Look at the success of the *Reader's Digest*, with its summaries of books or articles. These summaries can be read in less time than the original.

The art of writing good summaries is not easy. (George Bernard Shaw, the Irish playwright, once ended a letter to a friend with an apology for sending him a long letter — he said he had not had time to write a short one.) It is hard to be concise and to capture the most important points of a piece of writing or of a film. But, as with effective reading and viewing, breaking the process down into steps can help.

1. Identify your purpose.
   Ask the following questions:
   - Who am I preparing this summary for?
   - What is the audience likely to look for in a summary of this material?

2. Skim.
   Skim through the material to get a sense of its general intent. Keep in mind that you are looking for information that will be of interest to the people for whom you are preparing the summary. You may wish to underline or highlight key passages or scenes. Pay special attention to the topic sentence in each paragraph and the conclusion or to introductory frames of the material being viewed.

3. Read or view.
   Read or view the material more carefully and note important facts. If you are preparing a summary of written material, carefully underline points you will want to include.

4. Re-read or review.
   Read or view it through again. Delete any of the points you may have underlined or noted for inclusion earlier but now feel are not necessary. Trim away extra material. Summaries are only effective if they are brief.

5. Write.
   Organize your facts and write simply, briefly, and clearly. Include all the points that your summary should cover. Make sure that it answers such questions as who, what, where, why, how, and how much.

   Put the most important statement first. Summaries are not meant to make their readers search for the essence of what was written.

6. Edit.
   It is a good idea to put your summary away for a day and come back to it with a fresh look. Read it as if you were a reader of the summary rather than the writer. Ask yourself these questions:
   - Do you understand it?
   - Is it clear?
   - Are all of the important facts included?

   Check each statement for accuracy.
   - Are the figures accurate?
   - Are the names spelled correctly?
   - Is everyone quoted accurately?

   Cut out any unnecessary words or phrases. Summaries are better too short than too long.
   - Have you repeated anything?

   Rearrange your statements if necessary to make sure that the main statement is made first and that all supporting statements follow in logical sequence.

To prepare an effective summary
1. *identify your purpose*
2. *skim through the material*
3. *read or view the material*
4. *re-read or review*
5. *write the summary*
6. *edit the summary.*

APPLICATIONS

22. Choose a magazine article you have recently read or a television drama you have just watched. Write a summary of it that is suitable for a younger reader.

23. (a) Skim current periodicals for articles on a specific topic as decided by your teacher. (You will probably have to ask the help of your librarian.)

(b) Read one of the articles and prepare a summary for other students in the class.

24. Use the techniques of skimming and scanning to find the following information from your local telephone book:
    (a) The telephone number to call for telephone repairs in your area.
    (b) The area code to dial for a long-distance call to California.
    (c) The address and telephone number of your nearest Employment and Immigration office.

25. Having found the street address to (c) above, use a postal code directory to look up the postal code of this office.

26. In groups of two, each person should write a set of instructions showing, in separate steps
    (a) how to back in to a parallel parking space, or
    (b) how to soft boil an egg.
    Using the techniques of careful reading, read your partner's description and write down any steps you think have been missed.
    (c) Now, using your original set of instructions, represent the steps visually for someone who does not speak English. (Look at Figure 5-8 for an example of pictorial instructions.)

27. Summarize an article in the newspaper or an item on television that deals with one of the following topics: native land rights in British Columbia, the performance of a local sports team, interest rates in Canada.

CHAPTER SUMMARY

Reading and viewing are similar activities in that they require us to receive and interpret visually presented information.

Careful reading or viewing enables us to
- follow directions;
- gain maximum understanding of an issue or topic;
- distinguish the known from the unknown;
- evaluate style and content;
- identify techniques used;
- appreciate the aesthetic experience offered; and
- proofread and check for accuracy.

Rapid reading or viewing to absorb smaller sections of material while still appreciating the essence of the whole piece enables us to
- read or view for general interest; and
- pass time quickly.

Skimming through material to preview and select what should be read or viewed in greater depth enables us to
- extract main ideas;

- obtain a general overview;
- predict an outcome; and
- identify questions to be answered from other sources.

Scanning enables us to locate a certain section or identify specific information.

Steps to Effective Reading or Viewing
1. Identify your purpose.
2. Provide the right environment.
3. Skim through the material first.
4. Read or view the material carefully.
5. Evaluate what you have read or viewed.

The preparation of effective summaries involves the following steps:
1. Identify your purpose and your audience.
2. Skim through the material to be summarized to get a sense of its general intent.
3. Read or view the material to note all important points.
4. Re-read or review to trim and clarify your summary notes.
5. Organize and write your summary to make sure it answers such questions as who, what, where, why, how, and how much.
6. Edit for clarity, conciseness, and completeness.

MAKING IT WORK

1. As a member of a public relations firm, it is your job to prepare a fact sheet for the Prime Minister's office. Your teacher or librarian will supply you with a copy of a daily newspaper or current affairs magazine. Your assignment is to scan and identify topics and prepare a brief summary of each article to be forwarded to the Prime Minister's office.

2. In small groups, plan a business trip to another country. Identify the kind of business in which your company is involved and who you will want to see when you arrive. Using a variety of print and/or media sources, prepare a list of facts and information that you will need in order to plan and execute a successful business trip.

3. As a junior marketing research clerk in a large marketing firm, view a series of advertisements and list all of the techniques used to promote the sale of the product being advertised. Compare your list with that of other members of your class and revise it so that you will have a complete list of techniques used in media advertising.

4. Read the following case, then answer the questions that follow.

    One of the regular customers at a local bookstore where you work after school comes by several times a month. Each time he buys four or five lottery tickets and occasionally a newspaper. You have

learned to dread his appearances because he always stays for a while and causes a disturbance. Sometimes he knocks into customers as they stand looking at books. Other times he insists on being waited on out of turn. Often he is abusive to customers or clerks. Today is a particularly busy day and you are at the front counter as he comes in. He is no sooner in the door than he bumps into a customer and starts to shout at the person in a belligerent manner.
(a) How will you handle this situation?
(b) Why?

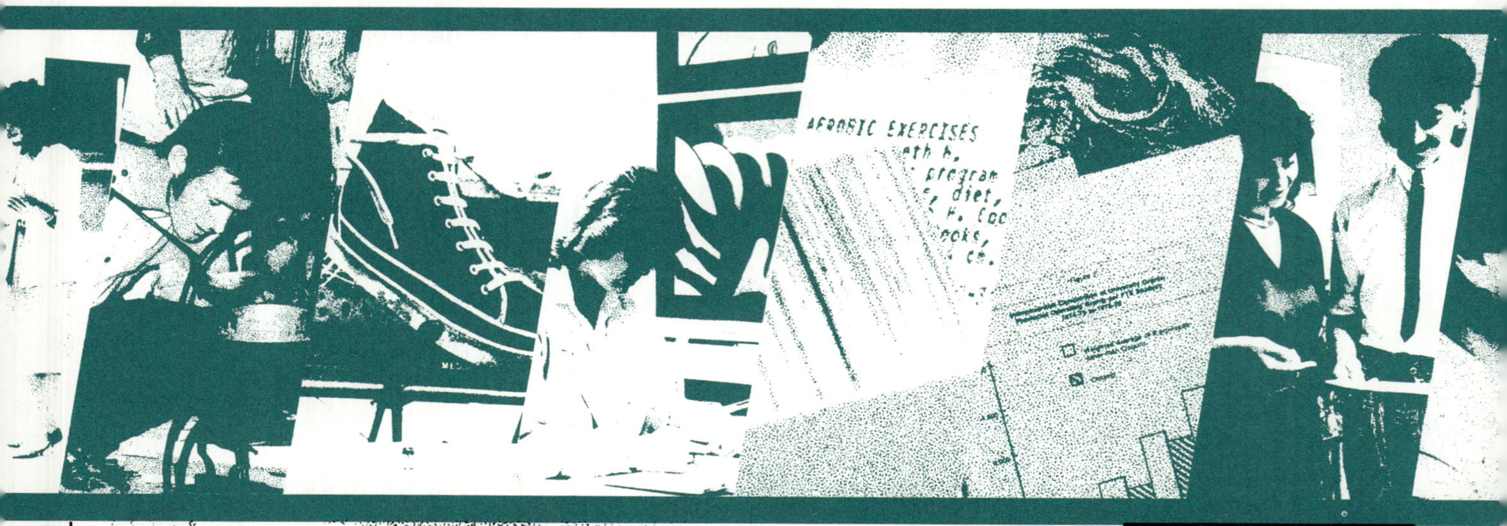
AEROBIC EXERCISES

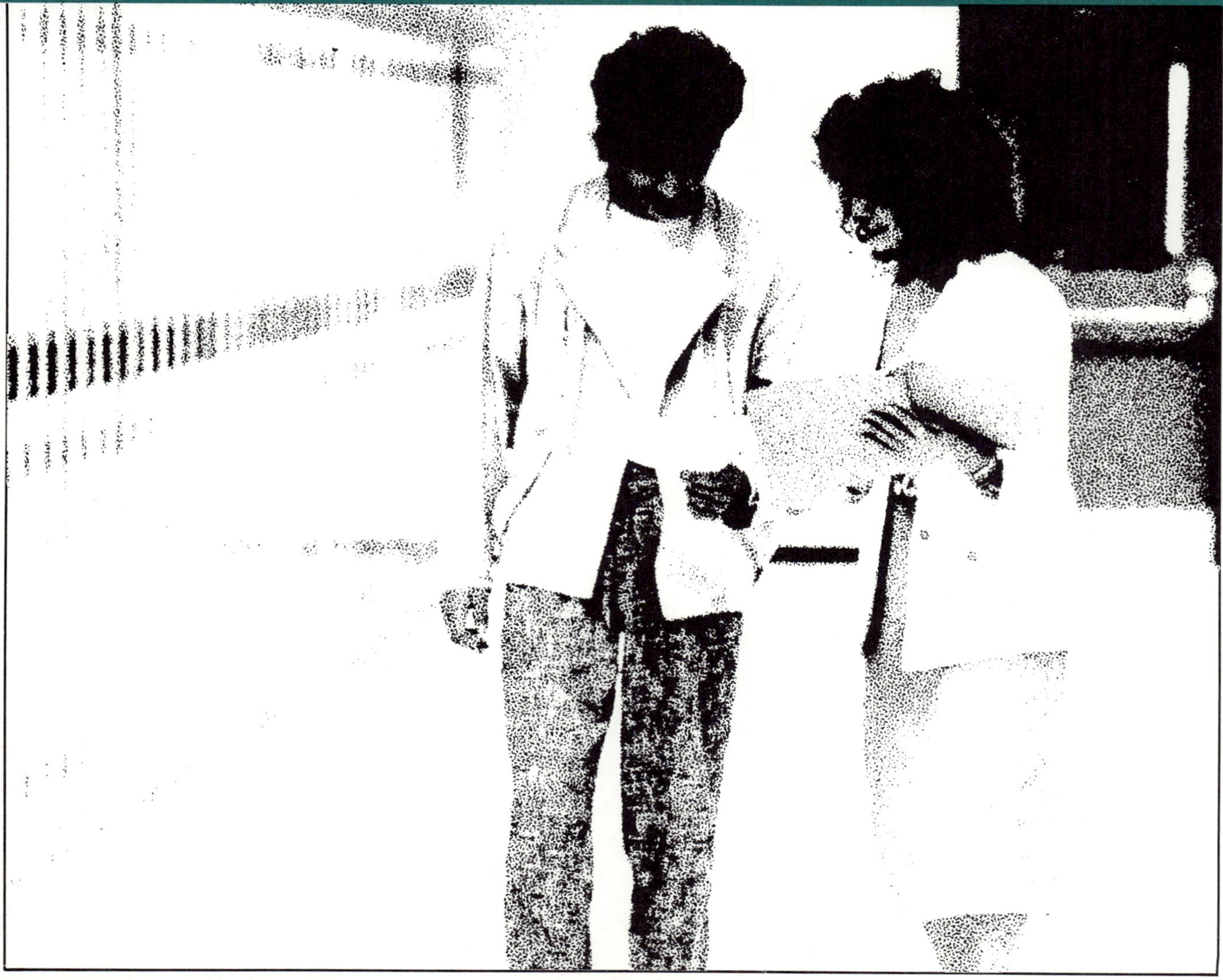

CHAPTER 6

Writing: The Prewriting and Drafting Stages

GOALS

At the end of this chapter you should be able to
1. identify the similarities and differences between writing and speaking;
2. discuss the advantages of word processing in writing; and
3. follow the steps involved in prewriting and drafting.

VOCABULARY BUILDING

word processing
random
keying
software packages
hard copy
right justification
headers and footers

VIEWPOINTS

In the following dialogue two students, Dominic and Vanessa, compare the problems they encounter when answering exam questions. They have just left the classroom where they were going over an exam paper.

VANESSA: That was a tough exam. How did you do on it, Dominic?

DOMINIC: Pretty badly. But I thought I had done all right on it. I had studied hard and I thought my answers were correct, but when we got the papers back today I couldn't believe my mark.

VANESSA: What happened?

DOMINIC: I had left out a whole lot that I knew. I'm so mad at myself!

VANESSA: Did you forget to put it into your rough outline too?

DOMINIC: I don't do a rough outline. I know we're supposed to, but I never have time. I have enough trouble trying to finish on time without doing extra work.

VANESSA: I have to do an outline. If I don't, I wouldn't be able to get my answer in any kind of order. I jot down everything I can think of and then organize it before I start writing the answer. My biggest problem is trying to break my answer up into paragraphs. I never know where one paragraph should end and the next one begin.

QUESTIONS

1. Do you organize your answers to essays or tests before you write?
2. Writing a test is just another form of communication — you are communicating your knowledge of a subject to your teacher. What barriers to effective communication apply in exam situations?
3. Some people find that nervousness prevents them from thinking clearly when writing exams. How could writing a draft and rough notes help such people?

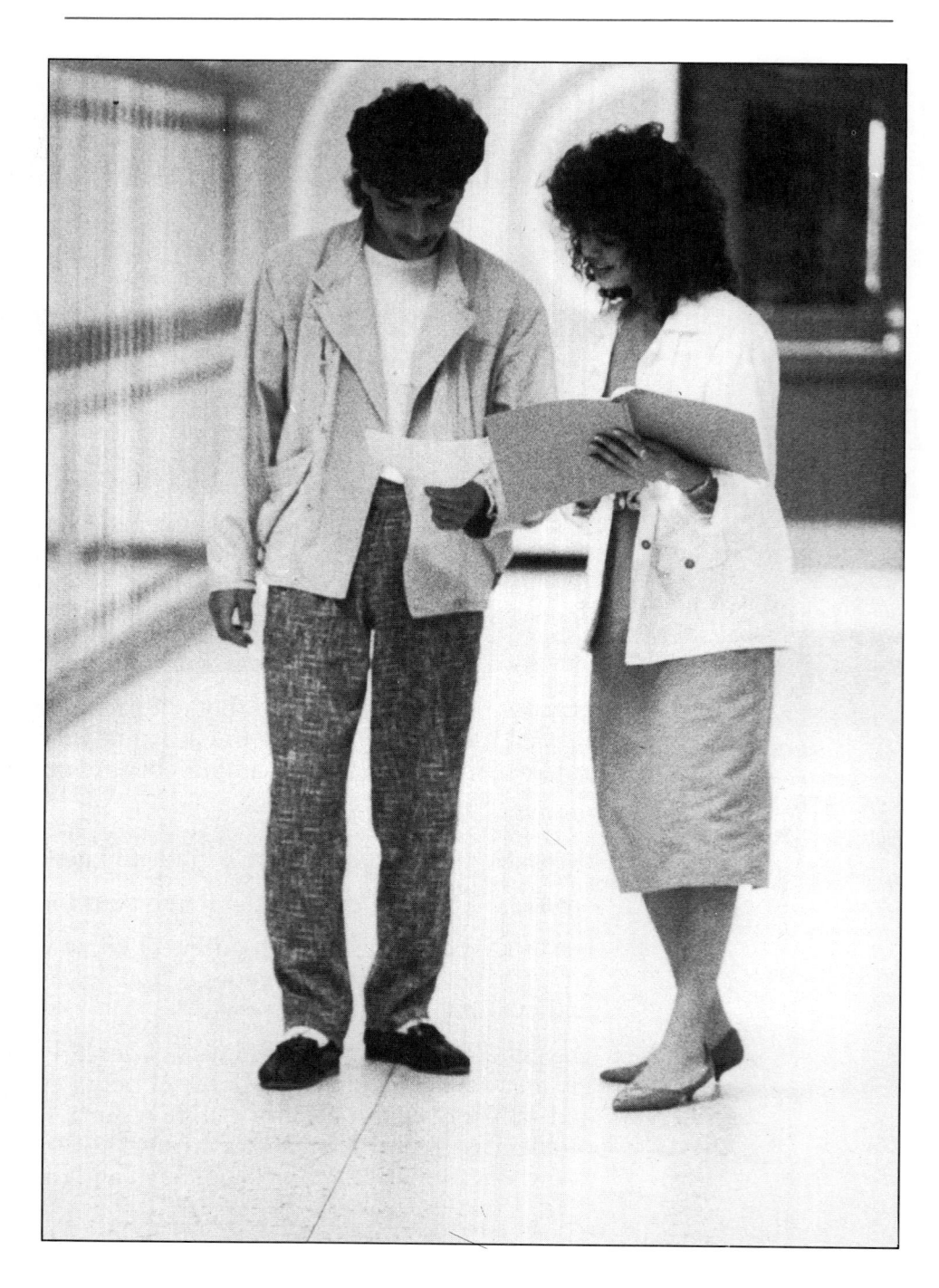

Figure 6-1
Planning can help you write, as Vanessa and Dominic discover.

INTRODUCTION

Expressing ourselves well on paper involves certain skills that can be developed. In this chapter, we will be considering many of the elements of writing and discussing how they can be handled to improve writing skills. Two of these elements, organizing material prior to writing and writing effective paragraphs, are common problems among students, as Vanessa and Dominic, whom you see in Figure 6-1, indicated in their conversation in *Viewpoints*.

One of the most basic skills of a writer is planning — deciding what to say, to whom to say it, and how to say it. The "how" part of the writing is what takes most of the planning. Careful planning can make the difference between a weak, poorly developed piece of writing and a powerful, well developed piece. Dominic, because he did not go through the planning stages with his exam answers, missed including information that would fully develop his arguments. In the last section of this chapter, we will investigate the steps involved in planning what to write.

WRITING AND SPEAKING

Many of the elements of writing and speaking are similar. As the sender of either a written or spoken message, you decide on the purpose of the message, what the message is, to whom you will send it, and how you want to say it.

In writing, you can plan what you have to say and control the process of communication to a greater extent than you can in speaking.

Topic

When you are writing, you address one main topic. For instance, if you are writing an essay about the effects of free trade with the United States on the Canadian economy, your efforts are focussed on just this topic. You will not digress to the acid rain controversy, or to the diversion of water from the Great Lakes to the American Midwest. With spoken communication, however, unless it is a formal presentation, the topics under discussion are always subject to change. You therefore cannot prepare yourself for conversation to the same extent you can for writing.

Pacing

Another feature of writing that differs from speech is pacing. When you write, you can pause, review what you have written, refer to your outline, consider how you want to illustrate an idea, and so on, before you continue. You proceed at your own pace.

With speaking, on the other hand, you cannot easily review what you have just said, and long pauses are not appropriate. The receiver may interpret long pauses as indicating you have finished speaking for the time being and are ready for feedback.

Rewriting

With writing you can exercise additional control by being able to rewrite as often as you wish before communicating the finished product. Have you ever wished that you could rephrase something you just said? Unfortunately, once we have spoken, we cannot take back or change our words.

With writing we can take the time and effort to make sure that the written message says what we want it to say. It is just a matter of rewriting until we are satisfied with the final product.

Writing and Word Processing

The invention of the micro chip has made personal computers small and economical for home and business use. The personal computer is put to very good use in the task of writing. Gone forever are illegible, handwritten drafts and reams of retyped pages. Using a word processor or a **word processing** software, a writer can input **random** ideas, that is, ideas in no particular order, then rearrange, alter, or add to them using quick, simple commands. In this way, the process of rewriting is greatly simplified. For instance, if you wish to add a paragraph in the middle of a section, you simply input the insertion at the point where it is required. The rest of the material will shift to make room.

Keying, the striking of letters on the keyboard to convey information, is the same on a typewriter or the computer. So if you are able to type, you can easily master word processing. Some **software packages**, or programs used for word processing, have a feature that checks your spelling and indicates when you have made a mistake so that you can correct it.

The **hard copy**, or the paper printout of a computer can be formatted to your specifications. If you want the printout to have **right justification**, or an even right edge like the print in a book, it is a simple matter to key in the appropriate command. In the same manner you can have **headers and footers**, information printed automatically at the top and the bottom of each page, such as the title, date, page number, and so on. You can also specify a set page length so that the pages will have a neat, uniform appearance. Figures 6-2 (a), 6-2 (b), 6-2 (c) compare the printout of a computer with handwritten and typewritten copies.

The appearance of a document can produce a positive or negative response from the reader. If you have access to a word processor, you can produce copy that is neat, clean, and error-free.

RISK TAKING

    Risk taking. What does that mean? Thrill seeking, adventure, opportunity, chance? There is a spectrum of meaning. At one end is the thrill seeker - the person who indulges in a dangerous activity to amuse those in attendance. A recent court case involved a fellow suing a resort for injuries he had sustained at the resort. The man had been a spectator at a competition and after having consumed a large quantity of alcohol during the course of the day, decided that he would attempt the same stunt as the competitors. The resort staff tried to dissuade him but he ignored their advice. He failed in his attempt and his injuries left him a paraplegic. In his ruling against the fellow, the judge commented, risk-taking activity, fr who participate cannot h on taking abnormal and complain of the conseque the activity challengin 'abnormal and unnecessa stunt was spur of the pre-planning, training,

Figure 6-2(a)

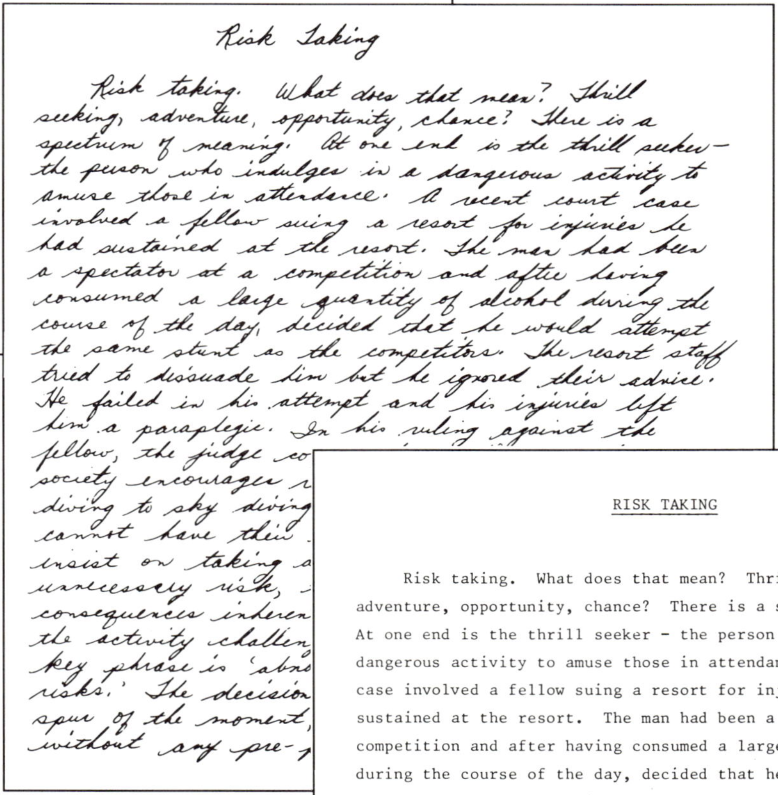

Figure 6-2
The copy printed on computer is visually more attractive than a handwritten manuscript. What differences are there between the copy printed on computer in (a) and the typewritten copy in (c)?

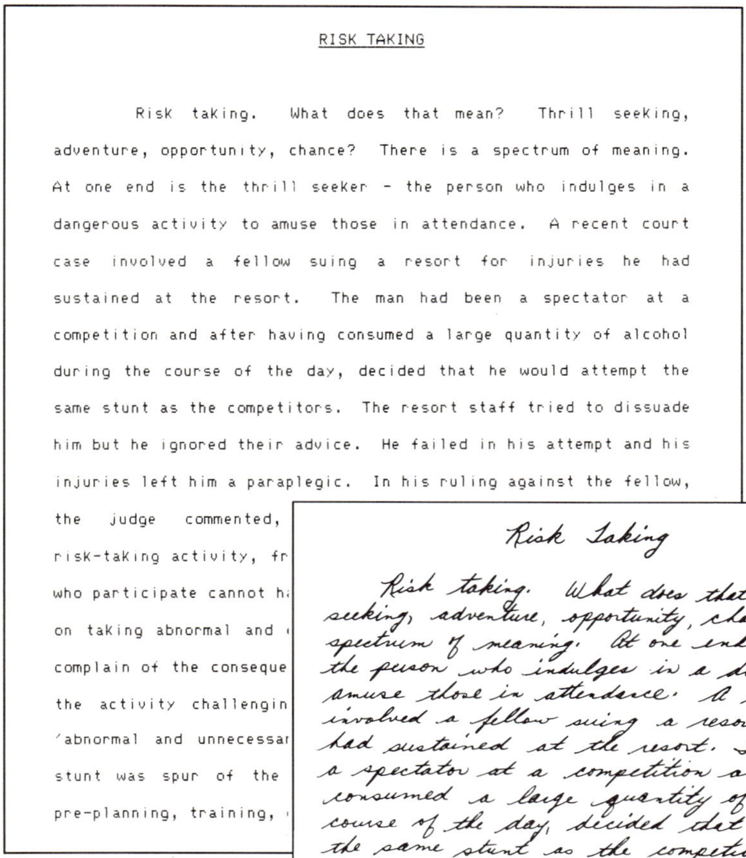

Risk Taking

  Risk taking. What does that mean? Thrill seeking, adventure, opportunity, chance? There is a spectrum of meaning. At one end is the thrill seeker — the person who indulges in a dangerous activity to amuse those in attendance. A recent court case involved a fellow suing a resort for injuries he had sustained at the resort. The man had been a spectator at a competition and after having consumed a large quantity of alcohol during the course of the day, decided that he would attempt the same stunt as the competitors. The resort staff tried to dissuade him but he ignored their advice. He failed in his attempt and his injuries left him a paraplegic. In his ruling against the fellow, the judge co society encourages diving to sky diving cannot have their insist on taking unnecessary risk, consequences inheren the activity challen key phrase is 'abn risks.' The decision spur of the moment, without any pre-

Figure 6-2(b)

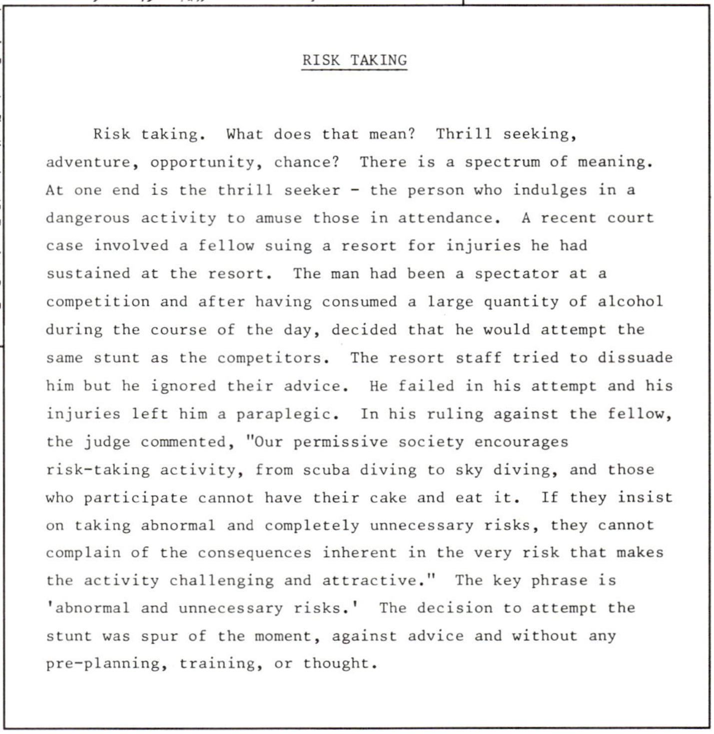

RISK TAKING

    Risk taking. What does that mean? Thrill seeking, adventure, opportunity, chance? There is a spectrum of meaning. At one end is the thrill seeker - the person who indulges in a dangerous activity to amuse those in attendance. A recent court case involved a fellow suing a resort for injuries he had sustained at the resort. The man had been a spectator at a competition and after having consumed a large quantity of alcohol during the course of the day, decided that he would attempt the same stunt as the competitors. The resort staff tried to dissuade him but he ignored their advice. He failed in his attempt and his injuries left him a paraplegic. In his ruling against the fellow, the judge commented, "Our permissive society encourages risk-taking activity, from scuba diving to sky diving, and those who participate cannot have their cake and eat it. If they insist on taking abnormal and completely unnecessary risks, they cannot complain of the consequences inherent in the very risk that makes the activity challenging and attractive." The key phrase is 'abnormal and unnecessary risks.' The decision to attempt the stunt was spur of the moment, against advice and without any pre-planning, training, or thought.

Figure 6-2(c)

WRITING: THE PREWRITING AND DRAFTING STAGES

THE WRITING PROCESS

Writing can be broken down into stages: prewriting, drafting, editing/revision, and publication. Your work, however, does not proceed in an orderly way through these four stages. Instead, you will probably repeat the drafting and the editing/revision stages several times before you are ready to go on to the publication stage. This is the stage in which the final polished product is made ready for presentation.

PREWRITING

In the prewriting stage you select the subject, define your purpose in writing about that subject, identify your audience, research the subject, and decide on an organizational pattern.

Subject

Sometimes you are assigned a subject or given a short list of topics from which to choose. When your choice is unlimited, however, it may take some time to select a subject. You may try looking through magazines or newspapers, or simply thinking about current issues that interest you until you hit upon a suitable topic.

Purpose

Writing can be said to have a general purpose and a specific purpose or specific purposes. Your general purpose in writing could be one of many. You may be writing to complete a school assignment, to make your feelings known to a local newspaper, to communicate with a friend in another part of the country, or to satisfy a personal urge to write a piece of literature or poetry. Within your general purpose you will have a specific purpose or several purposes such as informing, describing, explaining, persuading, or inspiring your readers.

Your purpose(s) in writing will determine what you say and how you say it, so it is important to have a clear idea of why you are writing when you start out.

The Audience

Think about whom you are writing for and how they can be reached most readily. What is your audience's background, education, and experience? The words you choose; the point of view you adopt; the examples you use; and the complexity of sentence structure — these are some of the variables that depend on the audience you wish to reach.

Compare textbooks used in elementary school, high school, and university. Look at a variety of magazines and trade journals. Compare the short stories of Stephen Leacock and Alice Munro. Can you detect differences in vocabulary, tone, and style? Do the differences relate to the audience?

Is your audience likely to agree or disagree with you? Knowing how your audience is likely to feel about what you have to say will help you to decide how to approach the subject. If you expect them to agree with you, then you will not have to convince them of your position. Instead, you will probably want to inspire them to do something.

If you feel your audience is likely to disagree with you, then it will be necessary to logically and objectively argue your position. It is good strategy to consider objectively your audience's arguments first. From there you can point out the weaknesses in their position, then present your own arguments against their position.

Knowing your audience — their background, education, and position — will guide you as you research and organize your information.

Preliminary Notes

The content of your writing may be based on personal knowledge and experience, or you may have to do some research as the students in Figures 6-3(a) and 6-3(b) are doing. Whatever the source, you will need to do some thinking about the subject. Discuss it with a friend or teacher to help generate ideas and clarify your thoughts. As ideas occur to you, jot them down. You need not worry about the order at this point.

Figure 6-3
Researching your topic is part of the planning stage in writing.

WRITING: THE PREWRITING AND DRAFTING STAGES

Outline

Once your preliminary list is made, organize the points into an outline. The way in which you organize the points will depend on the organizational pattern which you think is most appropriate. As you put your points in order, delete those that are not relevant. You will know at this stage what your central idea is, what you have to say about it, and what information you still need.

Suppose you are writing a paragraph explaining why "Star Wars" was your favourite movie. The outline might look like this.

Name of favourite movie: Star Wars
Reason for selection: 1. imaginative special effects
                       2. exciting plot
Details to support: unusual creatures
                   interesting spacecraft and space stations
                   space battles
                   much action throughout

Although an outline is brief, it is invaluable. It represents the plan you will follow when you write your paper, and consequently it keeps you on track. From your outline you can distinguish between main ideas and subordinate ones, and see clearly the relationships in the various ideas you are presenting.

Constructing an outline each time you write something is a useful practice to adopt. When writing your outline, decide how you want to organize your material. There are a number of organizational patterns you could adopt, as the following chart shows.

Prewriting includes
1. determining purpose and occasion
2. determining the audience
3. researching the content
4. preparing an outline
5. determining the organizational pattern.

Organizational Patterns

Organizational Pattern	Description
Chronological	Follows the sequence in which events occur, for example, by date or order of appearance (first, second, third).
Spatial	Follows a geographic plan or physical arrangement, for example, province by province, or clockwise/counterclockwise.
Topical	Breaks down a subject into parts, for example, the subject brickwork can be broken down into tools, mortar, bricks, and techniques.
Cause and Effect/ Effect and Cause	Describes the causes and the results, or in reverse order, the results and what caused them.

Comparison/Contrast · Comparison describes the similarities and differences; contrast, the differences only.

Problem/Solution · Identifies a problem, presents possible solutions, and chooses the best solution to the problem.

Specific to General/General to Specific · Starts with specifics and leads to the main idea or presents the main idea and makes conclusions about specifics.

APPLICATIONS

1. Prepare an outline for a three-paragraph writing assignment on one of the following topics:
   (a) the history of your village, town, or city
   (b) current issues before your municipal council
   (c) a pro or con stand on euthanasia
   (d) the future plans of a local business
   (e) a pro or con stand on eliminating the Canadian Football League
   (f) the activities of one of your community groups
   (g) your favourite artist
   (h) your best characteristics that would impress an employer

   Your teacher will indicate the amount of supportive detail required for each paragraph.

2. Choose a piece of writing consisting of at least three paragraphs.
   (a) Identify the organizational pattern used.
   (b) Explain why that pattern is effective.
   (c) Identify the main idea in each paragraph.
   (d) Explain how the transition is made between paragraphs.

3. Using the organizational pattern given, state the main idea and supporting details you would present in a paragraph for each of the following:
   (a) using cause and effect, your part-time job or a new piece of clothing
   (b) using contrast, two brands of a product or two forms of transportation
   (c) using comparison, ballet and figure skating or dogs and cats
   (d) using the chronological pattern, the development of a baby animal during its first year or what you did yesterday
   (e) using the spatial pattern, the layout of a room or an outdoor scene from a magazine. Number the parts of the picture to indicate the order in which you will describe the content

DRAFTING

When you have selected an organizational pattern and prepared an outline, you are ready to write your first draft. Be generous with your paper. Double spacing and wide margins will make it easier when you are editing your draft.

Your main objective at this point is getting your ideas down on paper, so write quickly, without concern for grammar, spelling, and cohesion. These areas can be addressed later when you are editing. But remember to follow your outline.

The development of your central idea will follow the outline and the organizational plan you have adopted. You develop your argument or thesis by providing examples, details, comparisons, contrasts, or cause and effect relationships. How you choose to develop the central idea will depend on the nature of your subject matter and your purpose in writing. Make sure that your development is as complete as possible. Your readers will be convinced only if you give them enough specific information to lead them logically and clearly through to your conclusions.

In later drafts you will be fine tuning your writing — incorporating revisions you feel will improve your composition.

Writing is done quickly, and in a format to allow for revisions, with double spacing and wide margins.

APPLICATIONS

4. Using the outline developed in Question 1 on page 119, write a draft on the topic that you chose to do.

5. Using the outline developed in Question 3 on page 119, write about the topic you chose to do. Use the organizational pattern stated for the topic.

6. Dominic, in the section *Viewpoints*, had problems when he wrote exams and tests because he did not go through the prewriting stage in preparing his answers.

   (a) Conduct an informal survey of about ten friends or classmates to find out how many of them during a test prepare their answers by writing preliminary notes and an outline.
   (b) Prepare to write a short essay on your conclusions about students' exam writing techniques. First, write preliminary notes and an outline based on the evidence you gathered in (a).
   (c) Write a first draft of the essay based on your outline.

7. How important do you think the skills of prewriting are to a journalist? Prepare to write a short essay on this topic by writing preliminary notes, an outline, and a first draft on this topic.

CHAPTER SUMMARY

The advantages of writing over speaking
- being able to prepare material for one main topic
- being able to pause between thoughts or to refer to an outline
- being able to rewrite material prior to its publication

Some advantages of word processing
- text is in print, not handwriting
- revisions are easily and quickly made
- hard copy can be formatted for neat appearance
- software may have a built-in dictionary option

There are four writing stages
- prewriting
- drafting
- editing
- publication

Prewriting
- determines the purpose and occasion
- determines the audience's role or position, background or education, knowledge of the subject matter, attitude toward the subject matter
- researches the content
- prepares an outline
- determines the organizational pattern

Drafting
- is done quickly
- is done in a format to allow for revisions

MAKING IT WORK

1. Arrange for the editor of your school yearbook to visit your class to talk about the planning and researching stages in prewriting.

2. Invite people from your community to participate in a panel discussion on writing. Some suggestions for panelists are an attorney who does summations for juries, an advertising copywriter, a journalist, a novelist or poet, a freelance writer, a politician, a company executive, or a songwriter.

3. Read the following case and then answer the questions that follow.

    Marcus was waiting to speak to the supervisor of the data management department. There was no one in the outer office and Marcus was standing casually by the secretary's desk. Having nothing else to do, Marcus began reading the material the secretary was working on.

WRITING: THE PREWRITING AND DRAFTING STAGES

It was a memo to the supervisor of the security staff outlining an incident that had occurred the previous evening. Upon returning from a coffee break, one of the computer operators on the midnight shift had been startled to find two police officers in the computer room. After several minutes of questioning, the police officers were satisfied that the operator was a company employee and not an intruder. The operator had been very agitated by the occurrence and reported it to the supervisor. The data supervisor wanted a full explanation from the security supervisor of why and how the police officers came to be in the computer room.

Later, as Marcus and his friends were entering the lunchroom, they passed the supervisor of the security staff. Marcus commented to his friends, "If he doesn't watch it, he isn't going to be around much longer. Wait until I tell you what's been going on around here at night."

(a) Is Marcus' behaviour ethical? Support your answer.
(b) What might be some possible results of his comments to his friends?
(c) How could this situation have been prevented?

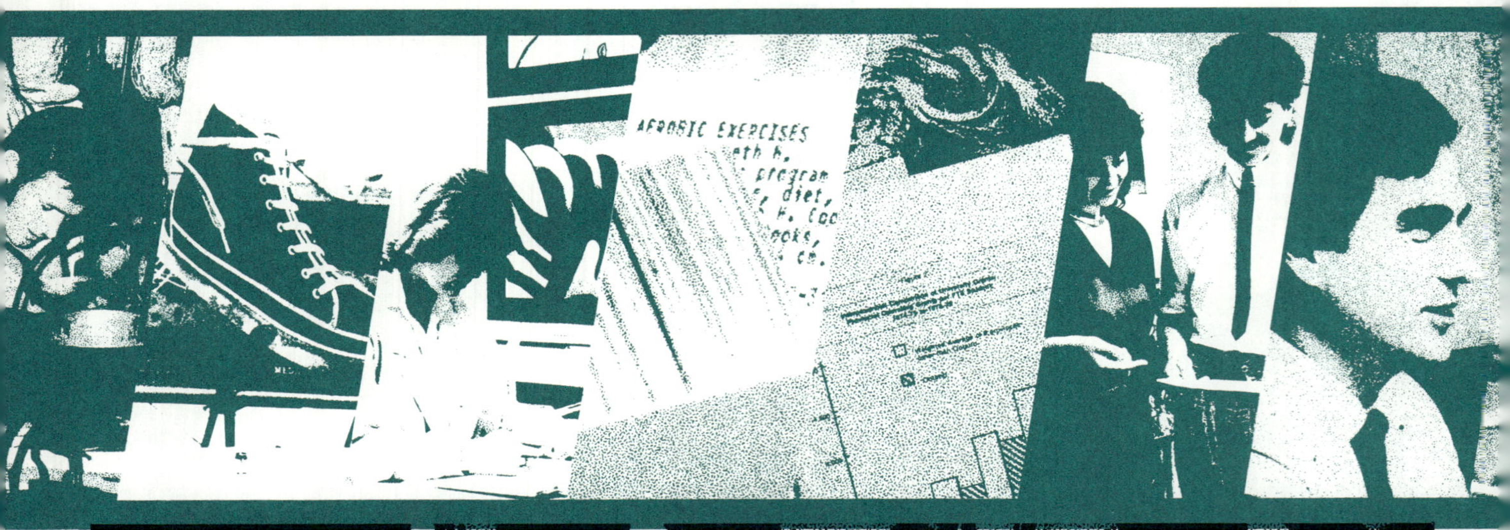
AEROBIC EXERCISES

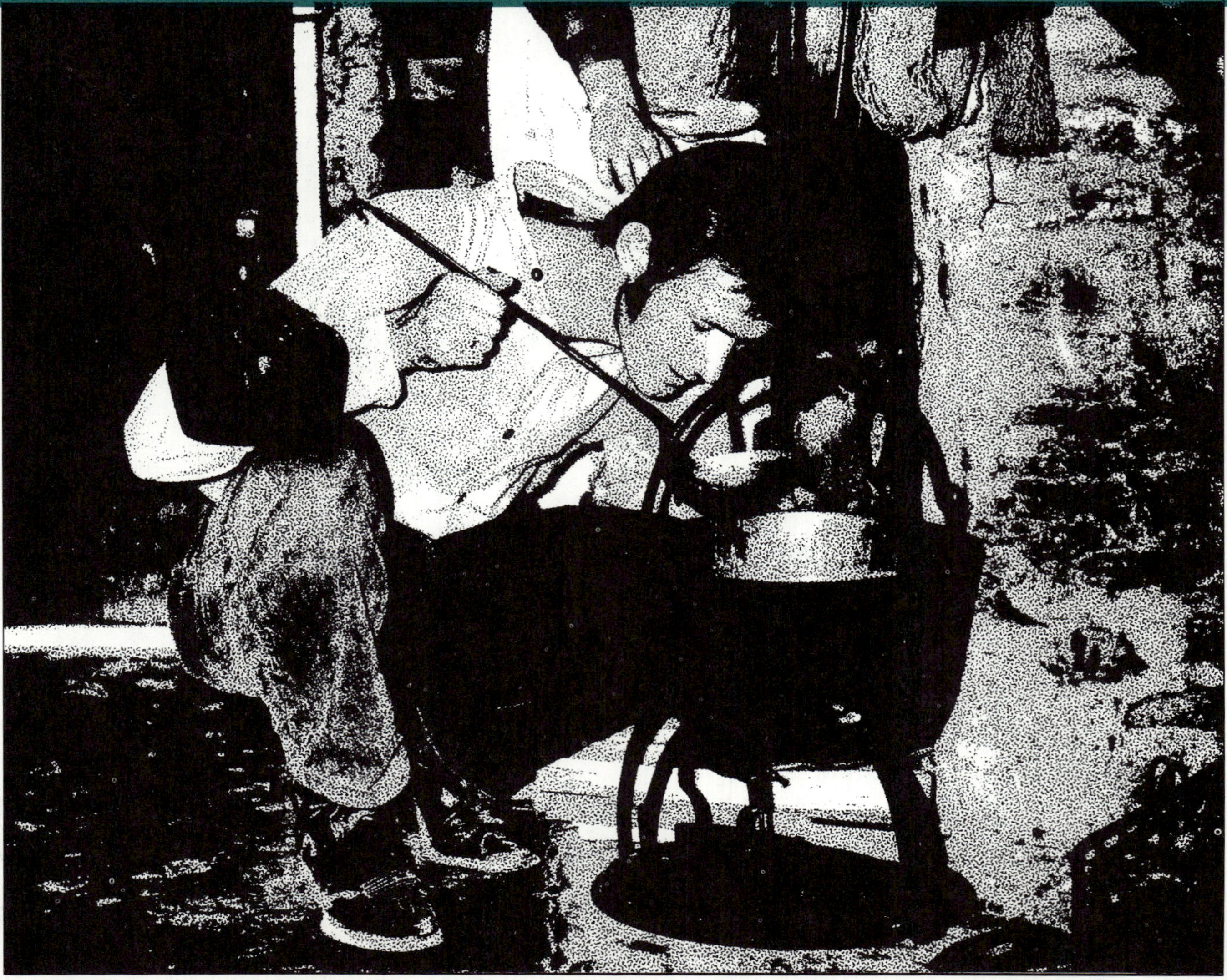

CHAPTER 7

Writing: Editing and Publication

GOALS

At the end of this chapter you should be able to
1. edit a draft of written work;
2. demonstrate an understanding of the role words, sentences, and paragraphs play in clear and correct writing; and
3. prepare a piece of written work for publication.

VOCABULARY BUILDING

editing
idiom
synonym
homonym
malapropism
redundant

VIEWPOINTS

Planning and writing a draft are only the first two stages of writing. What you have written has to be polished and revised. Perhaps you are like Dominic in the dialogue in Chapter 6 and do not spend enough time on the first two stages of the writing process. Or perhaps you are like Gerry in the dialogue that follows, and have trouble with the editing process.

Gerry is sitting in the library trying to get an essay into shape when Lionel comes in.

LIONEL: Hey, Gerry, I thought we were going to play tennis this evening.

GERRY: I can't, Lionel. I've got to get this essay done by tomorrow morning.

LIONEL: It doesn't look as if you're getting much done. What's the problem?

GERRY: Well, I know what I want to say and I've written a draft — actually, Vanessa helped me do that. But I know it's full of spelling mistakes and errors and it looks a mess, but I'm not sure what I should do to tidy it up.

LIONEL: I know what you mean. I had to read an essay out in class the other day, and I must have used the wrong word at one point, because some of the kids started to giggle. So, since then I always check words I'm not sure of in the dictionary.

GERRY: I guess I should do that too. Would you read over my work to make sure it makes sense?

LIONEL: Sure. And maybe when we're done we could print it out on my brother's computer.

GERRY: Great! Thanks, Lionel. If we get our game of tennis in tomorrow night, maybe I'll even let you win.

QUESTIONS

1. What other resources in the library, apart from a dictionary, could Gerry use?
2. Gerry and Lionel are going to use a computer to print out the essay. What other uses could they have put the computer to in the writing process?
3. What do you think Lionel should look out for as he reads over Gerry's essay?

Figure 7-1
Gerry, whom you met in the section Viewpoints, *works on the editing stage in the writing process.*

PART ONE: COMMUNICATION IN SCHOOL AND EVERYDAY LIFE

INTRODUCTION

Editing is the process of reviewing and revising your work to arrive at a polished final product. One of the most important parts of this process is checking for errors in word usage or in sentence structure. Gerry, in Figure 7-1, felt that he had mastered the processes of planning and writing a first draft, but was not confident about his ability to judge the appropriateness or correctness of words. Perhaps you have felt the same way too.

In fact, words, sentences, and paragraphs are the tools of a writer. Used well, they add clarity and shape to your ideas and thoughts when you commit them to paper. In this chapter, we will examine more closely the skills needed to use these tools correctly. By applying these skills to the process of editing, and by taking care to present your work in a neat and readable format, the work you have put into planning and writing will pay off.

EDITING

The first stage of editing is reading your manuscript carefully. A good strategy is to read each draft three times, each time with a different purpose.

First Reading

The first reading will give you an overview of your work. It is not for making changes. As you read, try to adopt the reader's point of view. Is the title appropriate? Are you drawn into the work by the opening statement? Is the central idea clearly presented? Is it logically and fully developed? Are all statements understandable? What additional supporting material is needed? What extraneous material can be deleted? Does it end effectively? During this first reading make marks in the margin where you encounter difficulties of any sort.

Second Reading

During the second reading, stop at any of the marks you made during your first reading and make changes as necessary. Check the accuracy of any quotations or numerical data.

Third Reading

On your third reading, check the language and style. If you must reread a sentence, then rewrite it. If you do not understand it, neither will your readers.

Keep the following questions in mind as you read through your draft.
- Does the material follow a logical order?
- Does each paragraph have a topic sentence?
- Does each paragraph have unity?
- Is there a smooth transition between paragraphs?
- Are the sentences grammatically correct?
- Is the punctuation correct?
- Are all words spelled correctly?
- Are the words specific?
- Is the language level appropriate for the readers?

This third reading should be a check on two aspects of your writing. The structure should be unified and the word usage should be correct and appropriate. To help you achieve these goals, let us look more closely at the building blocks of your essay — words, sentences, and paragraphs.

LANGUAGE AND WRITING UNITS

Written language, more than spoken language, requires structure to give it meaning. We cannot clarify our written thoughts with gestures, inflection, variations in pitch and volume, or facial expressions the way we do when speaking. Instead we provide clarity through our choice of words and the structure of our sentences and paragraphs.

Words, sentences, and paragraphs are the units with which written language is built. There are skills related to the use of each of these three units that we shall deal with in this section. First, we shall examine how we use words.

WORDS

Much of the misunderstanding in communication is the result of an inappropriate choice of words to express a thought. Using a dictionary, when it is possible, helps to avoid some of the difficulties. Making a continual effort to increase your vocabulary also helps.

Denotative and Connotative Meanings

As mentioned in Chapter 1, words have denotative (dictionary) meanings, and connotative (associated) meanings. The reader's previous exposure to a particular word will have created ideas associated with it, forming that person's connotative meanings. To illustrate the difference between denotative and connotative meanings, consider the word "dog." The denotative meaning is a carnivorous quadruped, mainly domesticated. Connotative meanings might be a friendly, loving domestic animal, or a vicious animal used to guard property. What the reader has read about dogs or has personally experienced with them will determine the associated connotative meaning. Consequently, the same word may elicit quite different reactions from a number of readers.

Specific Versus General Language

Because words imply different meanings to different people, the writer is faced with the task of choosing words that convey the thought precisely. Using specific words rather than general ones will help to prevent misunderstanding.

Figure 7-2 illustrates the difference between general and specific words.

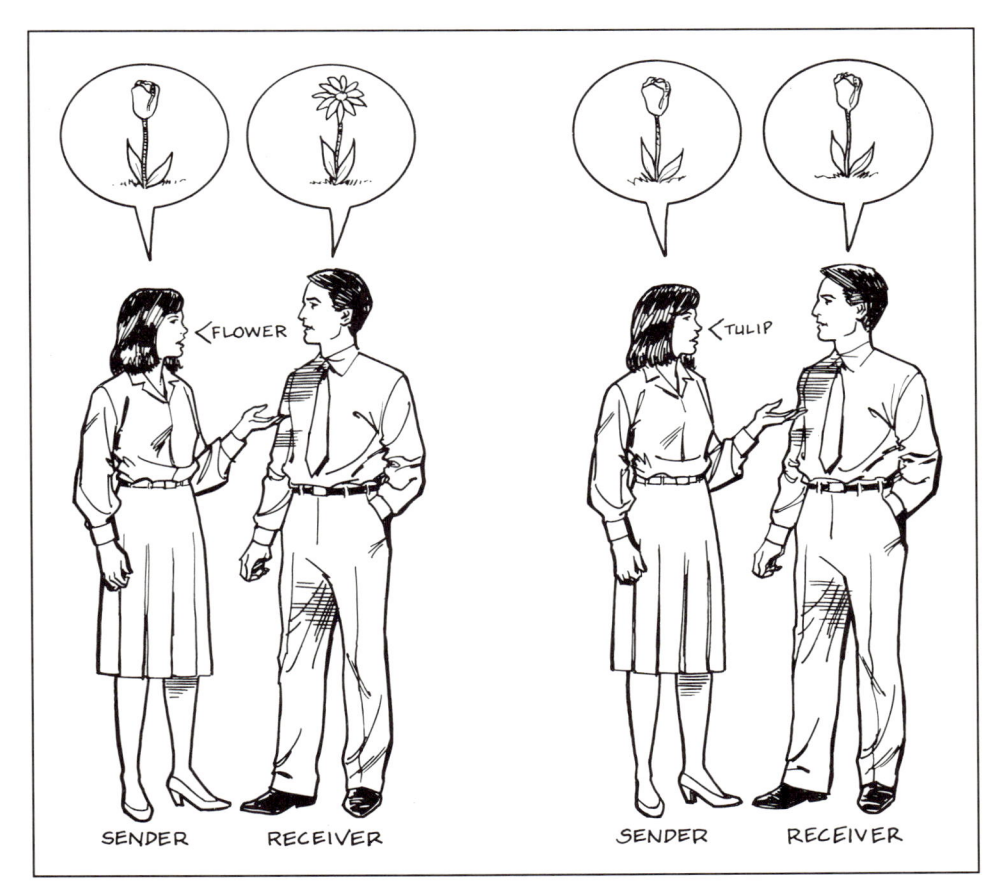

Figure 7-2
If someone says the word "flower," they may be thinking of a tulip while you are thinking of a daisy; more specific language is required in this case.

Variations in Use of Words

The English language, like other languages, is constantly changing to reflect current technology and society. Words are dropped from usage and new words are invented or borrowed from other languages. *Thee* and *doth* are seldom heard now, while *simulcast* and *hologram* are words found only in newer editions of dictionaries.

WRITING: EDITING AND PUBLICATION

Our language varies with time and also with geography. Countries and regions develop words specific to their area, reflecting their customs and society. For example, Australians speak of the *outback*, Americans of *hillbillies*, and Canadians of *fiddleheads*.

An **idiom** is an expression whose meaning cannot be derived from the individual words from which it is composed. See Figures 7-3(a) and 7-3(b). *Turn a deaf ear* and *bite the bullet* are examples. Idioms vary with geography and with time. As old idioms become overworked, they are abandoned and new idioms are generated.

Figure 7-3(a)
To fly off the handle: A sudden wild burst of wrath is often referred to as "losing one's head" or "flying off the handle." Both terms have the same origin — a loose axe head. If an axeman were to lose the head off his axe while chopping, the consequences would be dangerous and unpredictable. The same kind of trouble results when uncontrolled anger is let fly.

Figure 7-3(b)
Potluck: Coming from the days when a pot always hung simmering over the fire, "pot-luck" means making no special preparations. An unexpected guest would be welcome to share what was in the pot, often with no idea what it contained.

PART ONE: COMMUNICATION IN SCHOOL AND EVERYDAY LIFE

Synonyms, Homonyms, Malapropisms

Have you sometimes known the word you need but you cannot remember it? If you can think of a **synonym**, a word that means the same or almost the same, then you can usually find the word you want. Just look up the synonym in a thesaurus and your word should appear alongside it.

A thesaurus is also helpful if you are having difficulty finding a word with a particular shade of meaning. For instance, you might want a word like helper, but referring more to someone you work with. From a thesaurus you could choose from many synonyms provided: *helper*, n. *assistant, co-worker, partner, ally, colleague*. Each of these words creates a more specific image than "helper" and helps to make your writing more precise.

A thesaurus can also help you avoid repetition and the use of overworked words. Using the same word several times can be monotonous, so try substituting synonyms for variety in your writing. Words such as *very, nice, good, bad, thing*, and *get* are overworked. Try to avoid their use by finding a more accurate and vivid synonym in a dictionary or thesaurus.

Homonyms are words that sound alike but have different meanings and are spelled differently, such as aloud, allowed; site, cite, sight; and wear and ware.

If a writer, instead of using the correct word, uses a homonym or a word that sounds similar by mistake, the error is called a **malapropism**. A serious tone can be destroyed by a malapropism. Take for example this sentence from a threatening business letter: "If your car payment is not made within forty-eight hours, your car will be repressed." How would you react to such a letter? Sometimes writers use malapropisms intentionally to create humour. Look at Figure 7-4 for an example of this.

Figure 7-4
In this extract, Charlie Farquarson describes the Winnipeg General Strike, and uses malapropism to create humour. List as many words as you can that are examples of malapropism.

Some mettle workers in Winnypeg went even further out. They'd heard about yer Roosian Evolution got up by yer Marks Brothers, Tropsy, and Lemin, and they figgered they could try the same kinda Bullshyvism at yer Porridge and Main. All they did was sit on their rights fer a six week general strikeout, but the way them Mounties rid their horses agin them, you'da thought they had decomposed King Mackenzie and had him abdicatered.

WE GOT A WRITE, EH, TO MORE PAY!

ON STRIKE

WRITING: EDITING AND PUBLICATION   131

When choosing your words, consider
1. *denotative and connotative meanings*
2. *specific versus general language*
3. *variations in use of words*
4. *synonyms, homonyms, and malapropisms*
5. *redundancy*
6. *level of usage.*

Redundancy

Some expressions such as "new innovation" are said to be **redundant**, that is they say the same thing twice. Below are more examples of common redundancies:

free gift - a gift is a present given without cost or obligation
general consensus - consensus is general agreement
proceed ahead - proceed means to go ahead
combine together - combine means to put together
large in size - large implies size

In the above examples you need only one word to express the idea: innovation, gift, consensus, proceed, combine, and large.

Level of Usage

When choosing words to express your thoughts, keep the level of your intended audience in mind. The following chart summarizes the levels of usage.

Level	Characteristics	Applications
Formal	no contractions no idioms technical and specialized words	legal documents essays public speeches academic writing scientific reports
Informal	contractions idioms shortened words, e.g., phone	conversations and other informal speaking situations newspapers magazines business correspondence
Regional	words peculiar to different parts of the country	conversations with others who understand the words
Slang	usually popular for a short period of time, such expressions can become meaningless, e.g., swell	conversations only if the expression adds flair
Incorrect	inappropriate expressions, e.g., ain't, could of	should never be used

PART ONE: COMMUNICATION IN SCHOOL AND EVERYDAY LIFE

APPLICATIONS

1. Define the following Canadian words or phrases: muskeg, dust-bowl years, kayak, voyageur, screech, and coho.

2. Using language books from your school or community library:
   (a) List five Canadian words derived from each of the following:
     - the French language
     - the Inuit language, Inuktituk
     - the Native Indian languages
   (b) List three words characteristic of the following:
     - your geographic region
     - another Canadian geographic region

3. Present your lists to the class and explain the meanings of the words.

4. Canadian English spelling and pronunciation are influenced by American and British usage. Write a paragraph to support this statement.

5. Rewrite the following sentences replacing the italicized word. State whether the italicized word is too general or overworked.
   (a) The carpenter *fixed* the roof in a half hour.
   (b) What *nice* children!
   (c) My new *car* will be ready this afternoon.
   (d) She *said* that if elected, she would not increase taxes.
   (e) I just finished reading a *terrific* novel.
   (f) We just planted an *apple* tree in our backyard.

6. Choose a colour and write at least six descriptions that suggest various shades of that colour. For example, purple could be purple-black bruises, regal mauve velvet, pale lilac hills, or hypnotic violet eyes.

7. List three names you would choose and three names you would not choose for a child. State the reasons for each choice, for example, its connotation or sound.

8. Use each of the following words in a sentence that shows its meaning.
   (a) deprecate, depreciate
   (b) stationary, stationery
   (c) deceased, diseased
   (d) principal, principle
   (e) legible, eligible

SENTENCES

Using the smallest units or words, we construct larger units or sentences. If we build them well, sentences will express our thoughts clearly as well as grammatically. However, there is even more to sentence writing than a clear, grammatical expression of our thoughts. Sentences, if skilfully constructed, will show the relationship of ideas and facts rather than just state those ideas and facts. There are many ways in which we can say something. What we want is the most *effective* way of saying it.

Active and Passive Voice

Which of the following sentences are more forceful?
1. I was terrified skiing down the slope for the first time.
2. Skiing down the slope for the first time was terrifying for me.
3. Our star player hit the ball right over the fence.
4. The ball was hit right over the fence by our star player.

Sentences (1) and (3) are written in the active voice, that is, the subject is performing the action described by the verb. In sentences (2) and (4) the subject is the receiver of the action. It is being acted upon. Sentences (2) and (4) are written in the passive voice. Most people would agree that sentences written in the active voice, for example (1) and (3), are more direct and have greater impact.

If the subject is not known, however, it will not be possible to write the sentence in the active voice. Then the passive voice will be used, for example, "The corner store was robbed just as the clerk was about to close up." If we knew something about the robber, we might say, "A man wearing a black ski mask robbed the corner store just as the clerk was about to close up."

Sometimes the use of the active voice emphasizes the wrong element of the action. Consider these two sentences:

Active: Construction workers completed the new theatre just in time for opening night of the international film festival.
Passive: The new theatre was completed just in time for opening night of the international film festival.

The main idea is the completion of the new theatre, not who completed it, so in this case the passive voice is preferable.

Types of Structure

A sentence, no matter how short or long, must have at least one verb and one subject, which may be implied. For example, "I am." and "Go!" are sentences. In the second example "you" is understood as the subject. A unit composed of a subject, a verb, and any modifying phrases, adjectives, or adverbs is called a clause. When sentences have more than one clause, they are classified according to the type of clauses they contain. See Figure 7-5.

Main clauses make independent statements, that is, they can form a sentence on their own. A sentence with one main clause is called a simple sentence. A sentence with two or more main clauses is called a compound sentence. Another kind of clause is called a subordinate clause because it expresses an idea that is less important than the idea

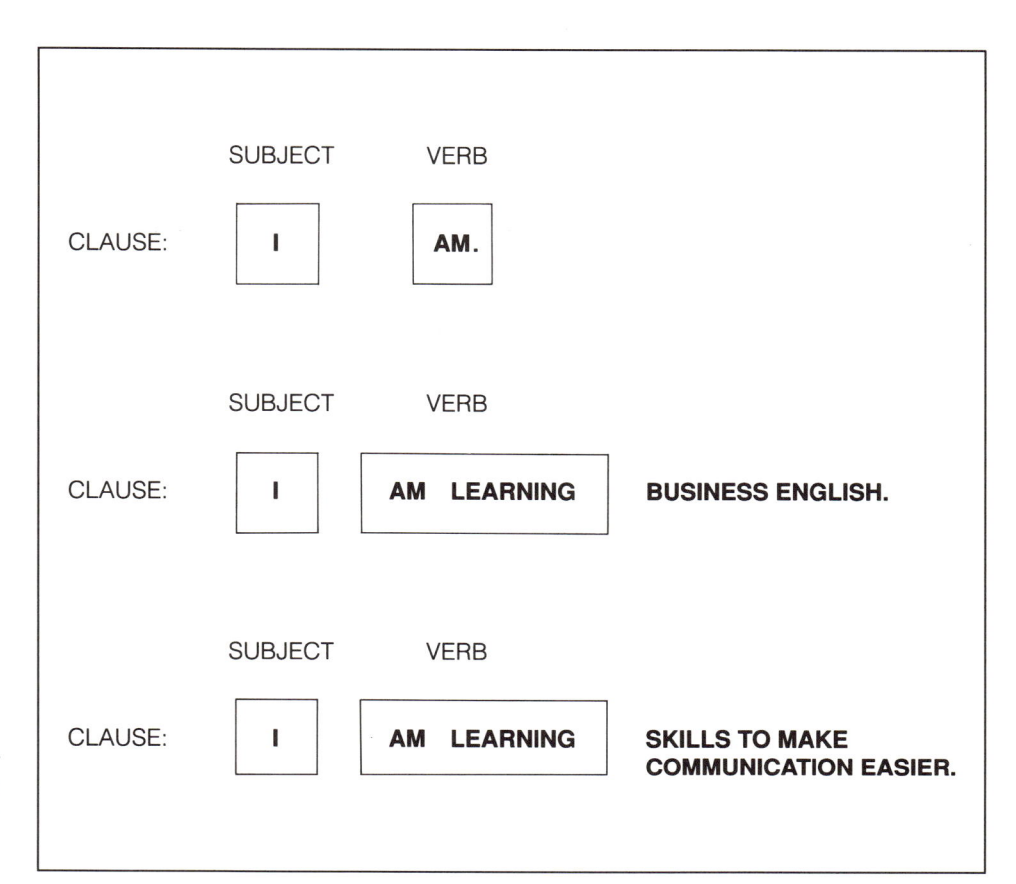

Figure 7-5
Clauses consist of a subject and a verb, and may contain other phrases or words as well.

	SUBJECT	VERB	
CLAUSE:	I	AM.	
CLAUSE:	I	AM LEARNING	BUSINESS ENGLISH.
CLAUSE:	I	AM LEARNING	SKILLS TO MAKE COMMUNICATION EASIER.

expressed by the main clause. Subordinate clauses cannot form sentences on their own and therefore do not make independent statements. The three types of subordinate clauses are noun, adjective, and adverb clauses. Sentences that contain one main clause and one or more subordinate clauses are called complex sentences. If a sentence contains two or more main clauses and one or more subordinate clauses, it is called compound-complex. Examples of simple, compound, complex, and compound-complex follow.

Simple:	The woman hobbled down the street.
Compound:	The woman hobbled down the street and she spoke to many people.
Complex:	As the woman hobbled down the street, she spoke to many people.
Compound-Complex:	As the woman hobbled down the street, she spoke to many people and she paused occasionally to chat with old friends.

Now look at Figure 7-6 to see how these sentences are broken down into clauses.

Using different sentence structures adds interest and variety to your writing. However, compound-complex sentences should be used sparingly because they are usually longer and more difficult to comprehend.

WRITING: EDITING AND PUBLICATION

SIMPLE	SUBJECT VERB **THE WOMAN HOBBLED DOWN THE STREET.** ———— MAIN CLAUSE ————
COMPOUND	SUBJECT VERB **THE WOMAN HOBBLED DOWN THE STREET** ———— MAIN CLAUSE ———— **AND** SUBJECT VERB **MANY PEOPLE SPOKE TO HER.** ———— MAIN CLAUSE ————
COMPLEX	**AS THE OLD WOMAN HOBBLED DOWN THE STREET,** SUBORDINATE CLAUSE SUBJECT VERB **MANY PEOPLE SPOKE TO HER.** ———— MAIN CLAUSE ————
COMPOUND COMPLEX	SUBORDINATE CLAUSE **AS THE OLD WOMAN HOBBLED DOWN THE STREET,** SUBJECT VERB **MANY PEOPLE SPOKE TO HER,** ———— MAIN CLAUSE ———— **AND** SUBJECT VERB **SHE PAUSED OCCASIONALLY TO CHAT WITH OLD FRIENDS.** ———— MAIN CLAUSE ————

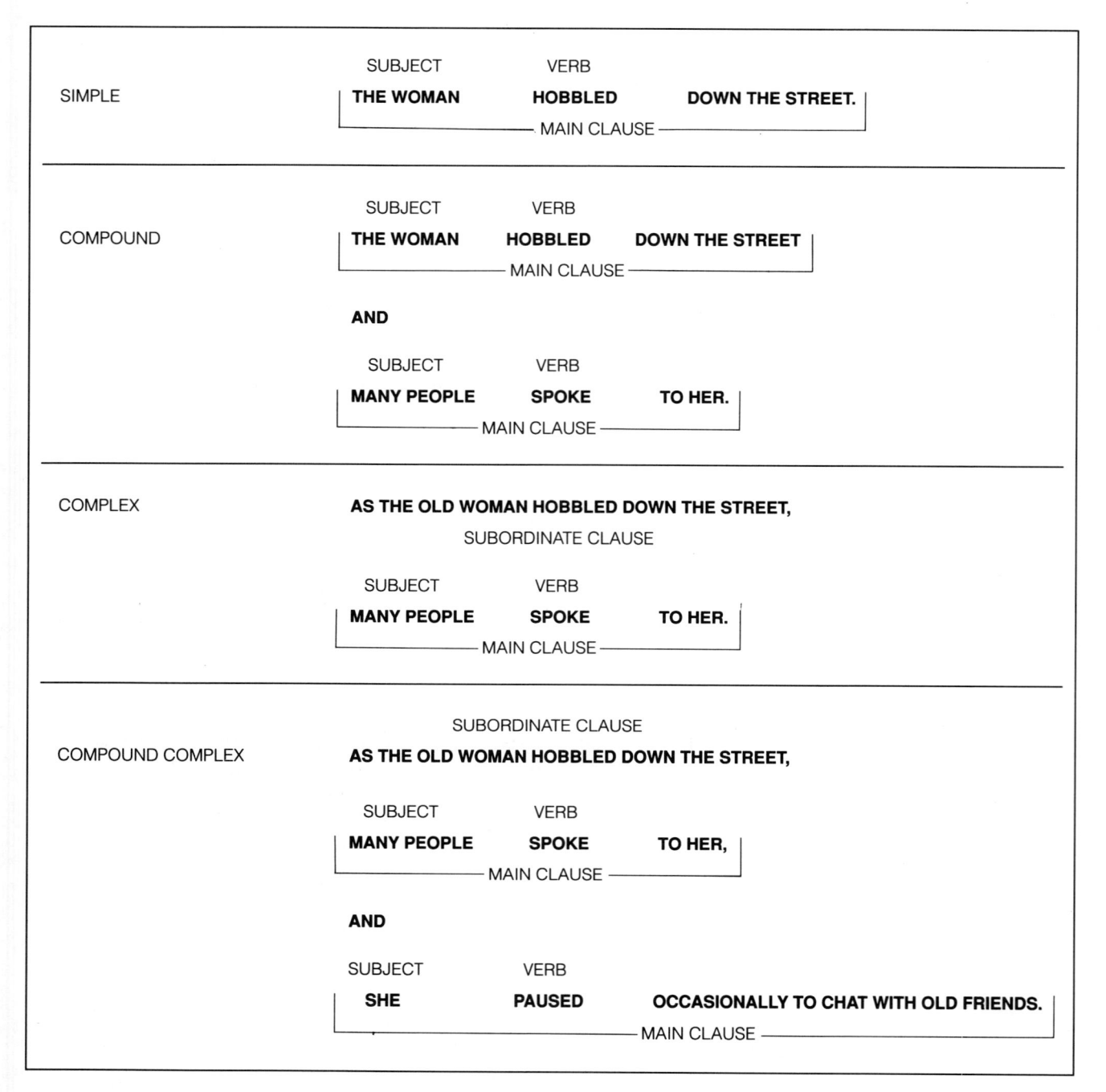

Figure 7-6
Types of sentences

Sentence Length

If all sentences are the same length, they are monotonous to read. Vary the length for interest. Also keep in mind that readers may have difficulty following your train of thought if you use too many long, involved sentences or too many short, disconnected ones.

Sometimes a writer wants to create a particular effect that can be achieved in part with controlling the sentence length. For example, using many short sentences in sequence creates a brisk, choppy effect.

Connecting Words and Phrases

Connecting words and phrases help to bring out the relationship between ideas. Consequently, they make it easier for your reader to follow the flow of thought. Some of the relationships connecting words and phrases can indicate are cause and effect, comparison, contrast, additional information, examples, summary, and time relationships.

Examples of connecting words and phrases include:

after all	nevertheless	for example
although	consequently	in addition
on the other hand	similarly	specifically
meanwhile	generally	otherwise
for instance	however	therefore

Of course, overuse of these words and phrases will produce a cluttered effect. Used in moderation, however, they will help to clarify your writing and make it more unified and smoother to read.

Word Order

Vary word order so that not all of your sentences begin with the subject. This will help to maintain interest and prevent monotony.

Notice how the following sentences can be written in different ways.

- I saw the wind blow the child's hat down the street and ran to try to catch it.
- When I saw the wind blow the child's hat down the street, I ran to try to catch it.
- Seeing the wind blow the child's hat down the street, I ran to try to catch it.
- I ran down the street trying to catch the child's hat which was blown by the wind.
- The wind blew the child's hat down the street and I gave chase.
- Running down the street, I tried to catch the child's hat which was being blown by the wind.

Words can also be arranged to emphasize the most important element. In general, the most emphatic position in a sentence is the end, the second most emphatic at the beginning, and the least emphatic in the middle.

Parallel Construction

When a pair or series of words, phrases, or clauses are similar and equally important in a sentence, they should be expressed in a similar way. Their construction should be parallel. If you use a phrase for one idea, you should also use a phrase for another idea of similar importance. The use of parallel construction will make your ideas clearer and will make relationships more obvious.

WRITING: EDITING AND PUBLICATION

Some examples of non-parallel and parallel sentences follow. Notice how much clearer the parallel sentences are.

Non-parallel:
Singing in the choir, playing an instrument in the band, and hockey practice were three of the activities the student had to schedule.
Parallel:
Singing in the choir, playing an instrument in the band, and practising hockey were three of the activities the student had to schedule.

Non-parallel:
The ceremony to open the new building was both a long event and very dull.
Parallel:
The ceremony to open the new building was both long and dull.

Non-parallel:
The new basketball coach was a well-rounded athlete who liked to swim, cross-country ski, sail, and was good at archery.
Parallel:
The new basketball coach was a well-rounded athlete who liked to swim, cross-country ski, sail, and practise archery.

In the last example, if you want to emphasize the parallel structure, you can insert "to" before each verb so that it reads, "to swim, to cross-country ski, to sail, and to practise archery."

When writing sentences, consider
1. active or passive voice
2. types of structure
3. sentence length
4. connecting words and phrases
5. word order
6. parallel construction.

APPLICATIONS

9. For each of the following sentences, state whether the active or passive voice has been used and change any with a passive voice to an active voice.
   (a) Hailstones smashed the greenhouse roof.
   (b) There were hundreds of people crowding the parade route.
   (c) It has been brought to my attention that some employees are late in arriving.
   (d) A soft voice can be more effective than a loud voice.
   (e) The reason he left school was that his marks were below 50.

10. Correct the errors in the following sentences.
    (a) Irregardless what the final decision is, we will help you implement your plan.
    (b) Diamonds and emeralds are examples of precocious gems.
    (c) I should of read the book before I wrote the test.
    (d) The filum was ordered last week.
    (e) A lot of my friends are graduating after this semester.

11. Working in pairs, compose a simple sentence. Change the sentence to
    (a) a compound sentence
    (b) a complex sentence
    (c) a compound-complex sentence.
    Repeat the exercise. Share one of your groups of sentences with the class.

12. (a) Write seven short sentences about the neighbourhood in which you live. On a separate sheet of paper rewrite your sentences, varying the sentence length and word order, and using connecting words or phrases.
   (b) Exchange your original sentences with another student. Rewrite the other student's sentences following the instructions in (a).
   (c) Compare your rewritten versions noting similarities and differences in the way the sentences were altered.

PARAGRAPHS

Writing well-constructed, grammatically correct sentences with well-chosen, vivid words will, of course, improve your writing. However, if you are unable to construct effective paragraphs you may never get your point across.

Structure

Paragraphs should have one clear, dominant, or central idea. Everything else contained in the paragraph should contribute to the development of that idea.

The central idea should be contained within a topic sentence. The rest of the sentences will then support, explain, or clarify the topic sentence. A topic sentence is usually placed at the beginning of a paragraph, followed by the material that supports it. Another placement of a topic sentence is at the end of the paragraph with the supporting material leading up to it. The topic sentence then sums up or draws a conclusion from the preceding sentences in the paragraph.

Sometimes a topic sentence that begins a paragraph will be repeated with modifications at the end of the paragraph. The emphasis of the repeated topic sentence will often be slightly different in light of the material that preceded it.

After writing a paragraph, ask yourself two questions. Is there any material in the paragraph that is unrelated to the central idea? Are the sentences in a logical sequence? Testing the structure in this way will help you to overcome any problems with paragraph writing.

Length

How long your paragraph is will depend on how much material you need to develop your topic sentence. If you find it running beyond seven or eight sentences, perhaps you are inserting too much detail. Alternatively, you may have material for two central ideas and hence, two paragraphs.

Very short paragraphs may indicate that you are not developing your central idea sufficiently. The result may be a very jerky progression of ideas that is missing the necessary supporting detail.

Connectives

If your paragraph is coherent, the reader will be able to see how each sentence relates to the previous one. There will be a smooth flow of thought and logic. Using connecting words and phrases, as pointed out in the section on sentences, will help make relationships clearer and reading smoother.

Just as the thoughts flow smoothly and logically through the paragraph, they should flow from paragraph to paragraph. The reader should be able to make the transition easily from one paragraph to the next. Sometimes connecting words and phrases can help produce a smooth transition. Look at Figure 7-9 on page 147 for an example of good paragraph transition.

When writing paragraphs, consider structure, length, and connectives.

APPLICATIONS

13. Choose a descriptive paragraph by a Canadian author such as Susanna Moodie, Farley Mowat, or Pierre Berton.
    (a) Identify the types of sentence structure used in the passage.
    (b) Rewrite the passage using only simple sentences.
       What are the major differences between your passage and the original? Which do you prefer and why?
    (c) Rewrite your passage of simple sentences using a variety of sentences. Compare all three passages and state which is the best and why.

14. Rewrite the following sentences to correct faulty, non-parallel construction.
    (a) On my next holiday I intend to swim, relax, and I'm going to go see the sights.
    (b) The students, the staff, and the way the school looked made the school an inviting place.
    (c) My supervisor told me that I was punctual and that I worked hard.
    (d) Gretchen was undecided whether she should apply for college or to seek employment.
    (e) Your essay is to be double spaced and should have wide margins.

15. Working in groups of four, have each group locate an excerpt from written material or a speech that exemplifies parallel construction. Present the excerpt to the class explaining why the parallelism is effective.

16. Choose a piece of material consisting of at least three paragraphs.
    (a) Identify the organizational pattern used.
    (b) Explain why that pattern is effective.
    (c) Identify the main idea in each paragraph.
    (d) Explain how the transition is made between paragraphs.

MAKING CHANGES TO YOUR DRAFT

We have looked at some of the ways you can make words, sentences, and paragraphs work for you in making your writing clear and correct. These are the techniques you should use to polish your draft. After you have changed your draft, your manuscript will be cluttered with marks and rewriting.

Editors and proofreaders use standardized marks and symbols to speed up the process of marking up a manuscript. Learning how to use the proofreader's marks will make the job of editing faster and easier. Figure 7-7 shows some of the more common symbols and a sample manuscript that has been edited using them. If you are using a computer, you will not need to mark up a manuscript. You can edit on the screen.

Figure 7-7
Proofreaders' symbols and how they are used

Symbol	Meaning	Example
⌒	close up space	Meet me in the b oardroom.
ℯ	delete	Meet mey in the boardroom.
ℯ̄	delete and close up space	Meet me in tʰhe boardroom.
#	insert space	Meet me inthe boardroom.
∧	insert letter or word	Meet me ˄the boardroom. (in #)
⁋	indent paragraph	⁋ Meet me in the boardroom.
no ⁋	no paragraph	no ⁋ Meet me in the boardroom.
⊙	add period	Meet me in the boardroom ⊙
⌄	add comma	Bring the report, the statement and your checklist to the boardroom.
⌄;	add semicolon	Meet me in the boardroom; the president will also be there.
⊙:	add colon	Meet me in the boardroom and bring the following items: the report the statement and your checklist.
⩘	add hyphen	Bring the mail-order slip to the boardroom.
⌄'	add apostrophe	Bring the company's annual report to the boardroom.
≡	capital letter	≡meet me in the boardroom.
/ℓc	lower case letter	Meet me in the ℬoardroom. (ℓc)
— ital	set in italic type	Meet me in the *boardroom*. (ital)
rom	set in roman type	Meet me in the boardroom. (rom)
∼ bf	set in boldface type	Meet me in the **boardroom**. (bf)
∪ tr	transpose letter	Meet me in the boardrom.

WRITING: EDITING AND PUBLICATION

Whichever way you make your changes, do another draft incorporating your corrections. While you are editing your next draft, pay more attention to beginning and ending your composition effectively. A good beginning will attract your reader's attention and lead directly into your topic. Beginnings that work are clear statements of an opinion, a proposition, or a fact. Sometimes a short anecdote or a quotation that is relevant to your topic can be an effective way to begin. To end your composition, try to bring what you have said to a logical conclusion. Sometimes restating what you said at the beginning, in the light of the information you have presented, can be an effective closing. Another way of closing is to summarize in a sentence or two the main points you have made.

The drafting and editing steps should be repeated until you have what you feel is a good, final draft. Ask someone whose opinion you respect to read your final draft and tell you if you have communicated what you set out to do. Minor alterations that your reader suggests can be incorporated in your final copy. Major problems though, will mean re-thinking and re-writing your composition. Just remember, good writers must be willing to make as many drafts as necessary to produce a composition with which they are satisfied. The process may seem long, but it is worth it.

PUBLICATION

The final form of your composition may be handwritten, typewritten, or printed by a computer printer. Whichever method is used, remember that its physical appearance will make the first impression on your readers. The effort put into the writing and editing stages can be lost if your final product is poorly presented. Small or faint type, or poor handwriting, will cause problems for your readers and they may lose the flow of thought as a result.

Headings can help your readers to follow your logical progression of thoughts. Main headings should be differentiated from subheadings. The use of upper and lower case, underlining, and boldface, if a computer is used, are some of the ways to set them apart. The treatment used in this book is one example of how to distinguish the levels of headings. Just remember to be consistent in your treatment of headings.

How the text is placed upon the page is another consideration. Double spacing and 4 cm margins at top, bottom, and sides is a standard format, acceptable for most purposes.

Editing includes
1. *first reading for an overview, making marks only in the margin*
2. *second reading, making the changes noted*
3. *third reading to correct language and style.*

Publication factors to consider are appearance and readability.

APPLICATIONS

17. Your teacher will indicate the length and choice of topics you are to write about from the following list. Again, remember to write preliminary notes and a first draft, and to edit your work when you are finished.

    (a) Reply to a newspaper editorial of your choice.

(b) Explain a farming or industrial process of your choice.
(c) Describe an athletic event or a stage production in which you participated.
(d) Describe your reaction to a film or a videotape of your teacher's choice.
(e) Assess the popularity of the current provincial government.
(f) The word "malapropism" has its origin in a play. Using the resources of your library, identify this play, then write about the origin of the word. Use examples from the text which you located.
(g) Discuss the effective use of words by Wilfred Owen in "Arms and the Boy," or by Leonard Cohen in "Elegy" or "Suzanne takes you down," or by Miriam Waddington in "What is a Canadian" or "Grand Manan Sketches." Remember to read over the section on words in this chapter before you begin.

18. Create a collage based on a theme of your choice. Write a story or poem to accompany your collage.

19. If your provincial government makes funds available to students to operate summer businesses, obtain an information package and complete the forms following the instructions provided. If a package is not available, write about a business you would like to operate during the summer. Include a description of the business and how it will operate, the number of people to be employed, its location, initial capital required, projected income, and the amount of the loan required to start the business.

20. Think of an issue or idea you believe in. Write a short passage about it. In the process of writing, follow the prewriting, drafting, editing, and publication steps. Try to use each of the sentence structures and skills discussed in this chapter. Each time you use a different type of sentence, a connotative word, or the active or passive voice, number the word or sentence and on a separate sheet identify what it is. See how much variety you can put into your writing and how it affects your style.

21. Using an advertisement or the lyrics from a song, discuss the following points:
(a) the intended audience
(b) the intended effect
(c) the way that effect is created
(d) the importance of the vocabulary used

22. Develop either a crossword puzzle or a multiple choice game based on Canadian words.

CHAPTER SUMMARY

What editing involves
- a first reading for an overview, making marks in the margin to indicate where a revision is necessary
- a second reading, making the changes noted during the first reading
- a third reading, correcting the writing and style

Writing units
- words
- sentences
- paragraphs

Considerations in the choice of words
- denotative and connotative meanings
- specific versus general language
- variations in use of words
- synonyms, homonyms, and malapropisms
- redundancy
- level of usage

Considerations in writing sentences
- active and passive voice
- types of structure
- length
- connecting words and phrases
- word order
- parallel construction

Considerations in writing paragraphs
- structure
- length
- connectives

Publication factors
- appearance
- readability

MAKING IT WORK

We find the work of writers all around us — in books, magazines, and newspapers; or interpreted on television, radio, and stage. There is also a great volume of writing that does not receive such wide circulation. Examples are business correspondence, reports, proposals, and memos; and personal letters and notes. Whether writing is a person's livelihood, one facet of a person's job, or a personal task, it is undertaken with the same goal in mind: effective communication of thoughts, opinions, or information so that readers will understand the message.

Read the following newspaper article by Charles Gordon and then answer the questions that follow.

A Hammerlock on Absurdity

by Charles Gordon

Mila Mulroney was giving a speech in Florida last week, in the course of which she described the daily House of Commons question period as the equivalent of a daily press conference. "Brian," she added, speaking of her husband, the prime minister of Canada, "says it is our equivalent of Dallas."

That's ridiculous. Question period is not like Dallas at all. Only someone who has not been in the House of Commons very long would make such a demeaning comparison.

Question period is our equivalent of professional wrestling.

Dallas is about rich oil men and shady wives and people boozing around the swimming pool. There is none of that in question period and Brian Mulroney, assuming he was quoted correctly by his wife—and if a wife can't quote you correctly, who can?—should know better.

Professional wrestling, on the other hand, is full of mock outrage, phoney anger, cheap theatrics, manufactured grudges, pulled punches and overweight men.

We rest our case.

The customer knows professional wrestling is a fake, but he goes to watch it anyway because he likes the spectacle. He likes the idea of seeing good versus evil and knowing which is which. This is a very complicated world we live in and, outside of professional wrestling and the House of Commons, it is often difficult to tell.

That is why professional wrestling is making a comeback. A couple of weeks ago Mr. T and some other guy fought some bad guys and people flocked to see it in person, forked out big bucks to watch it on closed-circuit television.

There were all overweight people fighting. They seemed to be very angry at each other. They threatened each other for weeks before the fight. There was a grudge, having to do with somebody's honor. People loved it and the fight was very exciting and nobody got hurt in it.

Question period is like that. Yet, it has somehow, despite being televised daily, failed to receive the recognition and the audience it deserves.

Some of this must be blamed on inadequate production values. The television cameras are not allowed to roam around the chamber and catch the people insulting each other and making threatening gestures while somebody else is supposed to be speaking. A change there would help. There is no slow motion—although it is sometimes difficult to know for sure.

Most of the other components of a good professional wrestling match are already in place in the House of Commons. There is a referee. There are television cameras. There is an audience. There is make-believe.

Now there is even the makings of a good grudge, without which no truly significant wrestling match is possible. The grudge stems from the fact that the prime minister used to live in the house that the Opposition leader wants to move into and they are arguing about it. No one else in the country knows what all this is about, but it seems to mean something to the two families, and that's what matters. Letters have gone back and forth about it and even the wives are getting into the act. Any minute now, someone's honor is going to need defending and a great wrestling match will begin, live from the House of Commons.

To equate this with Dallas is insulting. Compared to question period, Dallas is wimpy.

Reprinted from the Ottawa Citizen, April 15.

Figure 7-8
This article takes a lighthearted view of Parliament's question period, the time set aside in the House of Commons for members of the Opposition to question members of the government about their performance. (As you will have seen on television, Members of Parliament often use this period for verbal attacks and criticism of one another.) Read this article before answering Questions 1 to 6.

1. For what audience was the article intended?
2. What is the purpose of the article?
3. Discuss the level of usage of words in the article and support your statements with examples.
4. Write an outline from which Mr. Gordon could have written his article.
5. The article begins by quoting Mila Mulroney. Using a *Who's Who in Canada* or other resource material, research the background of Mila Mulroney or any other current political figure and prepare a brief biography.
6. Write a one-page commentary on one of the following topics.
   (a) Why you agree with Brian Mulroney that the question period is equivalent to Dallas.
   (b) Why you agree with Charles Gordon that professional wrestling is a form of entertainment.
   (c) Your view of the question period in the House of Commons.
   (d) Your view of professional wrestling.
7. Use this article and the essay, "Freedom, Our Most Precious Heritage," (Figure 7-9) to answer the following questions.
   (a) Is there any way we can see through the use of language which of the authors is older?
   (b) In what ways are the structures the same or different?
   (c) Select words you think each author used in hopes of connoting other ideas or impressions.
8. Read the following case, then answer the questions that follow.

   Howard Hyatt is responsible for the public relations of a large oil company. Consumers who read about the large profits that his company makes are beginning to react in a very negative way. Howard's job is to improve his company's image. He could tell consumers, for example, that all profits are put into research designed to develop more efficient solar energy systems. He could also think of something else to say that will turn consumer opinion around.
   (a) What medium should Hyatt use for his message?
   (b) How should he design his message so that it will have the most effect?

Figure 7-9
This essay won an international essay contest. Read it over, bearing in mind what you have learned about words, sentences, and paragraphs in this chapter.

FREEDOM, OUR MOST PRECIOUS HERITAGE

Freedom, independence, autonomy, what reality is hidden behind these words that are so often used and abused by our society?

We are free! As for me, I'll take freedom! When I am 18 years old, I will finally be free! With what empty words we too often lie to ourselves.

Freedom exists only insofar as we use it wisely and toward a good end. To abuse it is to forge our own enslavement. If freedom is an inheritance to be defended, it is also a treasure to be conquered. Freedom is first and essentially within: It is the ability to make choices which in and of itself supposes the intelligent analysis of a situation, a great moral honesty and the firm desire to accomplish a project within the range of our capability.

Unfortunately, there are many constraints on individual freedom, the most dangerous of which are not necessarily the most brutal. Of course, there are countries where dictatorship reigns, where totalitarian regimes repress the people (Russia, Iran. . .). There, the citizens are deprived of the right to express an opinion, of freedom to choose those who are to govern them. They are judged pitilessly if they fail to observe the regime's laws.

But there exists a host of other ways, even more insidious, in which our freedom is impeded without our even being aware of it: the media and advertising that present material objects as indispensable, when in reality they are not at all. Consider the televised message that says: "But it's your right to be oldfashioned." The methods are good ones: flatter our vanity, intensify our thirst for comfort, our taste for the game or for the easy life. And "freely," we buy perfume, the latest dresses, and the most insignificant gadget.

To be free is to know how to assume responsibility. As it says in the New Testament: "When a king wants to declare war against an enemy, he wants to know if his 1,000 troops can defeat 10,000." Before choosing an activity, one must weigh one's capacities. A person cannot throw himself impetuously into some "adventure" without first weighing the pros and cons.

Once a decision is made, to be free means having the will to go all the way, not to give up at the first obstacle. Guy Lafleur retired—freely, no doubt. Only he can say what place honesty or cowardice took in his decision. No matter what the journalists say, Guy Lafleur alone can measure the personal effects of his action.

Faced with cigarettes or drugs, faced with advertising that invades and tries to impose choices, true freedom is translated by our wisdom and the evaluation of our choices.

Maybe the dove is the symbol of freedom. Its whiteness signifies pure intentions; flying freely, well above pettiness and preoccupations, it almost reaches heaven.

Properly speaking, freedom is not an inheritance. We inherit the desire and the will to be free; we are ready to fight—as our ancestors did—to defend it and to respect the freedom of others.

WRITING: EDITING AND PUBLICATION

PART · TWO

COMMUNICATION IN BUSINESS

Chapter 8   Business Communication
Chapter 9   Speaking and Listening in Business
Chapter 10   Speaking Skills in Making Presentations
Chapter 11   Reading and Viewing in the Workplace
Chapter 12   Writing Business Documents
Chapter 13   Business Report and Technical Writing

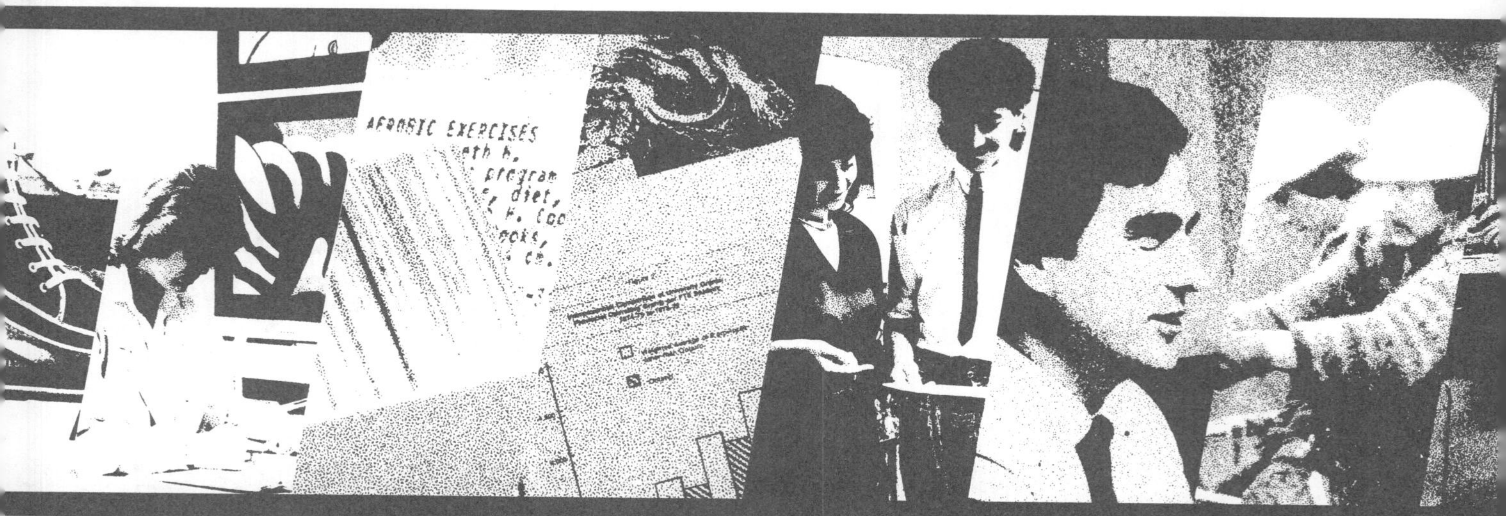
AEROBIC EXERCISES

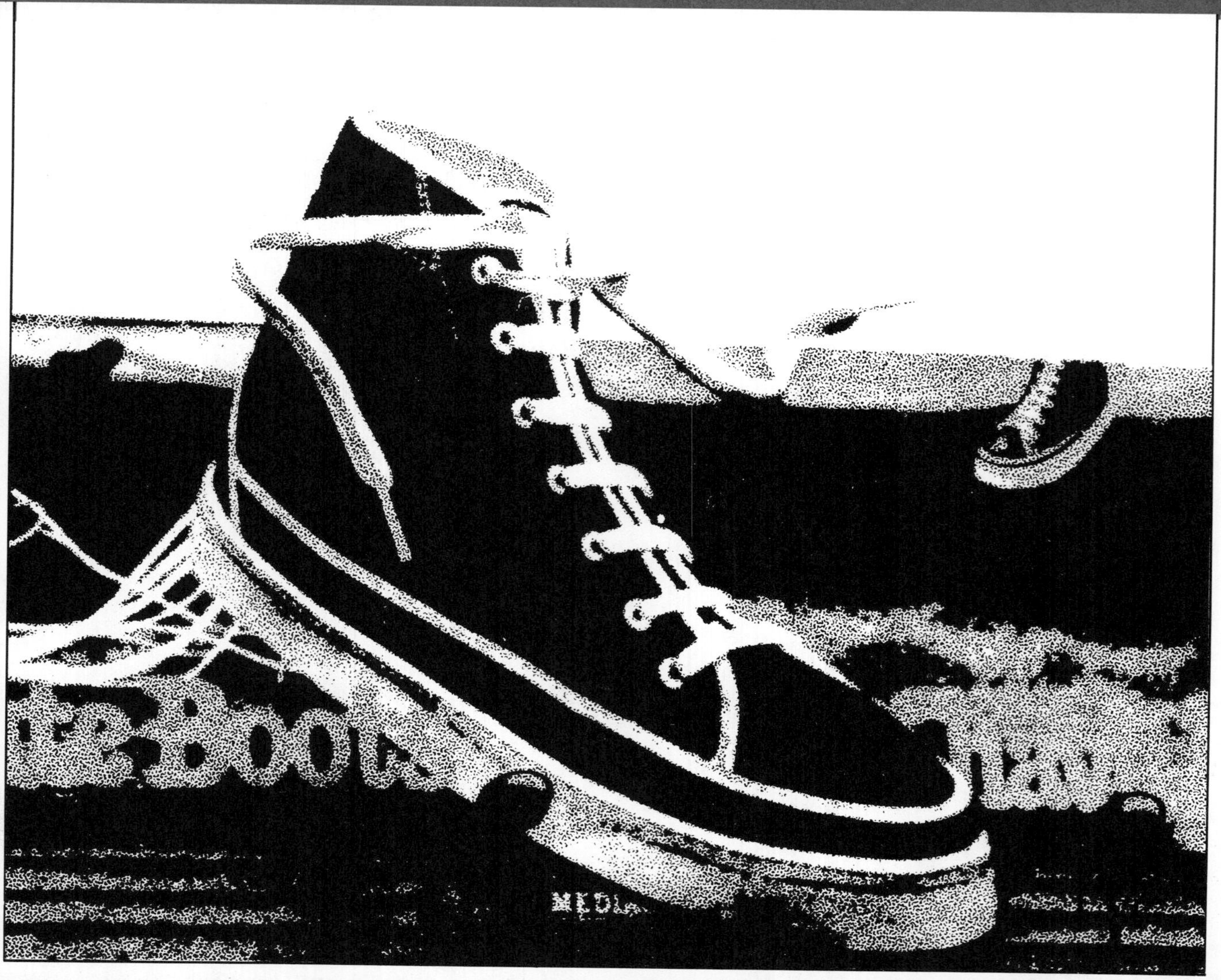

CHAPTER 8

Business Communication

GOALS

At the end of this chapter you should be able to
1. use the communication model for effective communication in business and industry;
2. apply a basic problem-solving model to solve business-related communication problems;
3. identify formal and informal lines of communication in a work-related setting;
4. recognize appropriate uses for different levels of business communications; and
5. identify barriers to effective communication in business and industry.

VOCABULARY BUILDING

chain of command
grapevine
categorize
stereotype

VIEWPOINTS

Wanda Bjornson is regional sales manager for a chain of record stores. She has just come from a meeting with the Vice-President of Sales, William Duplak, in which she was told that her region of Delta stores, the southern Alberta region, had shown the lowest profits for the last two quarters. She is under a great deal of pressure since Mr. Duplak hinted that if the situation did not improve, the company would have no recourse but to hire a new district sales manager.

Before going into the regular Friday morning meeting with her store managers, Wanda takes a few minutes to look over the figures that Mr. Duplak has given her. She notices that one of the stores, Mick Taguchi's, is showing a good profit margin for the period, unlike the other stores in her region. Wanda writes a few lines in her notebook, takes a few deep breaths, and enters the meeting room. Six people who have been sitting down talking, rise and greet her warmly.

WANDA: Hello, everybody. I'm glad to see you're all here. The roads this morning are treacherous. We'll make this meeting shorter than most so that you won't have to rush getting back to your stores. So, to get down to business, I've just been looking over the figures for the past two quarters. I'm probably not telling you anything that you don't know already, but there is a disturbing trend in our region. Costs seem to be on the increase and sales on the decrease. We need to turn this situation around as quickly as possible. Now one store that does not conform to this pattern is Mick's and I'd like him to outline what he is doing to create a good profit margin. What can you tell us, Mick?

MICK: Well, I think there are three or four things I've been doing that have helped. Firstly, I was appalled at the amount of pilfering last Christmas, so I rearranged the store. Now it is impossible to leave the store without passing by the cash desk. I also try to always have two people at the desk so that one can watch customers entering and exiting. With this system, pilferage has dropped 70 percent.

WANDA: That's a substantial drop. Your system must be working. You have security mirrors in your store too, don't you? Do they help?

MICK: Yes, I think they act as a deterrent, because people can see that one person at the desk is not heavily occupied and can glance at the mirrors from time to time.

WANDA: What else do you feel is contributing to the success of your store, Mick?

MICK: Last January I started having monthly in-store promotions. I get customers to fill in a form indicating first and second choices of records they would like to buy. We tabulate the answers and then place the forms in a draw box. On the last Saturday of each month we draw three forms and the winners are given their first choice records. The promotion has attracted a lot of new customers and it has also helped us in ordering the most popular stock.

WANDA: It must be a lot of work tabulating the choices though, isn't it?

MICK: It's a bit time-consuming, but we do it whenever there is no one in the store. And it doesn't have to be done meticulously; it's just to give us a rough idea of what people want. Each month we send a list of the winners and the survey results to the newspaper and get a bit of free coverage that way.

WANDA: It sounds like a good way to identify customer preference and advertise at the same time. Mick, I think you've given us some good ideas to think about. What I'd like to do now is suggest that we adjourn, and through the next week we can all think about ways to promote sales and reduce costs. Next Friday when we meet, I think we'll have some good ideas to evaluate, and from those ideas we can formulate a regional sales promotion. Any questions? Jenna.

JENNA: I like Mick's promotion and wonder if he would bring in one of the forms he hands out to customers?

MICK: Sure. I'll bring some to next Friday's meeting.

WANDA: Thanks, Mick. There's one more thing to do before next Friday, and this one I'll do myself. I'm going to recommend to the Vice-President of Sales, William Duplak, that Delta have a yearly incentive award for the store manager who shows the best percentage increase in profit. Maybe the prize could be a trip, or a compact disc player — something exciting.

TOM: Do you think Mr. Duplak will go for the idea?

WANDA: That I don't know, but I think it's worthwhile bringing it up. We were talking about the need to increase profits in this region this morning, so he should be open to ideas. Now, let's close the meeting, unless someone wishes to say something? No one? Fine. Remember now, come next Friday with your ideas for increasing profits. We'll have a brainstorming session and then work out a strategy that we can follow throughout the region. I know we can get the picture turned around with all the talent here. See you next Friday. Drive carefully.

QUESTIONS

1. Do you think Wanda's approach in letting her staff know that profits needed to be increased was effective? How would you have handled it?
2. Do you think Mr. Duplak was right in suggesting to Wanda that she might have to be replaced? Explain your answer.
3. Why did Wanda not let her staff see how upset she was after her meeting with Mr. Duplak?
4. Pretend you are one of the store managers and devise a few possible ways to cut costs and increase sales.
5. If you were an employee of Delta, who would you prefer as a supervisor — Mr. Duplak or Wanda?

Figure 8-1
Wanda, whom you met in the section Viewpoints, *must communicate effectively in order to produce the results expected of her and to be fair to the people she supervises.*

INTRODUCTION

If you were an employer, what basic attributes would you look for in potential employees? You would probably want someone who would work in harmony with others, perform tasks efficiently and conscientiously, assume responsibility, and demonstrate a willingness and ability to learn. Communicating clearly and concisely, both in speech and in writing, and solving problems that arise in daily dealings with others are the skills that support such attributes. Do you think Wanda, in Figure 8-1, shows these qualities? In this chapter we will be examining ways in which to improve these basic communication skills for business.

PROBLEM SOLVING

Problem solving is a skill in which people gain little experience or training until they are out of school and into a business setting. It is, however, a valuable skill to develop and practise prior to entering business because you will need to make use of it regularly in your work.

Sometimes you will find it necessary to deal with problems on your own; at other times you may be a member of a group charged with solving a problem that affects your co-workers. In either case, you can break the task into a few basic steps.

The steps to problem solving are as follows:
1. Identify and analyze the problem.
2. Gather and evaluate information.
3. Generate all possible solutions.
4. Select the best possible solution.
5. Implement the solution.
6. Evaluate the results.

These stages are shown in the diagram in Figure 8-2. We shall describe each stage of the process in turn and apply the process to Wanda's situation in *Viewpoints*.

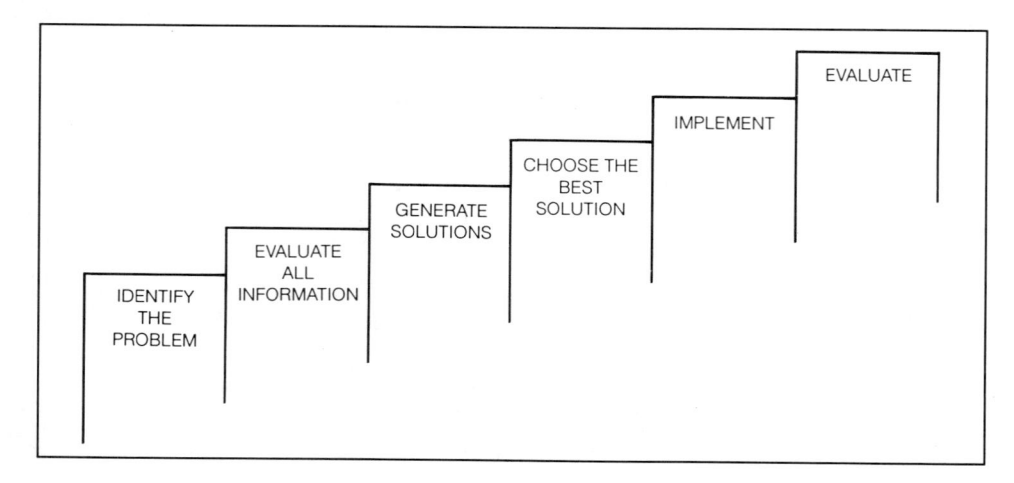

Figure 8-2
Basic problem-solving model: steps to effective problem solving

PART TWO: COMMUNICATION IN BUSINESS

Figure 8-A
Identify the problem

Identify and Analyze the Problem

Identifying the problem sounds simple, but in many cases, although you are aware of a problem, you may have difficulty putting it into words. Describing and defining the problem in words is a necessary step that will help you to gain a better understanding of it yourself.

It is also important to arrive at limits to the problem while you are defining it, otherwise it may seem unmanageable. If Wanda, in *Viewpoints*, were to sit down and define the problem she was facing, she might start like this:

The Problem:
Profits are lowest in my district and must be increased.
Limits:
Present situation — Average profit margin in region is 37 percent.
Acceptable situation — Average profit margin of 78 percent within the fiscal year for all stores in region.
Definition of the problem:
Profit margin needs to be increased by 41 percent in my region within the fiscal year.

Defining limits to the problem helps later when you are evaluating all the proposed solutions. The limits are also useful when assessing whether the solution you implemented has solved the problem or not.

In analyzing the problem, you are looking at it from many angles and asking questions such as: When did the problem arise? Why did it arise? What are the causes of the problem? What harm is caused by the problem? How many people are involved? What are the obstacles to solving the problem?

Once the pertinent questions have been answered, you will be in a better position to judge what information is needed for the formulation of solutions. Now you are ready to go on to the next step of gathering and evaluating information.

Figure 8-B
Evaluate all information

Gather and Evaluate Information

From attempting to answer the questions in step 1, you will have identified areas in which more information is needed. Once you know what information is needed, you can carry on to locate where to find the necessary information. You may wish to ask others for their opinions or their experience with regard to the problem area. There may be statistics or studies available that relate to the problem.

When the information has been gathered, you will want to evaluate it to make sure it is reliable and accurate. A solution that is based on inaccurate information will probably not go far in solving the problem.

Wanda's information included the statistics supplied by head office and, at the same time, her own experience with the managers and their stores.

BUSINESS COMMUNICATION

Figure 8-C
Generate solutions

Generate all Possible Solutions

This step of the problem-solving process involves brainstorming. If you are part of a group that has been given the responsibility of solving a particular problem, so much the better. The more ideas at this point, the more chances you will have of finding a creative and effective solution to the problem. Everyone should feel free to suggest as many solutions as possible. While the ideas are being put forth and written down, no criticism or discussion should take place, in accordance with the rules of brainstorming.

Wanda asked everyone to think up possible solutions over the next week. Presumably, each manager would go through the first two steps of the problem-solving process before coming up with suggestions. Then when they meet the following Friday morning, they would have the solutions ready for the next step.

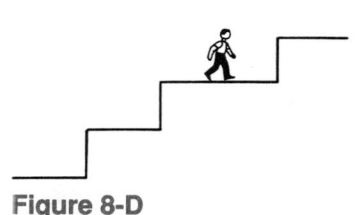

Figure 8-D
Choose the best solution

Select the Best Possible Solution

Selecting the best solution is a matter of evaluating each solution that you come up with. You must consider whether each solution that is proposed will solve the problem and produce the desired results. It may even be that a combination of more than one of the proposed solutions should be used to solve the problem. In such cases we are talking about requiring a planned strategy to arrive at a set goal, or solution.

In the Delta situation, Wanda and the managers might decide that Mick's plan of action, plus lowering the price of the most popular records by 5 percent for a six-month period to stimulate sales, would result in a satisfactory profit margin increase. In order to arrive at this decision though, they will have to evaluate each alternative solution, measuring each one against the goal — achieving a profit increase of 41 percent in the region within the fiscal year.

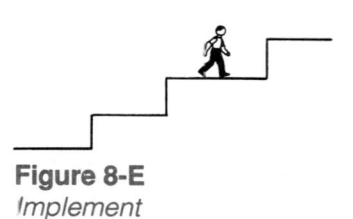

Figure 8-E
Implement

Implement the Solution

This step may be simple or it may be quite difficult depending on the complexity of the solution. If you are part of a group charged with finding a solution, it may be that your responsibility ends with advising management of your solution. At that point management will take over in implementing the solution. If you or your group must implement the solution, you will have to decide when and how to put it into effect. Perhaps your solution is a change in office procedure. The change may require a few simple steps: drafting a memo, having it approved, and circulating it to all employees. Alternatively, the change in procedure might be more complicated and involve designing and producing new forms, hiring and training a new employee, retraining certain employees in one department, or laying off employees. Such changes would require more planning and more time to implement. They might also require further meetings to present the proposed solution to management and to obtain management's approval.

Evaluate the Results

Selecting what you judge to be the right solution and implementing it may solve the problem. However, you are not finished with the problem-solving process until you (and possibly others) have evaluated the results to see if they have met the original goals set. Only then can you be satisfied that the problem has indeed been solved. If the goals have not been met, then it may be necessary to either modify the solution, or go through the problem-solving process again to develop a new plan of action in the light of the previous results.

In Wanda's case, the profits will be measured monthly, and after a year she will know if the goal of a 41 percent increase has been achieved. If the monthly profits decline instead, it will be necessary to look for different, or additional, solutions to the problem. The information gained from the solution already tried will be used to formulate a new strategy.

The six steps to problem solving which we have briefly discussed follow a logical sequence. Sometimes a problem will arise in business that evokes strong emotions in the people involved. An atmosphere of confrontation may make it difficult to deal with the problem in a rational manner. In such cases it is especially important to use an organized and logical method of dealing with the problem. Each step of the process should be approached fairly and objectively, and every member of the group should be encouraged to participate. Discussions must focus on the ideas being expressed and must not be allowed to touch on the personalities of the participants. Because the solution that is eventually selected will be the result of organized group communication, it will more likely meet with the support of everyone involved.

Figure 8-F
Evaluate the results

Steps in the problem-solving model:
1. identify the problem
2. evaluate all information
3. generate all possible solutions
4. choose the best solution
5. implement the solution
6. evaluate the results

APPLICATIONS

1. We have represented the problem-solving model as a staircase. Represent the six steps in another visual form. (You could, for instance, use a flowchart.)

2. Use the problem-solving model to analyze a problem you recently had at school. (A problem could be having to choose between a course you are good at but do not enjoy, and one that you enjoy but are not good at.) Break down the problem and alternative courses of action into six stages. Does the problem-solving model help you to find a solution to your problem? Explain your answer.

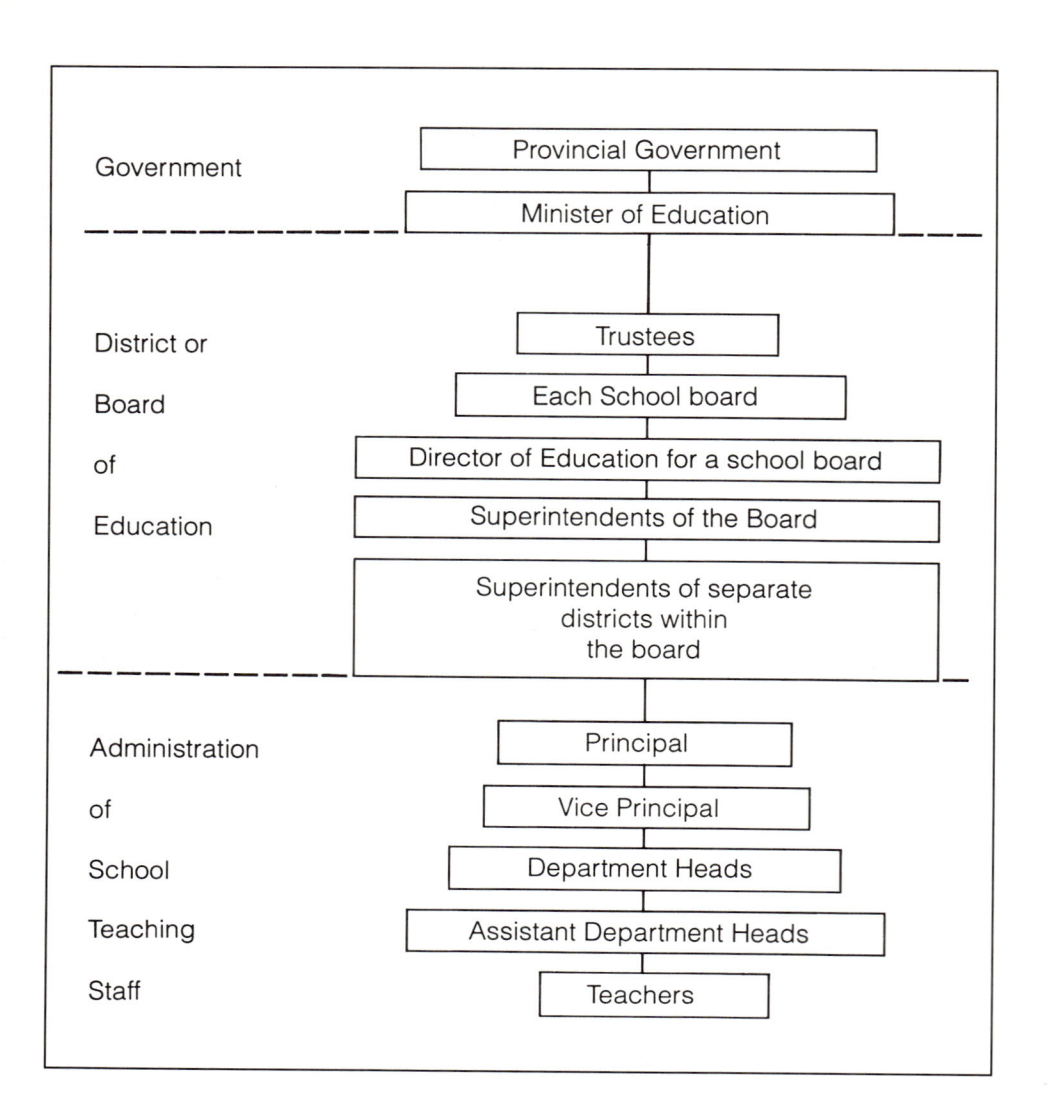

Figure 8-3
The formal line of communication in education

```
Government                    ┌─────────────────────┐
                              │ Provincial Government│
                              └──────────┬──────────┘
                              ┌──────────┴──────────┐
                              │ Minister of Education│
                              └─────────────────────┘
- - - - - - - - - - - - - - - - - - - - - - - - - - - -
District or                        ┌──────────┐
                                   │ Trustees │
Board                              └────┬─────┘
                              ┌─────────┴─────────┐
of                            │ Each School board │
                              └─────────┬─────────┘
                    ┌───────────────────┴───────────────────┐
Education           │ Director of Education for a school board│
                    └───────────────────┬───────────────────┘
                         ┌──────────────┴──────────────┐
                         │ Superintendents of the Board │
                         └──────────────┬──────────────┘
                         ┌──────────────┴──────────────┐
                         │  Superintendents of separate │
                         │    districts within          │
                         │       the board              │
                         └──────────────────────────────┘
- - - - - - - - - - - - - - - - - - - - - - - - - - - -
Administration                    ┌──────────┐
                                  │ Principal│
of                                └────┬─────┘
                                  ┌────┴──────────┐
School                            │ Vice Principal│
                                  └────┬──────────┘
                              ┌────────┴────────┐
Teaching                      │ Department Heads│
                              └────────┬────────┘
                         ┌─────────────┴─────────────┐
Staff                    │ Assistant Department Heads│
                         └─────────────┬─────────────┘
                                  ┌────┴────┐
                                  │Teachers │
                                  └─────────┘
```

LINES OF COMMUNICATION

Communication within a business can be of a formal or an informal nature. We will discuss how each type takes place.

Formal Communication

Just as a business is run in an organized manner, so must its business communication be conducted in an organized way. All employees need to know of decisions taken that affect them and their work. Management needs to be given information gathered by employees to help them in making decisions that will affect the running of the company.

Your school is part of a province-wide system of education. The parts within the system are held together by a **chain of command**, or an established network, through which information is passed. See Figure 8-3. Curriculums, data, rules, requests for information, decisions, and notices will pass up and down the chain of command. If all the links in the chain make sure that the next person in line receives the communication, then everyone affected will be notified. It is important that everyone in the system understands and uses the communication network, otherwise a break in communication would result. The communication systems in businesses are modelled along similar lines, with a chain of command for passing information.

Formal communication can also take place when information is passed among workers who are at the same level in the chain of command. The workers could communicate by memos, telephone calls, or in person. If a regular exchange of information between department A and department B has not been established, and you need information from department B, you might ask your department supervisor to get the information. The communication network between the two departments, A and B, might consist of: you (employee A) to supervisor A to supervisor B to employee B to supervisor B to supervisor A to you (employee A). Once you and employee B have exchanged information through this route, the network might be shortened and the next exchange could be between you and employee B directly.

Informal Communication

Informal communication involves no network, and occurs among employees of equal or near equal status. If, for instance, you were informed that you had to work late, and you had just made plans to meet a friend after work, you might ask a co-worker to take your place. Asking your supervisor for approval of the change could be accomplished informally. Alternatively, sending a memo requesting approval would be a more formal approach.

Another type of informal communication in business is the office **grapevine**, a person-to-person method of relaying information. This method often results in information being slightly altered, or lost, as it is passed along. The end product in some cases can be very inaccurate and unreliable. What you hear about people and events through the grapevine may be unfair or untrue, and may be a poor basis for judging them.

Communications can be
1. formal
2. informal.

APPLICATIONS

3. List five examples of formal lines of communication used in your school and discuss the effectiveness of each. Identify how these lines could be changed to improve communication.

4. Examine samples of formal communication supplied by your teacher. Determine potential breakdown in communication and assess their impact.

5. Identify five different ways that informal communication occurs in your school environment. What other methods of informal communication are used in business?

BUSINESS COMMUNICATION

LEVELS OF BUSINESS COMMUNICATION

In Chapter 3 you examined three levels of communication:
- internal, working out a solution to a problem in your mind
- interpersonal, conversations with one or more other people
- mediated, communication conducted through a medium other than face-to-face interaction

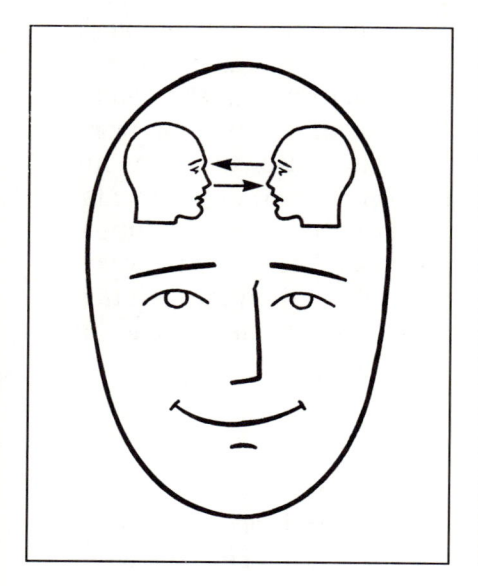

Figure 8-4(a)
Internal (or inner thought) communication level

Figure 8-4(b)
Interpersonal communication level

Figure 8-4(c)
Mediated communication level

160   PART TWO: COMMUNICATION IN BUSINESS

In addition to these three levels of communication, business and industry regularly use two additional levels — person-to-group and mass communication. Each of the five levels has its own specific points of value as well as its own unique applications and style.

Person-to-Group Communication

Person-to-group communication takes the form of a speaker addressing an audience. Depending on the type of meeting, members of the audience may at times become the speaker, as in a question period.

The Delta meeting took the form of person-to-group communication in which Wanda communicated information to her group of managers. Training programs, business reports, upgrading seminars, and new product presentations are often conducted by a speaker communicating with people who are there to learn.

Careful preparation and good speaking techniques are essential for effective person-to-group communication. If you have an opportunity to attend a person-to-group communication session, make notes on how the speaker builds and maintains audience interest. Chapter 9 studies the skills involved in speaking in a business situation and after reading that material you will know better what to look for in a competent speaker.

Figure 8-5
Person-to-group communication level

Mass Communication

Many businesses today communicate with the general public through radio, television, and printed materials. Forms of printed materials used in communication are pamphlets, brochures, catalogues, books, magazine and newspaper articles, advertisements, and direct mail.

With the advent of computers, direct mail has become an important means of advertising. Mailing lists are compiled by computers so that, for instance, a business can advertise to a large group of selected individuals or businesses (special interest groups) located within a particular geographical area.

It is difficult to receive feedback from mass communication. However, if an advertising campaign results in a sudden increased demand for your product or service, you can assume that the mass communication has been successful. The use of response cards that are mailed back to the advertiser is one method of judging whether printed advertising has reached the target audience and has been read. Can you think of any other methods?

Communication in business can be
1. internal
2. interpersonal
3. mediated
4. person-to-group
5. mass.

Figure 8-6
Mass communication level

APPLICATIONS

6. List communication situations where you have used or been involved in each one of the five levels of communication — internal, interpersonal, mediated, person-to-group, and mass.

7. Which communication level is most common in each of the following communication situations?
   (a) doing your homework
   (b) classroom work in school

(c) lunchroom discussions
(d) watching a comedy program on television
(e) teaching swimming at the local pool
(f) writing a test in school
(g) completing the applications exercises in this book

8. As you will see from your answers to Question 7, during any particular communication situation there will often be two or more levels of communication operating at once. For each of the occupations given below, identify the different levels of communication that would be used in order of importance to that occupation.
   (a) student
   (b) teacher
   (c) counter server at a fast-food restaurant
   (d) president of a large company
   (e) homemaker
   (f) automobile mechanic
   (g) self-employed electrician
   (h) hockey coach

9. In small groups discuss the levels of communication for each of the people in Question 8. Why do you think there are disagreements about the ranking of communication levels for each of the occupations listed above?

10. From your discussions of Question 9, prepare a short report identifying why, in your opinion, an understanding of the communication process and the various levels of communication is important to people in business and industry.

FORMS OF BUSINESS COMMUNICATION

Business communication, like communication in other areas of your life, is expressed in verbal and non-verbal forms.

Verbal Communication in Business

Verbal forms of communication include written and spoken language. In business, written communication is of much greater significance than it is in a social context. Much of the information generated by business transactions needs to be recorded in writing. Letters, memos, forms, reports, messages, tables, performance appraisals, orders, invoices, statements, signs, posters, price tags, and instructions are some of the written materials that you will become familiar with in business. Can you name some other types of written materials used in business?

Written business communications are ideally concise, accurate, carefully organized, and courteous. Enough detail should be provided to make the meaning readily apparent, but not so much that the recipient becomes confused by irrelevant details. Chapter 12 discusses writing for business in more detail.

Examine the advertisement in Figure 8-7 and see if you can identify what is wrong with it.

Generalist Required
to break into a Billion-Dollar Consumer Product Business

Our multi-national company is expanding. If you are the number one human resources executive in a significant Canadian company, we want you to report directly to the president as

Human Resources Manager

Be a part of a dynamic team committed to growth.

Submit resume and salary expectations to

Aggressive Sales International

Box 331, *The Daily News*

Figure 8-7
What is wrong with this advertisement?

Figure 8-8 shows an advertisement that appeared in a local newspaper. Would you want to go for dinner? Let your imagination run freely and create other advertisements where, because of poor language skills, an inappropriate message has been sent.

Foul Supper

At the Town Hall,
Riverton
Saturday, October 22
6 p.m.
Tickets available at Jack Little's Pharmacy
Proceeds to the Riverton Curling Club
Adults $4.00   Children $2.00

Figure 8-8
Would you go to this dinner? Incorrect language can mean that the wrong message is communicated.

Spoken communication in business includes talking person-to-person or on the telephone to co-workers, clients, customers, suppliers, and prospective employers. It may also include giving presentations to clients or co-workers. Chapters 9 and 10 discuss speaking for business in some detail.

Non-Verbal Communication in Business

We have already discussed non-verbal communication in a general sense in Chapter 1. In business, non-verbal communication consists of the image you project to people within your company, to customers, and to suppliers. A tidy, well-groomed appearance, good posture, and a self-confident, friendly manner will help you to communicate an appropriate, business-like image. The use of eye contact, a pleasant tone of voice, and good speech characteristics (fluency, enunciation, pronunciation, and word choice) will strengthen that image and contribute toward your success in business.

We also communicate a non-verbal message by the distance we stand from a person with whom we are talking. Have you ever found yourself backing away from someone you are talking to? The conventional distance between two people talking together, called "personal space" by Desmond Morris, varies from country to country. In Canada, most people begin to feel uncomfortable talking to one another if they are less than one metre apart. In some parts of the world, it is acceptable to be much closer together while talking, and to accentuate conversations with physical contact. Most Canadians, however, unless they know the people with whom they are conversing quite well, will avoid touching while talking.

BARRIERS TO EFFECTIVE BUSINESS COMMUNICATION

The barriers to effective business communication are similar to those encountered in personal communication, as outlined in Chapter 1. In the workplace these barriers may be more serious, in that our success in business may depend on our ability to overcome them. Some of these barriers are listed below. They are **categorized**, or put into groups, as barriers stemming from poor attitudes, from lack of ability, and from environmental shortcomings.

Sender/Receiver Attitude Barriers

- defensiveness
- emotions
- hostility
- lack of interest
- lack of trust
- resistance to change
- fear
- distortion or omission of information
- excesssive competitiveness
- insecurity

BUSINESS COMMUNICATION

Sender/Receiver Ability Barriers

- poor personal judgement
- weak sense of timing
- inappropriate voice tone, modulation, or expression
- limited language
- inaccurate reading of non-verbal communication
- inability to think clearly
- lack of motivation
- lack of knowledge

Environmental Barriers

- no feedback
- noise distractions
- visual distractions
- distance problems
- ineffective medium
- inappropriate group size
- poor organizational structure of group

Barriers to effective communication can be
1. *sender/receiver attitude barriers*
2. *sender/receiver ability barriers*
3. *environment barriers.*

APPLICATIONS

11. List examples of how each attitude, ability, and environmental barrier listed above could hinder or block effective business communication. Discuss your answers with the class.

12. Discuss with the class how each barrier could be overcome.

13. From your own experience, name the barriers which you have encountered and state how they affect communication.

14. Add other barriers that you can think of to each of the three groups.

SAFEGUARDS FOR EFFECTIVE BUSINESS COMMUNICATION

Once you are aware of the possible barriers to communication in business, you can deal with them as they arise. Following are a few recommendations for overcoming or avoiding communication barriers that you may encounter.

1. Concentrate on the message you are receiving and if necessary, repeat instructions to make sure you have not missed any information. If you allow your mind to wander, you risk receiving an incomplete message.

2. Determine who your audience is and present your message in a form that is appropriate to them. Make sure that your listeners understand your message completely. Read the feedback you are

receiving in order to monitor your listeners' understanding and attention. The feedback will tell you if you need to alter your direction, change your pace, repeat parts of your message, or start over again. An assumption that listeners operate from the same reference point and understand your message is not safe to make.

To avoid communication barriers
1. *concentrate on the message being received*
2. *design your message to suit the receiver*
3. *be objective*
4. *be sensitive to the feelings of those involved*
5. *do not stereotype*
6. *give advice only when it is needed*
7. *use a variety of channels to reinforce an important message.*

3. Consider the information being discussed objectively. Your opinion of the sender should not interfere with or prejudice your judgement of the matters under discussion.
4. Be sensitive to the feelings of others in your communication. Offer praise in public when it is due. Correct a problem or make a complaint in private. In group meetings or discussions, help to draw the quieter members of the group into the communication process.
5. Treat people as individuals. **Stereotyping,** or putting a standardized or conventional image on people, by race, ethnic groupings, sex, or age can lead to unfair and wrong conclusions and can discourage valuable input from individuals.
6. Give advice only when the other person asks for it or needs it. Generally, people prefer to solve their own problems. They may wish to have a sympathetic listener, but most often, they do not want advice.
7. Use more than one channel to reinforce important messages. If you are giving oral instructions to a co-worker that might be forgotten, take a minute to confirm them in writing.

APPLICATIONS

15. Think of an occasion when a message you gave recently was misinterpreted by the receiver.
    (a) Write a short summary of the incident.
    (b) Look over the list of safeguards above and decide which would have prevented the misinterpretation.

16. Do you think it is the responsibility of the sender or the receiver to overcome communication barriers? Look over the safeguards listed above to see how many of them apply to the sender and how many to the receiver to help you answer the question.

17. Use your research skills to find copies of the two poems "The Average" by W. H. Auden and "Warren Pryor" by the Canadian poet Alden Nowlan. In each, the main character and his parents are involved in work and business situations. Both parents and child in each poem are ultimately unhappy because they have failed in their communication. Analyse the poems by examining the details listed in the chart on page 168.

18. Refer to the chart that you prepared in Question 17. How could the characters in each of these poems have used a problem-solving model, such as the one outlined in this chapter, to avoid the communication errors described?

Warren Pryor   The Average

Plot
Parents' feelings
Child's feelings
Family's conflict
Effective words and phrases used to convey meaning
Family's problem
Child's problem
Barriers to effective communication
Ways to more effective communication

19. Think back to a recent situation in your own life in which poor communication led to a specific problem. Write out the steps you could have taken to avoid the problem.

CHAPTER SUMMARY

Steps to Effective Problem Solving
- identify and analyze the problem
- gather and evaluate all the information
- generate all possible solutions
- select the "best" solution
- implement the solution
- evaluate the results

Lines of communication can be formal or informal.

Levels of communication in business settings
- internal, or occurring in the mind
- interpersonal
- mediated, or conducted through a medium
- person-to-group
- mass communication

Communication in business can be verbal and non-verbal.

The barriers that inhibit business communication
- negative attitudes on the part of the sender or receiver
- lack of verbal ability on the part of the sender or receiver
- environmental barriers

Safeguards against ineffective communication
- concentrate on the message
- make sure the listener understands the message
- consider objectively the information being discussed

- be sensitive to the feelings of others
- treat other people as individuals
- give advice only when necessary
- use more than one channel or medium to reinforce your point

MAKING IT WORK

1. Write a script with a classmate in which Wanda Bjornson gives the reasons for low record sales, or presents the new higher sales figures to the chairman of the board for Delta record stores.

2. Read the following case, then answer the questions that follow.

    Pierre was hired to display merchandise in a large department store in town. He has worked there now for almost five months. Claudette, his supervisor, gives him several opportunities every day to voice any disagreements he may have with her. Each time Pierre chooses not to disagree. Whenever Claudette suggests a way to display certain kinds of merchandise, Pierre is quick to agree with her. In fact, whenever she asks for his opinion, he will try to read her mind. He will try to decide what she wants to hear and then say that. For example, Claudette asked him whether he thought they should go to the trouble of setting up another new display, or just rearrange the merchandise that was set up last week because it seems to be selling well. Pierre responded with "Whatever you think. You've more experience than I have."

    Pierre is really afraid to disagree openly with Claudette. He remembers an occasion just after he started work at the store when she was angry and reprimanded him in front of the other store clerks and even some of the customers. Since that day, Pierre goes out of his way to avoid any conflict with Claudette.

    Pierre realizes that his refusal to verbalize any kind of negative feedback to Claudette is hurting his career. He knows that he is a very creative person with some interesting ideas on merchandise display. It is frustrating for him to be always implementing someone else's design ideas and having no recognition of his own talents. He also knows that if he does not take the initiative to promote some of his own ideas soon, he will not gain experience in merchandise display and will not be able to learn from his job.

    (a) What alternatives does Pierre have?
    (b) Is it likely that Claudette would realize that Pierre's constant agreement might be due, in part, to her style as supervisor?
    (c) What kind of communication should take place in order to break down the barriers that exist between these two individuals?

3. Read the following case, then answer the questions that follow.

    You are one of twelve clerks in the order department of a large manufacturing company. The job requires you to take orders over the telephone and send a card to each customer confirming that the order has been processed. Each order clerk is given an order quota for the week and everyone tries very hard to reach the assigned quota. Those who process extra orders, over the quota, are paid an attractive bonus.

You have noticed lately that your colleagues are short and abrupt to customers on the telephone. You have also noticed that the confirmation cards are often illegible. You realize that everyone has to work quickly in order to reach the quota. On the other hand, you are disappointed that poor customer relations are the result. Your supervisor says she is too busy to listen in on customer order calls, but trusts that order clerks will check on each other.

(a) What can you do to improve the customer relations skills of your fellow workers?
(b) What should you do to change the way orders are taken and confirmed?
(c) What are the barriers here that prevent effective communications between customer and order clerk, between order clerk and supervisor, and among the order clerks themselves?

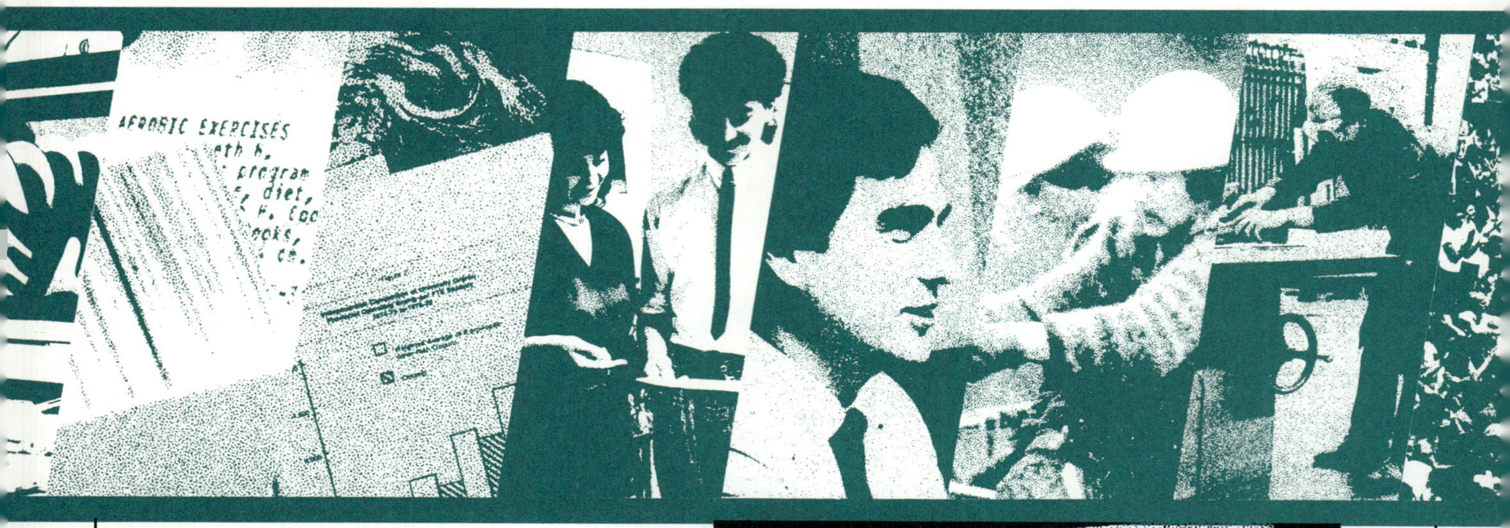
AEROBIC EXERCISES

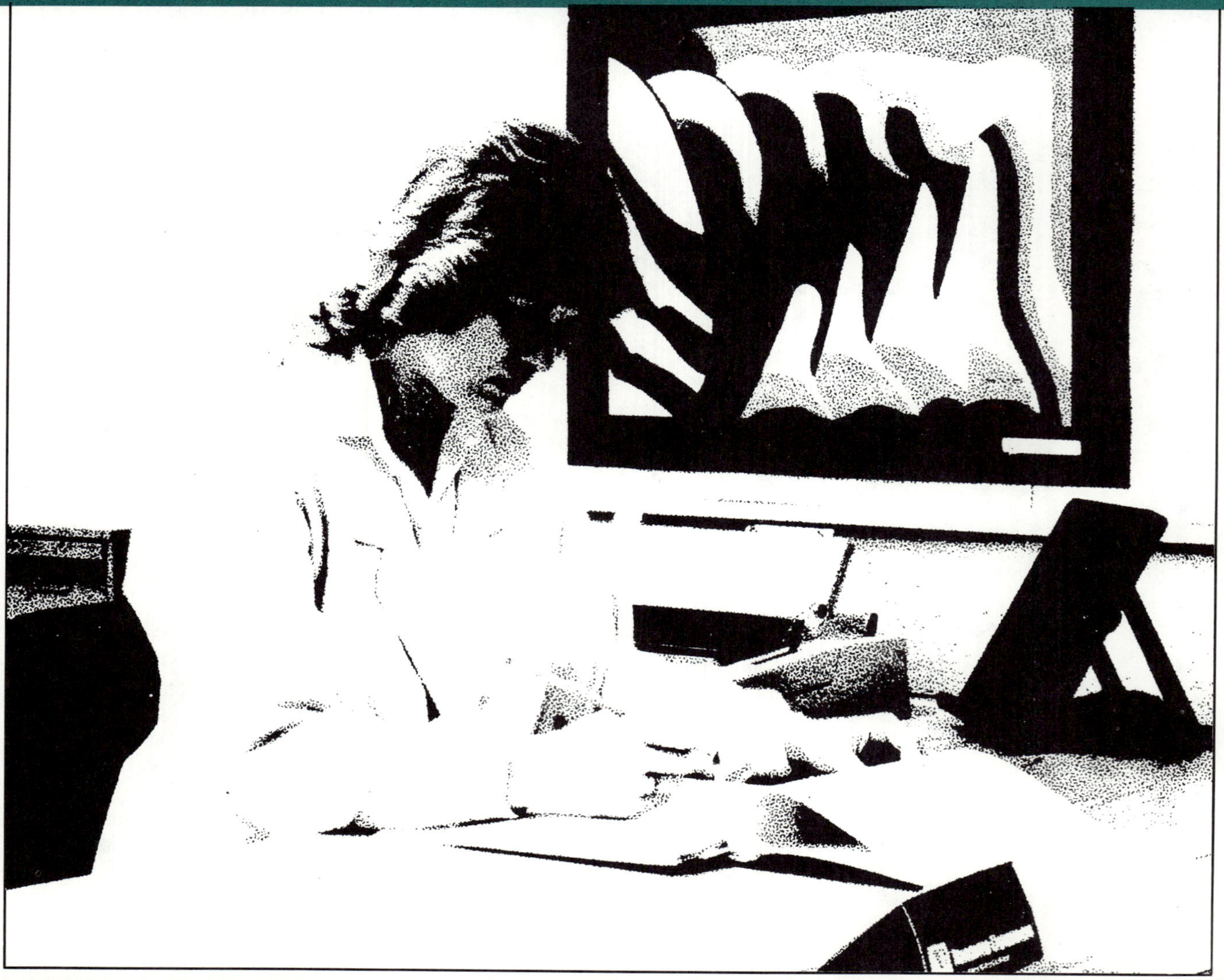

CHAPTER 9

Speaking and Listening In Business

GOALS

At the end of this chapter you should be able to
1. identify the importance of body language during an interview;
2. give and receive instructions;
3. acquire good telephone skills;
4. identify topics to be discussed during a job evaluation interview; and
5. work co-operatively in a group setting.

VOCABULARY BUILDING

dispel
demeanour
probationary period
counter-productive
job description
aspirations
rapport

VIEWPOINTS

Diane Tedesco, whom you met at the beginning of Chapter 4, has applied to Eastern Publishing for a summer position that she saw advertised in the newspaper. She sent in a letter of application and a résumé and a week later received a letter from Andre Fournier, the School Division Sales Manager at Eastern, asking her to come for an interview. She has just been shown to Andre's office.

ANDRE: (Rising from his chair, coming round to the front of his desk and extending his hand in greeting) How do you do, Diane. I'm Andre Fournier, Sales Manager for the Schools Division.

DIANE: (walking forward and shaking Andre's hand) How do you do, Mr. Fournier.

ANDRE: (returning to his chair and gesturing to one on the other side of the desk) Sit down please and tell me a bit about yourself. Why do you want to work at Eastern Publishing?

DIANE: I want to study sales and marketing at college and I thought the position of assistant to the promotions manager here would be good experience.

ANDRE: Yes ...

DIANE: Your ad said that there would be contact with the public and telephone work. In my summer job last year I especially enjoyed those aspects of the work.

ANDRE: (Looking at Diane's résumé) Let's see — you worked at a real estate office last summer as a receptionist, so you have lots of experience handling telephone calls. May we call the manager for a reference?

DIANE: Yes, my manager, Mrs. Law, said she would give me a reference.

ANDRE: Have you filled out one of our application forms, Diane?

DIANE: Yes, the receptionist gave me one while I was waiting to see you. She has it.

ANDRE: That's fine. Now then, what other experience or skills do you have that you think might be useful for this position?

DIANE: I've taken word processing and accounting at school and I help out in the guidance department for three hours each week. That job involves answering the telephone, booking interviews, filing, typing forms, and helping students find college calendars and other materials that they are looking for. Also this year I was on the school yearbook committee and I learned about layout and paste-up. Oh yes, I've used a photocopier that reduces and enlarges copies.

ANDRE: So, it sounds as if you are familiar with general office procedures. How fast are you at word processing?

DIANE: I think I can do about 50 words per minute, but with more practice I would be faster.

ANDRE: Well, Diane, I'm going to ask my secretary to take you down to meet Ms. Slaney, the promotions manager. She will show you around her department and you can ask her questions about the job. (rising from his desk and walking with Diane towards the door) I want to thank you for coming in for this interview. We'll let you know our decision at the end of this week.

DIANE: Thank you, Mr. Fournier. I've enjoyed talking to you.

QUESTIONS

1. Can you think of any other skills or experience that would help Diane to get the job?
2. Would Andre Fournier have sent Diane to see the promotions manager if he did not think that she might be a good person to fill the position? Why?
3. If you were Ms. Slaney, what questions would you want to ask Diane?
4. If you were Diane, what questions would you want to ask Ms. Slaney?

Figure 9-1(a)(b)(c)(d)
The skills of speaking and listening are just as important now that you are entering the working world.

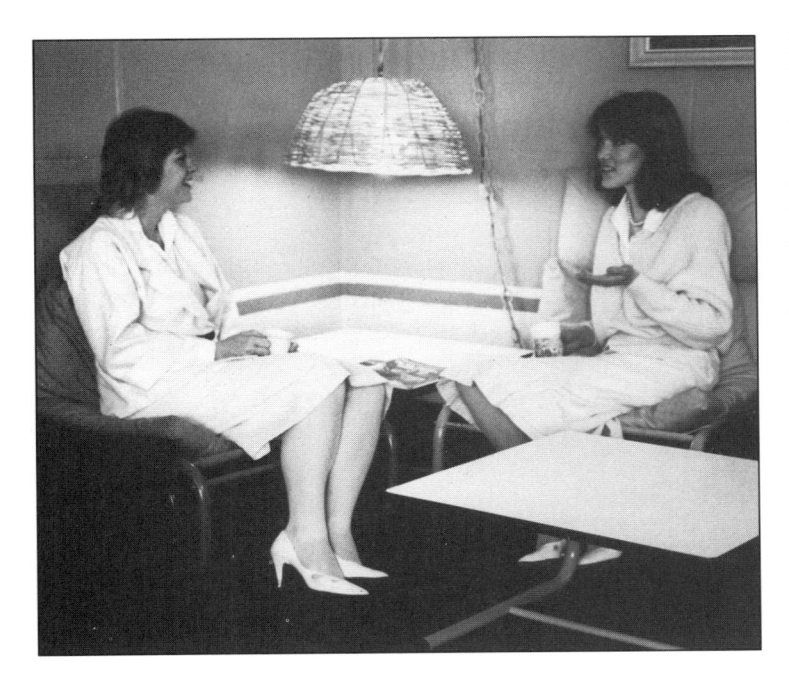

SPEAKING AND LISTENING IN BUSINESS

INTRODUCTION

Look at the photographs on page 175, and you will see how important the skills of speaking and listening are in a job. Whether you are being interviewed for a job, as Diane is in the section *Viewpoints*, or whether you are already working, interpersonal communication is vital to your everyday dealings with your employees, with customers, and with your co-workers.

In Chapters 2 and 4, listening and speaking skills were discussed in a general context. Now we will examine these same skills in the specific context of the workplace. Interpersonal communication within the work environment will be discussed from the perspective of
- a prospective employee;
- an employee interacting with customers and management;
- an employee interacting with peers; and
- a supervisor interacting with employees.

AS A PROSPECTIVE EMPLOYEE

The first time you meet the employer is usually at an employment interview. It will almost certainly be your last time if you make a poor impression. Have you ever heard the expression "first impressions are lasting"? There is a lot of truth to it. Very often the interviewer will decide within the first few minutes of the interview whether or not you are an applicant whom the company would want as an employee. Consequently, your first impression is crucial. Obviously, you should arrive in good time for the interview. Rushing in at the last moment or late will communicate not only that you lack organization, but also that you lack respect for other people and for conventions.

Let us examine the first few minutes carefully. Pretend you are a camera person filming the interview in *Viewpoints*. The scene begins with Diane entering Andre Fournier's office. Your camera is inside the office focussed on Diane as she walks in the door. Now freeze the shot. What do you see? Describe Diane's general appearance. Her clothing? Her facial expression? Her posture? The image your camera has captured is the same image Andre sees.

Within seconds Andre has decoded Diane's non-verbal message. From her body language his impression is
- she knows what clothing is appropriate for an interview and presumably will know what to wear for the job as well;
- she has good posture, as well as a pleasant and open expression; and
- she appears composed, self-confident, and alert.

This first impression, as we discussed before, is important for Diane. A negative impression at the beginning of the interview would mean she will be fighting an uphill battle for the remainder of the interview. Even good qualifications and an excellent work record might not **dispel**, or drive away, a negative first impression.

Figure 9-2
Based on your first impression of her appearance, do you think that Diane will get the job she is applying for?

Figure 9-A
Checklist for an applicant

Checklist for an applicant

How do you look to an interviewer?

- Are you dressed appropriately?
- Is your clothing clean and without small tears or buttons missing?
- Is your hair clean and neat?
- Are you smiling, reflecting a pleasant personality?
- Do you look at the interviewer?
- Do you create an overall impression of a person who is self-confident and able to get along with people?

Continuing the action, Diane walks toward Andre. He reaches out his hand in greeting and says, "How do you do, Diane? I'm Andre Fournier, Sales Manager for the Schools Division." Diane shakes his hand and responds with "How do you do, Mr. Fournier."

Again we shall stop the camera to examine what is happening in detail. Diane's handshake is firm, not weak or aggressive. She looks Andre in the eyes as she replies to his greeting. She repeats his name in a clear voice verifying that she has heard his name correctly and that she is pronouncing it accurately. In each of these details Diane has shown herself to be polite and self-confident.

The interview allows Andre to assess Diane's personal characteristics and qualifications, and it allows Diane to learn about the company and what is expected of her if she takes the job. If she were looking for a full-time position, the interview would provide an opportunity to find out what her prospects for advancement within the company would be.

SPEAKING AND LISTENING IN BUSINESS

Both interviewer and interviewee are practising comprehensive and critical listening. Comprehensive listening is required to understand a question; critical listening is required to understand and evaluate an answer. Andre and Diane are also providing feedback in the form of verbal answers, requests for clarification, and body language.

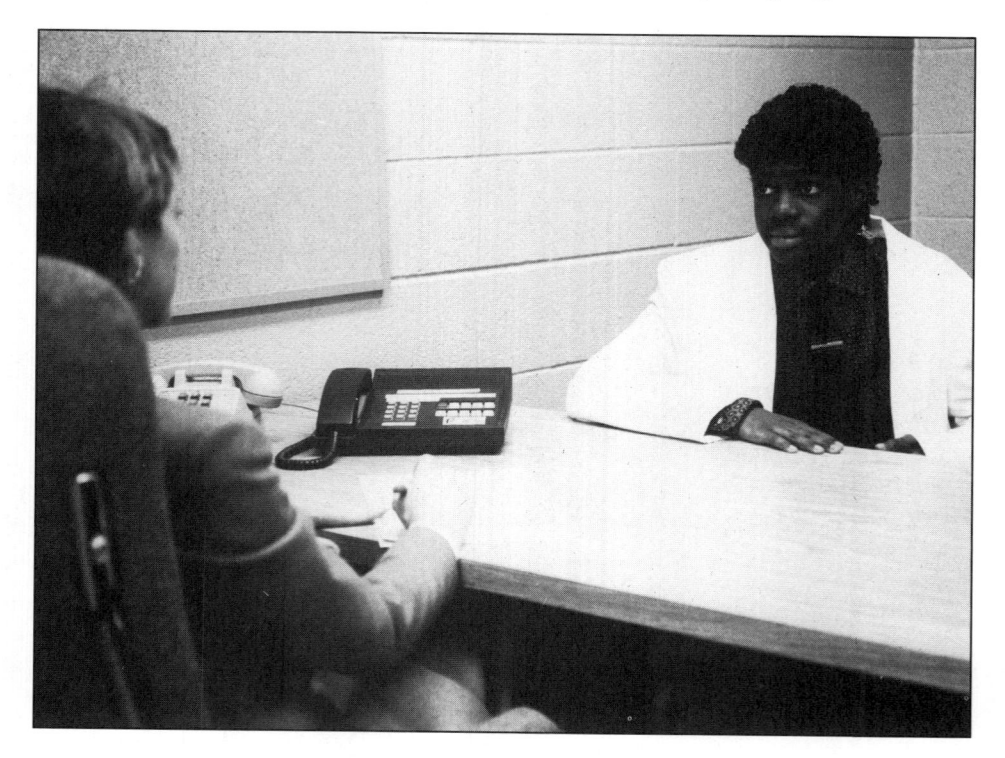

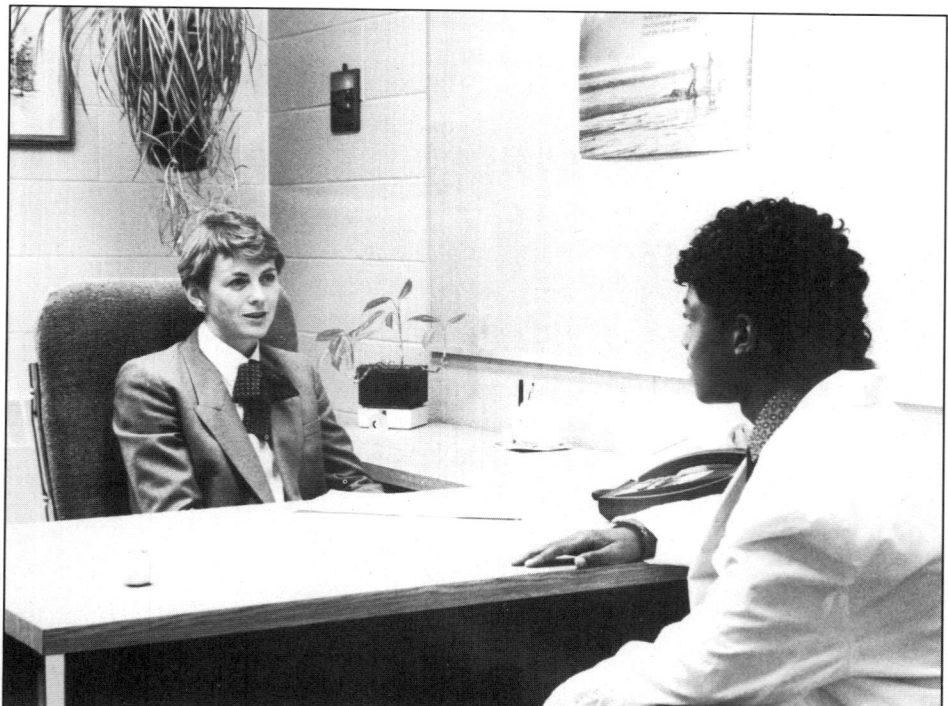

Figure 9-3(a) and (b)
In an interview, both the interviewer and the person being interviewed should provide feedback both verbally and through body language.

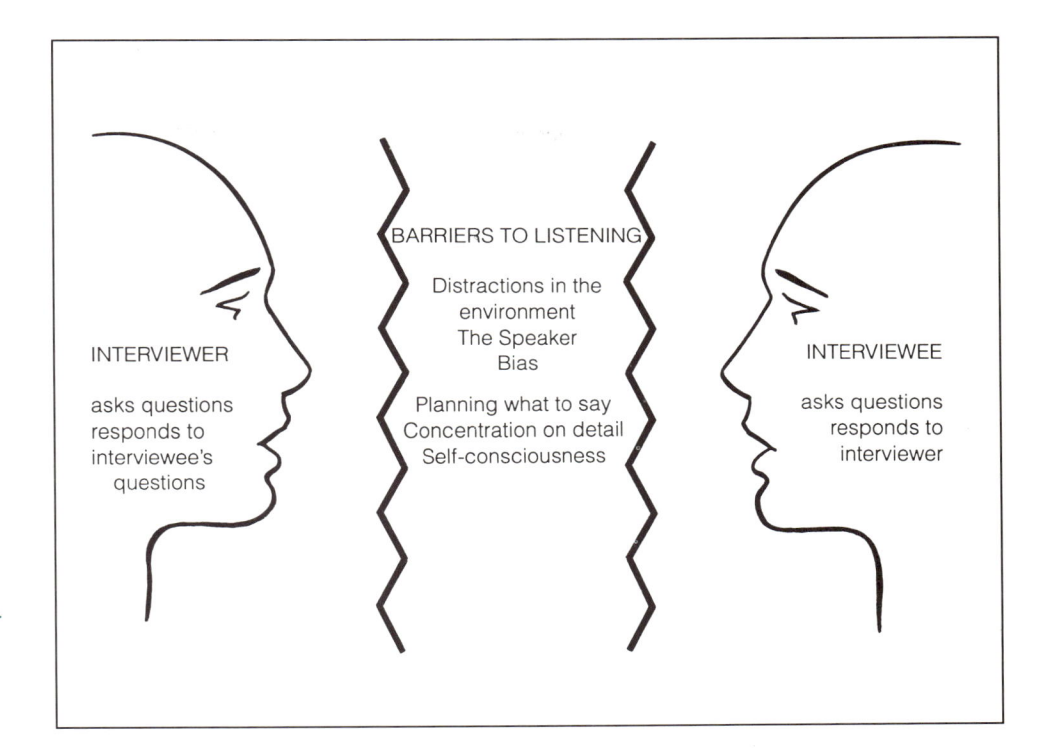

Figure 9-3(c)
During an interview barriers to effective communication, as well as feedback, can occur.

INTERVIEWER
asks questions
responds to interviewee's questions

BARRIERS TO LISTENING
Distractions in the environment
The Speaker
Bias
Planning what to say
Concentration on detail
Self-consciousness

INTERVIEWEE
asks questions
responds to interviewer

Once again the camera is rolling. Andre asks Diane "... what other experience or skills do you have that you think might be useful for this position?" This is Diane's prime opportunity to convince Andre that she is the right person for the job. She can expand on information that is only touched on in her résumé, such as experience or skills gained as a volunteer, relevant courses taken at school, or special abilities related to leisure interests or hobbies. She may wish to stress some aspects of her previous work experience that required similar skills to the position for which she is being interviewed. This is Diane's opportunity to present herself in the best light possible.

From Andre's point of view, Diane's answer will provide him with more than just information about her skills and experience. He will be evaluating her reply to know how she communicates under stress, how she organizes information, and how prepared she is for the interview. If she is well prepared, she will have anticipated such a question and will have worked out an answer in advance.

Now we will get to the end of the scene. The camera is rolling. Andre rises from his desk and walks toward Diane saying "I want to thank you for coming in for this interview. We'll let you know our decision at the end of the week." Diane replies, "Thank you, Mr. Fournier. I've enjoyed talking with you." Now freeze the action. Andre's expression is warm and friendly. He is smiling as he ushers Diane out of his office. Diane returns his smile and makes eye contact as she thanks him.

From Andre's tone of voice and friendly expression, Diane infers that the impression she has made is positive. Since he is sending her to meet the woman who would be her boss, he must think that she has the necessary skills for the job. He wants Ms. Slaney to meet

SPEAKING AND LISTENING IN BUSINESS

Diane to see if she will be compatible in that department. For a job at the entry level (a junior position) or a summer job such as this one, compatibility and a willingness to work can often count for more than previous experience and specific skills. Compatibility and willingness to work cannot be communicated in your written résumé, they must be communicated in conversation with your potential employer. It is therefore important, if you want the job, that you indicate by the way you meet and greet others that you enjoy interacting with people and that you are a friendly person. A willingness to work can be communicated by your interest and enthusiasm, and by the questions you ask about the job.

Interviews are not just arranged for the employer to find out about you. It is important for you to find out about such things as salary, hours of work, and benefits so that you can compare one job with another. In that way you can make a decision that is in your best interests. Asking specific questions about the job and the working conditions indicates to the employer that you have some business knowledge.

For most jobs you will not be the only applicant. If all the other variables were equal — skills, experience, and qualifications — the applicant who can communicate best, verbally and non-verbally, will be the one selected for the job. Projecting a positive physical image through dress, bearing, and expression communicates a non-verbal message to the employer that you have confidence and self-respect. Being prepared, choosing words carefully, listening attentively to questions and information, paying attention to feedback from the interviewer, and speaking clearly are some of the verbal communication skills you learned in Chapters 2 and 4. These are the qualities that an employer will be looking for in the successful applicant. For more information on how to conduct yourself in an interview and on the questions you should be prepared to answer and to ask, read Chapter 15.

A few job interview tips are
1. shake hands firmly
2. maintain eye contact
3. dress appropriately
4. be prepared
5. be interested.

APPLICATIONS

1. Choose a career that interests you and interview an employer in that field. Find out what the employer feels is appropriate dress for a job application interview, and what the employer looks for in a prospective employee, as far as personal characteristics are concerned, and why. Your teacher will tell you whether to prepare a written account of your findings or to report orally to the class.

2. Working in groups, role-play the beginning of a job interview, including the entrance, introduction, and seating of the employer and prospective employee. If you have completed Question 1, dress appropriately for the interview situation. Following each session of role-playing, discuss how well the list of interview tips was applied.

AS AN EMPLOYEE

Once you have accepted a position and become an employee, you will be using your communication skills constantly in many different situations. We shall discuss the following general situations which include:
- making introductions;
- giving and receiving instructions;
- placing and receiving telephone calls;
- face-to-face contact with customers; and
- job evaluation interviews.

Making Introductions

During your first day on the job as a new employee, you will be introduced to many people. It is quite understandable that you will probably not remember everyone's name. However, no introduction should be treated as unimportant. If you did not meet your immediate supervisor at the time of your interview, then this introduction will likely be your first. An example of such an introduction is:

> Mrs. Gottlieb, this is Abdullah Cabar, your new sales trainee.
> How do you do, Abdullah. We're glad to have you join us.
> How do you do, Mrs. Gottlieb. I'm looking forward to working with you.

"How do you do" is always acceptable as a response, accompanied by the person's name — "How do you do, Mr. Santos." Unless your enunciation is excellent, avoid the expression "Pleased to meet you." Although this reply is perfectly acceptable, it often ends up sounding like "Please ta meecha."

There will also be times when you will need to initiate an introduction. An example is "Hello, I'm Abdullah Cabar. I just started last week in the sales department." From this introduction, Abdullah and the other employee can begin a conversation centered on the positions they hold and then move on to other topics.

When you need to introduce one person to another, remember to present the person of lower rank to the person of higher rank. The name of the person of higher rank should be mentioned first. An example is "Mrs. Gottlieb, I'd like you to meet my friend Sonja Nordenson who is here as a co-op student this fall. Sonja, this is Mrs. Gottlieb, my supervisor." Three colloquial expressions to avoid when making introductions are "meet up with," "shake hands with," and "I'd like to make you acquainted with." "I'd like you to meet," "May I present," or simply "This is" are considered polite and acceptable.

Giving and Receiving Instructions

You may recall from Chapter 4 the guidelines for showing someone how to operate a piece of equipment or how to carry out a particular task. They are as follows:
- Organize materials or equipment before you begin.
- Position the viewers as close as possible for ease of viewing and hearing.
- Describe what you are going to do.
- State the instructions in sequential order, including common errors or dangers.
- Maintain eye contact as much as possible to gauge understanding.
- Use verbal as well as non-verbal communication.
- Pay attention to feedback that may indicate lack of understanding, and repeat or rephrase instructions when necessary.
- Use specific words to minimize confusion.
- Summarize the instructions you have given.

When you are the receiver rather than the sender of instructions, careful listening is, of course, most important. If the speaker is demonstrating the use of equipment, hand movements and gestures will also play an important part in the communication. For example, if the instruction is "Flip this switch before turning this dial to 8," or "Enter these invoices, but hang on to these for another day" you will know what to do only if you pay close attention to the speaker's hand movements. Make sure that you are positioned in such a way that you can see and hear easily. If you do not understand any part of the instructions, ask for clarification.

Receiving instructions requires comprehensive listening; that is, you are listening to understand the message. Repeating the instructions to yourself will help you to identify any aspect that is unclear. For instance, it would be difficult to repeat to yourself the instruction, "flip this switch," if you did not know to which switch the speaker was referring. You could then ask for clarification. For difficult instructions, repeating them aloud in your own words can help you to learn them and to identify any areas of uncertainty. You might say, for example "I am to turn on the second switch and then turn the small dial to 8." If you might forget some parts of the instructions, make notes you can follow until the procedure is memorized.

Acquiring Telephone Skills

Business, as we know it today, relies very heavily on the telephone as a communication channel. The telephone provides a vital link between the business and its clients, suppliers, advisers, advertisers, and government regulators. Because information can be relayed and received instantly, the telephone is used throughout all levels of business. Telephone skills are therefore essential for all business people.

We are so familiar with using the telephone for social communication that we may assume our telephone skills are adequate for business. This is not necessarily true. The use of the telephone in business requires a much higher degree of precision and courtesy. In fact, your ability to transmit information precisely (both sending and receiving), to treat business contacts in a courteous manner, and to make a good impression on behalf of your company through the skilful use of the telephone can determine your success in an organization.

Having A Positive Telephone Personality

Do you know what main component of the communication process is missing when we communicate by telephone? It is, of course, non-verbal communication. In face-to-face communication, the message and feedback are sent by voice, facial expressions, and gestures. On the telephone your message and feedback depend on the words you choose and the quality of your voice alone.

In a business call, your voice creates an impression in the mind of the person at the other end of the telephone line. It is this impression by which the other person will judge you and your company. Therefore make sure that your voice conveys positive qualities to create the right impression.

If possible, listen to how your voice sounds on a tape recorder. Your telephone voice is very similar. Does your voice sound pleasant and natural? Can you hear a "smile" in your voice? Can you hear and understand each word without straining? Do you speak at a pace that a listener can follow easily? Does your voice sound interested or disinterested? Check your tone, volume, pitch, and enunciation with a business listener in mind. In business, as in social situations, your tone will vary depending on the circumstances of the call, how well you know the other person, the other person's position, and the general business atmosphere of your company. You would not, for example, use the same tone to answer the telephone in a funeral chapel as you would in a take-out pizza restaurant. How well you know the other person and that person's position will also dictate the tone as well as the content of your message. You would use a more formal tone and phrasing when speaking to the president of a large corporation than you would to an order desk clerk you know on a first name basis from daily telephone contact.

Have you ever tucked the telephone under your chin when you were speaking? Most likely your listener had to ask you to repeat yourself because your voice was indistinct. Eating and drinking while using the telephone also result in indistinct messages and often an irritated listener. Remember to hold the receiver a little distance away from your mouth and speak directly into the mouthpiece.

Another telephone skill that is very important in business is providing verbal feedback. The person with whom you are communicating on the telephone of course cannot read your body language to know if you are understanding the message. It will be necessary for your feedback to be in the form of words and tone of voice. Verbal cues such as "yes," "I see," "I understand," and "that's right" are appropriate in business, whereas "yeah," "uh huh," and "sure," should be reserved for casual social conversations.

Figure 9-4

> How would you rate yourself on the following characteristics of a good telephone personality? Copy out this chart and record your score
>
> (1 = excellent, 5 = unsatisfactory)
>
> | | |
> |---|---|
> | natural sounding | 1 2 3 4 5 |
> | sincere | 1 2 3 4 5 |
> | friendly | 1 2 3 4 5 |
> | polite | 1 2 3 4 5 |
> | interested | 1 2 3 4 5 |
> | willing to help | 1 2 3 4 5 |

Receiving Telephone Calls

A business telephone should be answered promptly. A caller, having to wait for several rings for the telephone to be answered, may feel with some justification that the business is not being run efficiently.

Medium-sized to large companies channel incoming calls through a switchboard and have a standard way of answering which should be learned by new employees. The operator may answer, for example, "Good morning, Antello Paper Products." In a smaller company, "May I help you?" may follow the company name. The operator will then transfer the call to the appropriate department or individual. Since the caller has already been told the name of the company by the switchboard operator or receptionist, the next person to answer will identify which department or office the caller has reached and who is speaking. Examples are, "Hello, Sales Department, Joanne Lee speaking," or "Ms. Warren's office, Peter Kala speaking." This specific information will let callers know that they have reached the correct company, department, or individual. If you need to transfer the call to another person, tell the caller what you are going to do and then make the transfer quickly. Sometimes, you will find it necessary to put a caller on hold. When this occurs, ask the caller, "May I put you on hold?" Most callers would rather be put on hold for a minute than have to make a return call. If the caller is on hold for more than a minute, check back to ensure the person wants to continue to wait. When the person requested is not available, use tact and judgement when telling the caller, and offer to take a message. Look at Figure 9-6 for some of the things to say and not to say in such a situation.

If you are already talking on another line or waiting on a customer when a call comes in, it is acceptable to excuse yourself, answer the telephone, ask the incoming caller to wait for a minute, and get back to the person with whom you were dealing. The caller should not be kept waiting more than a minute. If it is going to be longer, take the name and number and call back as soon as possible.

Always keep a pen and pad near the telephone to take messages. Many businesses use preprinted telephone message pads, such as the one in Figure 9-5, to make the task simpler. Information that should be written down is the caller's name, telephone number, the name of the party being called, the time and date of the call, and any message

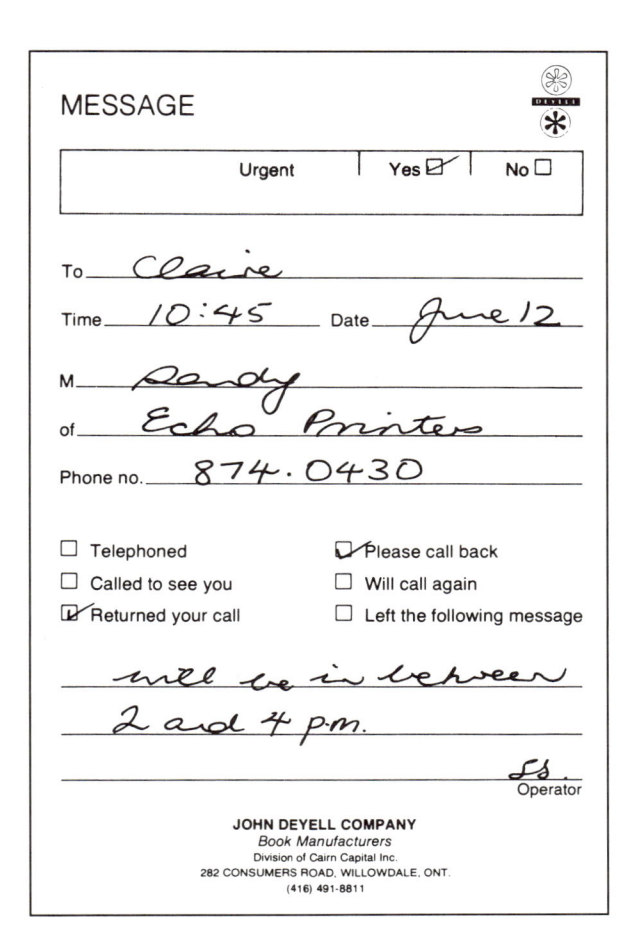

Figure 9-5
Preprinted telephone message forms help to ensure that the message is complete.

```
MESSAGE
                    Urgent    Yes ☑   No ☐

To     Claire
Time   10:45      Date  June 12
M      Randy
of     Echo Printers
Phone no.  874-0430

☐ Telephoned           ☑ Please call back
☐ Called to see you    ☐ Will call again
☑ Returned your call   ☐ Left the following message

         will be in between
         2 and 4 p.m.
                                    JS
                                    Operator
         JOHN DEYELL COMPANY
             Book Manufacturers
         Division of Cairn Capital Inc.
     282 CONSUMERS ROAD, WILLOWDALE, ONT.
              (416) 491-8811
```

the caller wishes to leave. Verify with the caller that the information you have written down is correct before you hang up. Do not be afraid to ask the spelling of the caller's name. Business people are used to this request and as they recognize the need for accurate spelling, they willingly comply. If the message is lengthy and rapidly given, you will have to summarize it. The note-taking skills you practised in Chapter 2 will help in writing quick summaries.

Figure 9-6
Knowing the right thing to say is important in business.

If a caller asks to speak to someone who is not available

DO SAY	DO NOT SAY
... is expected shortly	... has just gone to get a cup of coffee
	... hasn't arrived yet this morning
... is in a meeting	... is meeting with a client, First Choice Decorating.
... is away from the office this afternoon	... I don't know where he/she is
	... has left for the day (This response has a negative effect — the caller may assume the person has gone home early. In fact, the person may be at a meeting at another location, or have left because of illness.)

SPEAKING AND LISTENING IN BUSINESS

When giving information to a caller that must be written down, speak slowly and distinctly. It is a good idea to offer to repeat the information or to ask the caller "Would you like to read the information back to me?"

You may, at some time, have to deal with an angry caller. A natural reaction is to return the anger. However, it is important to remember that the caller is not upset with you, but with the company. Listen carefully to the caller's complaint and make notes. When the caller has finished speaking, review your notes and ask for clarification on any points if needed. Then either outline how you intend to deal with the complaint, or tactfully explain to the caller why the complaint is unjustified. Empathy and courtesy work wonders in dealing with angry callers. It is difficult to remain angry when the other person is being concerned, pleasant, and helpful.

Placing Telephone Calls

You have more control when placing a call because you know why you are calling and you can plan in advance what you wish to say. Most routine business calls are to give or obtain information. Reviewing what you wish to accomplish and anticipating questions that may be asked, before you place the call, will help to ensure that your call is efficient and successful.

Before you lift the receiver, have a general idea of how you will begin the conversation and how you will explain the purpose of your call. Preparing in this way for a conversation will help make you feel more confident when you place the call. Another useful practice is to jot down in point form the information you wish to relay or obtain. Then as each point is addressed, you can tick it off or write down the answer. This procedure will help you to transmit and receive information efficiently and also help you to recognize when to end the call.

When you place the call, identify yourself and your company immediately, then the purpose of your call. At the end of the conversation thank the other person for the information, or if you are providing the information, make sure that the information is complete from the other person's standpoint.

If you are ordering supplies by telephone, planning is essential. Know what items, catalogue or order numbers, quantities, sizes, and colours you want. Be prepared to provide such information as the name of the business, full address and telephone number, a purchase order number, delivery date, method of delivery, street directions, and method of payment. When you have finished, the order clerk should repeat the information you have given. If not, ask to have the order repeated to make sure the correct information has been written down. It may prevent having the wrong item shipped and subsequent delays.

When you are making an appointment by telephone, tell the receptionist your name (and spell it if necessary), the date, the time the appointment is desired, and the reason for the appointment. With this information, the person with whom the appointment is made can be prepared by reading background information or by speaking with others who have been involved in previous discussions. If an appointment must be rescheduled, give the name, date, and time of the appointment, explain briefly the reason for rescheduling and ask for a new date and time.

Telemarketing

Selling by telephone is a skill that seems to come naturally to some people. For others, it takes time to learn the technique and much practice. Successful salespeople project a natural and friendly manner and a knowledge and enthusiasm about their product or service. Projecting these qualities by telephone will require some practice, especially if you are one who feels uncomfortable making telephone sales calls. Many businesses offer training courses to improve the telephone skills of their sales personnel.

Before you place a sales call, take a few minutes to prepare. Assemble any information you might need, including the name of the person to be contacted, note the points you wish to communicate, and know how you will open the conversation. Prepare a few relevant questions in advance to ask when you need to keep the conversation going. When you make the call, use the person's name as you introduce yourself and your company, for example "Hello, Mr. D'Alessandro, my name is Sandra Scott. I represent Eastern Publishing." Then you can communicate your sales message. It may take some time to polish your sales techniques and your communication skills and it may also take some patience on your part while you are learning from experience.

Face-to-Face Contact with Customers

Situations in which you meet with customers in person, unlike telephone situations, provide you with the opportunity of using body language. This added dimension to the communcation process can be used to your advantage. The image you project by means of body language can help or hinder you and your company in your dealings with customers. Suitable attire, good posture, a friendly, self-confident **demeanour**, or behaviour, and eye contact are ways in which you can communicate effectively through body language.

Many of the same techniques and courtesies used in telephone communication can be applied to face-to-face business dealings. Appropriate tone of voice, good speech characteristics (fluency, enunciation, pronunciation, and word choice), prompt attention to customer needs and complaints, and careful note-taking are important when dealing with customers in person as well.

Performance Evaluation Interview

Most companies have a **probationary period**, that is, a trial period, usually of three months, after an employee is hired. During this

---

When giving instructions
1. *organize materials/equipment*
2. *maintain eye contact*
3. *keep a close distance*
4. *state instructions in sequential order.*

When receiving instructions
1. *repeat instructions to yourself*
2. *ask for clarification if required*
3. *paraphrase instructions out loud*
4. *jot down instructions if necessary.*

period the company assesses the employee's skills, attitudes, and performance. At the end of the probationary period, the supervisor will ask the employee to attend an evaluation interview.

The purpose of the interview is to let you know how well or poorly you are performing, from the management's point of view, and to allow you to discuss the job from your point of view. If the evaluation is negative, your supervisor should tell you what you need to do to achieve a more satisfactory performance, what assistance is available to you, and what the consequences of a second unsatisfactory evaluation will be. Your input is needed. The interview is not meant to be a one-sided conversation with your supervisor doing all of the talking.

Be prepared to listen carefully and to accept criticism. Try not to interpret the criticism as an attack on you. Instead, it is meant to be a comment on how you can improve your performance. Being oversensitive to criticism will be **counter-productive**, or having an effect opposite to the intended effect, so try to listen objectively and do not allow any of the barriers to effective listening to interfere.

The job evaluation interview gives the employee an opportunity to discuss the **job description**, or the list of duties and responsibilities a job entails, and make suggestions for changes in duties. If you are having a problem with some aspect of the job, now is the time to discuss it in a reasonable (not argumentative) manner. It may be that your supervisor will modify the job description if you present a strong case to support your position.

In addition to discussing present conditions, the job evaluation interview gives you the chance to express your **aspirations**, or ambitions, so do some preparation beforehand. Consider if there is another job within the company that would interest you in the future. Compare the skills required for that job with your present skills. During the interview discuss your suitability for the position and how you can become better qualified for it. By voicing your interest, the supervisor will be better prepared to make a recommendation on your behalf if the position becomes open. Look at Figure 9-7 for a summary of effective evaluation interviews.

A good telephone personality comes with
1. *pleasing tone of voice*
2. *clear pronunciation*
3. *moderate rate of speech*
4. *proper handling of the mouthpiece.*

APPLICATIONS

3. (a) Work in small groups to complete this assignment. Assign one student to demonstrate a piece of equipment, preferably business or technical equipment. Have the other students listen to the instructions and then have one student follow the instructions given in the demonstration and operate the equipment. As a group prepare either an oral or written report stating the strengths of the demonstration and suggestions for improvement.

    (b) Evaluate in writing your own personal abilities to follow the instructions, and how you could improve the way that you receive instructions.

4. Working in groups, each group completes one of the following exercises.

> **Effective Evaluation Interviews**
>
> *Topics to be discussed:*
>
> *Duties:* The employee and employer should discuss the employee's duties to ensure that they both agree about the job description
>
> *Evaluation:* Both positive and negative comments need to be discussed. Positive comments reinforce good job performance and make negative comments more acceptable. If the employee does not agree with the evaluation, an explanation should be given. By listening to one another, either may change their views.
>
> *Areas requiring improvement:* If the evaluation is negative, the employee should be told what is necessary to achieve a satisfactory evaluation, what assistance is available to the employee, and what the consequences will be for a second unsatisfactory evaluation.
>
> *Concerns/suggestions:* The employee should raise any concerns regarding the job or suggestions for changes in duties.
>
> *Future plans:* Discussion of future plans may include a change in positions, a leave of absence or retirement.

Figure 9-7
Effective Performance Evaluation Interviews

When receiving calls
1. *answer promptly and identify yourself*
2. *inform caller if transferring call*
3. *speak slowly if relaying material to caller*
4. *note caller's name, number, and message if taking a message*
5. *remain calm if caller is angry.*

    (a) Prepare a bulletin board display illustrating the differences between telephone and face-to-face communication, or the history of the telephone equipment including equipment available to assist handicapped people. Discuss your display with the class.
    (b) Locate a film or videotape on telephone personality or telephone techniques to show the class. Introduce the film or videotape and follow the screening with a discussion of the content.
    (c) Prepare a tape of short telephone conversations using examples of good and poor telephone personality. Play the tape for the class and discuss the strengths and weaknesses.

5. Working in pairs, practise the following telephone conversations:
    (a) A call to the dentist to arrange an appointment for yourself and another member of your family.
    (b) A call to a municipal library enquiring about a film on how to use the telephone.
    (c) A call to your insurance agent to find out the cost of insurance for a car you are thinking about buying. (The agent is not in when you call.)
    (d) A call to the dry cleaner. The jacket you picked up yesterday has several black marks on it and you are very angry.

6. Using the telephone directory, locate the following information: the exchanges you can call free from your exchange, directory assistance for a number outside your area, how to call a zenith number, the number for the municipal public works department, the

SPEAKING AND LISTENING IN BUSINESS

number for the provincial Ministry of Health, the number for External Affairs Canada, the number for the local school board, and the numbers for two automotive repair companies.

7. You are in charge of investigating the cost of spring and winter jackets. Make a list of the information you will want to obtain from the manufacturer. When you are finished, form groups to compare the lists.

8. Your community group is having a fund-raising food booth at the local fair. You are in charge of buying the food. Make a list of the items you need to purchase. As you do this, make a list of questions you want to ask your club president to clarify your list of purchases. Reorganize your list of purchases according to suppliers. Then write beside each item the information you want to know. Role-play the conversation you would have with each supplier.

9. Using the information in Question 8, role-play the telephone call(s) to order the supplies.

10. Collect three examples of job descriptions and compare the three. Use the library or contact businesses for the information.

11. Invite a local business person to discuss job evaluations and job evaluation interviews with the class.

When placing calls
1. know who you want to speak to
2. list information you want to give to or obtain from the person.

Telecommunications

In the past to ensure that a message containing complex details or numbers was accurately transmitted to the receiver, the message was sent by mail. That way the receiver had the information on paper exactly the way the sender had written it, and the possibility of the receiver making errors in writing it down from either a telephone or face-to-face conversation was avoided. Today, however, with the need for faster communications and the increase in communication between businesses in various countries, telecommunications is replacing the mail.

Telecommunications is the term used to describe the various methods of changing messages into electronic signals which are then sent over telephone wires or through space by means of satellites.

Companies having computer terminals can use electronic mail to send messages between terminals within the company or to terminals in other companies. The message is keyboarded on one terminal and transmitted electronically to another terminal. At the receiving terminal, the message may be displayed on a visual display unit (screen) or printed.

In addition to words and statistics, graphics may also be transmitted electronically. Graphics are sent using a facsimile machine. At the sending location, the facsimile machine scans the copy converting the copy into electronic signals. These signals are transmitted to a receiving facsimile machine at the other location. The signals are then converted back into the original copy.

The technology used in telecommunications is also used in teleconferencing. Teleconferencing allows people in different locations to conduct meetings. Each location is equipped with a screen, and the image of the person speaking appears on the screen. Teleconferencing eliminates the travelling expenses and time required when people from a variety of locations wish to hold a meeting.

Figure 9-8
Telecommunications have changed our way of communicating with one another. Read this article to help you answer Question 12.

PART TWO: COMMUNICATION IN BUSINESS

12. Read Figure 9-8, then write a short essay on the changes that advances in communication have made to the efficiency of business communication. (Remember to write an outline and a draft of your essay first. You may want to refer to Chapter 6 for help.)

AS A PEER

Unless you are the sole employee, you will have daily contact with your fellow employees. You will learn quickly who is efficient, who shirks responsibility, who is reliable, who is trustworthy, and who is comfortable to associate with as a friend. It will be necessary to maintain a good working relationship with people whom you would not choose as friends. To do this, you must make an effort to be tolerant, friendly, and supportive. Open hostility, caustic comments, and other negative behaviour will do you more harm than the person to whom it is directed. Tact and courtesy are much more effective.

Employees can come into conflict over many job situations — competition for promotion and overlapping responsibilities are two examples — and it is necessary to resolve the conflicts as they arise, while they are still manageable. Employers know that when two employees do not get along, job performance will suffer, as will general morale since others will be drawn into the conflict and will feel the need to take sides. The interpersonal communication skills stressed in the earlier chapters of this book apply to relationships with your co-workers. Much of the conflict can be avoided by practising them.

As a new employee, try to join in as many different groups as possible at coffee break and lunch. Being able to call people by their names will make you feel more at ease in your job, and the word will spread that you are a friendly person. Being willing to pitch in and help other employees who are temporarily overloaded with work when your own work is caught up will also contribute to your being accepted by others.

At times you may need to complete a task with one or more employees and it may be left up to the group how to handle the task. In any group situation, each participant is responsible for contributing in a positive manner. You will be expected to offer your suggestions and opinions clearly and concisely, and to support them with facts. When listening to others, keep an open mind, and if you disagree, do so in a friendly, objective manner. Diverting the group to other topics, not taking the matter seriously, showing disinterest through body language — all these are forms of negative group behaviour. Chapter 3 covered this topic in more depth.

Examples of positive and negative group participation are shown in the chart below.

Be ...	Avoid Being ...
1. Concise e.g., "This job is similar to the large copying job we did two months ago."	Vague "Well, uh, I seem to remember a job. Now when was it? Perhaps some of you remember it. It was something like this one but not quite."
2. Able to Support Opinions with Facts e.g., "I don't think the copier on this floor can handle the job because it becomes overheated on runs of more than 200 copies."	Unable to Provide Facts to Support Opinions "I don't think the copier on this floor can handle the job."
3. Constructive e.g., "We may have trouble implementing your suggestion, but perhaps we could alter it slightly. What if the copies were run back-to-back?"	Negative "That will never work."

APPLICATIONS

When working in a group
1. *make your points concisely*
2. *support your opinions with fact*
3. *listen with an open mind*
4. *disagree in a friendly manner*
5. *refrain from distracting behaviour.*

13. Write a paragraph on one of the following topics:
    (a) Why you like being in a group with a certain person.
    (b) What annoys you about group work.
    (c) Why you think some people distract rather than help the group.
14. Write an evaluation of your contribution to one of the groups in which you worked. Include suggestions for your improvement.

AS A SUPERVISOR

Supervisors are usually positioned between employees and management. See Figure 9-9. Their listening and speaking skills must enable them to communicate effectively at both levels. We will investigate the supervisor's role, as it relates to communication, at both levels.

Supervisor/Employee

The supervisor communicates with the employee in many situations, such as interviewing, assigning work, giving directions, helping to overcome problems, resolving conflicts, and conducting evaluations.

Figure 9-9
The supervisor is involved in two communication processes — employee/supervisor and supervisor/management.

In each situation, the supervisor must be able to express thoughts clearly and concisely and to listen to the employees' questions and comments.

Any person in a position of authority will operate much more effectively by developing **rapport**, or a sympathetic relationship, with employees. This can be achieved to a great degree through listening attentively and empathizing, and acting in a fair manner. A supervisor who feels superior to the employees does not empathize, and communicates the superior attitude through body language and verbal communication. Rapport with employees will not be possible under these circumstances. On the other hand, where rapport has been established, employees will feel comfortable in discussing problems with their supervisor, and in suggesting ways in which the problems can be solved.

Supervisor/Management

When dealing with management, the supervisor receives instructions, is given responsibilities, and is subject to job evaluation. Once again, if a rapport is established between management and the supervisor, two-way communication is possible and problem solving can be a mutual effort. It does not matter how up-to-date the machinery and equipment are in a company. If the personnel cannot communicate satisfactorily, the company cannot operate efficiently and successfully. Interpersonal communication skills are essential to the smooth running of any business.

SPEAKING AND LISTENING IN BUSINESS

CHAPTER SUMMARY

Tips for job interviews
- shake hands firmly
- maintain eye contact
- dress appropriately
- smile

Tips for giving instructions
- organize the materials/equipment beforehand
- maintain eye contact
- ensure an unobstructed view for the audience
- state the instructions in a sequential order

Tips for receiving instructions
- repeat the instructions to yourself
- ask for clarification
- paraphrase the instructions out loud
- jot down the instructions if necessary

Characteristics of a good telephone personality
- pleasing tone of voice
- clear pronunciation
- moderate rate of speech
- proper handling of the telephone mouthpiece

Tips for receiving calls
- answer promptly
- identify yourself
- inform the caller if you transfer the call
- speak slowly if relaying information to the caller
- note the caller's name, number, and message when taking a message
- remain calm when dealing with an angry caller

Tips for placing a call
- know who you want to speak to
- list the information you want to give or obtain from the person

Topics for discussion during a job evaluation interview
- duties
- evaluation
- areas requiring improvement
- concerns/suggestions
- future plans

Positive participation in a group
- make your points concisely
- support your opinions with fact

- listen with an open mind
- disagree in a friendly, objective manner
- refrain from distracting behaviour

MAKING IT WORK

1. Business people, who travel often as part of their work, usually have a travel agent make the necessary arrangements. In a large company, there may be an employee who is responsible for booking transportation and accommodation. In a smaller company you would usually contact a local travel agency or telephone the airlines and hotels directly.

   The skills of effective speaking and careful listening that you learned about in this chapter are important for a travel agent or an employee who deals with travel arrangements. It helps if such people also have a helpful attitude and enjoy working with people. Accuracy is important in order that time is not lost through faulty connections. And, since people may not know at first the amount of money they can spend on flights and accommodation, patience in explaining the various options is an important trait for a travel agent.

   (a) Do you think you have the characteristics to be a travel agent? Explain your answer by assessing your speaking and listening skills.

   (b) Match the vocabulary used by agents in Column A with the definitions in Column B.

   Column A
   - repeat business
   - visa
   - passport
   - layovers
   - itinerary
   - ports of call

   Column B
   - issued by the government, it identifies people and clears them for leaving or returning to a country
   - scheduled stops for ships
   - clients who call again and again
   - document allowing a person to enter a country and stay for a period of time
   - waiting period between flights
   - list of flights, hotel reservations, and car rentals, with dates and times

   (c) What are travellers' cheques? What are their advantages? How do you obtain them? How do you cash them? Write a short summary that answers these questions.

   (d) Practise your telephone skills by phoning two local banks to find out

   (i) if there is a charge for using travellers' cheques, and what it is; and

   (ii) what travellers should do if they lose their travellers' cheques.

(e) Invite a travel agent to speak to the class about the use of computer terminals by travel agents.
(f) Obtain a train or airline schedule. Write an explanation of how to read the schedule and the meaning of the symbols used.
(g) Create a collage, poster, or poem related to travel.

2. Invite a "hot line" counsellor to speak to the class on therapeutic listening over the telephone.

3. Read the following case, then answer the questions that follow.

Larry works with Dave in a camera shop in the mall. When Larry started, Dave said he was easy going, had always got along well with past staff, and would always be direct if there was anything Larry was doing that displeased him. Larry felt he was doing a good job and so was very surprised when Dave told him one day that he could not tolerate Larry's lateness any more. Larry remembered being a few minutes late a couple of times, but Dave had not seemed angry at the time.
(a) What do you think has caused this situation?
(b) What should Larry and Dave do now?
(c) How could it have been prevented?

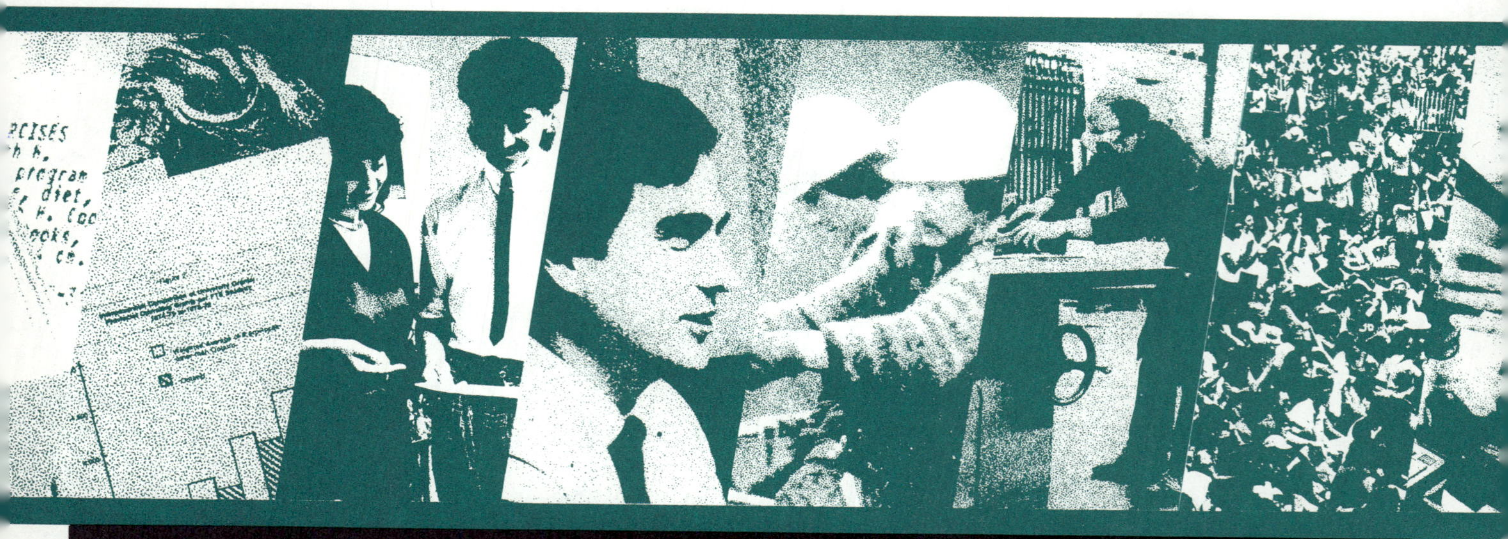

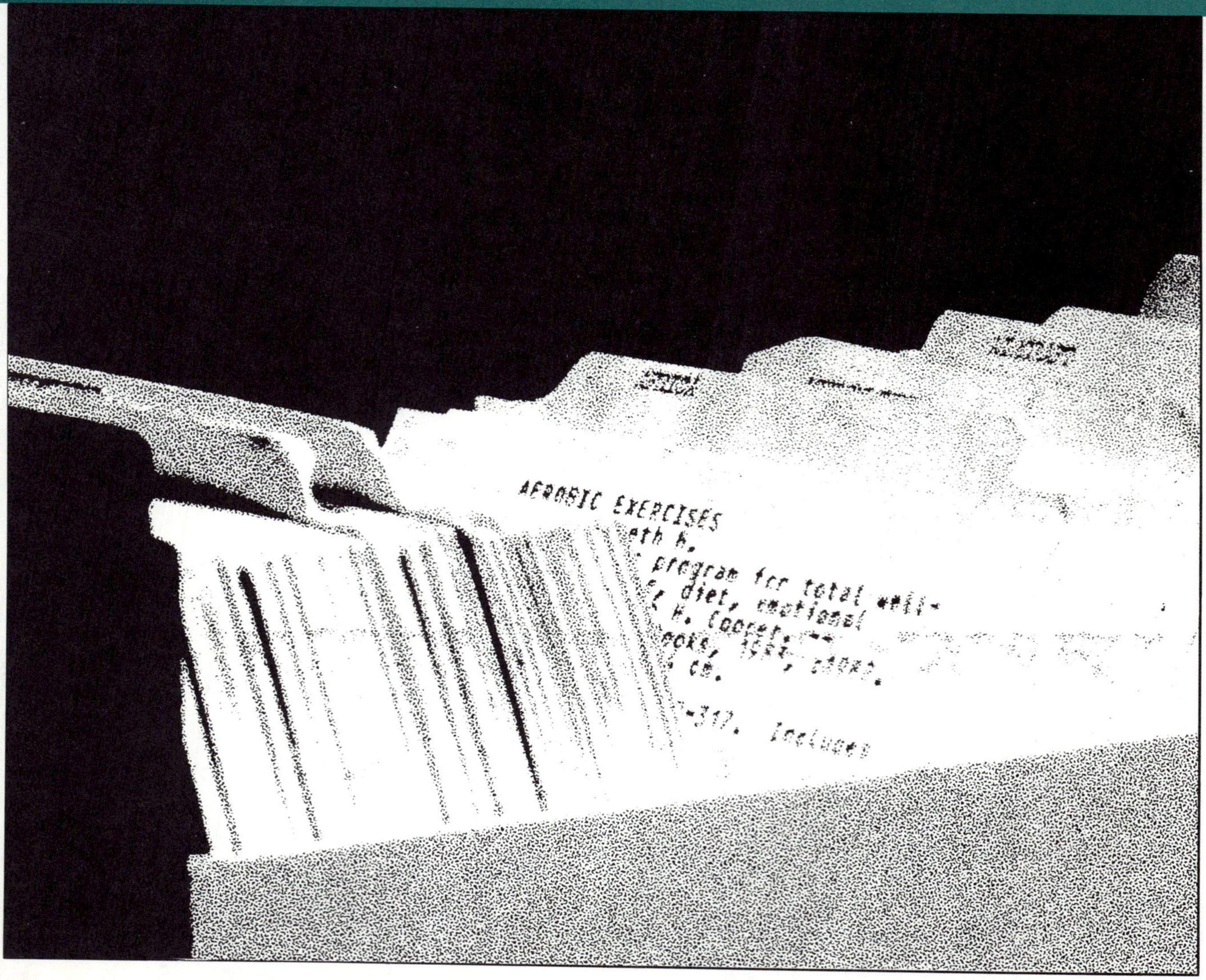
AEROBIC EXERCISES

CHAPTER 10

Speaking Skills In Making Presentations

GOALS

At the end of this chapter you should be able to
1. differentiate among informative, persuasive, and entertaining presentations;
2. identify sources for research data; and
3. construct a planning model for a presentation.

VOCABULARY BUILDING

modem
cross-reference

VIEWPOINTS

Diane, whom you met in the section *Viewpoints* in Chapter 9, got the job with Eastern Publishing. Her supervisor is Anna Slaney, the promotions manager. Anna is approaching Diane's desk, carrying several file folders under her arm.

ANNA: Well, Diane, how are you getting along with those calls I asked you to make?

DIANE: I'm almost finished, Anna. I think by noon they'll all be done.

ANNA: Good, because I want you to help me get ready for the summer sales conference. I'm going to give a presentation on how special promotions have helped the sale of our books. I'd like you to prepare the overhead transparencies for my presentation.

DIANE: I think I would enjoy doing that.

ANNA: Well, here's the material you should use. (Anna places the file folders on Diane's desk and opens the top one.) Now, you're going to have to adapt this one and this one to make them clearer. (Anna removes the second file folder from the pile and opens it.) And I think you will probably want to include these sales figures here. You'll find figures for other years and for books that were promoted conventionally, for comparison. Anyway, I'll leave it up to you how you want to treat the data. I'll be going out of town for three days starting tomorrow. Do you think you could have the transparencies done by the time I get back?

DIANE: Yes, I think so.

ANNA: All right, I'll leave you to it then. (Anna starts to leave the room but turns around to add something to her instructions and sees Diane looking at the material with a confused expression on her face.) I'm sorry for not being very considerate, Diane. I didn't ask if you had any questions.

DIANE: I'm not sure what you want me to do. I've never prepared transparencies before.

ANNA: Quite right, I didn't explain myself very well. I'm just in such a rush this morning, and you learn so quickly that I sometimes forget you've only been here a short while. Let's see ... I have half an hour free at eleven o'clock. Why don't we meet then in my office and go over this in more detail?

DIANE: Thank you, Anna. That will give me a chance to look over the material so that I can clear up what I don't understand.

QUESTIONS

1. If Anna had not noticed Diane's confusion, what do you think Diane should have done?
2. Do you think employees are entitled to as much consideration as employers? Support your answer.
3. Presentations can be informative, persuasive, or entertaining. Which of these three do you think Anna's presentation will be? Explain your answer.

Figure 10-1
Presentations can persuade, inform, or entertain. In business, they most often perform the first two functions.

INTRODUCTION

In Chapter 9, we looked at a few types of business communication — interviews, job evaluation interviews, contacts with customers, meetings, and telephone conversations. Another kind of interpersonal communication used in business is a form of public speaking, usually referred to as a presentation (Figure 10-1). In Chapter 4 we discussed some of the elements that contribute to an effective presentation. We looked at speech styles, body language, characteristics of good voice quality, and characteristics of good speech. In this chapter we will examine the following:
- types of presentations;
- planning before the research;
- researching the topic;
- preparing an outline;
- audio and visual aids;
- preparing a model; and
- delivery techniques.

TYPES OF PRESENTATIONS

Informative

Many presentations are designed to inform the audience. The information they present can be a description, such as an overview of the company's organizational structure, or an explanation of the company's policy and procedures with regard to profit sharing. Informative presentations can also instruct or direct employees in some aspect of operations. For example, the presentation might instruct employees in the safe and correct operation of a new computer, or the presentation might direct them in the proper handling of supplies and paperwork in the storeroom.

In planning an informative presentation, consider how much time you are allowed and restrict the scope to fit the time period. Begin your presentation with a statement of purpose, then arrange your material according to an appropriate pattern. In Chapter 6 we discussed various organizational patterns — chronological, spatial, topical, causal, comparison/contrast, and problem/solution. The nature of the material you are presenting should suggest the most effective organizational pattern. To help your audience follow and understand the sequence, enumerate your points using such expressions as "first ..., second ...," when giving instructions.

Tailor your choice of words to the audience. You should be able to judge whether or not technical terms will be understood, whether they should be explained, or whether they should be omitted entirely.

Informative presentations are often made more interesting and understandable by the use of visual aids. Models, charts, diagrams, overhead transparencies, or real objects can often clarify the information in a way that words cannot. Make sure that visual materials are properly labelled and that the information can be read easily by the audience.

Persuasive

A persuasive presentation is meant to influence ideas or actions. You may wish to propose the purchase of new machinery, to state the case for a wage increase, or to request a change in land zoning for a new warehouse. Persuasive presentations are made in all areas of business: within the company (interdepartmental, management/staff); between company and client; between company and financial institution; and between company and government agency.

The headline of an advertisement, or the part written in larger type, is designed to get the attention of readers. If the headline does not get attention, the copy will not be read. Similarly, in a presentation, you should take the time to write an opening that will engage the immediate attention and enthusiasm of your audience. Without their complete attention and interest, you will not be able to persuade them. First impressions are lasting. Once you have stimulated interest, you will be less likely to lose your audience.

Knowing your audience is key to giving a persuasive presentation that does persuade. How often have you heard someone say "Give me a good reason why I should agree with you"? A good reason, however, will vary from person to person. You may feel that you should take the car to go shopping because it will be faster than walking. Someone else, however, may not view your desire for speed as a good reason for taking the car. Similarly, in business, different individuals and different groups will have their own objectives, priorities, and ethics. The board of directors of a company may not see the need for new machinery, whereas the management may feel it is essential in order to remain competitive. Management may feel that staff members are receiving fair salaries, whereas the staff feel they should be paid more. The business community may feel that profit and efficiency are good reasons for a new multi-tiered parking lot. The municipal government may be more influenced by social needs and feel that a community centre would be a better use of the land. When giving a presentation, you should be familiar with the views of the group or the person you are addressing in order to present "good reasons" with which they will agree. In the example of borrowing the family car, you may present the argument that shopping at night is safer using a car.

In order for the audience to be swayed by your arguments, your credibility must be established. Support reasons for action or for a change of view with well-documented research, reliable statistics, personal experience, or the testimony of experts.

Besides being convinced by the logic of a presentation, the audience can also be persuaded by the psychological and emotional basis of a presentation. For example, most people like to feel that they belong to a group. Consequently, they may be motivated by appealing to this need through stressing "teamwork" and "team effort." An example of appealing to the emotions is the use of visual material depicting impoverished children to promote charitable donations. Advertising copywriters always consider the psychological and emotional "motivators," that is, the reasons why people might buy a product, when they write their advertisements. Some of the reasons are: to feel important, to have fun, to be different, to save money or time, or to be healthy.

In a persuasive presentation, organization of your arguments can follow either deductive or inductive reasoning. Deductive reasoning begins with a generally accepted idea and then applies it to specific instances. If, for instance, you know that the audience agrees with the premise that everyone should be paid the same wage for the same job, you will start with that idea. Then you will move on to show that filing clerks in the accounting department are being paid less than filing clerks in the advertising department, although they perform essentially the same job. By deductive reasoning, the accounting department clerks should be receiving the same wage as the advertising department clerks. You might be trying to persuade a company to buy scrubbers for the removal of air-borne pollutants that contribute to acid rain. You know the audience believes that acid rain damages the environment. You might therefore start with an affirmation of that belief, continue with a description of the methods for reducing acid rain, go on to an appeal for responsible action on the part of companies contributing to acid rain, and finish with a suggestion for the most efficient way in which that particular company could act responsibly (by buying scrubbers). Use deductive reasoning when you know that the audience agrees with your main premise and needs only to be convinced of specific instances or applications.

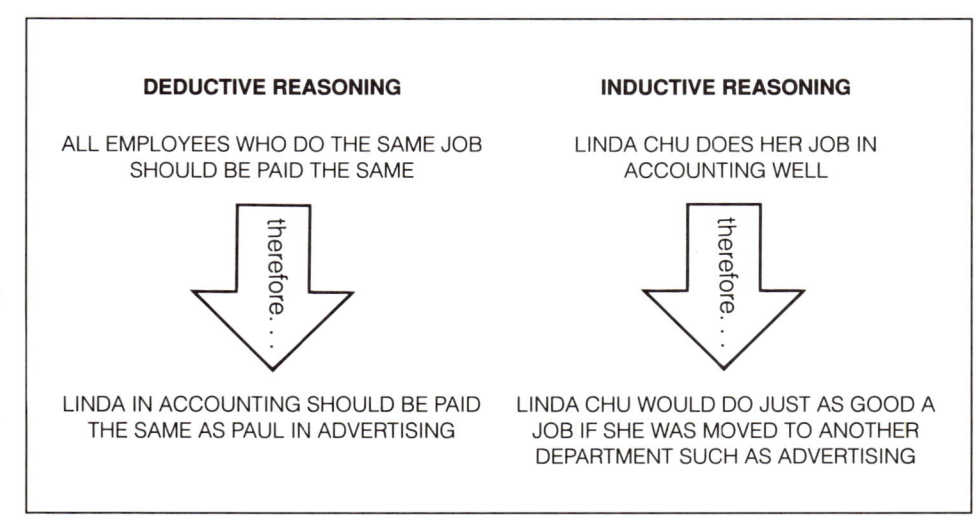

Figure 10-2
Deductive reasoning works from a general idea to specific examples or situations; inductive reasoning works from a specific example or situation to a more general one.

DEDUCTIVE REASONING

ALL EMPLOYEES WHO DO THE SAME JOB SHOULD BE PAID THE SAME

therefore...

LINDA IN ACCOUNTING SHOULD BE PAID THE SAME AS PAUL IN ADVERTISING

INDUCTIVE REASONING

LINDA CHU DOES HER JOB IN ACCOUNTING WELL

therefore...

LINDA CHU WOULD DO JUST AS GOOD A JOB IF SHE WAS MOVED TO ANOTHER DEPARTMENT SUCH AS ADVERTISING

Inductive reasoning begins with a specific instance and progresses to a general idea. Look at Figure 10-2 for a visual explanation of the difference between this and deductive reasoning. Suppose you were supporting the election of a provincial premier to the office of Prime Minister. Using inductive reasoning, you would begin by demonstrating ways in which the premier was effective at the provincial level. You would then point out similar areas the premier would be involved with at the federal level. For example, if the premier had attracted new industries to the province, you might point out the need for new industries across Canada. Your next step would be to bring the audience to the conclusion that because the premier was effective in provincial politics the same would hold true in federal politics. Inductive reasoning is used to persuade the audience that if a specific idea is true or valid, a related general idea will be as well.

The strategy you use in planning your presentation will depend largely on the audience you will be addressing. You will need to know whether inductive or deductive reasoning will work best for your particular audience, what reasons will have the most support, to what degree will it be necessary to establish your credibility, and to which emotional or psychological need to appeal. Knowledge of the audience will provide the fundamental direction for the organization and content of your presentation.

Entertaining

Humorous, entertaining presentations are delivered mainly in the evening as after-dinner speeches. They are seldom required during the day. If you are asked to give an entertaining speech, choose a topic that fits the occasion. When an individual or a group is being honoured, you could use anecdotes or a narrative relating to them. You may wish to personalize your talk by including names of people in the audience in any anecdotes. Use humour only if you feel comfortable with it and only if the humour is kind. For a talk to be successful, the audience must feel that the speaker is at ease and enjoying the event, and that no one is being made to feel uncomfortable.

Presentations can be
1. informative
2. persuasive
3. entertaining.

APPLICATIONS

1. Cut two advertisements from newspapers or magazines. Name the psychological need or emotion to which the advertiser is appealing. Discuss how this is reinforced by the
   (a) headline
   (b) copy
   (c) typeface
   (d) visual elements, including artwork, photography, and colour.
   Prepare a written report and present your material to the class.

2. Prepare a magazine advertisement for a product of your choice. In small groups discuss the psychological need or emotional appeal for each advertisement and how it is achieved.

3. Watch a television commercial or listen to one on the radio. Is the message different when an audio medium is used as opposed to a visual medium?

4. In small groups, discuss why celebrities are used to sell products. How effective do you think this method is? What is the relationship between the product and the actor?

5. Comment on whether athletes should appear in advertisements for alcohol or tobacco companies or whether such companies should sponsor sporting events.

6. Working in pairs, write a radio advertisement and record it on a cassette tape. The advertisement can be for the school store, a school dance, or other student activity. It should be no longer than 30 seconds.

7. Make up two examples illustrating both inductive reasoning and deductive reasoning. Think up your own topics or use the following:
   (a) why athletes buy brand X running shoes
   (b) why people should exercise their right to vote

8. Prepare a bibliography of three reference books of humorous anecdotes. Briefly describe the format of each book.

PLANNING BEFORE THE RESEARCH

After you have decided on a topic but before you begin your research, you should give some thought to who the audience is, where and when the presentation will be held, and the purpose of the presentation.

Audience

Some of the information you will want to know about the audience is age, occupation, intellectual level, economic level, and special interests. Knowing how large your audience will be is also helpful. Your treatment of the topic, the vocabulary you use, and the examples you provide to support your ideas and facts will be tailored to the particular audience who will be present. If you were a police officer describing the role of the police in society to students, your presentation to a group of elementary school children would differ radically from your presentation to senior high-school students. Also, audiences tend to be more attentive if the topic is of interest to them. If you work into the presentation comments and examples to show the audience how they can benefit from listening to the material, they will be more attentive.

Location

Where the presentation is to be given must also be taken into consideration. Knowing ahead of time the size of the room and the arrangement of chairs and tables may affect the type of presentation you decide to make. For example, visual aids developed for a small room would not necessarily be successful if used in a large auditorium.

Time

You will need to know the time of day and the time period allotted to your presentation. People are less attentive late in the afternoon and immediately after a meal, so a presentation made at those times will need to be delivered in a lively fashion. You will need to first grab your audience's attention with an unusual or an enthusiastic opening that has been carefully prepared.

The length of time allowed for your presentation will determine the number of main points you can present and develop. In a talk of less than five minutes, restrict yourself to one or two main points. In a thirty-minute presentation, four or five points can be comfortably developed. Knowing the number of main points will guide you in writing your statement of purpose and in researching your topic.

Purpose

A statement of purpose will make it clear in your mind what material you should be gathering. This statement will be a guide for you to keep your research and material on track and to decide on the style of presentation you will follow. Some examples of purpose statements are as follows:
- To inform the audience of the site, design, and construction period of the new head office building.
- To persuade the audience to vote for me in the election because of my political experience, dedication to the job, and ability to represent my constituents' point of view.
- To entertain the audience while outlining the civic contributions of the Citizen-of-the-Year, Mrs. Maureen O'Brien.

You are ready to begin researching your topic when you know the audience, location, time, and purpose of your presentation.

RESEARCHING THE TOPIC

When gathering your information, it is helpful to write each idea on a small index card or strip of paper. See Figure 10-3. When all these cards or strips have been assembled, they can be arranged in order and any extraneous material discarded.

Research data come from either primary sources or secondary sources. Personal knowledge is a primary source whereas published knowledge is a secondary source.

Home Canning Cook Book   641.42

Better Homes and Gardens

If the foods were incorrectly processed, it is possible that botulism-causing bacteria were not destroyed.   p. 17

Steps to proper freezer packaging p. 88

Figure 10-3(a) and (b)
Specific or general information can be quickly recorded on index cards.

Primary Source

A primary source is an original source, that is, the source from which the information originated. You could be the primary source, or someone else who is an authority on the subject.

It is much easier to speak about a topic you are familiar with than one that is entirely researched from secondary sources. It is unlikely, however, that you would be asked to speak on a subject with which you are unfamiliar. With your statement of purpose in mind begin writing down ideas as they occur to you. Spread this task out over more than one day, because often an idea noted one day will generate additional ideas the next day. Once your ideas are noted, decide whether you are comfortable with the existing material, or whether you need further research to support your views.

Additional primary source data may be gathered from interviews with people knowledgeable in that field. Prepare a checklist of the material you require and the questions you will ask to elicit the information. The interview can be conducted in person, by telephone, or by letter.

Secondary Source

The library offers many secondary (intermediate) sources of information — articles in newspapers, magazines, and journals; and material in books, encyclopedias, and government documents. The card catalogue is a good starting place. It is organized by titles, authors, and subjects. If the catalogue is computerized, you can conduct a quick search by subject matter that will yield a list of books related to the subject and, if desired, a brief description of particular books of interest.

To locate magazine articles on a particular subject, start with the *Reader's Guide to Periodical Literature, Business Periodicals Index, The Applied Science and Technology Index*, or any other relevant magazine index your library has. By looking under the subject area, the specific article title, or the author's name, you will be able to find the name of the magazine, date of publication, and page number (Figure 10-4). Some libraries copy newspapers onto microfilm. Then, if you wish to locate a particular article, you need only know the name of the newspaper and the date when the article appeared.

More and more libraries have access to data banks. Using a telephone connected to a computer, the telephone number is dialed to access the data bank, the mouthpiece is placed in a **modem**, or a device that converts computer signals to telephone signals and vice versa, and the request is keyboarded on the computer. The data bank searches its files for material related to the subject requested and the library's computer printer then prints brief descriptions of available sources.

When using a data base, remember that you will be charged for computer time, usually by the minute. Requesting information on a broad topic will be expensive and will yield a great deal of irrelevant material. Therefore, try to narrow your subject request as much as possible. For example, if you were researching employee strikes in the oil industry in Alberta, asking for a search of "strikes" would result in volumes of computer printout. Narrowing the search to "strikes in Alberta" would give you the material you wanted but there would still be irrelevant material included. By asking specifically for "strikes in Alberta in the oil industry," you would get exactly the material you wanted.

Recording Sources

While you are doing your research, record your sources of information for future reference. You may wish to return to a particular article to gather more information, to volunteer this information during your presentation, or to provide it if requested during a question and answer period. Supporting your views by quoting the experience and research of authorities increases your credibility, as we mentioned earlier. For example, you might say "Rosemary Stewart in her book, *The Reality of Management*, states that as an organization grows larger, the gap between management and worker widens."

The source can be noted on the same card as the quotation. Alternatively, you can use separate cards for source and quotation or a paraphrase of the quotation, with the two cards **cross-referenced**, or coded so that although they will be kept in separate places, either one can be retrieved by referring to the other. The book mentioned above could be noted on one card as

Stewart, Rosemary.   *The Reality of Management.*
Pan Books Ltd., London, 1963
"As an organization grows larger, the gap between management and worker widens." p. 172

or on two cards as

1. Stewart, Rosemary. *The Reality of Management.* Pan Books Ltd., London, 1963, p. 172	1. "As an organization grows larger the gap between management and worker widens." p. 172

The number "1" is the cross-referencing code number in this case. The cards would be filed separately, but either one could be found by reference to the other.

If you quote a source directly, use quotation marks around the quote on your card to indicate that the words are those of the author rather than your own. If you paraphrase the material, do not use quotation marks, but do still note the source.

Research data comes from
1. primary sources
2. secondary sources.

APPLICATIONS

9. Look at the picture of a periodicals index in Figure 10-4, and answer the following questions.

   (a) Imagine you want information about atomic power in Canada. Write out in full the titles of periodicals where such information is located.

   (b) After reading over the information given in "Finding Information," find out in what periodical information about Sherry Atkinson is located. Write out the reference in full.

   (c) You are giving a presentation on the need for more funding for Canadian arts. Write out in full, the reference to the article that will be most useful to you.

10. Select a topic related to business or technology and find three pertinent newspaper or magazine articles by using a magazine index or newspaper file. Indicate the search word(s) you would use for a data base search. Submit your answer in writing.

11. Using the same topic you chose in Question 10, develop a list of ten questions you would ask if you were interviewing someone on this topic.

PREPARING THE OUTLINE

A presentation is much like a return trip. You have a starting point (the introduction), you cover a certain amount of territory (the body of material), and you eventually return to your starting point (the conclusion). Although we talk of these as being separate sections, they must flow together in your presentation.

Introduction

The introduction must immediately catch the attention and interest of the audience. There are several different devices that can be used for

Figure 10-4
Indexes of periodicals list information by author and by subject. Read over the information in "Finding Information" carefully before answering the applications at the end of this section.

Finding Information / Pour trouver de l'information

The *Canadian Periodical Index* is an author, subject and corporate name index. Articles are listed under English subject headings only, but French cross-references guide the reader to French articles, or articles with French summaries, under the corresponding English heading. Poems and short stories are listed, by title, under the two form headings POEMS and SHORT stories.

Dans l'*Index de périodiques canadiens* l'accès aux articles dépouillés se fait par l'auteur, le sujet ou le nom de la société enregistrée. Chaque article est classé sous un descripteur en anglais, mais un terme équivalent en français donne accès au descripteur en anglais, sous lequel se trouvent des articles en français ou les articles ayant un sommaire en français. Tous les poèmes et les contes sont classés sous les rubriques POEMS et SHORT stories.

SUBJECT ENTRIES / ENTREES

REMOTE sensing systems
  Canada from space: eye in the sky satellites produce vivid views of earth's surface. William C. Heine. il port map *Can Geographic* 106 no 6: p42-55 D '86-Ja '87 87-01242

An article by William C. Heine on remote sensing systems entitled "Canada from space: eye in the sky satellites produce vivid views of earth's surface" appears on pages 42-55 of the December 1986 - January 1987 issue of *Canadian Geographic*. The article contains illustrative material, including at least one portrait and one map. A final citation number acts as a unique identifier for each article and facilitates user correspondence with *CPI*.

Un article par William C. Heine sur la télédétection, intitulé "Canada from space: eye in the sky satellites produce vivid views of earth's surface", se trouve aux pages 42-55 du numéro décembre 1986-janvier 1987 de la revue *Canadian Geographic*. L'article comprend au moins une illustration, un portrait et une carte. Un dernier numéro permet aux usagers d'identifier chaque article et de correspondre facilement avec *CPI*.

8   CANADIAN PERIODICAL INDEX

ARTS and crafts (cont.)
  Statements of quality. Andrew M. Tomcik. il *Ontario Craft* 12: p33-5 Mr '87 87-11778
    Ontario
  Guild of all arts: Spencer and Rosa Clark led the way. Kay Kritzwiser. il *Ontario Craft* 12: p13-15,23 Mr '87 87-11771
ARTS and industry
  Funding withdrawn [Montreal Jazz Festival]: Rothmans, Molson take tougher stand on sponsorships. Stan Sutter. *Marketing* 92 no 8: p1,3 F 23 '87 87-12770
  See also
    Art patronage
ARTS and state
  Audiences on rise as subsidies fall in Britain. Paulette Roberge. *Financial Post* 81 no 11: p38 Mr 16 '87 87-13150
ARTS festivals. *See* Festivals
ARZT, Donna E.
    about
  Author offers theories on cause: public interest law lures many Jews. Rose Kleiner. *Can Jewish News* 27 no 35: p10 Ja 15 '87 87-10322
ASBESTOS
  Institut de l'amiante poursuit ses efforts. Guy Mercier. *Affaires* 59 no 6:S23 f 7 '87 87-14164
ASHEIM, Geir B.
  Hartwick's rule in open economies; with French summary. bibliog *Can J Economics* 19: p395-402 Ag '86; correction 20: p177 F '87 87-14393
ASSEMBLY of first nations
  AFN knocks [federal government] land claims policy. *Windspeaker* 4 no 45: p2 Ja 16 '87 87-10493
ASSET-BACKED financing
  Securitized debentures latest new twist [Canadian Oil Debco Inc]. Barry Critchley. port *Financial Post* 81 no 8: p23 F 23 '87 87-13012
ASSOCIATION canadienne pour la santé, l'éducation et le loisir. *See* Canadian association for health, physical education and recreation
ASSOCIATIONS, Co-operative. *See* Co-operative associations
ASSURANCE chômage. *Voir* Insurance, Unemployment
ASTHMA
  Sustained release tablets help asthmatics in Israel. *Can Jewish News* 27 no 33: p17 Ja 1 '87 87-11599

ASTROLOGIE. *Voir* Astrology
ASTROLOGY
  Zodiaque et finances: le Capricorne: transiger avec le long terme. Chantal Andrée Berclaz. il *A+ mag Affaires* 10 no 1: p70 f '87 87-12948
  Zodiaque et finances: le Verseau: réussir en toute liberté. Chantal Andrée Berclaz. il *A+ mag Affaires* 10 no 1: p72 f '87 87-12949
ASTRONAUTICS. *See* Space flight
ASTROPHYSICS
  Black hole of Andromeda: a B.C. astronomer makes a startling discovery. Stephen Weatherbe and Paul Bunner. il port *Alberta Report* 14 no 10: p33 F 23 '87 87-11931
ATHABASCA University
  Fastest university in the West: despite frustrations, unique Athabasca grows by 85%. Linda Caldwell. il port *Alberta Report* 14 no 12: p30 Mr 9 '87 87-12157
ATHLETES
  Athletes in Action strike out [religion in sport]. Ted Schmidt. il *Catholic New Times* 11 no 3: p11 F 8 '87 87-13722
  Bruce and Helga McKay. Diane McDougall and Jennifer Harris. il *Verve* 2 no 8: p18 N-D '86 87-11354
  Dave Murray and Stephanie Sloan. Diane McDougall and Jennifer Harris. il *Verve* 2 no 8: p17 N-D '86 87-11353
  Gary and Sheila Beckie. Diane McDougall and Jennifer Harris. il *Verve* 2 no 8: p19 N-D '86 87-11355
  Hockey interuniversitaire canadien: certaines variables descriptives; avec sommaire en anglais. J. Roger Proulx and Normand Chouinard. il port tab graph *CAHPER/ACSEPL J* 53 no 1: p25-9 ja-f '87 87-13071
  Hugh and Toni Spooner. Diane McDougall and Jennifer Harris. il *Verve* 2 no 8: p22 N-D '86 87-11357
  Paul and Jane Barry. Diane McDougall and Jennifer Harris. il *Verve* 2 no 8: p20 N-D '86 87-11356
  Playing doubles: working out with the one you love can be the greatest challenge you've ever faced! Diane McDougall and Jennifer Harris. il *Verve* 2 no 8: p16-20,22 N-D '86 87-11352
  See also
    Hockey players

Taxation
  Taxation in Canada of nonresident performing artists and behind-the-camera personnel; with French summary. Norman Bacal and Richard Lewin. bibliog *Can Tax J* 34 no 6: p1287-1330 N-D '86 87-12694
ATHLETISME. *Voir* Track and field athletics
ATKINSON, David Scott. *See* Scott-Atkinson, D
ATKINSON, Sherry
    about
  Move over old boys... meet a new breed of deal makers. il port *Report on Business Mag* 3 no 10: p21-5,27 Ap '87 87-11849
ATLANTIC pact. *See* North Atlantic treaty organization
ATLANTIC provinces
  See also
    Churches - Atlantic provinces
    Immigration and emigration - Atlantic provinces
    Mines and mineral resources - Atlantic provinces
    Railroads - Atlantic provinces
    Women - Atlantic provinces
    Economic conditions
  Regional wages for development: governments should lead in recognizing that wages lower than in Ontario are essential to the development of Canada's peripheral regions. James Kadyampakeni. *Policy Options politiques* 8 no 2: p32-4; French summary p39 Mr '87 87-10964
  Savoir faire: well, not quite. Rick Williams. il *New Maritimes* 5 no 6: p15 F '87 87-12028
    Economic history
  Regional industrial growth during the 1890s: the case of the missing artisans. Kris Inwood and John Chamard. tab graph *Acadiensis* 16 no 1: p101-17 autumn '86 87-11162
    History
    Bibliography
  Recent publications relating to the history of the Atlantic region. Eric L. Swanick, ed. *See* issues of *Acadiensis* 87-14364
ATLANTIC provinces library association
  From the president's desk. Richard H. Ellis. *APLA Bulletin* 50 no 4: p2 Ja-F '87 87-10015
ATLANTIC salmon. *See* Salmon
ATOMIC energy of Canada limited
  Slowpoke: salespitch generates more heat than light. Mitchell Beer. il *Alternatives* 14 no 1: p45 F '87 87-12210

210 PART TWO: COMMUNICATION IN BUSINESS

this purpose. They include using humour, asking a question, using a narrative or illustration related to the topic, establishing common ground with the audience, and using a dramatic gesture or statement. Choose a device with which you feel comfortable and which is appropriate to the occasion.

Humour, if successfully used, can put the audience at ease. If it flops, however, it can work against you. Humour works best when the joke or anecdote is related to the audience or topic. There are many books available that contain jokes and humorous stories categorized by topic.

Opening questions can be either rhetorical or action questions. A rhetorical question does not require a response from the audience, but it will stimulate thought. An action question requires the audience to respond, usually by a show of hands. The response allows the speaker to gauge the audience's knowledge or attitude. If an action question is used, the speaker should incorporate the response into the material that follows, or adapt the material to the response.

A narrative or illustration that leads into the topic might be the recounting of a personal experience, a literary excerpt, or an historical event. In some cases, a picture or slide may stimulate interest in the topic.

Establishing common ground is a technique that helps to create a bond between you and the audience. You may point to a similar background, a shared experience, or common beliefs.

The use of a dramatic gesture or statement can heighten an audience's interest and also pique their curiosity. A person dressed to represent a character can produce a dramatic effect as well as humour. A mock crime at the beginning of a discussion on the reliability of eye witnesses gets attention and provides a reference for later discussion.

Once you have gained the audience's attention and interest, state your purpose. You may also wish to provide background information, define key words, or establish the scope of your speech. If you are speaking about a new safety regulation, state the regulation so that the entire audience will be sure to understand the remainder of your presentation. Words that are central to your theme should be defined so that everyone will be aware of your particular connotation. For example, the word "employees" may, for the purpose of your presentation, include only full-time employees. The audience will need to know this particular usage. If you are presenting only one solution to a problem or one side of an issue, it will be important to outline your scope or range, otherwise the audience might feel you were ignorant of other valid approaches.

Some effective introductions to a presentation are
1. *using humour*
2. *asking a question*
3. *using a narrative or illustration related to the topic*
4. *establishing common ground with the audience*
5. *using a dramatic gesture or statement.*

APPLICATIONS

12. Write the opening for a presentation about one of the following:
    (a) your favourite sport
    (b) how videos have changed rock music
    (c) how advertisements insult people's intelligence

13. In small groups, present the introduction you wrote in Question 12. Write an assessment of your performance, based on how you felt the audience reacted to it.

Body

With the opening out of the way, it is time to move smoothly into the body of your presentation. Here you are presenting main points and supporting evidence. It is essential to organize the information so that the audience can follow your line of thought. If they cannot, all your research and preparation are wasted. Selecting an appropriate organizational pattern, adhering to it, building bridges that lead from one point to the next, and using visual aids to clarify material, where appropriate, will provide a trail for the audience to follow.

To select an organizational pattern that suits your material, refer to Chapter 6 where chronological, spatial, topical, causal, comparison/contrast, and problem/solution organizational patterns are described in detail. The question to ask when selecting a pattern is "If I were listening to this presentation, which pattern would be easiest for me to follow?"

The transition from one point to another should be smooth so that your audience is carried to the next part of your presentation without a break. There are several ways to link points. When you indicate the end of one section, you can at the same time prepare the way by introducing the next section. You might say, for example "Now that we have covered the elementary functions of the word processor, let us look at some specific business applications." Another way to proceed from one point to the next is to number the points, and refer to them as "first, second, and third." A rhetorical question can also bridge material, for example "What, then, is a possible solution to this problem?" Without building these bridges, your presentation may seem incoherent and the audience will have difficulty in following your reasoning.

Once you have presented all your points and supporting information, it is time to move into the conclusion of your presentation.

Conclusion

Your closing remarks should be just as well planned as the opening of the presentation, if you want to leave your audience with a positive final impression and a sense of completion. Going straight from the body of your presentation to "Well, that just about does it" can leave your listeners up in the air, and can undo all the good points and convincing arguments you have laid out.

Effective conclusions make use of techniques such as a summary, a quotation, a challenge, a restatement of purpose, a completion of an idea raised in the introduction, or an illustration. The technique used should be appropriate to the presentation, and the concluding remarks should be brief.

In a summary, you reiterate the main points presented in the body of the presentation. This type of conclusion is useful if you wish to stress the points you made rather than the purpose of the talk. You would use this type of conclusion if, for instance, the purpose of your presentation was to inform employees of the procedures to be followed in some area of their work.

If you decide to use a quotation to conclude your talk, make sure it is pertinent, meaningful, and brief. It may be from the writing of an expert on the topic, a piece of literature, a song, or a slogan.

Persuasive presentations often end by challenging or requesting the audience to take action. You may be asking them to buy a product or service, sign a petition, make a donation, or begin to work toward a goal.

Restating your purpose is an effective way to end a presentation that was intended to persuade, or an informative presentation focussed on one central theme. The concluding remarks are a restatement of the purpose, worded differently from the introduction to reflect the information you have presented in the body.

If, in your introduction, you posed a question, or laid out an unfinished story or idea, you will want to answer it or complete it in the conclusion. This device gives a nice rounded effect to the presentation with the introduction and conclusion forming a unit. The audience feels satisfied that the incomplete information is now complete.

Reshowing a visual aid used in the introduction is another way to unify your presentation. This technique would be used in conjunction with one of the techniques outlined above.

Some ways to conclude a presentation effectively are through
1. *a summary*
2. *a quotation*
3. *a challenge*
4. *a restatement of purpose*
5. *a completion of an idea raised in the introduction*
6. *an illustration.*

APPLICATIONS

14. Using the same topic that you used to write an introduction to in Question 12
    (a) outline the content of the body in point form
    (b) write a conclusion
    Your presentation should take no longer than two to three minutes.

15. Again, in small groups, present your speech and rate your own presentation based on the feedback you receive from your audience.

AUDIO AND VISUAL AIDS

Audio, audio-visual, or visual aids can reinforce and clarify material. They can also add interest. Listening to a tape of someone reciting material or of the operating sound of a piece of equipment may help your audience to understand your point. Films, videotapes, tape-slide presentations, or excerpts from any of these can improve your presentation by adding variety. Some of the visual aids that you may be able to prepare or assemble are charts, diagrams, pictures, models, real objects, overhead transparencies, and flip charts. If you do decide to use audio or visual aids, keep the following tips in mind.

- Mark in your notes when you are going to use an aid so that you do not forget it.

- If you are using equipment, be sure you know how to operate it. Practise with it beforehand until you can use it with ease.
- Identify the aid for the audience. Untitled graphs and unnamed objects will be of little use.
- Stand to the side of the aid so that you do not block the audience's view. Never turn your back on the audience or your voice will be inaudible.
- Use a pointer rather than your finger and point to the specific parts of the aid as you refer to them.
- Continue eye contact with the audience as you refer to the aid. Turning your head down or away from the audience affects your voice projection.

If you are constructing a visual aid, be sure that it is large enough to be seen by everyone. If it is light in colour, a contrasting dark background will increase its visibility. If dark, use a light background. Label only significant parts and check to make sure the spelling is correct. Your display should be sturdy and visually appealing.

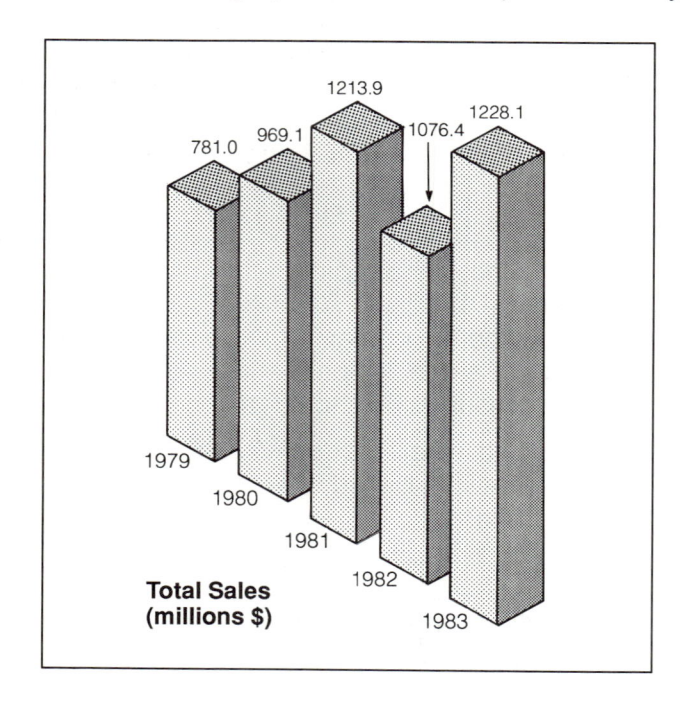

Figure 10-5
Visual aids enhance a presentation. This one shows how a company's sales have increased, and the information is presented simply and clearly.

Overhead transparencies are popular with speakers as they can be produced easily and inexpensively. Audiences enjoy them too, for they can add interest and variety to a presentation if carefully prepared and skilfully used. In addition to the suggestions given previously for aids in general, the following suggestions regarding transparencies will improve your use of them.
- Each transparency should reflect one idea. Use no more than six lines with no more than six words per line. If your transparency has been well planned, you should not need to write additional words on it during the presentation.
- Make sure that the print is large enough to be read easily.

- Coloured backgrounds, overlays, cartoon characters, and clip art can enhance the content.
- Number the transparencies so that they can quickly be put in order if they become disarranged.
- Before your audience arrives, test and adjust the focus of the overhead projector.
- Do not turn the machine on until you are going to use it. Have a transparency on the light table whenever the machine is on.
- To avoid distractions, turn the machine off between transparencies and do not wave the transparencies in the air.
- Maintain eye contact with the audience rather than watching the screen.
- Use a pen to point to the transparency.
- For special effects a piece of paper can be used to cover the transparency and then moved to reveal portions of the content. By placing the paper between the light table and the transparency, the paper will not fly off the machine.
- When you are finished with the transparencies, move away from the projector so that you will not be tempted to start straightening them. Only when your presentation is over should you pack them up.

With all visual and audio aids, remember that they represent a support for your message. They should not become more important than your message.

Now that we have looked at the parts of a presentation, let us look again at the presentation as a whole, and how to plan what you are going to say.

PREPARING A MODEL

When planning a presentation, it may help to follow a model. The following model incorporates the ideas discussed in this chapter.

A Planning Model
 1. Introduction
    A. Introductory device
    B. Purpose
    C. Background material/term definition/scope
 2. Body
    A. First major point
       - subsection 1
       - subsection 2, etc.
    B. Second major point
       - subsection 1
       - subsection 2, etc.
 3. Conclusion

The number of major points and subsections will vary according to the length of your talk and the particular material you are using. If your material is very complex, you may need to break down the subsections into smaller units.

Writing the body first usually makes writing the introduction easier. The conclusion should be written last to tie in with the introduction.

DELIVERY TECHNIQUES

Speeches may be delivered extemporaneously, delivered from notes, or read. A speech that is read out is the least desirable because there is little interaction with the audience and they may lose interest. It may also sound stilted. An extemporaneous delivery sounds more natural and allows maximum audience contact. The following points summarize the delivery techniques explained in Chapter 4.

1. Note key words or phrases on cards or on a piece of paper.
2. Rehearse the presentation under conditions as close to the actual as possible. Have a friend or relative as an audience when you rehearse.
3. Practise the gestures and head movements you plan to use.
4. Practise using any aids to develop familiarity and ease with them.
5. Speak aloud in order to assess pitch, rate, volume, tone, fluency, enunciation, and pronunciation.
6. Be aware of any annoying habits that could negatively affect the audience, such as swaying, jingling coins, foot tapping, and excessive hand movements.

The three parts of a speech model are
1. introduction
2. body
3. conclusion.

APPLICATIONS

16. Using the same topic from Question 12, prepare a visual aid to enhance your presentation. Discuss your choice with your teacher before preparing it.

17. Using the planning model, prepare in note form a presentation, no more than three minutes in length, on one of the following topics:
    (a) baling hay
    (b) how a particular sport is played
    (c) why students should purchase a yearbook
    (d) student absenteeism
    (e) the student's council
    Be prepared to present your speech to the class.

18. In small groups, have one student give the prepared presentation of the topic chosen in Question 17.
    (a) The rest of the group should take notes, and at the end of the presentation, ask questions to clarify any points of which they are not sure.
    (b) Write a short report that outlines the main arguments used by the speaker and that analyzes the presentation to find out how the material was organized.

19. Prepare a presentation using the information you have learned in this chapter on one of the following topics:

(a) how taking a Business English course will help you when you leave school
(b) your responsibilities in a part-time job
(c) what you have gained from any volunteer work you did

Remember to follow the planning model. Prepare a visual aid with your teacher's help. Be prepared to speak to the class for three minutes on your chosen topic.

CHAPTER SUMMARY

Types of presentations
- informative
- persuasive
- entertaining

Points to know before beginning research
- the prospective audience
- the location
- the time of day and the length of the presentation
- the purpose

Tips on researching the topic
- use primary sources (original sources such as interviews)
- use secondary sources (intermediate sources such as books)
- record the sources

The planning model for preparing an outline
- Introduction
    introductory device
    purpose
    background material/term definition/scope
- Body
    first major point
        subsection
    second major point
        subsection
- Conclusion

MAKING IT WORK

1. Refer to the dialogue in the section *Viewpoints*, and answer the questions that follow.
    (a) If you were Diane, what questions would you want to ask Anna about her presentation in order to prepare the visual aids she would need? (You may want to know, for instance, the size of the sales meeting so you would know how large to make overhead transparencies.)

(b) If Anna wanted to present sales figures of certain books, do you think it would be better just to write the figures out to be shown as overheads, or do you think it would be better to present the figures in the form of a graph? Give reasons for your answer.

2. Read the following case, then answer the questions that follow.

Three months ago, Erica was hired as the assistant to a hospital administrator. As Erica would like to become a hospital administrator eventually, she has asked the administrator to let her handle as wide a range of responsibilities as possible. One of Erica's responsibilities is to attend the hospital board meetings.

After one such meeting, a board member approached the administrator and asked about Erica's job performance. The board member did not wish to be critical but mentioned that Erica seemed uncomfortable around the board members and was reluctant to join in conversation with them or to express opinions on matters. Knowing Erica's future plans and her great potential, the administrator felt Erica's behaviour must be discussed with her.

Why do you think Erica behaves the way she does? If you were the administrator, what would you say to Erica? What can the administrator or Erica do to change her image?

3. Read the following case, then answer the questions that follow.

Simon worked for four years as a welder before being promoted to supervisor. When he was a welder, Simon had experienced no trouble getting along with the other welders, most of whom were older. Now as supervisor, Simon is beginning to feel that the welders are not taking him seriously. Sometimes when he needs a job done quickly, the welders seem to do it at their pace instead of at the pace Simon expects. Also, if Simon is around at break time, some of the welders still kid him the way they did before he became a supervisor. Simon feels that this is no longer appropriate.

Simon is not sure what to do. Should he become more aloof? Maybe he should be more heavy-handed with the group? Should he give up the supervisor's job? Maybe he is being too sensitive?
(a) What advice would you give Simon?
(b) Do you think this is a problem common to people who are promoted from within a group? Why or why not?
(c) How might it be avoided?

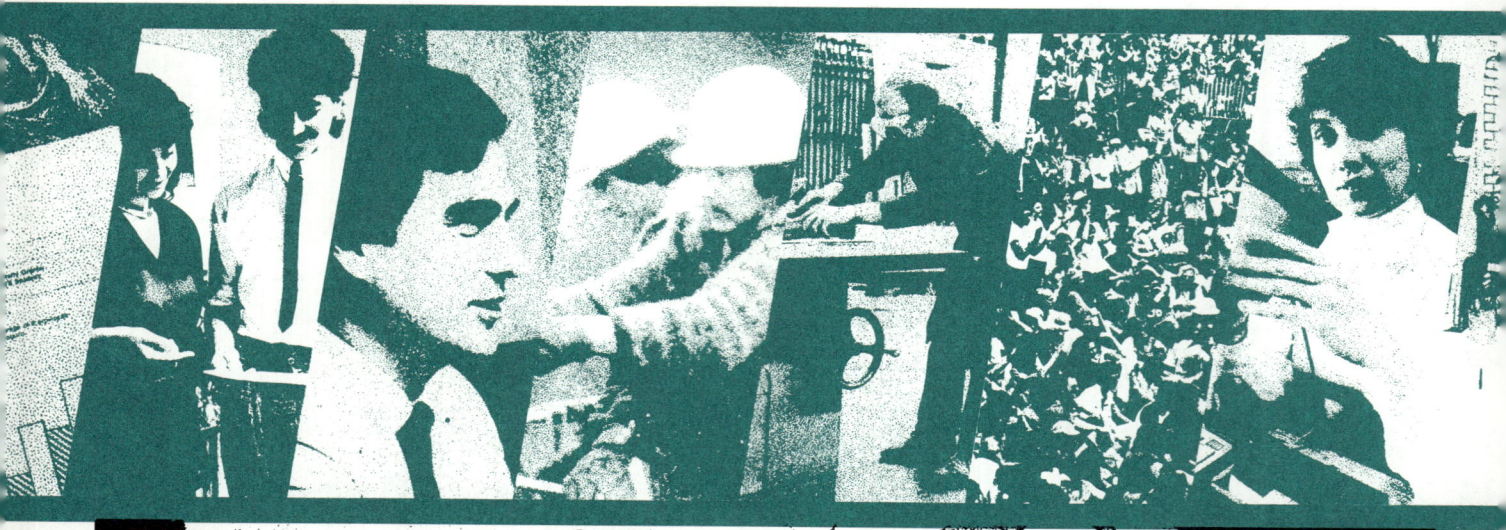

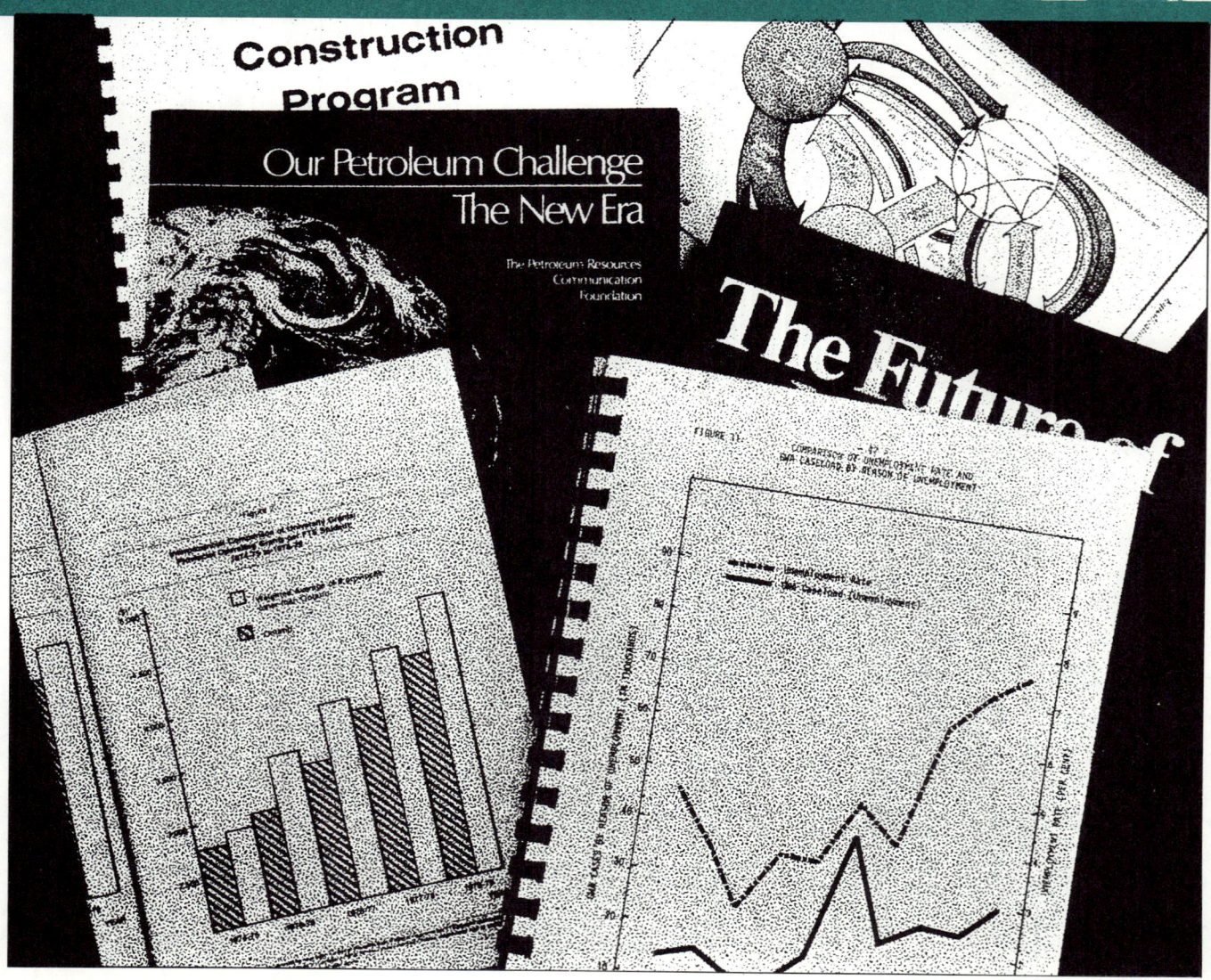

Construction Program

Our Petroleum Challenge
The New Era

The Petroleum Resources
Communication
Foundation

The Future of

CHAPTER 11

GOALS

At the end of this chapter you should be able to
1. select appropriate business material for reading and viewing;
2. apply the reading/viewing process to a variety of business and industry materials; and
3. become more assertive as a reader.

Reading and Viewing in the Workplace

VOCABULARY BUILDING

evaluate
passive
assertive
procedures manuals

VIEWPOINTS

Remember Erica in *Viewpoints* in Chapter 1? She helped her younger brother Jorg deal with leaving his part-time job for other employment. Now she has problems of her own. She's working full-time as an administrative assistant with Korman Manufacturing. Today Erica is talking over her situation with her aunt Jan, who has worked in business all her life, while they have lunch together.

JAN: And how's the new job, Erica? Your mother tells me you're finding it a bit of a challenge.

ERICA: Well, yes. I'm not as happy as I thought I would be. Sometimes I wish I had stayed at my old job. I knew what was going on there.

JAN: What seems to be the problem? You've always been so good with figures and you're taking that evening course in bookkeeping.

ERICA: Oh, the accounting part of the job is fine. I understand that, and I know the procedures pretty well by now. I guess the problem is the vocabulary I have to learn. There are so many technical terms and abbreviations I need to understand.

JAN: But won't it come to you with experience?

ERICA: I thought it would, but I still feel as lost after a month as when I started. Sometimes I feel like quitting. You know I hate to feel that I'm not doing my job well.

JAN: Is there anyone in the office whom you can ask for help?

ERICA: Well, there's the office administrator, Mrs. Knuttell. She was really kind to me when I started and is always asking me how I'm doing. But she's so busy, I feel a nuisance when I keep bothering her.

JAN: But maybe she could suggest things you could read to familiarize yourself with the field you're working in. Have you noticed whether there are trade magazines lying around the office?

ERICA: There's a whole shelf of magazines and books on Mrs. Knuttell's bookshelf labelled "Resources." Maybe I could ask her if I can read them during my lunch hour.

JAN: Good idea. She'd probably be impressed by your initiative! And anyway, I'm sure you're doing much better than you think. It's always hard when you start a job in a new field. It's a long time ago, but I can remember when I started as a typist with James Gregory and Sons. You wouldn't believe how little I knew about the company.

ERICA: Thanks for the suggestion, Aunt Jan. I feel a lot better now that I know what I can do.

QUESTIONS

1. What material do you think Mrs. Knuttell would keep on her shelves as resources for the staff?
2. Reading is just one of the communication skills you have been learning about in this book. In what ways would the skills of listening and speaking help Erica learn about her new job?
3. Sometimes, we learn a lot about our work environment through talking informally with other staff at coffee breaks and lunch breaks. What do you think are some of the pros and cons of spending breaks "talking shop"?

Figure 11-1
In the world of business, we are surrounded by material to be read or viewed. The skills outlined in this chapter will help to make sense of this material.

INTRODUCTION

Starting a new job is a little like travelling to a foreign country. At first you do not know anyone and everything seems unfamiliar. In the preceding section Erica, whom you see in Figure 11-1, feels alone and lost. Her new job means she must get used to a new work environment as well as new vocabulary.

In *Viewpoints* in Chapter 5, we met Sol and Kyle, who were preparing for their trip to Greece by reading about the country they were going to visit. You can prepare for a new job in much the same way, by using the skill of reading. Reading, along with day-to-day listening, speaking, and viewing, will help you keep up-to-date with the specialized language used in your field.

Effective reading skills will help you to learn about the industry you are involved in and acquire an understanding of the specialized vocabulary it uses. Reading skills will also help you to carry out the daily requirements of your job.

In our work, we read, view, and process information. To do this we use the same reading techniques as those outlined in Chapter 5. For instance, Erica in *Viewpoints* needs to apply the techniques of careful reading in her job. She checks invoices and proofreads final copy as part of the work she does every day. To make use of the resource material kept on Mrs. Knuttell's bookshelf, Erica will use the techniques of skimming. She will be looking for information that is useful to her from a large volume of material, not all of which will apply to her company.

In this chapter, we will look at the reading or viewing process as a way of researching or finding out about an aspect of a business or industry. Then we will look at how reading techniques help in the day-to-day environment.

RESEARCHING A BUSINESS OR INDUSTRY

Define the Purpose

Before you start, identify for yourself what you want to get out of your reading. Do you want to find out specific information, or do you want to get the "feel" of a more general topic? Erica would probably start by reading general information about the field of manufacturing that her company is involved in, then move to more specific information as her knowledge increases. It is a good idea to ask yourself these questions before you start to read.
- Why am I reading or viewing this material?
- What do I hope to get out of it?
- How will I use the information or ideas I gain from it?

After you have identified the purpose of your reading or viewing, you will be able to move on to the next step.

Select Appropriate Material

After you have established the kind of material that would be of most use to you, you should search it out. Erica has simply to go to Mrs. Knuttell's bookshelf. Your search for material might be more difficult, and involve the use of the resources of a number of libraries. Up-to-date material on particular industries can usually be found in trade and technical magazines, in company fact sheets, current industry films or videos, and booklets or pamphlets on particular topics. Some of these are illustrated in Figure 11-2.

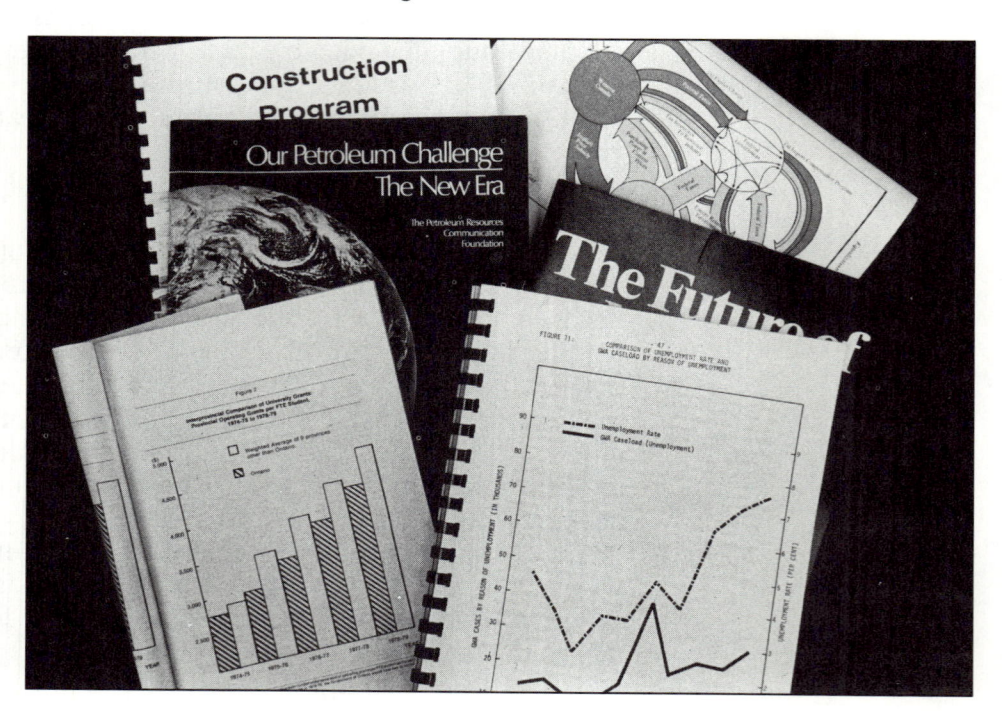

Figure 11-2
Reading or viewing the resources that are available on a specific topic provides valuable background information.

Most companies have a great deal of material available, which describes their industry or outlines the particular skills and techniques their employees use on the job. This material should be readily available to employees. If, however, you are looking for information about a company or industry before you are actually employed there, your search may be more difficult. Libraries and guidance centres are good places to start.

What material should you look for? The daily newspaper is an excellent source of current information, not only on business and industry, but about the world in general. Magazines, too, are a good source of information, and can be divided into three groups. There are popular magazines, general-scientific magazines, and trade or technical journals.

The popular magazine is designed to appeal in a general way to a large number of people. It usually contains a variety of material such as short stories, accounts of travel, political and economic discussions, and other items of interest to the general public. This type of magazine is generally available at the local branch of your library, or you may have copies of such magazines lying around your house.

General-scientific magazines, on the other hand, appeal to a smaller number of people who are more interested in issues of science and mechanics. The trade and technical journals are published for the benefit of a limited number of people who are interested in one particular technical field. Articles published in these journals contain information about a specific trade or profession and are carefully written. In addition, the advertisements in trade journals are of considerable value to the reader. They contain important news about recent technical developments in that field.

Before beginning to read, define your purpose and select the appropriate material.

APPLICATIONS

1. Members of the class should each bring the same issue of a newspaper and read whatever they want for twenty minutes.
   (a) At the end of that time, identify the pages that were read by most of the students, and those that were read by the least number of students. Discuss why some sections are more popular than others.
   (b) Examine the same-day issue front pages of different newspapers. Determine how many stories are the same and discuss differences in the treatment of these stories. What do these differences reveal about the audience the newspapers are aimed at?
   NOTE: Keep your copies of newspapers. We will be using them later in this chapter.

2. (a) Find the names of a popular magazine, a general-scientific magazine, and a technical or trade journal.
   (b) Summarize an article in the popular magazine and an article in the technical or trade journal, using the skills of summarizing that you learned in Chapter 5.
   (c) What differences can you note about the way the articles were written in the popular magazine and in the technical or trade journal?

3. In groups of three, have one person act as researcher, one as writer, and one as reporter.
   (a) The researcher should go to a department of the school to find out what magazines are used in fields related to that area of study and note the names of any magazines that the department subscribes to.
   (b) The writer should borrow a copy of each of the magazines used by the department and analyze, from the index of each, what information each magazine presents. The writer should write a short report outlining what material is contained in each magazine.
   (c) The reporter should interview a member of the department to determine the usefulness of each magazine, and write a short report on the findings.

(d) As a group, classify all the magazines collected into the three main groupings: popular magazines, general-scientific magazines, and trade or technical journals.
4. As a class, prepare a report describing the kind of magazines sent to the school and the uses to which they are put.
5. (a) As a class, identify areas of business or industry that might be of interest to members of the class.
(b) One student should act as a spokesperson for the class and talk to the person at your school who is responsible for booking films and videos for classroom use. The student should report back on what films or videos are available in the subject area of most interest to the class.
(c) Another student should act as a spokesperson and speak with the community public librarian about audio-visual materials that are available on the topic of most interest to the class.
(d) The two students should report back to the class. The class should then decide on the five or six items of interest to most of the students.
(e) In groups of two or three, arrange to view each video and prepare summaries to share with the other members of the class.

Once you have identified your purpose in reading or viewing, and selected the materials you will use, you can begin the reading process itself. You should follow the same stages in reading as were outlined in the discussion of reading in Chapter 5.

Provide the Right Reading Environment

Even though reading or viewing as ways of learning may be pleasurable activities, a sunny spot on the beach is not likely to be as productive an environment as a study desk and chair in a quiet corner of the library. The careful selection of the right environment to support a particular reading or viewing purpose will help you understand and retain more information.

Scan and Skim Through Material

When Erica first looks through the resource shelf in Mrs. Knuttell's office, she will probably spend a lot of her time just scanning and skimming to identify the articles that she needs to read more carefully. Likewise, if you are reading for business, you will probably want to spend a moment scanning the table of contents or index of a book or magazine and skimming through the pages to get an idea of the type of information presented. (An example of the table of contents page of a magazine is shown in Figure 11-3.) If you are viewing for business purposes, you will probably want to glance at the description of the film on the package, and run the whole video or film through once so you have an idea of the information that it contains.

Skimming through the material will help you get a general idea of the material covered. Likewise, identifying difficult words and discovering their meaning (either from the way they are used or by checking in a dictionary) will also help you. Furthermore, if you look at the way the article is organized by identifying the main ideas or headings, you will have a better idea of where the material you need is located.

Figure 11-3
The Table of Contents of a book or magazine can be scanned to find the material you require. This Table of Contents is from a magazine which contains information about careers in environmental studies.

READING AND VIEWING IN THE WORKPLACE

Read or View the Key Parts

Skimming will have enabled you to identify what the material to be read or viewed is about, and scanning will have helped you identify particular parts which you want to read in detail. You are now able to concentrate on reading or viewing to get the information you need to match the purpose you have already defined. In this way, all your attention can be focussed on the material at hand. You will be able to read or view just what you want, understand it better, and remember it longer.

Evaluate

As you read, **evaluate**, or judge the worth of the material. Identify occasions when the writer is stating opinions without supporting them with facts. Most writers write from a specific standpoint, and it is important to recognize that there may be a different point of view. Above all, be wary of any writers whose bias makes them prejudiced or causes them to use stereotypes, or conventional images, when describing human behaviour. For instance, a writer who always portrays managers as men and employees as women may not be aware that women can and do perform supervisory roles as well as men.

As you evaluate what you have read or viewed, it may help if you try to relate it to your personal experience. If, for instance, you read that part-time workers are not as committed to their work as full-time workers, and you know from your experience and from talking to others that this is not so, bear this fact in mind as you read. It may be that the writer is writing from a different standpoint or a different background from yours, and this will influence whether what is written is relevant to your situation.

Summarize or Record What You Have Learned

Have a purpose and the right material and then go on to
1. *provide the right reading environment*
2. *scan and skim through the material*
3. *read or view the key parts*
4. *evaluate*
5. *prepare a summary or record.*

If the information is important to keep, set up file folders or use a loose-leaf notebook in which to record and store the information. Remember, material that is summarized well and arranged in an orderly way can be added to and referred to much more easily. Information that you cannot find again or that you cannot understand when you re-read it, is of no value to you. Chapter 5 outlined the techniques to use in summarizing.

APPLICATIONS

6. Look at the Table of Contents in *Environmental News*, shown in Figure 11-3.
   (a) Identify which articles are feature articles (ones that appear just once) and which are regular columns (ones that appear in every issue).

(b) If you were interested in a job as a ranger in a Provincial Park, which article would be of most interest to you?
(c) What is the subscription fee for the magazine and how often is it published?

7. From the newspapers you used in the applications on page 225, read any part of the newspaper you choose for 10 minutes, then
   (a) identify the reading styles you used for different sections of the newspaper; and
   (b) explain why you used a particular reading style for a particular section.

8. Identify whether the following are opinions or facts.
   (a) The weather is cold today — the temperature is 10°C.
   (b) The weather is too cold for us to enjoy a walk.
   (c) Men are paid, on average, more than women in equivalent jobs in Canada.
   (d) Women should always put their families before their jobs, but men should put their careers first.

BECOMING AN ASSERTIVE READER OR VIEWER

The reading process outlined in the steps above will, after a while, become almost automatic. When this happens, your effectiveness as a reader will improve enormously. By following the first steps, you will be able to zero in on the material you need. By following the last steps, you will be able to exercise your critical powers as you read. How will this help you?

A selective and critical reader is not **passive**. All too often, readers and viewers feel they have lost some of their assertiveness and fallen under the control of the writer or presenter of information. You probably know from experience what it is like to suddenly realize that you have been reading or watching television passively without exercising judgement over the information being presented. By following the reading or viewing process, this situation can be avoided. You will become more active and **assertive** as you read or view.

The following hints will help you achieve this assertiveness in the reading process.
1. Select an appropriate reading/viewing style.
   Determine your purpose and then decide whether to skim, scan, or carefully examine the material. This decision will help you take a more active role in your reading or viewing process.
2. Use the appropriate reading/viewing style.
   The best comprehension does not always come with using a slow speed. You will usually remember more if you force yourself to use your maximum speed for the particular reading/viewing rate required.

3. Set a time schedule.

   Whenever possible, set a realistic time aside for specific reading or viewing assignments. Using a time schedule for this kind of activity will increase and encourage greater efficiency. Set goals that have clear time lines attached.

4. Control the external conditions.

   Try to establish an environment that is comfortable and that provides the proper lighting, temperature, and ventilation. You will then be better prepared to devote your full attention to the task at hand.

5. Improve your vocabulary.

   Use a word list, glossary, dictionary, and thesaurus as aids to developing a wider vocabulary. Pay attention to words and to how they are used.

APPLICATIONS

9. Identify a trade or industry that you are particularly interested in. Using the resources of your library, examine trade and technical magazines that deal with this field. Choose an article that you are interested in and read it using the reading process.
   (a) Write a list of any new words you come across with their meanings.
   (b) Write a short report on what you have read.
   (c) Be prepared to report back to the class on any steps of the reading process that you had trouble with.

10. Locate five advertisements in the trade magazine you used in Question 9. For each, write a short description outlining their value to individuals in that particular trade or industry.

11. Read through a financial magazine and prepare a list of unfamiliar terminology. Check the meaning of each term in the dictionary and prepare a glossary of terms for financial reading.

DAY-TO-DAY READING IN BUSINESS

The skills of scanning and skimming to find the information you need are useful in day-to-day business reading. As well, your performance in business depends on your accuracy and your ability to use a job-related vocabulary, so the skills used in careful reading are also important in business settings.

Erica, in her job at Korman Manufacturing, deals with paperwork which she must read carefully. You can see some of the materials she has to read in Figure 11-4. To order supplies, she uses catalogues. This type of reading requires her to know how to use indexes and to have an eye for detail in selecting the correct order numbers and related data. She uses **procedures manuals**, or booklets describing the way personnel in a company carry out certain tasks, in her job. She also deals with invoices and needs to check the information in them carefully. From the materials that she reads in her job, Erica learns about the activities of her company.

KORMAN MANUFACTURING   **PROCEDURE 2**

PROCEDURE   DATE PREPARED: April 6, 198_
CAPITAL PURCHASES   PREPARED BY: G. MACPHERSON
                                  APPROVED BY: F. KORMAN

As a matter of procedure, no capital purchases above $1000.00 are to be made without the knowledge and approval of the Vice President, Finance and Administration.

All Capital Purchases are subject to normal Purchase Order Procedures.

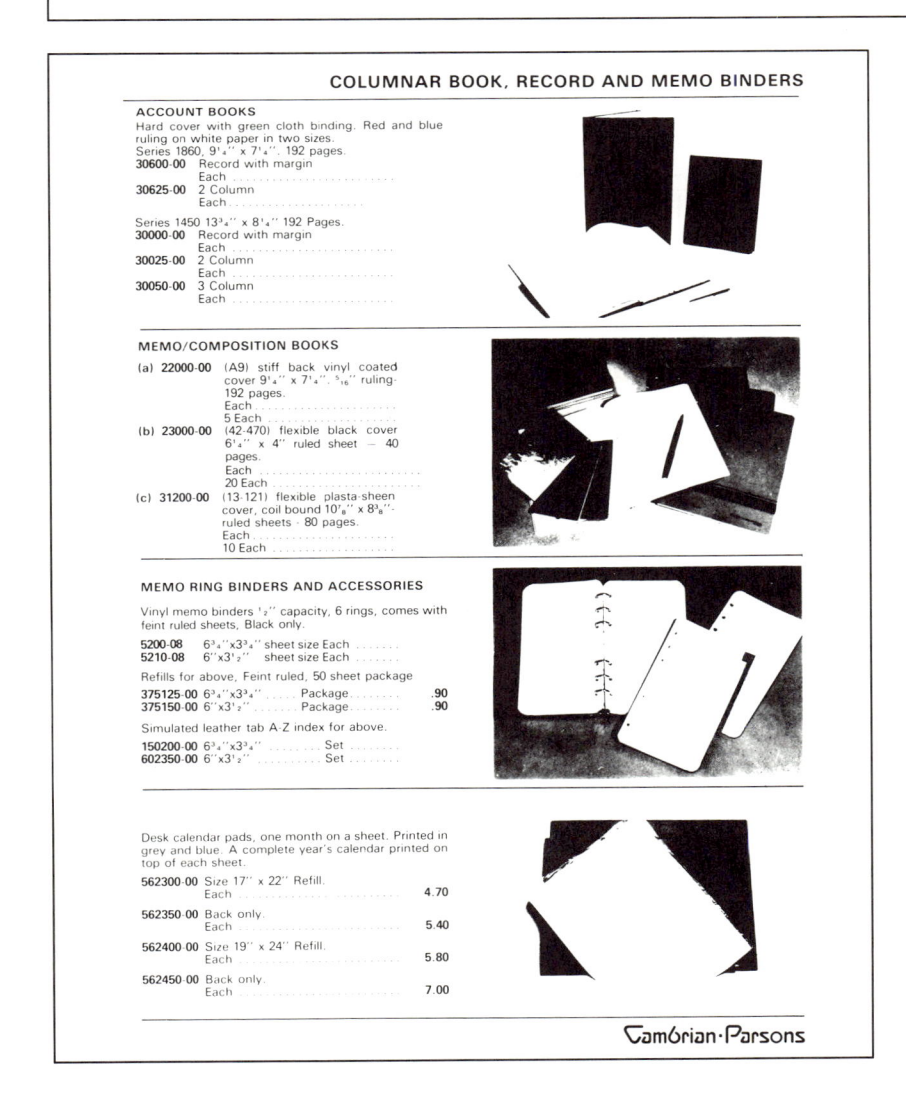

Figure 11-4(a)
Procedures manuals show how to perform certain tasks in the office. They are invaluable for ensuring that all employees follow the same rules in their jobs.

Figure 11-4(b)
Supply catalogues require that the reader scans indexes, skims pages, and reads carefully.

READING AND VIEWING IN THE WORKPLACE

An invoice is a detailed list of goods sold or services provided, together with the charges and the terms of payment. An invoice is not a summary of a customer's account. That is called a statement. The information in an invoice includes a list of items or services, unit costs or hourly rates, quantity prices, discounts, and shipping information and charges.

Invoices can be mailed to the customer at the time the product is shipped or the service has been performed. Alternatively, an invoice can be enclosed with the product together with a packing slip or in place of a packing slip. In some companies invoices are sent out once a month for jobs that have been completed during that period.

Accountants use invoices to avoid mistakes such as paying for the wrong material or for the wrong amount of material. As an accountant, you can use an invoice to alert you to mistakes or even misconduct on the part of suppliers or the company you are working for. If the company regularly pays $40.00 a month for a subscription service, an invoice for over $200.00 for the same service can alert you to an error or an overuse. Invoices can be used in business to check trends. If your company is spending an increasing amount of money on outside photocopying services, then the purchase of an inhouse photocopier could save costs. Another way is to cut down on the amount of photocopying.

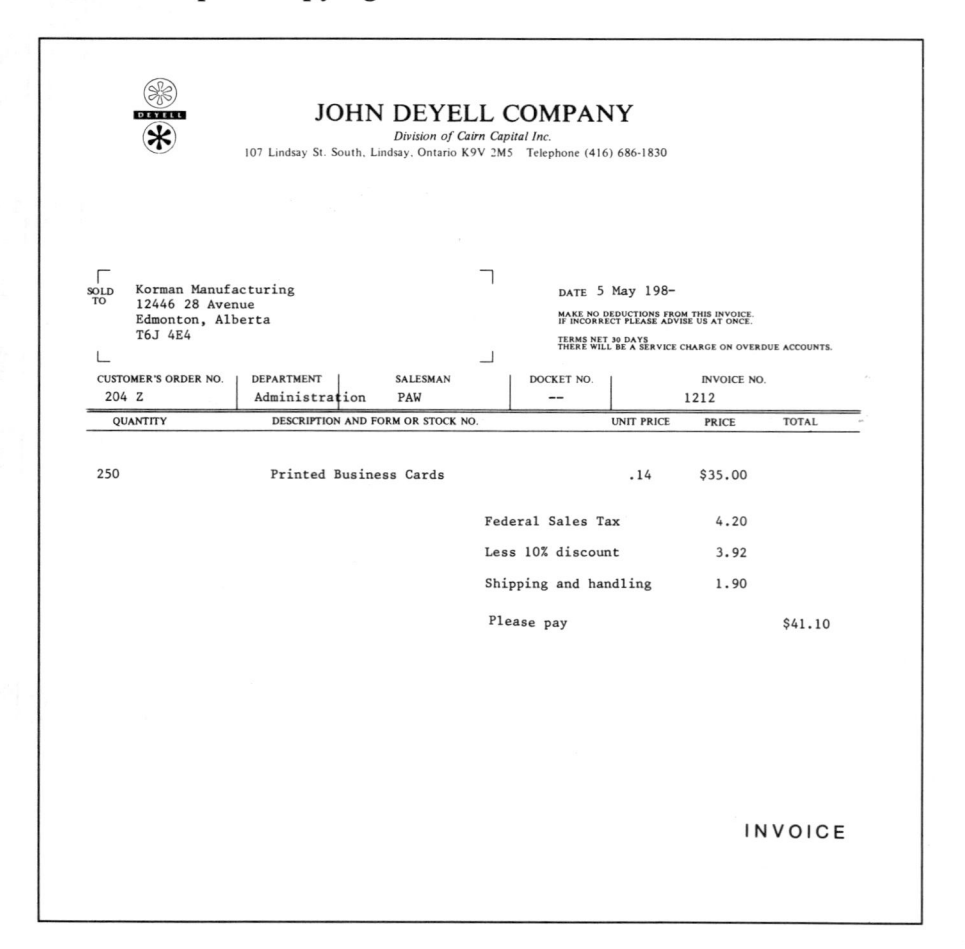

```
                    JOHN DEYELL COMPANY
                      Division of Cairn Capital Inc.
         107 Lindsay St. South, Lindsay, Ontario K9V 2M5   Telephone (416) 686-1830


  SOLD   Korman Manufacturing                DATE  5 May 198-
   TO    12446 28 Avenue                     MAKE NO DEDUCTIONS FROM THIS INVOICE.
         Edmonton, Alberta                   IF INCORRECT PLEASE ADVISE US AT ONCE.
         T6J 4E4                             TERMS NET 30 DAYS
                                             THERE WILL BE A SERVICE CHARGE ON OVERDUE ACCOUNTS.

  CUSTOMER'S ORDER NO. | DEPARTMENT     | SALESMAN | DOCKET NO. | INVOICE NO.
       204 Z           | Administration |   PAW    |    --      |    1212
       QUANTITY        | DESCRIPTION AND FORM OR STOCK NO. | UNIT PRICE | PRICE | TOTAL

        250              Printed Business Cards              .14        $35.00

                                              Federal Sales Tax         4.20
                                              Less 10% discount         3.92
                                              Shipping and handling     1.90

                                              Please pay                       $41.10




                                                                 I N V O I C E
```

Figure 11-5
An invoice is the bill for a specific order. Read this one carefully to help you answer Question 12.

APPLICATIONS

12. Look at the example of the invoice in Figure 11-5 and identify the following:
    (a) purchase order reference number
    (b) invoice number
    (c) the vendor's name and address
    (d) the customer's name and address
    (e) a description and listing of items
    (f) unit cost
    (g) quantity cost
    (h) discount
    (i) shipping charges
    (j) date of order
    (k) date of shipment
    (l) person who pays the shipping fee
    (m) total amount due

13. Look at the supply catalogue of the memo book in Figure 11-4(b) and identify the following:
    (a) the catalogue number
    (b) the colour it is available in
    (c) the unit price

14. Look at the example of a procedures manual in Figure 11- 4(a) and
    (a) identify who originated the procedure
    (b) define "capital purchases." (If you do not already know the meaning of this term, see if you can tell from the context in which it is used.)
    (c) If you were a new employee at Korman Manufacturing, which other part of the procedures manual would help you understand how to make a capital purchase?

15. With a business teacher, identify other forms used in business. Prepare a display of each type of form, and identify how, why, and when it is used. Identify special words used on each form and explain their meaning.

16. Using information which you can obtain from your local library, research the history of newspapers and prepare a short report.

17. Debate on the following statements.
    (a) "Television has made newspapers obsolete."
    (b) "You can't believe everything you read in print."
    (c) "Freedom of the press is a dangerous right."
    Your teacher will tell you which side to take.

18. Prepare a display of articles which you have clipped out of local newspapers about current business or industry issues. Tie your display together by concentrating on an aspect of business you are particularly interested in.

19. Prepare a display of a variety of different kinds of newspapers and identify the kind of audience for each.

READING AND VIEWING IN THE WORKPLACE

20. As a class, keep a clipping file on current business or economic topics. Students should contribute articles to this file on a regular basis and discuss trends in class.
21. Develop a profile of local beliefs and values gathered from local news stories, editorials, and advertisements.
22. Collect the work of an editorial cartoonist over a period of time and describe the cartoonist's philosophy through an examination of the cartoons.

CHAPTER SUMMARY

Tips for improving your reading or viewing process with business materials
- define your purpose before you start
- select appropriate material
- provide the right reading environment
- scan or skim through available material
- read or view the key parts
- evaluate
- prepare a summary or record

Tips for becoming an assertive reader or viewer
- select an appropriate reading/viewing style
- use this style consistently
- set a time schedule
- control the external conditions
- improve your vocabulary

In daily business reading, use the scanning and skimming techniques when consulting indexes or when finding pertinent information, and use the skills of careful reading to concentrate on details.

MAKING IT WORK

1. Select a profession or an industry of interest.
   (a) Research the job requirements for a job that appeals to you within that field.
   (b) Try to arrange through your guidance teachers or co-operative education program leader a visit to a place of employment that is a part of that industry or profession.
   (c) Research through articles in trade and technical journals the industry or profession you are interested in.
   (d) Make up a vocabulary list of words that are used in the area you investigated. Provide an explanation for each of the words.

2. (a) Interview a local journalist to determine
    (i) who reads a specialized kind of newspaper (You may choose a sports magazine or a financial newspaper, for instance.); and
    (ii) how journalists for that particular paper research, organize, and present information to their readers.
   (b) Prepare a short report for the class.

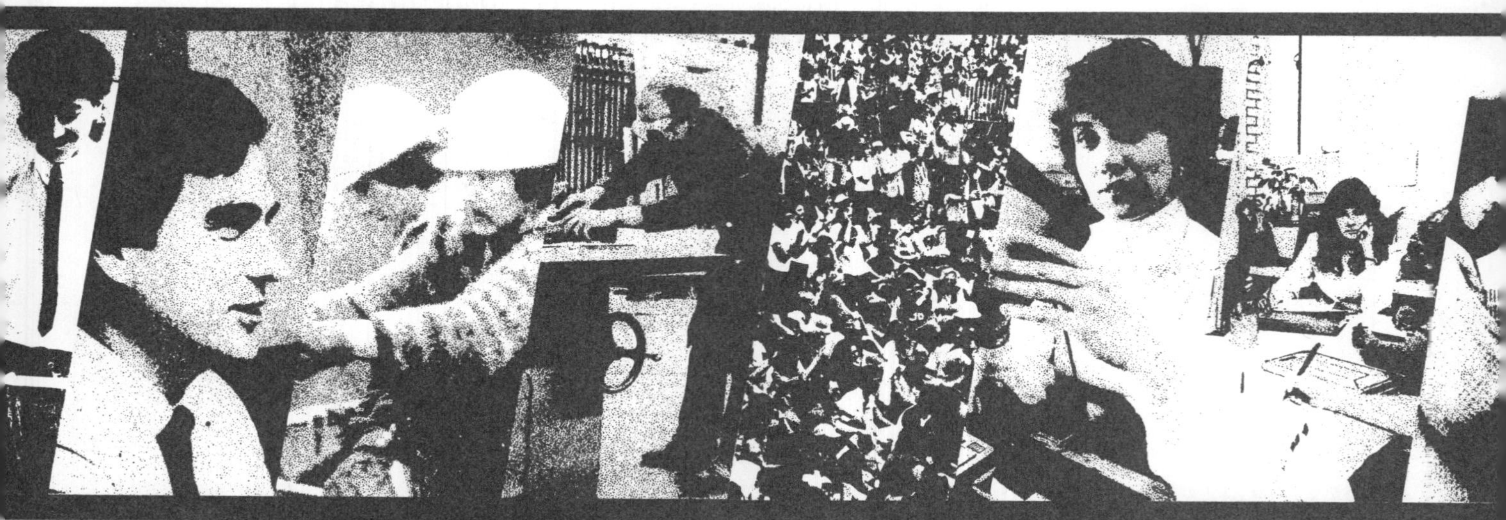

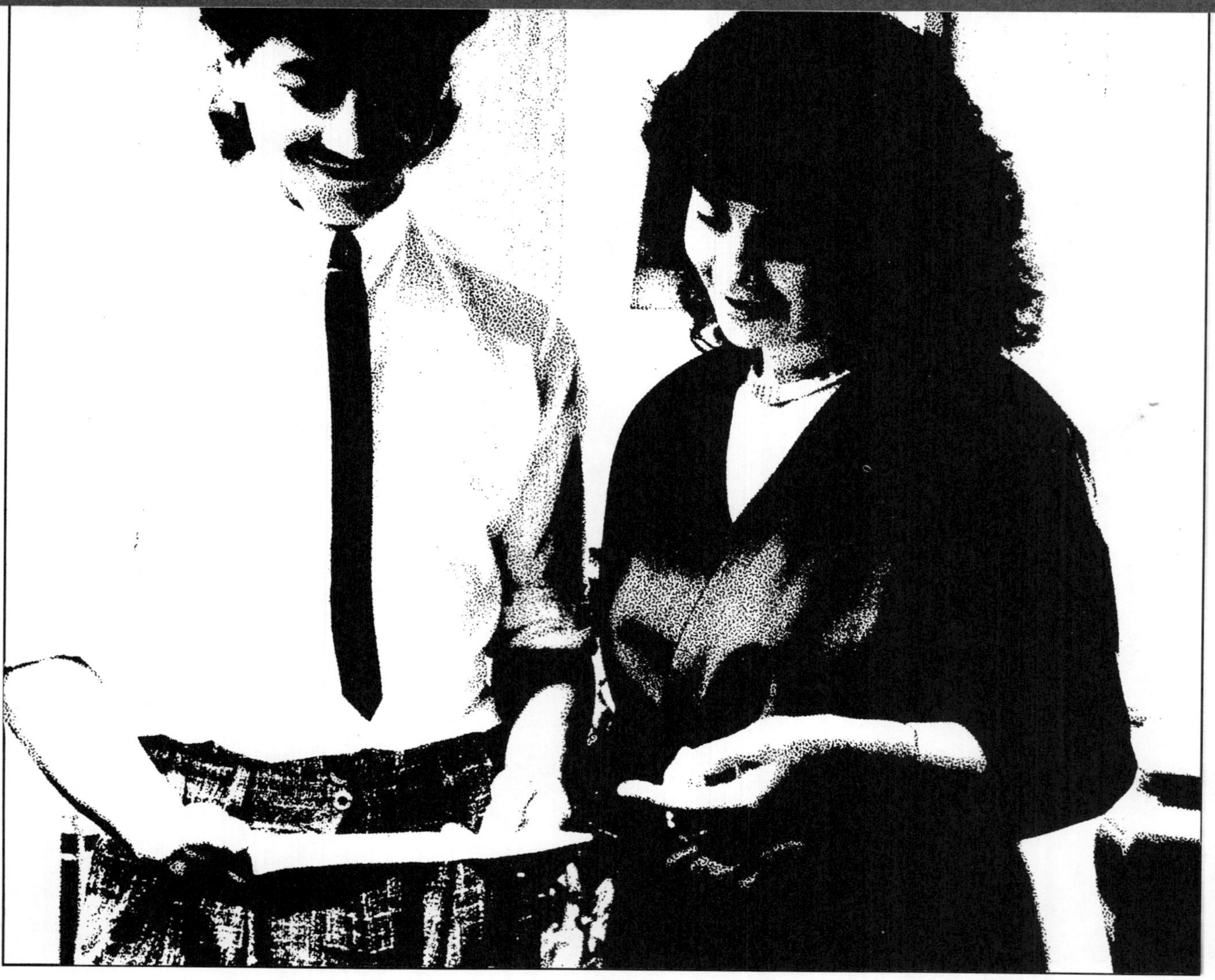

CHAPTER 12

Writing Business Documents

GOALS

At the end of this chapter you should be able to
1. identify the characteristics of effective business writing;
2. compose business documents using the writing model: prewriting, writing, editing, and publication;
3. identify and use a writing plan for business letters and interoffice memorandums;
4. discuss and revise letters and memorandums; and
5. compose and format news releases.

VOCABULARY BUILDING

maxim
stilted
pompous
anecdotes
brash
rectifying
go off on tangents
brevity
unabashed
hyperbole

VIEWPOINTS

Dominic decided to work for a year in Eastern Publishing's Customer Service Department before enrolling in a community college program. At Eastern he handles telephone and mail enquiries regarding customers' orders.

This morning Dominic has spent an hour working on a letter, but he is dissatisfied with what he has written. He decides to ask Christina for assistance. She has worked in Customer Service for five years — longer than anyone, and trains new staff in the department.

DOMINIC: Christina, do you have time to help me for a few minutes? I'm having trouble with this letter.

CHRISTINA: Sure, Dominic, what's the problem?

DOMINIC: I can't seem to get the right tone. One draft sounds too formal and the other one too casual. Here's the situation. The customer has returned a book, claiming we sent him the wrong one, but when I examined it, I found that the cover was marked and several pages had their corners turned back as markers. In my letter I'm trying to tell him that I can't give him a refund because the book is used and that I'm returning the book to him. Dealing with this would be so much easier on the telephone.

CHRISTINA: All right, let's see what you've written. (Christina reads the two drafts shown in Figure 12-1.) Yes, I see what you mean. The first letter sounds too stiff and the second one is too friendly.

Figure 12-1(a)

> It would appear to me that your request is unacceptable due to the fact that the cover and several pages have been damaged. Obviously, the book has been read. As we cannot resell the book, it will be returned to you and no refund will be issued.

> Unfortunately I'm going to have to return this book to you. If it wasn't for the damage to the cover and pages, I could issue you a refund. As it is, I can't help you, much as I'd like to.

DOMINIC: When I'm talking to customers on the phone, I know what to say by listening to them. With letter writing, though, I'm not getting any feedback from the customer, and I feel I'm talking into a vacuum.

CHRISTINA: I know the problem. This is what I do. When I draft a letter, I make a list of the main points I want to get across and arrange them in a logical sequence. Then I try to put myself into the position of the customer. I ask myself how the customer would reply to each point. The replies help me to be sure I am covering all the information I should be finding out in the letter. Now, why don't you start over with your letter. Make an outline of the main points, think of the customer's replies to each, and then write your draft. When you're finished, if you like, I'll take a look at it. Is that any help?

DOMINIC: Thanks, Christina. That is a help. (Dominic returns to his desk and begins writing. Within five minutes he approaches Christina's desk with the new draft.)

CHRISTINA: Well, that didn't take you long. Let's see how it reads now. (Christina reads Dominic's draft shown in Figure 12-1(b).) That's fine. The tone is business-like but not too formal and you have said everything you need to. (Hands letter back to Dominic.)

Figure 12-1(b)

> The damaged condition of the book you returned to us makes it unsaleable. The cover was marked and several pages were folded back. Since the book cannot be resold, you will not be receiving a refund as you requested. Instead, the book will be returned to you under separate cover.

DOMINIC: Putting myself in the position of the customer really helped. Thanks for the advice, Christina.

QUESTIONS

1. List the main points Dominic would have written before writing his final draft.
2. If you were the customer, would you feel that the final draft offered sufficient explanation of the company's actions? What, if anything, would you want added to the letter?
3. Is the final draft of the letter an improvement over the first two drafts? Why or why not?

Figure 12-2
If you were Christina, what would you say to Dominic about the drafts of his letters?

WRITING BUSINESS DOCUMENTS

INTRODUCTION

Writing a business letter or memorandum does not have to be a difficult task, as Dominic in Figure 12-2 found out. Following some of the steps outlined in previous chapters for organizing and presenting material can help you when you are writing business correspondence.

In this chapter we will be looking at various kinds of letters and memorandums that are encountered in business, and applying to them some of the rules and guidelines you have already learned. To begin with, we will examine the characteristics of effective business writing.

CHARACTERISTICS OF EFFECTIVE WRITING

Salespeople, while interacting with clients, create an impression of the companies they represent. In the same way, a business document represents the company that sends it, and creates an impression in the mind of the receiver. What is the impression that both salespeople and business documents are trying to make? Likely they want to give the impression of a well-run company, interested in providing quality products and/or service to customers.

How would you go about creating a favourable impression of your company? Whether you are representing your company in person or in the form of a printed document, you will make a good impression by following these points:

- focussed on the customer/reader
- courteous
- correct
- concise
- clear
- complete
- neat

We shall discuss these qualities as they apply to business writing in the sections that follow.

Focussed on the Reader

The "You" Approach to Writing

The **maxim**, or statement of a general truth, in writing is to "put yourself in the reader's shoes." What is your reader's point of view? If you were writing a letter to persuade a customer to buy your company's product, what arguments would you present? Telling the customer what *you* stand to gain from the sale would not meet with success. Instead, what you must use as a persuasive tool is a statement of the benefits the customer will enjoy by buying your product. The

following are some examples of the benefits you might stress to the customer if you are selling a new solar calculator:
1. You save money on batteries or electricity.
2. You save time, not having to shop for and replace batteries.
3. You feel good by conserving non-renewable energy supplies.
4. You feel you are in step with current technological developments.

The reader, your customer, is more likely to continue reading and to take the action you are encouraging, when you make the benefits clear.

Talking to the reader

Write as though you were talking to the reader. This way you will not sound **stilted**, or stiff and formal, nor will you sound **pompous**, or overly self-important.

On the other hand, in trying to sound natural, be careful that you do not use slang, and that you do not sound as though you are writing a personal letter. Often personal letters adopt a light, breezy tone and contain **anecdotes**, that is, short narratives about interesting events. Humour is frequently used in personal letters and thoughts may be expressed as they occur to the writer, not necessarily in logical sequence. To "talk to the reader" in a business letter, however, it is necessary to express thoughts clearly and sequentially. The vocabulary and tone should be appropriately businesslike and suited to the subject matter and reader.

Courteous

When you represent your company to customers, you are expected to treat them in a friendly and courteous manner. An employee who is **brash**, or impudent, with customers will not last long. In the same way, any letters you write on behalf of your company should be carefully and courteously worded. If the language or tone offends the customer, the message may be lost.

In Figure 12-3, both letters contain the same essential points — thanking the client for the business, informing the client of the policy number, requesting the client to include the policy number in future correspondence, and indicating the willingness of employees to answer questions. However, the tone of the second letter is more friendly. Why? Read the two letters again observing the frequency of the word "you." If you were the client, which letter would you respond to more positively?

In the second letter, the company's appreciation is expressed more personally by the phrase "Thank you" rather than by the statement about what "we" feel. In addition, the request for including the file number in future correspondence is stated as an advantage to the client. In the first letter this request is stated as an advantage to the insurance company. The client is more likely to respond positively to the personal wording and personal benefits of the second letter. Overall, the first letter is written from the insurance company's point of

> We would like to acknowledge the receipt of your request for life insurance coverage.
>   The policy number we have assigned you is LOM36921. We ask that you include this number in any correspondence with us. This will make our job easier.
>   If there are any questions, please call.

> Thank you for giving us the opportunity of meeting your life insurance needs. It is a pleasure to know that you feel we are the company best suited to you.
>   Your new policy number is LOM36921. We ask that you include this number in any correspondence with us. Your policy can then be retrieved more quickly, thus providing you with better service.
>   If you have any questions about your new policy, please call and ask any one of our staff to assist you.

Figure 12-3

view, whereas the second letter is written with the reader's point of view in mind.

The tone of a letter is determined in part by the choice of words, as you have seen, and also by the sentence structure. Although the first letter contains the essential points, it is abrupt and choppy. This effect is due to the use of short sentences. The second letter, by expanding on the central idea of each paragraph and varying sentence structure and length, is more courteous and conversational in tone.

Correct

Correctness is essential in all business correspondence. Several elements should be checked for accuracy whenever you write a business document.

First, are the details of your document correct? Circulating a document containing incorrect information may cause problems for the parties concerned, depending on how critical the information is. Also, careless errors may leave the reader with the impression that you (and your company) did not consider the matter to be important enough to take sufficient care when writing the document. When you discover an error you have made in a document, it will be necessary to write a follow-up letter or to place a telephone call **rectifying**, or correcting, the mistake.

Second, are the spelling, punctuation, and grammar correct in your letter? Such errors are distracting to the reader. Spelling errors are easily avoided by checking in a dictionary whenever you are unsure. The rules of punctuation and grammar must be learned either in school or from books on the subject.

Third, have you used language that is biased against either sex? Avoid the use of "man" or "woman" as a suffix in job titles. For example, use "foreperson" instead of "foreman" and "chairperson," "moderator," or "presiding officer" instead of "chairman." If you are referring to someone who could be either male or female, avoid using "he," "him," and "his." In such situations you can (1) reword the sentence to eliminate the pronoun, or (2) change to the plural so that you can use "they", "them," and "their."

Concise

To write concisely is to state your message completely, in as few words as possible. Businesspeople are annoyed at having to read long, wordy letters that **go off on tangents**, or change suddenly from one thought to another. On the other hand, **brevity**, or shortness of expression, can sometimes result in abruptness, as we saw earlier. At other times, if the letter is too brief, information may be missing or it may be insufficiently explained. A balance must be struck between the extremes of wordiness and brevity.

Keep your writing concise by avoiding wordy expressions such as the following.

Instead of ...	**Write**
as a general rule	generally
at a later date	later
at the present time	now/at present
at such time, at which time	when
costs the sum of	costs
despite the fact that	although
for the purpose of	for
for the reason that	because/since
held a meeting	met
in a position to	able to
in receipt of	received
in spite of the fact that	even though/despite
in the event that	in case/if
in very few cases	seldom
pertaining to	about/of
reason is due to	because
this will acknowledge receipt of	thank you for sending

Sometimes, in an attempt to be concise, a writer may use one unfamiliar word to replace several words. A reader, not knowing the meaning of the word, could misinterpret the letter's content. It is best to use familiar words and appropriate business and technical terms that you are sure will be understood.

WRITING BUSINESS DOCUMENTS

Figure 12-4
How would Charles Dickens have written the beginning of A Tale of Two Cities *if he were writing a business letter instead of a novel?*

'It was the best of times, it was the worst of times, it was the age of wisdom, it was the age of foolishness, it was the epoch of belief, it was the epoch of incredulity, it was the season of Light, it was the season of Darkness . . .'

Examine the opening paragraph from *A Tale of Two Cities* by Charles Dickens in Figure 12-4. If the author had intended to write a business letter instead of a novel, how might he have worded this passage?

Clear

Clarity is essential in business documents; ambiguities can lead to costly errors. Vocabulary, sentence structure, and cohesion of sentences and paragraphs contribute to a clearly worded document.

The level of knowledge of the reader on the topic will determine whether or not technical vocabulary should be used. To determine how persuasively you must word the material you are presenting, you must gauge the probable interest of the reader in the topic. In many cases you will have no information about the background of the reader and it may be necessary to word your document in such a way that it will be clear to someone with no knowledge of the subject.

At one time the accepted style for writing business documents was formal and stiff. This writing style is no longer considered desirable. Use language you would choose for conversations with a co-worker or supervisor, but refrain from using slang expressions. For additional guidance on word choice, refer to the section on words in Chapter 7.

Ideas that flow in a logical progression are more likely to be followed easily, and tight, rather than loose and rambling sentence structures, will also help. Short and medium length sentences are the easiest to understand, and varied sentence length and structure, the most interesting to read. Check though, that each sentence is complete and not just a fragment. Sentences should be grouped into paragraphs containing one central idea. Paragraphing adds clarity by indicating which are the main ideas and which the supporting material.

Aim for cohesion within sentences and paragraphs so that the relationships between ideas and information are clear.

Complete

Taking short cuts does not always reduce the time required to do a job, especially if the job has to be redone as a result. Deciding to write a document in final form without any preparation often results in points being omitted and a lack of coherence. It takes only a few minutes to plan a document and the time is well spent.

When writing a business document, follow the same writing model discussed in Chapter 6. The stages of the model are

- prewriting
- writing
- editing
- publication.

Before any writing or information gathering is done, make sure you are clear about the purpose of the document and the audience for whom it is intended. Is the document meant to inform, to persuade, or to enquire? What is the reader's role or position, background or education, knowledge of the subject matter, and attitude toward the subject matter? The answers to these questions will guide you in choosing vocabulary and in establishing an appropriate tone.

Once your purpose and audience are known, you are ready to develop an outline using the following steps.

Step One
Jot down all the points to be covered in the document, not in any particular order, just as they occur to you.

Step Two
Review the points and cross out any that are not relevant. Add any that may have been missed in step one.

Step Three
Decide on the organizational pattern you will use. Then identify the points that will be grouped together. This can be done by colour coding or numbering the points.

Step Four
Decide on the order in which the points will be raised. When you have developed a satisfactory outline, you can begin writing from it.

The opening and closing paragraphs are normally brief. Usually, the opening paragraph should indicate the subject of the document and refer to any relevant previous communication. The closing paragraph usually recommends the action that should take place, to be initiated either by the writer or by the reader. In stating the action that is recommended, avoid "-ing" endings. "Let us hear your views before the end of the month" is more forceful than "Hoping to hear your views before the end of the month."

After writing the document, it is important to re-read it and make any revisions that will make an improvement. Check for accuracy in this editing stage as well.

Neat

The publication stage, in which your document is produced in its final form, requires your attention to appearance. A consistently neat format with headings, where appropriate, will help to make your document attractive and easier to read and create a good impression for you and your company. In the next section we will discuss how to put documents in various formats.

Business documents should be
1. *focussed on the reader*
2. *courteous*
3. *correct*
4. *concise*
5. *clear*
6. *complete*
7. *neat.*

APPLICATIONS

1. Explain what is wrong with the following sentences taken from letters to customers. Then rewrite the sentences to improve them.
   (a) It's your fault the food processor doesn't work. You should have read the instructions before using it.
   (b) We're so lucky to have such a prestigious firm as yours to do business with us.
   (c) We received your order of January 27. It will be shipped tomorrow.
   (d) Because you were so persistent, we corrected the error we made in your account.
   (e) I want to welcome you as a new client, and I have enclosed your new charge card.

2. Rewrite the following letters to improve their clarity.
   (a) In order to maintain a steady production of furniture, we are in need of a constant source of timber and we would like to investigate the possibility of signing a long-term contract with you if we can be certain of regular supplies of all kinds of wood suitable for furniture.
   Please let us know if you can supply us with all kinds of woods at reasonably low prices that compare favourably with those of your competitors and also please let us know your payment terms. Upon receipt of this information, we will draw up what we think will be a mutually acceptable contract and forward it to your legal department for their consideration.
   (b) It sure is too bad that the goods you ordered from us were damaged in transit. Absolutely, by all means, return any of the stuff that's damaged and we'll send you a credit memo for it. I hope you'll give us another chance before you switch to our competitor.
   (c) I have pleasure in acknowledging receipt of your letter of the 5th, together with a copy of your catalogue by the same post.

I am sending you herewith order No. 564, and shall be glad if you will execute it in accordance with the instructions contained therein. As this is a trial order, I trust you will devote your utmost care to its execution. If the goods give me satisfaction, I shall be in a position to place larger orders with you.

3. Suggest alternate words for salesman, stewardess, ladylike, man-made, man-hours, mankind, and businesswoman.

4. Rewrite the following sentences in two different ways to avoid the masculine pronoun.
   (a) Before approving a substantial loan, the loans officer is to phone the regional manager for authorization.
   (b) Each employee is to complete a Request for Vacation Period form and return it to his supervisor.
   (c) Every clerk is responsible for the daily balancing of his cash drawer.
   (d) When a courier cannot deliver a package, he is to return it to the dispatcher that day.

INFORMATION LETTERS AND MEMOS

A frequent purpose of business correspondence is sending and obtaining information. Falling into this category are letters of enquiry, letters accompanying orders or documents, thank you letters, letters of congratulation, and memorandums, or memos, on any of the preceding matters. (See Figure 12-5 for an example of a memo. The

```
TO          Roger Duran, Sales Manager
FROM        Danielle Boucher, Accounting Department
DATE        March 3, 19__
SUBJECT     Monthly Sales Statistics

Attached are the monthly sales statistics for
your department. Please check them for accuracy
and completeness. If they are correct, initial
the last page and return the report to me. Any
omissions or errors should be noted where they
occur before returning the report to me.

db

Encl.
```

Figure 12-5
The interoffice memorandum

format for memos is outlined in the appendix at the back of this book.) All of them should state
- the purpose for writing;
- the reason the reader is being asked for or given information;
- the information; and
- what action, if any, is expected of the reader.

Most information letters and memorandums are straightforward and tend to be short in length.

Enquiry

A letter of enquiry requests information of one type or another. It may be asking for information about a product or service. Notice in the following memorandum that the subject line highlights the purpose for writing.

> SUBJECT   Annual Report
>
> In order to prepare the annual report, each department is requested to submit its projected budgetary needs for the coming year. Please use the same format as last year. To help you in this regard, you will find a copy of your last year's submission. The deadline for this year's budget submission is December 5.

Transmittal

Business documents such as reports, forms, or cheques should be accompanied by a letter of transmittal which describes the document enclosed and what is to be done with it. The following is an illustration of a transmittal letter.

> Dear Mr. Sanchez
>
> Enclosed is a cheque for $327.00 in payment of the catering service you provided on October 4. Included in this amount is the cost of the flowers, as we had agreed.
>
> Thank you for the time you spent with me planning the menu.
>
> Sincerely

Thank You

Sincerity is the most important element in writing a thank you letter. Examine the following thank you note.

> Thank you for the lovely gift you gave me last week. Your thoughtfulness was very much appreciated. Even though my new job involves more travelling, I hope that we can keep in touch.

The note sounds sincere, but can it be improved? Read it again. What was the gift? How does the writer plan to keep in touch? Thank you notes should specify the favour or gift received and why it is useful, beneficial, or appreciated. The preceding thank you note could be used for any occasion by simply changing the last sentence, so it is not a good example.

Congratulations

Congratulatory letters are usually handwritten and mark a special occasion or achievement, such as a promotion, or recognize the extra effort of an employee that has resulted in a job well done. Again, sincerity is important. Often enthusiasm will be expressed as in the following example.

> Dear Gail,
>
> Congratulations on receiving your RIA! All those years of night courses, assignments, and exams are finally over. You've worked hard and deserve your degree.
>
> I'll call you next week so that we can arrange a date to celebrate your achievement.
>
> > Sincerely,

Acknowledgement

Only under special circumstances does the receipt of correspondence or merchandise need to be acknowledged by letter. It may be that if there is going to be a delay in resolving a matter, a letter should be sent to acknowledge receipt of the original correspondence. This acknowledgement will let the receiver know that the original letter was not lost and that the matter is receiving attention.

Some companies that routinely send acknowledgements use a form that covers all the common situations. This form will help the company to speed up the processing of correspondence. The following are examples of such a form.

1. We have received your dental estimation. When we have finished reviewing it, we will contact you.
2. To enable us to consider the claim recently submitted, please have the attached form completed by the dentist.
3. Attached is the receipt recently sent to us. To enable us to consider this expense, please have the attached form completed by the dentist.

Confirmation

Arrangements made orally, such as agreements or orders, should be confirmed in writing to avoid misunderstanding or errors. For example,

> Dear Ms Lobraico
>
> As discussed by telephone today, we would like you to speak to our department managers about stress. The presentation should include a discussion of causes, symptoms, and methods of dealing with stress.
>
> Arrangements have been made for your presentation to be in seminar room 205 from 9:00 a.m. to 12 noon on Thursday, June 10. Enclosed is a map giving directions to our building.
>
> If you have any questions, or if you need any audio-visual equipment, please let me know. I'm looking forward to your presentation.
>
> Yours truly

Form Letter

There are times when a business may find it necessary to send almost identical letters to a number of different individuals or companies. For example, a personnel department may confirm interview times with applicants by sending each applicant a letter. If this is a routine procedure followed for each position being filled, then it is more efficient to have a form letter than to compose a new letter for each position.

A form letter contains the information that is the same for each address. Space is left for any variables; that is, information that differs for each address. The following is an example of a form letter a personnel department may use.

> Dear
>
> Thank you for applying for the position of (name position). As discussed by telephone, your interview will be on (day and date) at (time) in the Personnel Department.
>
> Please call me if you have any questions about these arrangements.
>
> Yours truly
>
> C. R. Steinburg
> Personnel Officer

When writing information letters and memos, state
1. *the purpose for writing*
2. *the reason for asking or giving information*
3. *the information*
4. *the action, if any, expected of the reader.*

If a business has word processing or computer equipment, the form letter can be stored as it appears above. Each time the letter is to be used, the typist would key only the variables: date, inside address, salutation, position, day and date, and time. This information would be merged with the form letter to produce a letter that looked as if it had been individually prepared. A form letter can save time in processing repetitive letters, and at the same time retain an individualized appearance.

APPLICATIONS

5. Write a thank you letter to a relative for a birthday gift you were given.

6. You have been awarded a bursary donated by a local firm. Write a thank you letter to the firm.

7. You belong to the Record-A-Month Club and now want to cancel your membership. Write an appropriate letter inventing facts where necessary.

8. Collect examples of order forms from magazines or newspapers. List the similarities in the organization of the forms. Complete one of the forms. Then write a letter ordering the same product(s); assume that you do not have a form.

9. Write to a holiday resort requesting information about a summer or winter vacation.

10. Write a memorandum to the Personnel Department of a fictitious company requesting that you be able to take your holidays during the first two weeks of July. Mention in your memo that your supervisor has approved of your vacation.

11. You want the duplicating room to make 20 copies of a report on the renovations to the first aid station. You want five copies sent to J. Kruppe, President; three copies sent to W. Thiessen, Controller; five copies to P. Berenson, Plant Manager; and the remainder returned to you. Write the necessary memo to go to the duplicating room with the report.

12. As secretary-treasurer of a community organization, you sent out reminders to members who had not yet paid their dues. Subsequently, you received an abrupt note from one of the members insisting that there was a mistake. Upon checking the records, you find that the member was right; the member's dues had been paid. Write a letter apologizing for your error.

13. As Planning Assistant in the Marketing Division, you are responsible for the booking of hotel facilities for product shows. You have spoken to Carla Matte in Catering at the Gregory Hotel about renting the ballroom for the first Monday and Tuesday of next month. You need the room all day on both days and would like coffee and muffins for 60 people in the room at 8:30 each morning. Write a letter confirming these arrangements.

14. A customer has telephoned that he has lost his latest statement from your company and would like a photocopy sent to him. Write the letter you would send with the photocopy of the statement.

15. You are working the night shift as a security person for a local mall. When you were hired, you were told that you would be able to transfer to the day shift when an opening became available. Yesterday, when you reported for work, you saw a notice on the bulletin board about an opening on the day shift. Write a memorandum to the general manager of the mall reminding him of his original promise and your interest in working the day shift.

FAVOURABLE LETTERS AND MEMOS

Favourable letters include affirmative responses to routine requests, granting adjustments, and responses to credit requests. If the content of the letter or memorandum favours the reader, these three steps should be followed:
1. State the good news immediately.
2. State any necessary information.
3. End on a positive note.

A memorandum granting an employee's request for holiday time might read as follows.

SUBJECT   Summer Vacation

Your request to have a two-week vacation beginning July 7 has been approved. If you wish to change the beginning date, please notify us within the next two weeks. After that time, I may not be able to arrange a change.

Pleasant sailing.

The following is in reply to a customer who has requested an adjustment in her account.

Dear Mrs. Tien

Your account has been adjusted by $45.15.

As you had described in your letter of August 23, the entry of $45.15 for Downtown Hardware was incorrectly charged to your account. We have also ensured that there will be no interest charge relating to this entry on your next statement.

Thank you for drawing this matter to our attention.

To a customer who has asked for charge privileges, you might write:

> Dear Mr. Romanero
>
> Your request for credit has been approved to a limit of $5000.
>
> Our policy with company accounts is that the invoiced amount is due within 30 days of the date of the invoice. A two percent monthly charge is added to outstanding monthly balances. Accounts over 90 days are submitted to a collection agency unless an arrangement for late payment has been made with our credit manager.
>
> To prepare for our annual inventory count, we are offering a special discount on many of our in-stock items. Enclosed is a listing of the specials that may be of interest to you.
>
> Yours truly

When writing favourable letters and memos
1. *state the good news immediately*
2. *state any necessary information*
3. *end on a positive note.*

APPLICATIONS

16. As manager of a sporting goods store, you are often asked to sponsor community teams. In today's mail is a letter requesting your sponsorship of a midget hockey team. You decide to do this but need to know the number of sweaters needed. Write a letter to Marc Laroche, the team manager, to obtain this information.

17. You work in Customer Service and Mrs. T. McEachran has returned one of the toys manufactured by your company. The arms of the doll broke off shortly after it was purchased. Your company has had a number of these dolls returned and has decided to replace all returns. Write a letter to the customer saying that a new doll will be mailed the following day.

18. Your company has recently introduced a job-sharing plan. Requests to participate in the plan are submitted to the Personnel Department. Write a memo to Pat Taybour in the Data Processing Department informing her that her request has been approved for a one-year period. If she wishes to have an extension, application must be made two months before the year is up. This is in accordance with the company policy on job-sharing.

19. Discuss the following letter, then rewrite it making improvements based on your critique.

> Dear Sir
>
> On Thursday of this week, you will receive a voucher which will enable you to receive another turntable. I have investigated your case and I have found out that poor shipping and receiving was the cause of your poor conditioned turntable. Our merchandise is made from fine top quality material and is a fine listening pleasure, I am sure you will enjoy another turntable.

WRITING BUSINESS DOCUMENTS

> Upon receiving your new turntable return the old one to the store in which you purchased the turntable from. Also enclosed in this letter is a business card with the district manager's name on it if you have any problems with your new turntable, feel free to contract him anytime.
>
> Sincerely yours

20. Discuss the following letter and then rewrite it making the improvements noted in your critique.

> Gentlemen
>
> We have received your letter. Enclosed we have mailed our catalogue and price list. We would like very much to do business with your company.
>
> Yours truly

UNFAVOURABLE LETTERS AND MEMOS

At times you will have to write letters and memos that communicate ideas the recipient will not be happy to read. These unfavourable letters include refusing requests for information, having problems with orders, refusing credit, and refusing to grant adjustments or claims. When the content of the letter or memorandum is not favourable to the reader, these five steps should be followed.

1. Begin on a neutral note.
2. Introduce the topic.
3. Explain the reasons for the negative decision.
4. State the refusal clearly, avoiding the use of negative words wherever possible.
5. End on a pleasant note.

Compare the following memorandums. What would your reaction be to each one if you were the recipient? Why?

> SUBJECT   Expense Claim
>
>   Unfortunately, not all the expenses you are claiming for your recent trip to Boston can be approved. Procedure 9 clearly states that managers at your level must travel economy class. Consequently, you will be reimbursed for the cost of only an economy class ticket, not a first-class ticket.

When writing unfavourable letters and memos
1. *begin on a neutral note*
2. *introduce the topic*
3. *explain the negative decision*
4. *state the refusal clearly*
5. *end on a positive note.*

> SUBJECT   Expense Claim
>
> Your expense claim for your recent trip to Boston is now being processed.
>
> Among the items being claimed is a first-class return flight to Boston. Company procedure 9 states that regional managers will be reimbursed for economy class travel. Accordingly, your claim has been adjusted to an economy class fare.
>
> You should receive your cheque within five days.

APPLICATIONS

21. Rewrite Dominic's letter in *Viewpoints*, incorporating the ideas presented in the five steps for writing unfavourable letters and memorandums.

22. The publishing company you work for had a special mail order offer just before Christmas: customers who ordered three or more books received a free copy of *Canada Now*. Unfortunately, you have run out of copies of this book. Write a letter to be included in customers' orders indicating what has happened and promising that the free book will be shipped as soon as a new order of them is received by your company.

23. As manager of the sporting goods store referred to in the last set of activities, write to Marc Laroche to explain why you are unable to sponsor the hockey team.

24. You work in the payroll division. Today you received a memo from G. Mathieu of Data Processing asking to know the salary of another employee who is interested in buying Mr. Mathieu's car. Write to Mr. Mathieu refusing his request.

25. Discuss the following letter, then rewrite it making the improvements noted in your critique.

> Dear sir
>
> I am writing this letter to you for the benefit of my son Greg's education. I feel that your educational system is wrong. I feel it has no space for the child's imagination. In order for him to be successful I feel it is important for him to use his imagination. As I can see, you have not made any attempt to take this into consideration to the last letter I wrote. Therefore, I feel it would be best if I were to withdraw my son, starting Monday, April 16.
>
> Yours truly

WRITING BUSINESS DOCUMENTS

PERSUASIVE LETTERS AND MEMOS

Special requests for information or assistance, appeals for donations or contributions, sales letters, enquiry follow-ups, invitations to attend seminars, and letters of application — all fall into the category of persuasive letters.

Letters of application will be discussed in some detail in Chapter 15.

If you want to persuade your reader to take a particular action, then follow these steps:

1. State the request clearly or use an attention-getting statement if appropriate.
2. State why the request or action would benefit the reader.
3. State evidence to show that your request is reasonable.
4. State the exact action you want the reader to take. The action should be reasonable and a time frame should be included.

Writing a persuasive letter or memorandum is similar to preparing a persuasive presentation. Central to both is knowing as much as possible about your audience. With knowledge of your audience you will be better able to judge whether to use inductive or deductive reasoning. Choose acceptable supportive arguments. Decide what emotional or psychological needs should be appealed to. Determine your present degree of credibility and how it can be developed in the correspondence. For more guidance, re-read the section on persuasive presentations in Chapter 10.

Compare the following memorandums written by a secretary to her supervisor. What is your reaction to each one? Why?

SUBJECT   Purchase of microcomputer

Wouldn't it be great to have up-to-the-minute balances for our budget accounts? Not only that, our reports that go through several draft stages could be prepared faster! Well, both of these are possible.

All we have to do is purchase a microcomputer.

Here are all the cost details, delivery and installation information, and training requirements ...

SUBJECT   Purchase of microcomputer

I feel consideration should be given to purchasing a microcomputer for our office. Such a purchase will alleviate our two main office problems: the lack of up-to-the-minute account balances and the large amount of secretarial time spent on the retyping of revised reports.

Having investigated several microcomputers, I would recommend the following purchase ...

In the above examples, you are writing to your supervisor, and it is therefore inappropriate to give a sales pitch as in memo 1. If you are writing a direct mail sales letter, however, an attention-getting first sentence is not only appropriate, but essential. With the number of sales letters received each day, yours will be discarded without being read if you cannot catch your reader's interest immediately. Many direct sales letters have the attention-getting statement, called a "teaser," on the envelope to prevent readers from throwing the letter away unopened.

The following are examples of openings from direct mail sales letters.

Have you ever noticed how much harder people try when they work for a supervisor who takes a personal interest in their work?

If you have an **unabashed**, or unembarrassed, interest in your own success, you really should be in touch with the thoughts of the most successful businesspeople.

You'll agree that it's everything we promised ...

When I was a youngster, I recall asking my Dad ...
"When is the best time to advertise?"

Sales letters and letters asking for donations always include the last step mentioned above, that of specifying the action you want the reader to take. Often this statement is reinforced in a postscript such as the following.

Order today. Fill in the quick reply card enclosed.
P.S. This unusual offer expires in 30 days.
If you are definitely aiming at the top, fill out and mail the enclosed card.
P.S. Remember, your first issue is absolutely free.

Knowing your audience and the purpose of your letter will determine how colourfully you should word your letter. Emotional words, metaphors, and **hyperbole** (exaggeration that is not intended to deceive) may be acceptable in various types of sales literature, but in some correspondence they may sound insincere, or they may create a tone the reader finds objectionable.

When writing persuasive letters and memos
1. *either state the request or use an attention-getting statement*
2. *state why the request or action would benefit the reader*
3. *show evidence that your request is reasonable*
4. *state the exact action you want the reader to take.*

APPLICATIONS

26. Collect several direct mail letters and letters requesting donations. Write a brief summary outlining the similarities and differences between the two types of letters.

27. Analyze one of the letters you have collected. Indicate why it is or is not effective.

28. Your school yearbook committee wants to canvass the local business community to buy ads in the yearbook. Write a letter the committee could use for this purpose.

29. Pretend you are Marc Laroche, the manager of the midget hockey team mentioned earlier. Write the letter you sent to the manager of the sporting goods store asking for support for the midget hockey team.

WRITING BUSINESS DOCUMENTS

30. You have just started your own business to design and make women's clothing. As part of your advertising campaign, you decide to send a letter to each woman whose wedding engagement is announced in the local newspapers. Compose a suitable letter.

31. You have organized a group of students who will do lawn work, painting, and repair work during the summer. To advertise your services, you want to send a letter to all households that might be interested in hiring your group. Compose a suitable letter.

32. Your company has a suggestion box. Write a memorandum for the suggestion box asking that an additional feature be included in the employee orientation program. You want to see the company add a slide show to the orientation program that outlines the organizational structure of the company, names the executive officers, and explains how the various departments within the company interact.

33. Write a letter of complaint to the head office of a clothing chain store. You recently purchased an item of clothing and are not happy about the quality of the material. The store has refused to give you a refund or to replace the item.

34. Write three letters of adjustment in response to the letter in Question 33. In the first, give a full refund; in the second, a partial refund; and in the third, no refund.

35. You have been asked to prepare a memorandum for circulation among the employees on one of the topics below:
    (a) remind them about a safety practice
    (b) encourage them to keep the office neat
    (c) explain the parking regulations in the company lot
    In order to make the memorandum more effective, include a drawing along with the message.

NEWS RELEASES

Businesses and organizations like to have favourable news stories about themselves appear in the press or on the air to create good public relations. To ensure that the media will cover topics such as promotions, retirements, new product or service introductions, and special celebrations, the company usually provides the media with a news release (press release).

The news release should be written in standard journalistic format to make it easier to read and edit.
- Use double spacing, with 3.8 cm (1.5 inch) margins on all sides.
- At the centre top, type News Release.
- At the bottom of each page except the last one, type "more."
- At the bottom of the last page type "XXX" or "30" to signify there is no more copy. The number thirty was used by telegraph operators

to indicate the end of a transmission. It is currently used by journalists to indicate the end of a story.

Your news release should include the following elements:

Release date — If you want the information to be released immediately, indicate it by saying, for example, "For immediate release, December 3, 19__." If it is to be released on a particular day, you would say "For release on March 14, 19__" or "Do not release before March 14, 19__."

Headline — Write a brief descriptive headline that summarizes the content of the release.

Body — Your opening paragraph should contain the answers to the questions who, what, where, when, how, and why. Try to place the most important information in the first few paragraphs, because if the editor must shorten the release, the material will be deleted from the end sections. Figure 12-6 is an example of a news release that answers all the basic questions.

Contact Person — The name and telephone number of the person in your company who should be contacted about the news release should be given either at the top or the bottom of the release. This information is essential to the news editor who will be editing your release. If no contact is given, the release may not be printed. In some large companies the contact may be someone in the Public Relations Department, or there may be an employee who is given the responsibility for approving all press releases.

Before you send your press release to the newspaper, make sure that you have included all the facts and that you have verified them. Publishing incorrect information can harm your company's public image more than no information at all. Once you have prepared the information, obtain permission to send it to press from whoever in the company has the necessary authority.

A news release contains
1. *the release date*
2. *a contact person*
3. *a headline*
4. *double-spaced copy answering who, what, where, when, how, and why*
5. *"XXX" or "30" at the end.*

APPLICATIONS

36. Using Figure 12-6, identify
    (a) the date for release
    (b) the contact person
    (c) the headline
    (d) the newsworthy elements.

37. Marguerite van Alstine has just been appointed Municipal Administrator in your area. Marguerite and her family have lived in the locality for 15 years, and during that time she has been active in several community groups, including the United Way and the Girl Guides. Prior to her appointment, Marguerite had been the Treasurer of a nearby community and for the past six years had been the Special Assistant to the local Municipal Administrator. Her new position became vacant with the retirement of Dennis McGiven. The announcement was made by Mayor Jeremy Froud.

    As a member of the town administration, compose a news release for this situation. The information is not to be used until March 5.

WRITING BUSINESS DOCUMENTS

Figure 12-6
A news release answers the questions who, what, where, when, how, and why.

Information Sheridan

Sheridan College of Applied Arts and Technology

Trafalgar Road, Oakville, Ontario L6H 2L1
Oakville 845-9430, Clarkson 823-9730
Burlington 632-7081

For Immediate
Release: Thurs., Sept. 13, 1984

Contact: Information Services
Locals 285, 286, 301

SHERIDAN COLLEGE STUDENTS BENEFIT
FROM UNIQUE COMPUTER WRITING COURSE

Sheridan College is the first college in Canada to offer computer-assisted writing instruction through a unique software system called "The Writer's Workbench".

With the Writer's Workbench, a student keys in an essay, and the computer provides a six to eight-page printout of qualitative comments. Feedback is given on such items as readability, style, sentence variation, organization, and effective use of vocabulary.

"Innovative teachers will use this system as a tool to create a critical audience for their writing students," said Manager of the project and Co-ordinator of the Language Development Centre (Brampton Campus) Randy Smye. "Teachers of writing may soon be freed from the mind-numbing job of editing and evaluating student essays."

The Writer's Workbench was initiated at Sheridan through the Research and Development Division. Smye believes the Writer's Workbench will be the catalyst in producing more literate, creative and effective writers.

Smye has been working for the past six months with Spectrix Microsystems of Markham to program a Canadian-designed computer (Spectrix 30) with the Writer's Workbench program. The software package, created by Bell Laboratories in the U.S., is an extensive collection of computer programs for textual analysis.

Sheridan plans to include the Workbench in educational programs for the business community as well as for hundreds of students currently enrolled in English courses at the College.

Interest in the program is wide-spread — Smye has made presentations to the Metro Colleges English Teachers, Ontario Deputy Minister of Colleges and Universities Harry Fisher and the Educational Computing Organization of Ontario.

38. The following letter was written in response to an advertisement in a golf magazine. The advertisement was placed by a Florida company that sold golf balls suitable for driving ranges.

> In reply to your advertisement in *Golf Digest*, we are interested in obtaining a source of range balls for the Canadian market. We are currently supplying driving ranges and golf clubs in Ontario and western Canada and must establish a working relationship with other suppliers of good quality used golf balls.
>
> If terms and conditions are acceptable, I am hopeful that a long-term supply contract can be agreed upon. Would you please provide details regarding
> 1. prices and terms;
> 2. quantities available;
> 3. design and material used to strip range balls; and
> 4. method of shipment.
>
> In Canada the golf season runs from approximately April 15 to October 31. Customers place their orders in October for the upcoming season, and we are in need of dependable suppliers who can ship large agreed-upon quantities by March 15 of each year and lesser quantities from then until approximately August 1.
>
> If you are interested, please reply as soon as possible together with your name and telephone number so that I can call you personally.

(a) Study the letter carefully and then state its strengths and/or weaknesses.
(b) Write the advertisement to which you think this letter was responding.

CHAPTER SUMMARY

Effective business documents
- focussed on the reader
- courteous
- accurate
- concise
- clear
- complete
- neat

The writing model for business documents
- prewriting
- writing
- editing
- publication

Letters and memorandums should be formatted in an acceptable business style.

Information letters and memorandums
- state the purpose for writing
- state the reason the reader is being asked or given the information
- state the information
- state what action, if any, is expected of the reader

Favourable letters and memorandums
- state the good news immediately
- state any necessary information
- end on a positive note

Unfavourable letters and memorandums
- begin on a neutral note
- introduce the topic
- explain the reasons for the negative decision
- state refusal clearly, avoiding the use of negative words wherever possible
- end on a pleasant note

Persuasive letters and memorandums
- state the request clearly or use an attention-getting statement if appropriate
- state why the request or action would benefit the reader
- state evidence to show that the request is reasonable
- state the exact action you want the reader to take; the action should be easy to do and should include a time frame

A news release
- indicates the release date
- identifies the contact person
- provides a headline
- answers the questions who, what, where, when, how, and why
- ends with "XXX" or "30"

MAKING IT WORK

1. In this chapter we discussed the writing of letters and memorandums, documents which make up the bulk of written communication in business. The use of preprinted letterhead and memorandum paper was also mentioned. Letterhead, forms, and business cards are usually designed by an artist and printed by a printing house. There are many different types of jobs related to the printing business. Among them are designers, finished and assembly artists, scanning operators, strippers, platemakers, press operators, and production and sales personnel.

    (a) Design the letterhead for a company you would like to own.

(b) Prepare a collage from ads in the telephone book or newspapers to illustrate the various services offered by printing businesses.
(c) Using words and pictures cut out of newspapers and magazines, design an ad for a company of your choice.
(d) Discuss why a company will have a logo designed. Collect the logos from six businesses. Research the meaning of each logo and discuss its effectiveness.
(e) Define heraldry. If your community has a coat of arms, invite the designer or another person knowledgeable in heraldry to explain the meaning of the design. If your community does not have a coat of arms, study your province's coat of arms.

2. Friendly persuasion is important not only in letters but also in obtaining co-operation from those with whom you work closely or from whom you need special assistance. As in a letter, your approach when requesting help in person will determine your success. Make a list of suggestions on how to approach other employees when you require assistance.

3. Invite a business executive to speak to the class about writing. Ask the person to bring samples of drafts and final documents to show the class.

4. Invite writers from the local newspaper, radio station, or television station to discuss the types of material they write, the way they determine content, and the approach they take to the content.

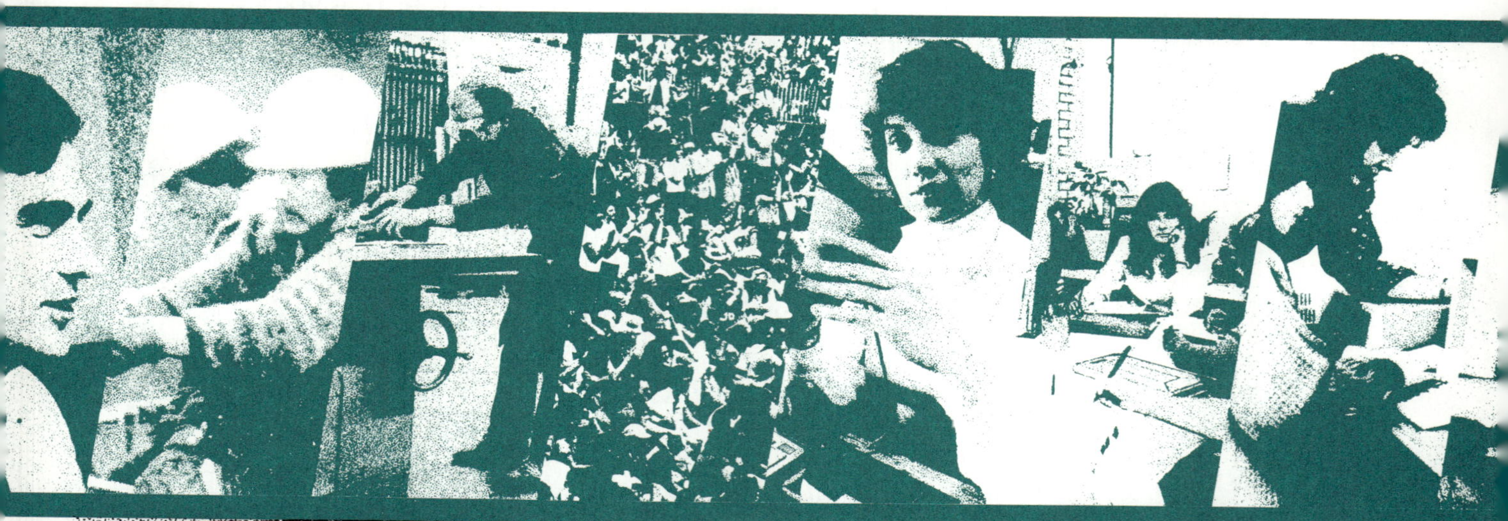

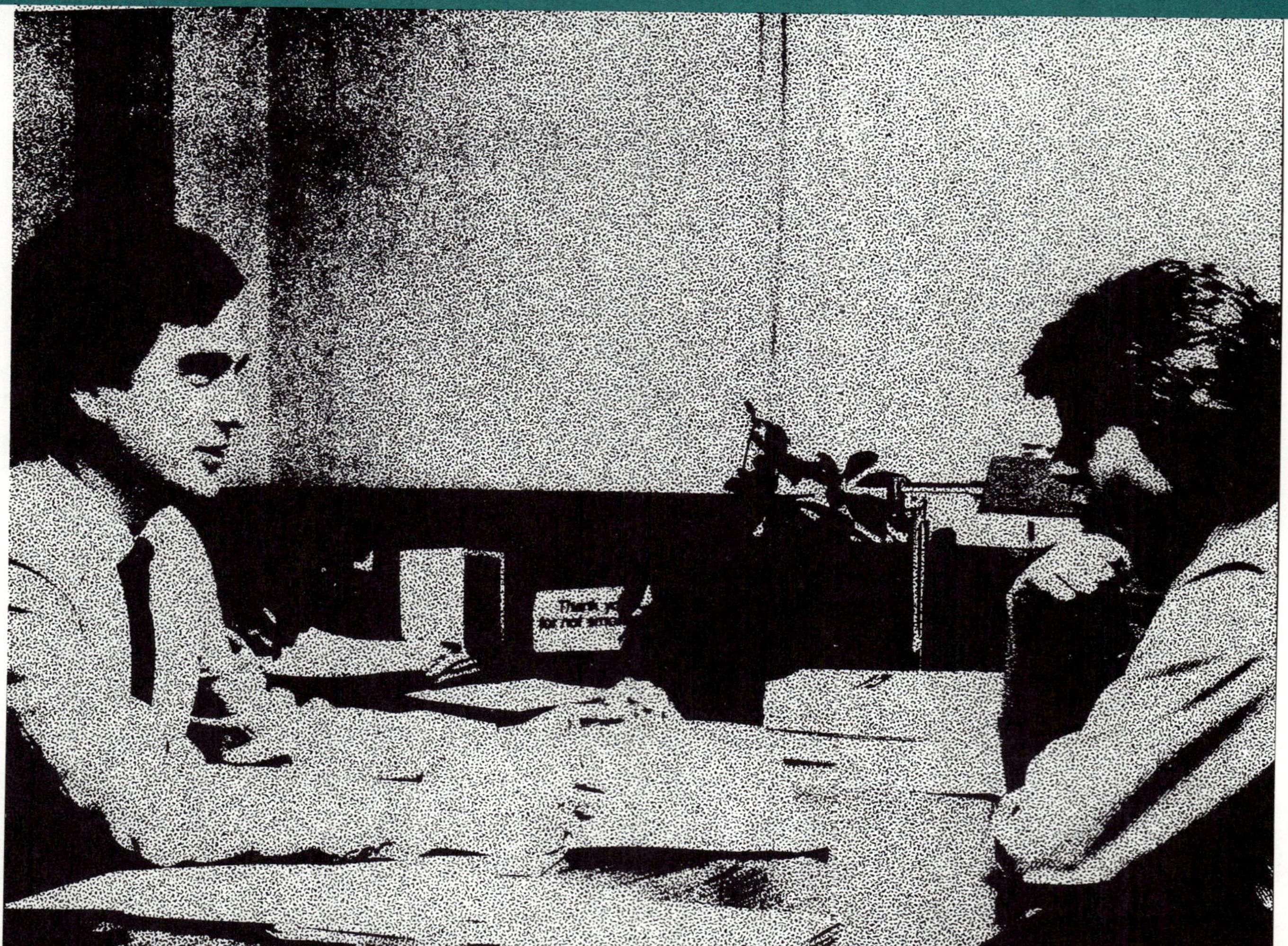

CHAPTER 13

Business Report and Technical Writing

GOALS

At the end of this chapter you should be able to
1. distinguish between the styles of informational and analytical reports;
2. identify the steps in report writing;
3. prepare visual aids appropriate for a report;
4. identify and explain the purpose of the various parts of a report; and
5. format a report attractively.

VOCABULARY BUILDING

onerous
preliminary
designate
warranted
respectively
axis
crosshatching
leaders
expend
appendices

VIEWPOINTS

Marcel, whom you met in Chapter 4, is also working at Eastern as part of his school's co-operative education program. Marcel's placement is in the Department of Human Resources. He is approaching Ken, who supervises the department.

MARCEL: Ken, I wonder if you could spare a bit of time to help me with a report I'm writing.

KEN: What's the report about, Marcel?

MARCEL: I've been asked to prepare a report on the company's flexible working hours policy. They want to know the impact the policy has had so far. I'm also to make recommendations for changes to the policy based on my findings.

KEN: And what help can I give you? Is it material you are looking for?

MARCEL: No, Leila gave me the company policy material and I interviewed all the department supervisors who have employees on flexible hours. I also wrote to the Provincial Government and they sent me the pamphlets they have published on flexible working hours. So it's not material I need at this stage.

KEN: You've been quite thorough in your researching. Now where do I fit in?

MARCEL: My problem is that I'm not sure how to deal with the pile of material I've accumulated. I think I need some guidance putting it together into a report. I was wondering if you had any reports on file that might help me. If you have, I'd like to borrow them to get some ideas on how to organize the report.

KEN: Yes, I think I can find a couple that might be of some use to you. You might also check Marketing. Some of their reports are fancier than ours. They use more graphs and colour that you might find interesting. Monica Tham is the person you could speak to there. I'll give her a call and let her know what you want.

QUESTIONS

1. Based on what you have learned from Chapters 6 and 7, what advice can you give to Marcel on organizing his material and getting started with the writing of the report?
2. What kind of graphic material could Marcel use in his report? What points would the material illustrate?
3. If you were Ken, would you offer to help Marcel organize the report, or would you provide him with sample reports to help him do the organizing himself? Why?

Figure 13-1
It is not unusual to be asked to undertake a task you have not practised at school, as Marcel is asked to do.

INTRODUCTION

One of the problem-solving tools used by decision makers in business is the report. The report gathers, summarizes, and analyzes information; it may also recommend solutions to a problem, if required. In this section we will be distinguishing between the various types of reports, examining the steps taken in writing them, and describing the structure and format of reports.

You may, like Marcel, be called upon by your employer to write a report on some aspect of the business. By learning in this chapter the procedures and form, the task will not seem so **onerous**, or burdensome, as it did to Marcel.

STYLES AND TYPES OF REPORTS

Marcel was right in asking for sample reports to study since there are many forms a business report can take. There are two basic styles of report — the formal and the informal, and two main types of report — informational and analytical. The style and the type of the report will depend, of course, on its purpose and audience.

Informal and Formal Reports

Formal reports are usually longer and more detailed than informal ones. The reason for the longer length is that the problems examined in the formal report are generally more complex. More information will be required and the subject will be analyzed in greater depth than in an informal report. Another difference is that the informal report is usually written for internal circulation, whereas the formal report can be written for either internal or external circulation.

Informational Reports

If you were asked to prepare an informational report, you would be expected to present facts or assemble background information that will assist managers in making decisions. No recommendations or evaluations will be required on your part. An informational report might provide current data on inventory on hand, on order, on back order, and in process for shipment. Another report might give the cumulative expenses involved in each job shipped and in production for the past six months. Annual reports, progress and sales reports, inspection reports, accident reports, procedural manuals, and training manuals are other examples of informational reports.

Analytical Reports

An analytical report goes beyond the reporting of facts. It makes recommendations on possible solutions to the problem being researched, or offers evaluations of the data or the various courses of action open. Analytical reports may be used as aids for managers making decisions about a problem or as guidelines for future action.

Proposals, feasibility reports, budget reports, and product analyses are examples of analytical reports.

STEPS IN WRITING A REPORT

As you read this section, much of the material will seem familiar to you. That is because it incorporates information and suggestions made in previous chapters dealing with making presentations and composing written material. The process is similar for preparing any written material. When writing a report, follow the steps outlined below:
- do a **preliminary**, or preparatory, analysis of the problem
- gather the data
- evaluate and organize the data into an outline
- draw conclusions and make recommendations, when required
- write, edit, and publish

Do a Preliminary Analysis

In this first stage of report writing, you will need to determine the purpose, **designate**, or specify, the audience, and define the problem (if you are writing an analytical report).

Knowing *why* you are writing the report can save a lot of confusion, frustration, and unnecessary work. Ask yourself the questions: Why am I preparing this report? Is it to present information? If so, why is the information needed? What will be done with it? Am I required to make recommendations? Am I expected to suggest a solution to a problem? When you have answered these questions, write out a statement of purpose on a card and keep it handy as you progress through the remainder of the steps. Referring to it frequently will help you to keep on track.

The importance of designating the audience has been stressed in other chapters of this book, but the repetition is **warranted**, or justified. Will the report be read by company personnel only, or is it to have a wider circulation outside the company? Knowing who the audience is will help you to select the appropriate style and tone. Most internal reports that will be read by management and possibly staff are written in a less formal style than those to be read by shareholders, government agencies, banking institutions, or clients. The vocabulary and contents will also be geared to the audience. Will the reader understand the technical terms, and be familiar with the company structure and aims? Will the reader need background information before an examination of the problem or an analysis of the data can be attempted? Addressing the report to the specific audience for whom it is intended helps to ensure appropriate wording, sufficient information, and the proper perspective.

For an informational report, stating the purpose is usually sufficient, but for an analytical report, defining the problem is necessary. Framing the problem by answering a series of basic questions beginning with what, why, when, where, and who will help to define the problem clearly. What do I want to know? Why do I need to know it?

When did this problem arise and when does it need to be resolved? Where in the company operation does the problem appear? Who will benefit from the resolution of this problem and how?

If, for instance, you were investigating the feasibility of introducing robotics to your company, some of the questions you might ask are: What do I need to know about robotics to evaluate their advantages and disadvantages? Why are robotics being considered? When did the need for robotics become apparent? When could robotics be introduced and when would the system begin to pay for itself? Where could robotics be applied efficiently within the company? Who could benefit from robotics?

When you are not familiar with the subject of the report, you will need help from others in answering these questions. Your supervisor may be able to provide some of the information, or will be able to direct you to those who are knowledgeable on the subject. Writing out a comprehensive definition of the problem is the next step. Your discussions with others and the answers you have compiled to the basic questions should help with this important step.

Gather the Data

Gathering data for a report is the same as gathering data for a presentation. Data can come from primary sources — your own knowledge and the information gained from interviewing others — or from secondary sources — videotapes and a wide variety of printed materials, including company files, handbooks, encyclopedias, journals, annual reports, and newspapers. Recording secondary sources and computer searches were discussed in Chapter 10. As suggested in that chapter, recording your data on index cards or strips of paper makes it easier to arrange and rearrange your material.

As you collect data, make sure that it is relevant to the problem by referring frequently to the statement of purpose or the definition of the problem. Does the data relate to the main points you want to make or explore? In the example of robotics, some of the main points might be start-up cost, maintenance costs, production results, union considerations, and benefits. Decide where the data fits in with your main points.

To simplify the task, combine similar data and depict material graphically if it lends itself to graphic treatment. Later in this chapter we will be discussing the uses of graphs and charts.

Evaluate and Organize the Data

When you feel that you have gathered all the necessary data, lay out your cards or pieces of paper on your desk. Start by labelling cards for each major point and placing these cards in a row across your desk. Then under each of the main points, place the relevant data cards or strips of paper. Figure 13-2 illustrates such an arrangement.

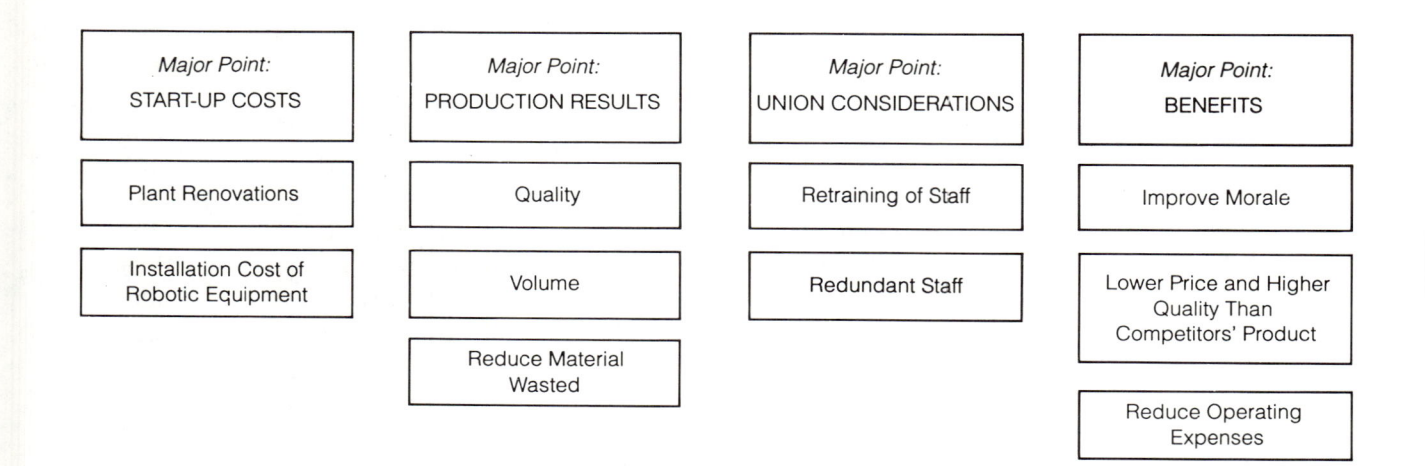

Major Point: START-UP COSTS	Major Point: PRODUCTION RESULTS	Major Point: UNION CONSIDERATIONS	Major Point: BENEFITS
Plant Renovations	Quality	Retraining of Staff	Improve Morale
Installation Cost of Robotic Equipment	Volume	Redundant Staff	Lower Price and Higher Quality Than Competitors' Product
	Reduce Material Wasted		Reduce Operating Expenses

Figure 13-2
Arrange your cards according to your major points.

If you end up with cards that do not belong under any main point, ask yourself if the information is necessary. In some cases you may find that you need to develop another main point that had not seemed apparent in earlier planning stages. In other cases the data may not be important enough to the problem to keep. Next, go back and re-read each card to verify that it is in the proper column. A card you thought was applicable on first reading may be irrelevant and should be discarded.

Taking each point in turn, read the column of cards under it to determine if there are any gaps requiring additional data. When you are satisfied with the material, choose an appropriate organizational pattern. A summary of the various organizational patterns is presented below. For an explanation of each pattern, refer to Chapter 6.

ORGANIZATIONAL PATTERNS

Chronological	Spatial
Topical	Cause and Effect
Comparison	Contrast
Problem/Solution	Specific to General

We mentioned earlier that reports could be formal or informal. Generally, reports that are prepared for distribution outside the company or for company executives are formal. All other reports are considered to be informal. In formal reports, no personal pronouns — I, me, you, we, us — are used. In informal reports, personal pronouns are acceptable and tend to make the report less impersonal.

Draw Conclusions and Make Recommendations

If your report is informational, this step will not be necessary. In an analytical report, conclusions are drawn and answers are offered to problems. Each conclusion or answer must be based on data presented in previous sections of the report. Consequently, no new data is presented at this point in the report.

The number of conclusions reached depends on the nature of the problem you are solving. In the robotics example, the conclusion might be: Robotics should be introduced on the assembly line with the installation completed within 18 months.

The recommendations follow the conclusion(s). They outline the actions that should be taken in order to implement the conclusion(s). Once again, using the robotics example, the recommendations might be: Based on the conclusion of this study, the following recommendations are made:

1. An announcement should be sent to shareholders and all company employees outlining the plan and its benefits.
2. A joint union-management committee should be formed to plan the retraining of employees.
3. A tender should be issued immediately for robotic equipment.

There are two plans to choose from for presenting the conclusions and recommendations. The first is the direct plan, in which you begin your report with a short summary, move to the conclusions and recommendations, and then present the analysis of the information you have gathered. The second is the indirect plan, in which the conclusions and recommendations are presented last. Informal reports usually follow the direct plan so that the reader is provided with the findings immediately. However, if the recommendations are not what the reader is hoping for, or if you are trying to persuade the reader to do something, use the indirect plan.

Write, Edit, and Publish

You are now ready to start writing the first draft of your report. For this first draft spelling, grammar, and cohesion are not particularly important. They can be corrected in a later draft. The important thing is to get your thoughts down on paper. When the first draft is completed, edit your work following the three-readings approach outlined in Chapter 7.

Summary of Editing
First Reading: Check if the purpose has been met. Place marks in the margin to indicate trouble spots.
Second Reading: Correct the problems noted during the first reading. Verify the accuracy of quotations and numerical data.
Third Reading: Locate and correct errors in language and style.

Once you have finished all the editing and revision stages, your report is ready for publication.

The importance of the appearance of published documents has been discussed before. In the same way that letters adhered to rules of format and appearance, reports do as well. The appearance of your report creates the first impression on the reader. The following is a sample format that can be used.

The introduction is considered to be the first page of the report. The title, in block capitals, is placed 5 cm from the top edge of the paper.

Business reports are
1. informational
2. analytical.

When writing a report
1. analyze
2. gather data
3. evaluate and organize data
4. draw conclusions and make recommendations as required
5. write, edit, and publish the report.

On successive pages, the title is placed 2 to 3 cm from the top edge, lined up with the left margin. On the same line, but placed at the right margin, the page number appears. Paragraphs are indented five spaces and may be single or double spaced, depending on company practice. A blank line is left between paragraphs. At the bottom of each page a 2 to 3 cm margin is left.

The left and right margins should be the same width as the bottom margin (2 to 3 cm) unless the report is being bound. For a bound report, you will need to move the type over to the right five characters to allow space for binding the left sides of the pages.

The letter or memorandum of transmittal, title page, summary, table of contents, and bibliography all appear on separate pages. The other sections of the report follow each other from one page to the next.

In the next section you will be taking a look at the use of visual aids for presenting information in reports.

APPLICATIONS

1. Obtain a copy of a company report. Annual reports may be obtained by writing to the head office of a company. If you have a part-time job or co-operative education placement, ask your supervisor at the company for a copy of a report prepared by the company. Analyze the report. State whether the report is informational or analytical, formal or informal. Identify the purpose, audience, and plan for the report.

2. You have been asked by your teacher to prepare an informational report about your part-time job, work experience position, or co-operative education placement. State whether the report should be formal or informal. Outline a plan for the report. The outline should contain three major sections. List three points to be included in each section.

3. Develop a plan for an analytical report to be presented to your principal on whether the parking lot at your school should be enlarged.

4. Using your school and/or community library, locate a handbook and yearbook. Write a brief description of the contents of each book.

5. Develop a plan and gather data for a report on one of the following topics:
   - job sharing
   - flexible hours
   - equal opportunity
   - mandatory retirement
   - sexual harassment

   Discuss the topic with your teacher to determine whether the report should be informational or analytical.

VISUAL AIDS

We discussed visual aids in Chapter 4 and noted how they can reinforce and clarify material in an oral presentation. Visual aids can also enhance a written report by drawing attention to written information, by making written points clearer, and by adding variety to the report to keep the reader's attention.

Tables, charts, graphs, photographs, maps, and diagrams are aids that can be used effectively in reports. Generally, material appearing in tabular form is referred to as a "Table" and other visual aids are referred to as "Figures." Each table and figure must be numbered and labelled precisely so that the reader is in no doubt as to its meaning and relevance to the text. The titles or captions should be concise, with no superfluous words.

Tables

Tables consist of data systematically arranged, usually in rows and columns. Readers are able to comprehend the data more easily when presented in this way than if the data were contained within the text. Consider the following paragraph from a report.

> From my visit to each of the five companies, I was able to ascertain the following about salaries. Acme Printers has a beginning salary of $200 per week, after three years, $300, and after five years, $500. However, Business Forms Ltd. has a beginning salary of $200, after three years, $325, and after five years, $450. On the other hand, Multi-Forms starts at $225, after three years is $325, and after five years is $425. Then, of course, there are Printers Inc. and Versatile Printing Ltd. with beginning salaries of $175 and $225, after three years, $250 and $300, and after five years $400 and $425 **respectively** (relating to each of the above in the order given).

Although the data is not complex, it is difficult to digest when written as part of the text. The reader is forced to study it closely in order to interpret the data. Consider the same paragraph presented in tabular format.

Table 3.1

Comparison of Weekly Salaries for Five Local Printers

Company Name	Beginning Salary	After Three Years	After Five Years
Acme Printers	$200	$300	$500
Business Forms Ltd.	200	325	450
Multi-Forms	225	325	425
Printers Inc.	175	250	400
Versatile Printing Ltd.	225	300	425

BUSINESS REPORT AND TECHNICAL WRITING

When the numerical information is arranged as a table, the reader can grasp it more quickly and easily. If the intent in the sample table was to compare the salaries at each of the levels, the high and low salaries can be picked out readily.

Factual information can also be presented in tabular form, for example, the table on organizational patterns in Chapter 6. The table of contents at the beginning of a book is another use of tabular format.

Graphs and Charts

Another way of presenting statistical data is by the use of graphs and charts, in which data is depicted visually. A visual presentation of data can be more effective than a tabular one when your purpose is to highlight a pattern of increase or decrease or to show relative sizes of different elements.

Line Graph

In the line graph, also called a line chart, the vertical **axis**, the straight line that forms one of a pair of intersecting arms in a graph, begins at zero and increases in equal increments as you move away from the origin. The horizontal axis measures another element in a similar fashion. Both axes are labelled to indicate what each measures. Figure 13-3(a) shows an example of a line graph.

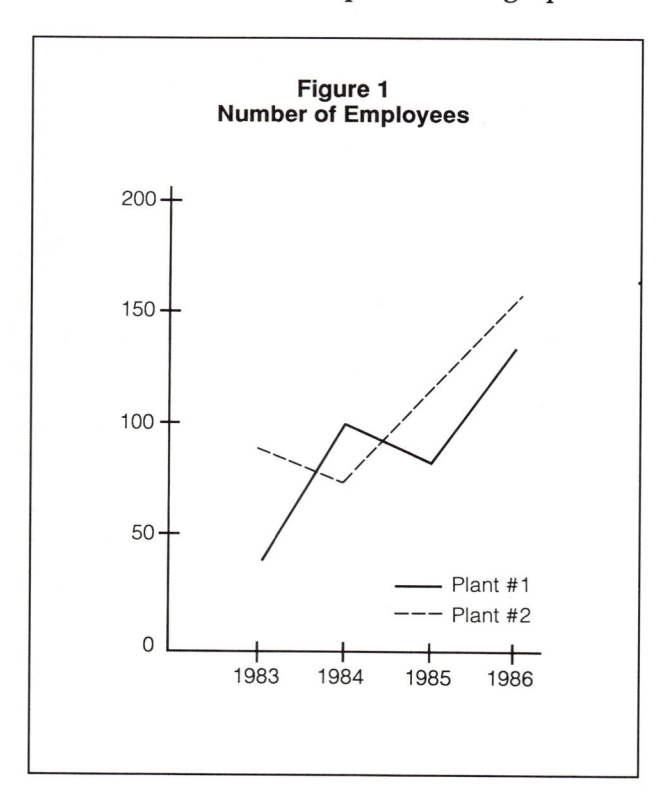

Figure 13-3(a)
Line Graph

274   PART TWO: COMMUNICATION IN BUSINESS

Bar Graph

The bars in a bar graph may be oriented vertically or horizontally. The bars will vary in length, but the width remains constant. When colour, shading, or **crosshatching**, shading done with a series of intersecting straight lines, are used, more factors than two can be represented. In some cases where there is a wide range of values along one of the axes, the axis would end up being much longer than the other axis. This problem is solved by inserting a break between zero and the first interval. See Figure 13-3(b).

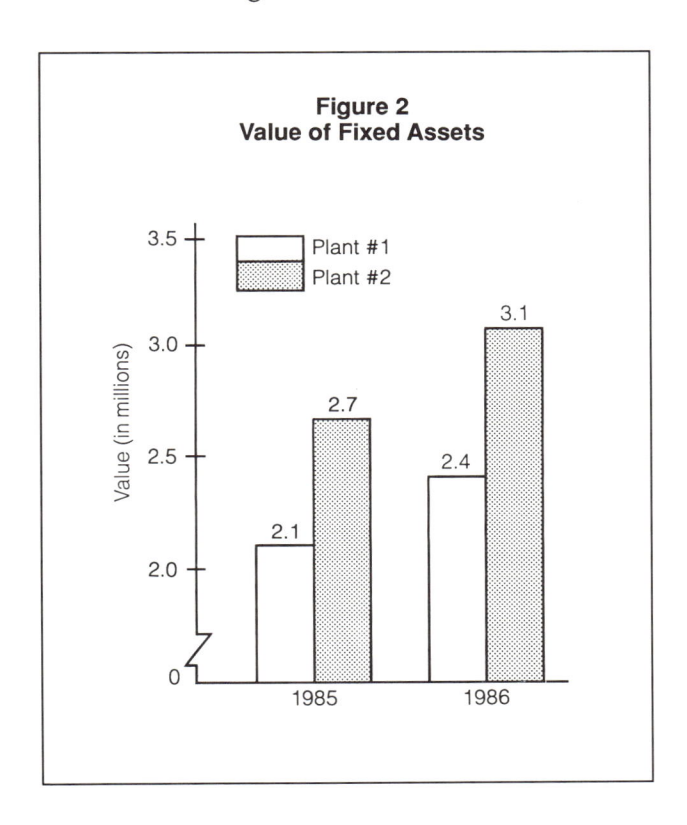

Figure 13-3(b)
Bar Graph

**Figure 2
Value of Fixed Assets**

Pie Chart or Circle Graph

A pie chart or circle graph shows how large a portion of the whole each element comprises. Often this type of graph is used to portray financial information. For example, the portion of each dollar granted to different departments of an institute is represented in a pie chart.

When making a pie chart or circle graph, you will need to calculate the number of degrees of the circle each of your elements should be given. Use the following mathematical formula:

$$\frac{\text{value of part}}{\text{total of all parts}} \times 360 = \text{number of degrees}$$

BUSINESS REPORT AND TECHNICAL WRITING

Breakdown of Expenses

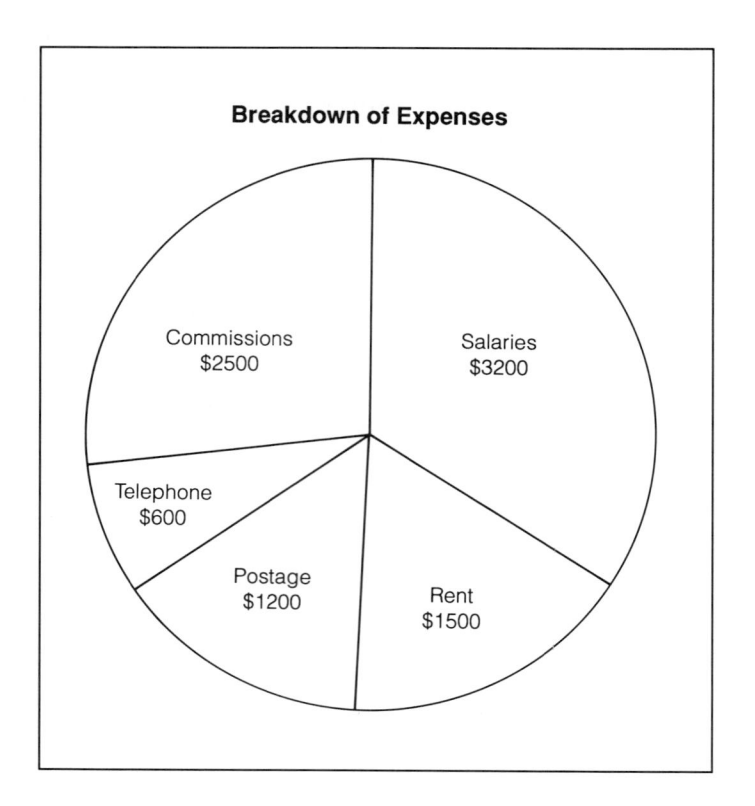

(Pie chart showing:)
- Commissions $2500
- Salaries $3200
- Telephone $600
- Postage $1200
- Rent $1500

Figure 13-4
Pie Chart

For the pie chart shown in Figure 13-4, the following calculations were made:

Total of all parts = 3200 + 2500 + 1500 + 1200 + 600 = 9000

Salaries = $\frac{3200}{9000}$ x 360 = 128°

Commissions = $\frac{2500}{9000}$ x 360 = 100°

Rent = $\frac{1500}{9000}$ x 360 = 60°

Postage = $\frac{1200}{9000}$ x 360 = 48°

Telephone = $\frac{600}{9000}$ x 360 = 24°

After drawing a circle, use a protractor to mark the degrees for each part. Start with the largest part at the 12 o'clock position and move clockwise in descending order of the size of the parts. The miscellaneous category, however, is always placed last regardless of its size. Place your labels of the parts within the circle. For those parts that are too small to label inside the circle, place the label outside and draw an arrow to the related part.

Organizational Chart

Organizational charts show the overall structure of a department or organization and the line of authority. They are read from the top to the bottom with positions of equal value located on the same line.

Look at Figure 8-3 on page 158 for an example of an organizational chart.

Flow Chart

Flow charts have developed out of the computer industry. They show the steps in a process from beginning to end, usually with choices to be made along the way. You can use the symbols used by computer programmers or design your own symbols. A flow chart is illustrated in Figure 13-5.

Figure 13-5
Flow Chart

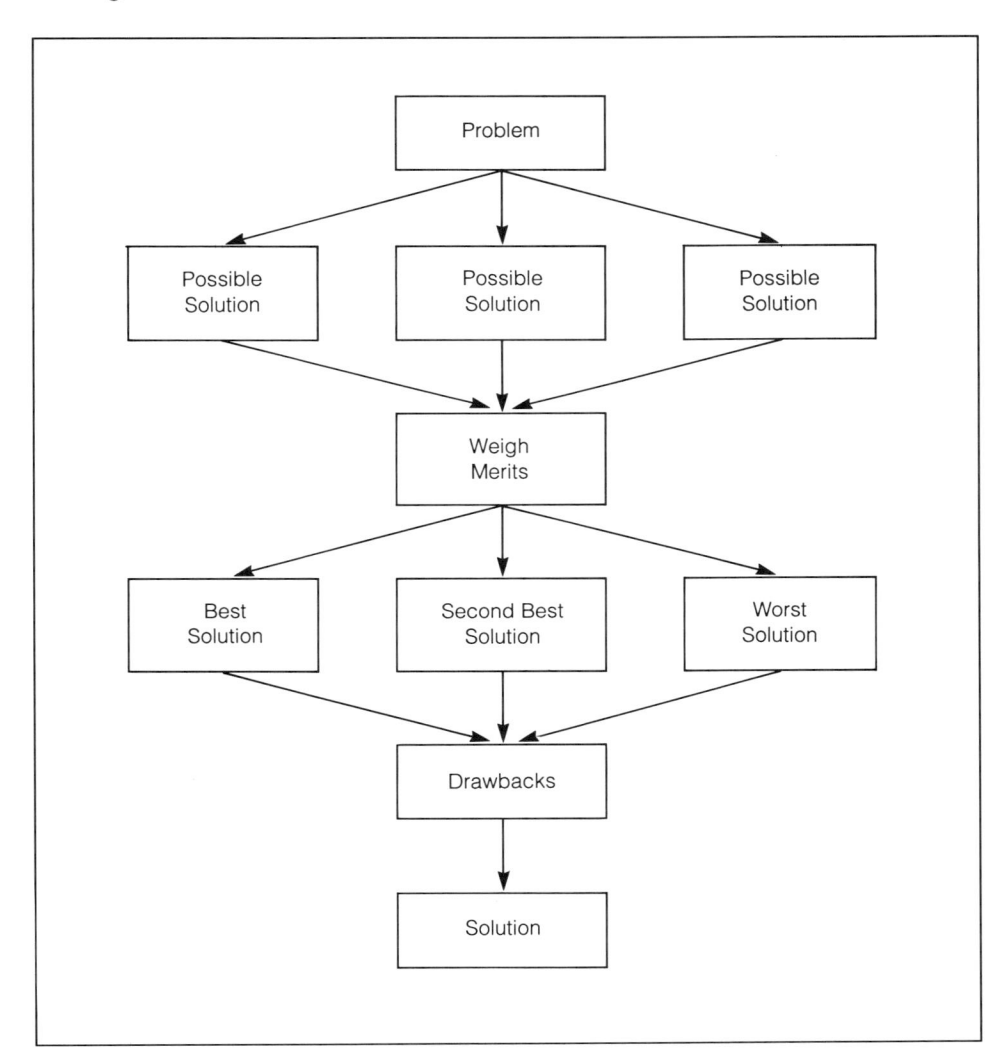

```
                    Problem
           ↙           ↓           ↘
    Possible      Possible       Possible
    Solution      Solution       Solution
           ↘           ↓           ↙
                  Weigh
                  Merits
           ↙           ↓           ↘
      Best        Second Best      Worst
    Solution       Solution       Solution
           ↘           ↓           ↙
                 Drawbacks
                     ↓
                 Solution
```

Visual aids in reports include
1. tables
2. charts
3. graphs
4. photographs
5. maps
6. exhibits.

Graphs and charts include
1. line chart
2. bar chart
3. pie chart
4. organizational chart
5. flow chart.

Other Visual Aids

If your report is a feasibility study on a new piece of machinery, you will probably want to include a diagram or photograph illustrating how it works or the various parts of which it is comprised. For another kind of report it may be useful to include a map to show the area under discussion.

BUSINESS REPORT AND TECHNICAL WRITING

APPLICATIONS

6. Using books in your school library, locate and photocopy examples of three different kinds of visual aids. Write a paragraph to accompany each example explaining the purpose of the aid and why the aid is better than written text.

7. Prepare a line chart to illustrate your school's enrolment during the last five years.

8. Using the information from Question 7, prepare a bar graph.

9. Prepare a bar graph showing both the school enrolment and Grade 9 enrolment during the last five years.

10. Prepare a pie chart to illustrate the current enrolment by grade at your school.

11. Prepare an organizational chart of your school.

12. Prepare a flow chart to illustrate the procedure for dealing with absenteeism at your school.

PARTS OF A REPORT

The complexity of your report will determine which of the following parts you will need to include.

A. Preliminary Parts
   Letter or memorandum of transmittal
   Title Page
   Summary or Abstract
   Table of Contents.
B. Body
   Introduction
      Background of the problem
      Statement of the problem
      Scope of the problem
      Methods of gathering data
   Data and Discussion of Data
   Ending
      Summary
      Conclusion(s)
      Recommendation(s)
C. Supplementary Parts
   References or Bibliography
   Figures (if not included in the Body)
   Tables (if not included in the Body)
   Appendix or Appendices

Preliminary Parts

Letter or Memorandum of Transmittal

The letter or memorandum of transmittal should either accompany the report or should be sent in advance to the person who authorized it. Either binding the letter with the report, or enclosing it in a separate envelope is acceptable. For internal reports, a memorandum of transmittal is often clipped to the cover of the report.

The letter of transmittal should include authorization to write the report, the subject matter of the report, and the method of sending the report. If you feel it is appropriate, you may include a synopsis of the problem and a summary of the conclusions and recommendations in the letter of transmittal.

Attached is the report on the feasibility of introducing robotics in our assembly plant as was requested by Management Council on November 27.

Although the report is limited to plant #1, the four areas discussed are applicable to all our plants. These areas are start-up cost, production results, union considerations, and benefits.

If clarification of the content or further research is required, I would be happy to make the necessary adjustments before the next Management Council meeting.

Figure 13-6
Body of a memorandum of transmittal

Title Page

Formal reports are usually bound within a front and back cover. The title page of the report should be just inside the cover (or it can be the front cover of the report) and should give the title, who the report is for, who prepared it, and the date as in Figure 13-7.

FEASIBILITY REPORT
ON
IMPLEMENTATION OF ROBOTICS

Prepared for
R. Pfaff, President

Prepared by
L. Meighan, Planning Department
December 30, 198_

Figure 13-7
Title page

Summary

The summary is considered by many people to be the most important part of the report since it is the part, if nothing else, that will be read. Busy executives have not the time to read everything that crosses their desks. They will often read the summary first and skim the remainder of the report for specific details. They may decide, on the basis of what is written in the summary, to pass it on to others for consideration or to put it aside until later. It is therefore important, if you want your report to be read, to write an interesting and informative summary. Some reports consist primarily of technical data and the reader depends on the summary to provide an overview that is easy to read.

The summary is a synopsis of the report. It briefly covers the background of the problem, the purpose and scope of the report, the methods used in gathering the data, the highlights of the data, and the conclusions and recommendations.

Table of Contents

The table of contents shows the reader what material is covered and how it is organized, and assists the reader in finding particular sections of the report. In short reports the table of contents will often be omitted. However, in longer reports it should always be included.

The headings of the sections, worded exactly as they appear in the report, are listed down the left margin, with headings of lower rank indented. The page on which the section begins is entered down the right margin as shown in Figure 13-8. Often a row of periods, called **leaders**, connects the left hand headings with the right hand page numbers. If leaders are overused, however, the table of contents will appear cluttered and less, rather than more, readable.

TABLE OF CONTENTS

Overview	1
Start-up Cost	2
Production Results	4
Union Considerations	6
Benefits	9
Summary	11
Conclusions	11
Recommendations	12
Appendix A: Five Year Forecast of Savings	14

Figure 13-8
Table of contents

Body

Introduction

The introduction outlines the background of the problem, states the problem, gives its scope, and describes the methods used to gather data. This section should also state who authorized the study, when, and the terms of reference, if given. See Figure 13-9.

The background information is intended to familiarize the reader with the circumstances that gave rise to the problem. You may wish to include a description of past events and work up to the present situation, or it may be sufficient to describe the present circumstances.

**FEASIBILITY REPORT
ON IMPLEMENTATION OF ROBOTICS**

Overview

This report has been prepared to address questions raised on this matter at the Management Council meeting in November.

During the past year, the Vice-President and three Plant Supervisors have toured five Canadian manufacturing plants presently using robotics on their assembly lines. At the November meeting of Management Council, this group reported that the technology was sufficiently developed and had a satisfactory operational record to warrant further investigation into installing robotics in our plant facilities.

The present feasibility report was set up to determine whether robotics would be a sound investment for the company at this time. Both long term and short term factors are considered. Data in this report have been confined to plant #1.

In preparing this report, I held discussions with three manufacturers of robotics equipment, the shop stewards of our two unions, and the company personnel who had been on the plant visitations during the past year. Technology magazines and scientific writing were also searched for material on robotics.

Figure 13-9
Introduction to a report

A clear and concise statement of the problem or the purpose of the report explains to the reader why the study was carried out and the report written. The section on scope describes what ground is covered by the report and identifies what the limits of the report are. Giving the scope of the problem and the limitations of the report will let the reader know what has and has not been included in the report and will prepare the reader for the information that follows.

The reader also needs to know the sources of information used in the report. Identify all primary sources that you used. For example, if you conducted interviews and circulated questionnaires, state the numbers of each and name those involved. Secondary sources are named as well unless they are numerous. If there are more than three or four, they should be identified in the references section. However, you could make a general statement about the nature of the secondary sources in the introduction.

Data and Discussion of Data

This section is normally the longest one in the report. It contains all the information the reader will need to understand how you approached the problem, dealt with it, and were led to the conclusions you make in the following section. You should organize the material in a logical manner so that readers can follow your facts and arguments easily and will not be confused. All data should have a direct relationship to the problem identified in the introduction.

Break up your material into main units with margin headings or centered headings, using an appropriate organizational plan. The headings will help the reader follow your line of reasoning, they will break the material up for easier reading, and they will provide additional information for the table of contents. In the report on robotics, for example, some of the margin headings would be: Start-up Cost, Production Results, Union Considerations, and Benefits. If the topic described by the margin heading is to be discussed in smaller units, then subsidiary headings may be used. These headings should be distinguished from the centered headings or margin headings. You might number them, underline them, capitalize the first letter in each word only, or use some system that will indicate to the reader that these headings are not as important as the centered or margin headings. Examine the headings in this chapter. Can you tell the rank of each one? What system has been used?

Visual aids should be referred to in the text and should be positioned in the text as close as possible to the place where they are mentioned. That way the reader can easily examine them as they are discussed.

Ending

Summary

An informational report ends with a summary of the major points. Most reports, however, begin with a summary as stated earlier.

Conclusions

Conclusions are not found in informational reports. They state briefly what you have drawn from the body of the report and answer the problem posed in the earlier sections. No new information should be presented in the conclusions section. If there are several conclusions, present your most important conclusion first and the remainder in decreasing order of importance.

Recommendations

Recommendations are written for analytical reports only. They are stated in a positive and convincing manner, using the active rather than the passive voice. Say "I (or we) recommend," not "It is recommended." Include what should be done, instead of what should not be done.

Sometimes writers **expend**, or use up, their energy on the research and presentation of the data in the body of the report and put very little energy into the ending. Remember though, that the purpose of the report is to find an answer to a problem, so the answer should be clearly presented in the conclusions and recommendations.

Supplementary Parts

References or Bibliography

This section contains the sources of the information used in the report. Any document that has been referred to in the report must be identified in the list of references or bibliography. In a list of references, the documents are often numbered and listed in the order they are referred to in the report. The same reference number is used in the text. A bibliography lists all the documents used in alphabetical order of authors' surnames. The author's name, the title of the document, publisher, date, volume and page numbers are given, as shown in Figure 13-10.

Figure 13-10
Bibliography

BIBLIOGRAPHY

Douglas, Paul, *Memory for Management*, Canadian Pendant Publishing Ltd., Edmonton, 1982

Faustmann, John, "John MacDonald had a firm. . .," *Canadian Business*, February 1986, pp. 60-69.

Shuman, John, et al., *Communication Skills for the World of Work*, John Wiley and Sons Canada Limited, Toronto, 1981.

Appendix

The appendix allows the writer to make material available to the reader without putting it in the main report. Documents such as newspaper articles, letters, excerpts from other reports, and charts may be put in the appendix section as long as they are relevant to the report. These documents are not essential to an understanding of the report, but may provide additional information that will support it. The material might be too technical for most readers to read, or its inclusion in the main body of the report might make it too bulky.

The order of the material in the appendix is the same as the order in which it was referred to in the body of the report, for example, Appendix A, Appendix B. If the material in the appendix is all the same kind, for instance, all tables, then only one appendix need be used. **Appendices** are listed in the table of contents.

APPLICATIONS

Reports may consist of
1. *preliminary parts*
2. *body*
3. *supplementary parts.*

Preliminary parts include
1. *letter of transmittal*
2. *title page*
3. *summary*
4. *table of contents.*

The body consists of
1. *introduction*
2. *data and discussion*
3. *ending.*

Supplementary parts of a report consist of
1. *bibliography*
2. *appendix.*

13. Prepare a report using the data gathered in Question 5 earlier in this chapter. Your report should include a bibliography or appendices. Discuss your report with your teacher to determine what parts of a common report are appropriate for your report.

14. Write the conclusions and recommendations for a report you have prepared on whether a new gymnasium should be built before a new library at your school.

15. Using the resources in your school library, prepare a bibliography for one of the following topics:
water pollution
nuclear energy in Canada
solar heating
use of computers in farming
diesel engines
Present your answer in the proper format for a bibliography.

CHAPTER SUMMARY

Types of business reports
- informational
- analytical

Tone of business reports
- formal, if they are sent outside the company or to company executives
- informal, if they are used internally

Use a Problem-Solving Approach to Prepare a Report
- do a preliminary analysis (purpose, audience, plan)
- gather the data
- evaluate and organize the data
- draw conclusions and make recommendations, when required
- write the report in proper format

Visual aids in a report
- tables
- charts
- graphs
- photographs
- maps
- exhibits

The parts of a report
 A. Preliminary Parts
    Letter or memorandum of transmittal
    Title Page

　　　　Summary
　　　　Table of Contents
　　B. Body
　　　　Introduction
　　　　　　Background of the problem
　　　　　　Statement of the problem
　　　　　　Scope of the problem
　　　　　　Methods of gathering data
　　　　Data and Discussion of Data
　　　　Ending
　　　　　　Summary
　　　　　　Conclusions
　　　　　　Recommendations
　　C. Supplementary Parts
　　　　Bibliography
　　　　Appendix or Appendices

MAKING IT WORK

1. Some companies and organizations publish newsletters which are distributed to subscribers. These newsletters may focus on particular occupations or topics. Read the following article taken from the IAPA publication, *Accident Prevention*.

   Questions
   (a) What does IAPA stand for?
   (b) Who would read this publication?
   (c) What is the central issue in this article?
   (d) What was the solution to the problem? Was it a logical solution?
   (e) In journalism, the answers to the questions who? what? where? when? why? should be answered in the beginning sentences. Using quotes from the article, show which of these questions has been answered in the first sentence of this article.
   (f) Describe the writing style used in this article.
   (g) Check in your library, at home, with your teachers, and at work to find copies of other newsletter publications. Post these on the bulletin board. Read an article from two other publications. What similarities do you notice in these publications?

2. In small groups, discuss what kinds of articles would be appropriate to include in a newsletter about your school. Each small group presents its ideas to the class. The class then compiles a list of suitable articles.

3. Publish a newsletter for your school based on the articles compiled in the previous activity.

4. Read the following case, then answer the questions that follow.

   On Thursday afternoon last week, as you were returning to your desk after your afternoon break, you were involved in an accident.

Figure 13-11
Newsletters in industry communicate developments to workers. This article will help answer the questions in Making It Work.

IAPA Accident Prevention — Profit from safety

Forktruck contest rules discussed

Some 30 division chairmen, section chairmen and forklift truck co-ordinators met at Toronto's Royal York Hotel recently at the invitation of IAPA president Ron Johnston to discuss safety measures for the Association's forklift truck competitions.

The main issue was the wearing of hard hats and approved footwear by competitors at the forklift truck contests. Several delegates expressed the view that drivers unused to wearing hard hats in their work environment might perform poorly during the competition, and that little if any danger exists during a contest. Mr. Johnston said he had reviewed all documents on this matter, and remarked that attempts to resolve the question by both the Administrative Committee and the co-ordinators had been going on since 1982.

However, Mr. Johnston said, as safety professionals, our job is to make accident risks as low as possible, if not non-existent. The Administrative Committee had reviewed the accident statistics for forklift trucks and the legal implications of an accident during a competition. The findings convinced the Committee that a policy was needed on the wearing of protective equipment during any competition.

The Administrative Committee had ruled that CSA-approved head protection and safety footwear will be worn by contestants and officials

continued on page 3

during any IAPA forktruck competition, and that the chief judge has the responsibility of ensuring the policy is observed. As Mr. Johnston said in a later letter to delegates, "we must be seen to be observing our own preaching."

Leo Cassaday, IAPA past-president, said he agreed that IAPA must maintain an image, and since the competition simulates the work environment as closely as possible, all safety precautions must be used.

A second concern raised at the meeting was the apparent lack of communication between the two levels of volunteers. Some delegates felt that decisions made by the Administrative Committee were not being communicated to the co-ordinators, nor were they being asked for their input. Mr. Johnston commented that the Administrative Committee does indeed listen to volunteers and takes value from what it hears. However, the Committee has the responsibility of making the final decisions, which are not arrived at lightly. Both Mr. Johnston and Mr. Cassaday assured delegates that steps are being taken to improve communications both up and down the organizational ladder.

In closing, Mr. Johnston thanked the volunteers for the professional manner in which they had brought their concerns to the meeting. He also reinforced his statement that they would receive proper response to their concerns.

IAPA's Kent Division is sponsoring the All Ontario Forklift Truck Competition at Chatham Memorial Arena, Chatham, on June 15. Narrow Aisle Reach Truck Competitions will be held by Humber Division on June 22 at A&P Food Stores in Toronto, and by Upper York and Don Valley Divisions on November 16 at Steelcase Canada Ltd., Markham.

Since IAPA's Forklift Truck Competition is to simulate the work environment as closely as possible, the Administrative Committee has ruled that hard hats and safety footwear will be worn by contestants.

VOLUME 32, NUMBER 5, MAY 1985

Another employee, Brett, who was carrying a large stack of papers, came around the corner by the water cooler too sharply. He bumped into the water cooler, knocking it over. Pieces of glass from the cooler cut your legs in several places. Although no stitches were required, the doctor advised you to stay home, and off your feet for a few days.

When you returned to work, you were asked to write a description of the accident.

Write a formal description, supplying any details you feel are missing from the information given.

5. Read the following case, then answer the questions that follow.

When Martina came into work this morning, her employer greeted her with the statement "I thought you were going to have that job finished before you left yesterday." Martina's initial reaction is to become defensive and to say one of the following: "The drawings didn't arrive until late in the afternoon, so it isn't my fault."

"I didn't think you'd be in until lunch today, so I was going to finish the work this morning."

"Last week some of the others were late in completing work."

Give Martina some tips on how to accept criticism. What could she say in response to her employer's question?

PART · THREE

SUCCESS IN BUSINESS AND INDUSTRY

Chapter 14   Teamwork in Business and Industry
Chapter 15   Job Search

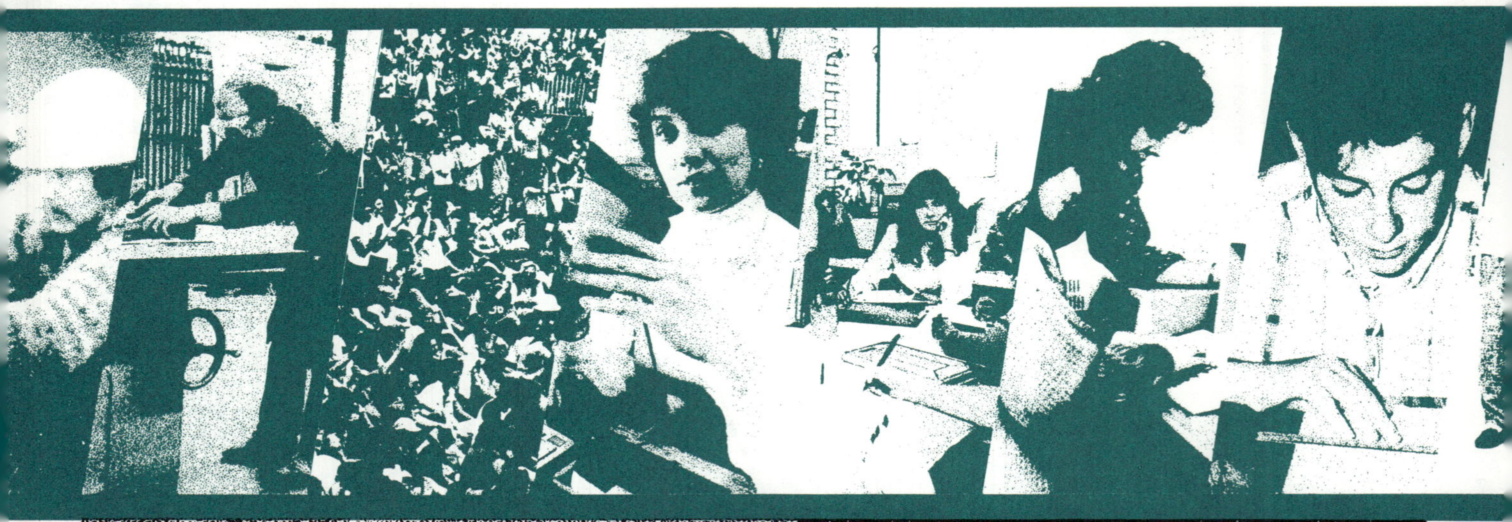

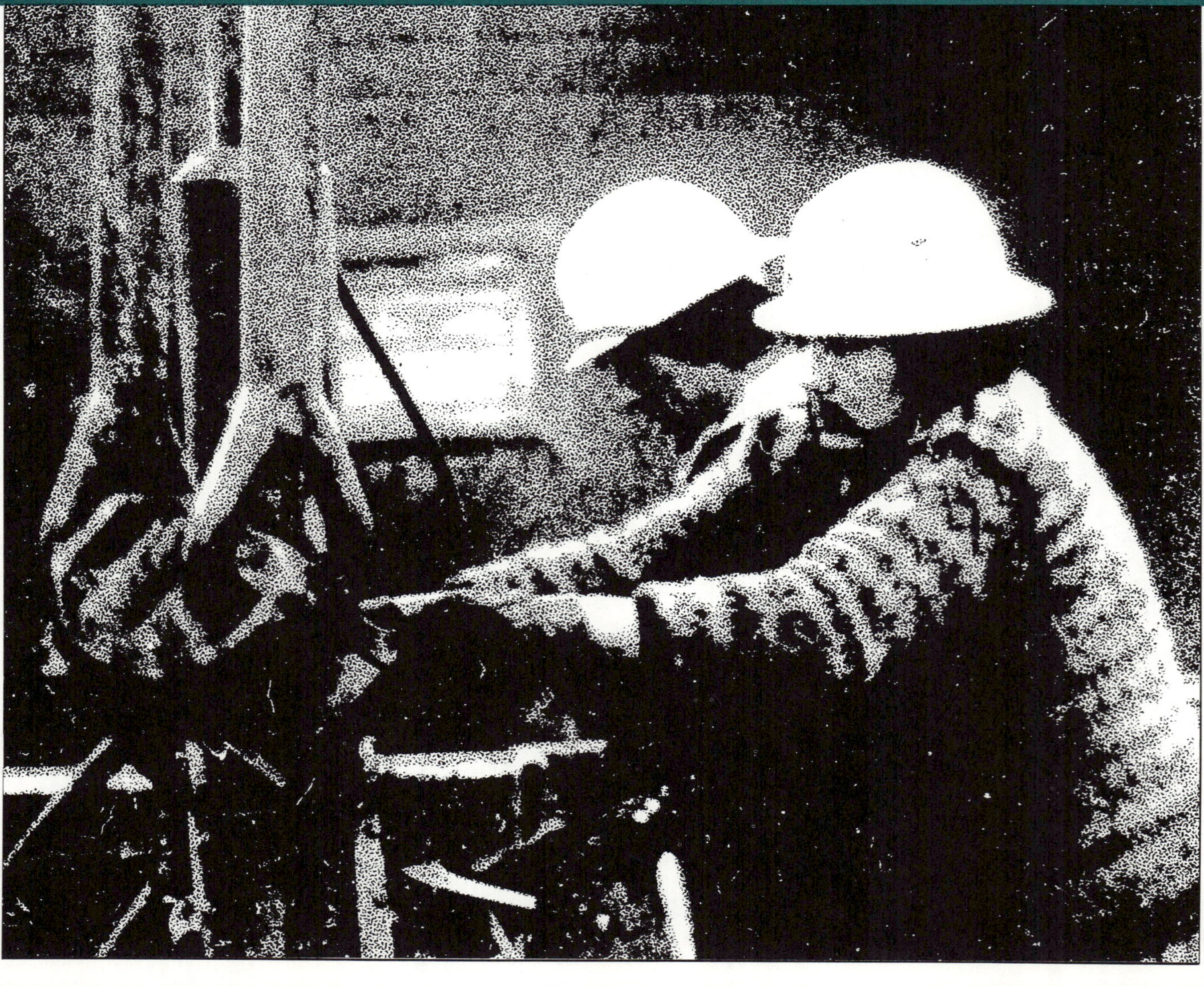

CHAPTER 14

Teamwork in Business and Industry

GOALS

At the end of this chapter you should be able to
1. understand the concept of teamwork in the business world;
2. identify and apply appropriate productive roles to work assignments on the job;
3. avoid non-productive roles and activities in the workplace;
4. understand a variety of different group structures used in business and industry; and
5. understand how an effective business meeting is organized and run.

VOCABULARY BUILDING

camaraderie
conformity
consensus
ad hoc
dissension
brainstorming sessions
moderator
concurrently

VIEWPOINTS

Adam drives his forklift over to the parking space beside the receiving door, steps onto the receiving platform, and hurries to the lunch room. Most of the other nine warehouse employees are already sitting at a long table engaged in conversation while waiting for Gord, the foreman, to start the meeting. Since meetings for employees of the Shipping and Receiving Department are infrequent, Adam thinks it must mean that something important has come up, or that Gord is upset about something.

Adam greets everyone and sits down across from Wendy and looks around the table to see if everyone is there. His inspection reveals that Josh is missing. Adam has noticed that Josh has been acting a little strange lately, as if he would prefer not to talk to anyone around the warehouse if he can avoid it. Since Josh is often hostile, Adam has never sought Josh out to talk to anyway.

A few minutes later Josh walks in and silently takes a seat at the far end of the table. No one greets him, but then he does not say anything or look at anyone directly to encourage a greeting. As Josh takes his place, Gord speaks.

GORD: All right, let's get this meeting started. We don't have all day. (Everyone settles down and looks toward Gord.) I spent last night trying to set up the vacation schedule according to what each of you wrote on your request form.

TINA: That took you all last night?

GORD: (He ignores the comment and proceeds.) Some of you have asked for vacation time when you know there will be a few others off as well. We can't operate with fewer than six employees at any one time. As you know, the last two weeks in August is the busiest time of the summer, yet that seems to be the time several of you choose to have your vacation. What I want to do today with everybody here is review each request to find out who is flexible. This place can't stop functioning while people go on holidays, and we can't ask some people to work three times as hard to keep things going.

JOSH: Well I for one don't have time for these kinds of meetings. I've worked here for twenty years — that's far longer than most of the bosses around here — and I've earned the right to whatever time I want for my vacation. When the rest of you have put in another ten or fifteen years, you'll have that right too.

ADAM: Josh, I'm getting married in August and I asked for the middle two weeks off almost a year ago.

WENDY: And my brother and his family are coming to visit from overseas at the end of August. So I need the time to show them around and visit with them.

JOSH: (looking at Adam with evident hostility) I didn't plan your wedding, you did. (looking at Wendy) And I didn't invite your company. You should have asked before you planned things.

UDO: Can we take a look at the schedule as it stands now, Gord? I asked for my holidays in August, but I can probably change them. My family is just going to the cottage and I think July will be fine with them.

GORD: (posting the schedule on the bulletin board at the front of the room) There it is. Any suggestions?

SONYA: Can you hire a student for the peak period?

GORD: No, that would just mean we'd have too many people here during the slow weeks. Another point I haven't mentioned yet is that in August we'll be right in the middle of contract negotiations and I'll be up to my ears in meetings. I'm going to need a senior person here in the warehouse to fill in for me while I'm away — that means either Josh, Lana, or Ainsley. Have you made special plans to go away, Josh?

JOSH: (getting up) I told you my plans. I plan to take the last three weeks in August off. And now I have to get back to work.

MATT: Let's just close the place down for two weeks during the slow period and be done with it. We aren't ever going to reach an agreement.

QUESTIONS

1. In groups of three or four, discuss what happened at the meeting. Name the people who made positive contributions to the work of the group and those who blocked it.
2. (a) As a group, discuss why you think Josh took the stand he did.
   (b) To what extent do you agree with Josh's stand? Why?

3. (a) In small group settings and then as a class, identify four or five options open to Gord at the end of the meeting.
   (b) Describe what you would do in this situation if you were Gord.
4. After the problem of vacation schedules has been resolved, what action can Gord take to improve the interpersonal relationships in his department? What can he do to build a team spirit?

Figure 14-1
It takes teamwork to get work done.

INTRODUCTION

During the early part of this century the word "team" was used most frequently to refer to a number of horses. Teams of horses helped to plough the fields, pull wagons, or move equipment. Later, the word was extended to describe a group of people making up one side in a game or an athletic event.

Nowadays, it is common to hear "team" applied to the employees in a business, as in a sales team, a marketing team, a design team, or an engineering team. Business teams such as these are made up of workers who contribute their professional and interpersonal skills to accomplish a common goal. The workers within a business team may very well perform different functions and have different skill levels, but they all have a common commitment to one another and to the goals of the company or group.

We have all seen how players in a sports team contribute their talents and co-operate for the good of the team. In the same way, members of a team in the world of work contribute their particular skills and knowledge, and co-operate with the other members with the result that tasks are performed more quickly, skilfully, and efficiently (Figure 14-1).

There are also personal benefits in working with others as a team. For many people teamwork is an enjoyable experience. There is a sense of loyalty and **camaraderie**, or good comradeship, among group members and this contributes to a good team spirit. Often the actions and attitudes of individual team members can act as a positive influence to stimulate other members to greater effort and achievement. When the job is done well, there is a shared sense of accomplishment and often a bond of friendship and respect develops among the team members.

Sometimes teamwork can have disadvantages as well. Teamwork demands a certain degree of **conformity**, or agreement with established rules and procedures. The members of a team may have to operate within a pre-set game plan, fulfilling their specific functions and responsibilities and recognizing the functions of other members. At times, it will take more time for the team to produce the required results than it would have taken if an individual had been solely responsible for the task. As an individual, you can make a decision and take action immediately. As a team member, you must allow each member of the team to participate in the decision making before action can be taken. Sometimes a difference of opinion among team members will delay the decision making, or the decision will be a compromise that is totally dissatisfying to everyone.

PRODUCTIVE TEAM MEMBERS

There are many roles that members can play in their association with the team. Some of these roles were introduced in Chapter 3. A number of them are supportive and productive; others are destructive and non-productive. A knowledge of these roles can help you to choose a role in which you can make a positive contribution to the team effort, and can help you in dealing with other members of the team. Once you are able to recognize what roles individuals are playing, you will be in a better position to neutralize any non-productive behaviour.

Productive Roles

Team members who assume productive roles do the following:

Clarify — ask for more information and explanations when needed; or pose questions that will help the group to consider important matters thoroughly.

Contribute — offer information; give opinions; and suggest direction.

Encourage — support other members of the group and help them make a contribution; promote positive attitudes; and keep the group working toward the goal.

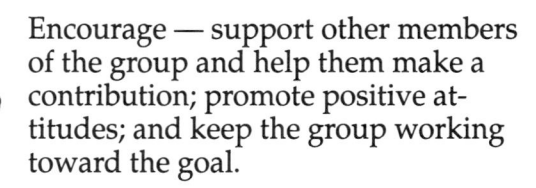

Facilitate — keep members' attention on the assigned task; break large tasks into manageable smaller work units to facilitate completion; and eliminate blocks that prevent decisions or action.

Initiate — get things going; organize group activities; introduce new ideas; raise new questions; or suggest new ways to look at things.

Summarize — look for **consensus**, or general agreement; show relationships; review proceedings; or identify major accomplishments.

Productive team members
1. clarify
2. contribute
3. encourage
4. facilitate
5. initiate
6. summarize.

Members of groups are not confined to playing only one of these positive roles. Through the course of a meeting they may easily play all of the roles at different times in order to further the work of the group.

TEAMWORK IN BUSINESS AND INDUSTRY

APPLICATIONS

1. Identify examples where individual students in your school have acted as productive team members.
2. As a class, list members of your local business community who are recognized as productive team players.

Figure 14-2
Productive team members

NON-PRODUCTIVE TEAM MEMBERS

The non-productive roles that team members can play tend to block the efforts of the group. They can also create unnecessary tension and conflict in meetings, making it more difficult for members to work together productively. Knowing the negative roles can help you to avoid playing them and to recognize when others are playing them.

Team members who assume non-productive roles do the following:

Say nothing (Figure 14-3) — do not volunteer information or opinions; refuse to become involved; and may refuse to vote on an issue or take any stand.

Figure 14-3
Team members who do not contribute

Dominate (Figure 14-4) — try to take over discussions; ignore ideas other than their own; want everything their way; see the interactions of the group as a series of power plays; and show disrespect for other members of the group.

Figure 14-4
Team members who dominate

TEAMWORK IN BUSINESS AND INDUSTRY

Seek attention (Figure 14-5) — try to capture the attention of other group members through what they say or through body language; boast about their accomplishments; and want special credit for any contributions they may make.

Figure 14-5
Team members who seek attention

Non-productive team members
1. say nothing
2. dominate
3. seek attention
4. block progress.

Block progress (Figure 14-6) — have their minds made up; refuse to listen to other team members; show more interest in their own goals than in the goals of the group; side-step issues by raising other concerns; avoid responsibility; dwell on minor arguments; and delay consensus.

Figure 14-6
Team members who block progress

PART THREE: SUCCESS IN BUSINESS AND INDUSTRY

APPLICATIONS

3. Survey the students in the class and prepare a list of those who are involved in some form of school or extra-curricular activity. These activities could include sports, students' groups, or community work. Have the students involved in group activities explain their particular responsibilities and their importance to the group.

4. Ask each student involved in a leadership role in the activities identified in Question 3 to describe any difficulties they would have in doing their work if they did not have the support of other group members.

5. Use each of the letters in the word "co-operation" as the first letter of a word or phrase that describes what you think the word co-operation means. To start off, you might consider the following: C — considerate of others, O — open-minded.

6. Ask a member of a sports team at your school to draw a set play of the team on the board. Ask the student to explain the individual roles of the players. Then have the student explain how teamwork is essential for a successful play.

7. Invite a coach into the class to identify what went right or wrong at a recent game. Consider some of the reasons for each right or wrong incident identified.

8. William Shakespeare said: "All the world's a stage, / And all the men and women merely players." We take our places in a variety of small groups and we play particular roles. Identify all of the small group or teamwork activities in which you have been involved over the past few months and assess your role in each group.

9. As a group, list the things you might do to help someone, who is withdrawn or reluctant to get involved, become a more productive member of your group.

10. In small groups, prepare and present a short skit that illustrates how someone who always tries to dominate a group effort might be controlled.

11. What tactics would you use to handle someone who seems to block progress at a meeting for which you were responsible? Give examples of how, when, and what you would say or do.

BUSINESS WORK GROUPS

Within business organizations, much of the decision making is carried out by groups. The structure and composition of these groups and the responsibilities of the individual members will vary depending on the nature of the tasks undertaken and the time frame within which they are to be performed. The types of groups described below are not necessarily separate and distinct. There is some overlap.

Permanent Groups

Some groups are formed when employees depend on one another's work to accomplish a common task. These groups can be termed permanent groups because the individuals that form them go on performing the same tasks over a long period of time. The management board of a company, composed of senior company officials such as president, vice-president, treasurer, production manager, and sales manager, is an example of a permanent work group. This group meets regularly and acts as a team to make policy decisions. Often a department within a company will function as a permanent group. They will have regular meetings at which they may assess the quality and quantity of work put through, how the work load might be better shared, or how a new project can be tackled.

Ad Hoc Groups

Ad hoc groups, that is, groups set up for a particular purpose only, are disbanded once they have achieved their goal. In the *Viewpoints* section, Gord could initiate an ad hoc group whose objective would be to help Josh feel part of the warehouse team again.

Another way of categorizing groups is to divide them into formal and informal groups.

Formal Groups

A group set up to perform a specific function or task on a continuing basis is sometimes referred to as a formal group. There will usually be a group leader, who is either appointed or elected, and a number of participants who may have specified duties to perform within the group, for example, the secretary or treasurer.

Informal Groups

Workers may gather in an informal group to provide mutual support, share ideas, and to work out problems as they arise.

Two additional categories sometimes used to describe groups are primary and secondary groups.

Primary Groups

Membership in a primary group depends on individual identity rather than function. A family group, for example, is a primary group. Family members leaving the group will not be replaced.

Secondary Groups

In a secondary group, function is more important than individual identity. Responsibilities are defined and members are assigned to carry them out. Group membership can fluctuate and when it does, responsibilities are reassigned with no overall negative effect on the group. Your student council is typical of a secondary group. Each year a new slate of officers is elected, but the change of membership does not affect the structure or purpose of the group.

Business work groups can be categorized as
1. *permanent and ad hoc groups*
2. *formal and informal groups*
3. *primary and secondary groups.*

APPLICATIONS

12. Organize into groups of three or four. Each group then interviews a representative of the local business community to determine the kind(s) of work team used in the company.
13. (a) Identify the kind(s) of work group each team represents.
    (b) Outline the goals of each team as identified in the roles played by each person in the team.
14. (a) Describe the interpersonal skills and effective teamwork components necessary for the team's success.
    (b) Identify the benefits and the difficulties involved in working in each kind of team.

EFFECTIVE TEAMWORK IN BUSINESS AND INDUSTRY

Businesses run more smoothly when employees work together harmoniously and productively. One of the ways that these conditions can be achieved is by promoting the development of a team spirit. When employees feel that they are contributing members of a productive group as well as part of the company's decision-making process, then they will be more likely to feel as part of the team.

The members of business teams get together in meetings to plan activities, set priorities and goals, discuss problems, and arrive at decisions. The meetings can be held on an ad hoc or on a regular basis. Usually the larger the business, the more likely there will be regularly scheduled meetings. Most of the decisions that must be made for the business to function are made in meetings by team members. They will identify problems, gather information, discuss options, and come to a collective agreement on the appropriate course of action. Once a decision has been implemented, certain members will be responsible for monitoring the results. If the results are not what the team hoped for, the team may call a meeting to modify the course of action.

KINDS OF BUSINESS MEETINGS

Figure 14-7
Meetings are times for sharing information, ideas, and responsibilities.

Meetings, like the one shown in Figure 14-7, are held to provide an opportunity for members to share ideas and information, to generate new ideas, and to share the responsibilities of running the business through decision making. The reason for holding a meeting and the number of people who will be attending often determine what form the meeting will take and where it will be held. For a small group discussing an issue such as holidays, as the warehouse group in *Viewpoints* did, the meeting can be called shortly before it is to take place, conducted on an informal basis, and held in an informal setting such as a lunchroom. For a meeting at which the company's future direction will be mapped out, there may be twenty or more management representatives attending, and a large private area such as a boardroom will be needed. For this kind of meeting, a chairperson will be appointed to run the meeting according to standard procedures. Descriptions of various kinds of business meetings follow.

Formal Meetings

Formal meetings are run by a chairperson who ensures that everyone has an opportunity to contribute and that each item on the prepared agenda is addressed. In order that everyone is prepared for the meeting, the agenda is circulated several days beforehand. The chairperson is responsible for starting and finishing the meeting on time, conducting the meeting in an orderly and efficient manner, and bringing about a decision on each item under discussion. When disagreements begin to develop into a battle of personalities, the chairperson tactfully intervenes and re-establishes an objective framework for discussion. The ability to handle **dissension**, or strong disagreement, skilfully and productively requires excellent interpersonal communication skills. Following the meeting, a summary of the issues raised, tasks assigned, and the decisions made will be circulated to those in attendance and to those invited who were unable to attend.

Informal Meetings

No pre-planning goes into an informal meeting, nor is there an appointed chairperson. Informal meetings are arranged to settle matters of immediate concern and usually take less time than a formal meeting since participants are addressing one or two matters only. Gord, in the section *Viewpoints*, could have called an informal meeting with Josh, Wendy, Udo, and Adam to resolve the specific problem of scheduling vacations during the busy time in August. He might have approached them by saying "Look, we have a problem with the schedule of vacations in August. Let's take a few minutes now to see what we can do to resolve the problem so that the rest of the warehouse won't have to work extra hours or double work loads during August."

Figure 14-8
An informal meeting

TEAMWORK IN BUSINESS AND INDUSTRY

Organizational Meetings

Planning, organizing, assigning responsibilities, and establishing routines are some of the functions of an organizational meeting. A sales department, for example, might hold an organizational meeting to plan a sales campaign, assign responsibilities, and establish routines and formats for collecting sales data for the next sales quarter.

Information Meetings

One of the ways in which the personnel in a company are kept posted on new developments and future plans is through information meetings. The manager and key people of a production department could hold an information meeting to instruct the department on how to demonstrate and use a new product.

Problem-solving Meetings

Problem-solving meetings allow a number of people to participate in resolving issues that touch on their areas of responsibility. These meetings can take the form of **brainstorming sessions**, that is, sessions in which members contribute all the ideas and possible solutions they can think of in a non-critical, non-evaluating atmosphere. Later each suggestion will be considered and assessed as members work toward a solution or decision on the issue under discussion. Sometimes the task of sorting through the suggestions will be assigned to a few of the members. This committee will report back later to the larger group, recommending the best course of action.

Panel Discussions

In a panel discussion, a few people, usually three or four, with different points of view discuss an issue. The discussion is run by a **moderator**, that is, a presiding officer who allows each panel member equal time to speak. At the end of the discussion, questions from the audience are answered by the panel members.

Symposia

A symposium (the plural is "symposia") is a meeting at which a series of papers on a related subject or theme are presented. Speakers are allotted a definite time period, usually less than an hour, within which to present their ideas and information. Often symposium speakers will reinforce their points with visual materials. At the end of each group of speakers, a chairperson summarizes the presentations. At a large symposium, several papers may be presented **concurrently**, or at the same time, in different meeting rooms.

Buzz Sessions

When a large group is divided into smaller work units in order to maximize participation, the smaller units are sometimes called buzz sessions. Each small group is given a specific issue or a facet of a problem to discuss. The findings of each buzz session are then presented to the larger group. See Figure 14-9.

Figure 14-9
A buzz session

ROBERT'S RULES OF ORDER

Robert's Rules of Order are the most followed procedures for running a formal meeting. They are as follows:
- All business, except routine matters, is brought before the assembly by means of a member's motion. The motion should preferably be presented in writing.
- After a report is read, a motion is made to adopt, accept, or agree to its position. If the report is an information report only, no action need be taken after it is read.
- A member must obtain permission from the chairperson before making a motion.
- All motions begin with "I move that ..."
- All motions are presented by a member of the organization and seconded by another.
- Discussion of the motion follows its presentation.
- All motions are voted on following a discussion of the motion.

TEAMWORK IN BUSINESS AND INDUSTRY

APPLICATIONS

15. As a class, obtain a copy of *Robert's Rules of Order* from your school library resource centre and prepare a summary of the procedures required for making a motion, seconding it, discussing it, amending it, moving a substitute motion, and taking a vote. Record each of the steps mentioned in the correct order.

16. Appoint a chairperson for your class and, following the procedures you have identified above, prepare and present a series of motions.

HOW TO MAKE A MEETING A SUCCESS

Responsibilities

For a meeting to be successful, participants must be aware of their functions at the meeting, and the responsibilities attached to their functions. The leader or chairperson, the recorder, and the participants play key roles at a meeting.

The leader or chairperson is expected to
- prepare an agenda;
- arrange an appropriate meeting place;
- provide the focus for the meeting;
- set the stage by giving the reasons for the meeting;
- outline the objectives or alternatives to be considered;
- identify any time constraints that might be a factor in reaching a decision;
- encourage full participation;
- ensure that the meeting adheres to the agenda and progresses in an orderly fashion; and
- control troublesome participants and unproductive dialogue.

The recorder or secretary is expected to
- record all important information, that is, take the minutes;
- record all decisions; and
- note which members are given responsibility for taking action following the meeting.

Taking the minutes involves noting the date, time, place, names of participants and absentees, items discussed, decisions made, and responsibilities assigned. The minutes should also list unfinished business, committee reports presented, new actions taken (including the names of those making and seconding motions), and the results of any voting. Figure 14-10 shows the typical minutes of a meeting.

All those attending a meeting are participants. They are expected to
- prepare themselves for the meeting, reviewing any background material that will enable them to make a more effective contribution to the discussion;

Figure 14-10
The minutes of a meeting

```
              MINUTES OF THE MEETING OF THE EXECUTIVE COMMITTEE
              HELD AT THE BOARD ROOM, 1540 MAIN STREET, WINNIPEG,
              MANITOBA, ON JULY 29, 19--, AT 10:00

   PRESENT:   JOHN PELLETIER, PRESIDENT, IN THE CHAIR

              W. G. BURNETT,   VICE-PRESIDENT,  MARKETING
              D. L. LUTKIN,    VICE-PRESIDENT,  FINANCE
              V. T. UNRUH,     VICE-PRESIDENT,  PERSONNEL
              A. J. VAN DYCK,  VICE-PRESIDENT,  OPERATIONS

              Mrs. L. Grosz, Manager of Personnel, was a guest of the meeting.

AGENDA        After discussion and UPON MOTION by Mr. Lutkin, the Agenda
              was adopted as presented.

MINUTES       UPON MOTION by Mrs. Van Dyck, the Minutes were approved as
              presented to the Meeting.

JASPER        Mr. Burnett reported on behalf of the Jasper Project Committee.
PROJECT       Two proposals to promote the Jasper Project were presented. A ski lodge
              could be converted into a sales training center at a cost of $25 000 or
              a new site could be built at a cost of $55 000. The reason for considering
              the new site is the difficulty in accessing the old lodge. The Executive
              Committee will review both proposals before the next meeting.

BOND          Mr. Lutkin stated that the latest increase in interest rates
ISSUE         has made the bond issue impossible at this time. This was discussed at
              some length, and the Committee decided to shelve the proposal.

JOB           Mrs. Grosz reported to the meeting that the pilot project begun
SHARING       in May appears to be very successful. Presently, 36 staff members are
PROJECT       participating in this project and initial reports show that they are happy
              with the scheme. A formal report will be forthcoming after the six-month
              trial period.

NEW           There was no new business to come before the meeting.
BUSINESS
              The date and time of the next meeting was set at 19-- 09 05. It
NEXT          will again be held in the Board Room.
MEETING
              The meeting adjourned at 11:25.


                                                   _____
                                                   CHAIRMAN


                                                   _____
                                                   SECRETARY
```

- join in the discussions;
- play positive and productive roles to help team members clarify, contribute, encourage, facilitate, initiate, and summarize;
- avoid non-productive roles and avoid saying nothing, dominating, seeking attention, and blocking progress; and
- use effective interpersonal and intrapersonal communication skills to facilitate an exchange of ideas and information.

You as a Participant

Sometimes you can try too hard to contribute to the success of a meeting. Although your intentions may be good, questioning every decision and finding an objection to every proposal can slow down or even block progress.

When you do have a legitimate objection, raise it immediately. Waiting until the other participants are arriving at a decision before you introduce your objection can waste time. Have an alternative to propose before you object to one that everyone else supports.

Words that introduce a value judgement and belittle the contribution of others, for example, inferior, unreliable, or silly, should be avoided. Likewise, insulting, blaming, or attacking another member is unacceptable behaviour in a meeting. When you must disagree, do so in an objective and tactful manner. It is not necessary to be disagreeable when you disagree.

Handling your own anger or the anger of another person that is directed at you is important if you want to be a productive participant in meetings. Remaining calm, being polite, and listening actively to what others have to say may be difficult, but it is necessary behaviour. Once things have calmed down and tempers have had a chance to cool, you and the other participant(s) may be able to find a solution that is mutually acceptable.

The message in a Chinese fortune cookie has this to say about anger, "Anger, like fog, distorts the way." Avoiding situations that will lead to angry outbursts will improve your chances of having a successful meeting.

Body language can also contribute positively to your meeting. A pleasant manner, an alert expression and posture, and a readiness to provide feedback to other members will indicate your willingness to contribute and to lend support.

Meeting Place and Room Arrangements

The communication environment is also important to the success of a meeting. The meeting place should be convenient, comfortable, and free from physical distractions. The chairperson should ensure that the room is appropriately furnished and that any special equipment is set up and in working order prior to the meeting. Often a chairperson will appoint someone to carry out this task.

The seating arrangement should correspond to and support the kind of discussion and the number of participants expected. A boardroom table lends itself very nicely to a decision-making meeting involving a small number of individuals (no more than fourteen). If small group discussions are desirable, round tables spaced to avoid interference from discussions at other tables, can work well. At an information meeting, a lecture-style setup often works best, with the main speaker addressing the rest of the participants from the front of the room.

An Agenda

Successful meetings are planned in advance. An agenda is the plan distributed to all participants well in advance of the meeting. Agendas are important for several reasons.
- The chairperson needs an outline of items for discussion, logically arranged, to make sure nothing is overlooked during the course of the meeting.

- The recorder needs an ordered record of each item to be discussed so that the minutes of the meeting will be complete.
- Participants can come to the meeting prepared to discuss the items identified on the agenda.

Agendas inform participants when and where the meeting will take place and usually include such items as old business, new business, items for discussion, action, and information. The agenda format will reflect the kind of meeting scheduled to take place and the items and issues to be discussed.

If you are planning to chair a meeting and/or write up an agenda, there are a number of books that will help you. Here are a few that are particularly helpful.

1. Bradford, Leland P.
   Making Meetings Work: A Guide for Leaders and Group Members (University Assoc., 1976)
2. Maidmand, Robert and Bullock, William
   Meetings! Accomplishing More with Better and Fewer (NASSP, 1985)
3. Wainberg, J.M.
   Company Meetings: Including Rules of Order (Canada Law Book Limited, 1969)
4. Shea, Gordon J.
   Managing a Difficult or Hostile Audience (Toronto: Prentice-Hall, 1984)
5. Bourinot, Sir John George
   Rules of Order (Toronto: McClelland & Stewart, 1963)

Electronic Meetings

In today's business environment, meetings are not always face-to-face encounters. Advanced technology is having a dramatic effect on the way businesspeople communicate and conduct meetings. In Chapter 3 you examined the concept of mediated communication — communication that requires the use of a mechanical device. Mediated business communication can involve a variety of electronic telecommunication equipment that permits conferences to be held by telephone with a number of callers connected simultaneously; by communication satellites that permit video conferencing with participants seeing one another and any visual aids on a television screen; and by computer conferencing using a network of computers. One of the main benefits of this new technology is the time saved. A meeting of the directors of a country-wide organization can be held by telephone or communication satellite and no time is spent bringing the participants together at one location, or wasted on telephoning or writing to exchange ideas, information, and views on issues requiring decisions.

Meetings are successful when
1. *the participants fulfil their responsibilities*
2. *the meeting place is appropriate and free from distractions*
3. *the agenda is planned in advance.*

APPLICATIONS

17. As a class, ask your school librarian to help you locate a number of reference books on the subject of meetings. Have each student select one of the topics discussed in this chapter, summarize what one book says about it, and share the information with the rest of the class. Present summaries of each topic in a formal oral presentation.

18. As a class, identify an issue of importance in your school and plan a meeting to resolve it. Arrange an appropriate meeting environment, appoint a chairperson, a recorder to record minutes, and run the meeting according to *Robert's Rules of Order*.

19. Select articles from your local newspaper that describe different kinds of meetings. Summarize the results of these meetings and determine why the particular meeting format contributed to or detracted from the results of the meeting.

20. (a) Appoint an individual in your class to act as a panel moderator and three or four others to serve as panel members. Research the topic of current telecommunication conferencing in business and organize a panel discussion.
    (b) Appoint a recorder for the session and have that person prepare a report on the information presented.

21. Make a list of ten problems you would like solved in your school. Study the list and decide what type of meeting would best suit a successful discussion of the problem.

22. In groups of seven, select a single problem. Place yourselves in the roles of leader, recorder, and five participants. By following the ideas found in this chapter, study the problem and conduct a meeting for the class.

CHAPTER SUMMARY

Teamwork involves co-operation and loyalty, and also conformity. Productive team members
- clarify
- contribute
- encourage
- facilitate
- initiate
- summarize

Negative roles are non-productive. Negative team members
- say nothing
- dominate
- seek attention
- block progress

Groups perform valuable roles in business settings. They can be permanent, and last for a long period of time, or ad hoc, and set up for a specific short-term purpose. They can be formal or informal.

Groups where identity is more important than function are called primary groups. Function is most important in secondary groups.

Teamwork is important for meetings to be successful. Decisions are made in meetings based on agreements made collectively and the results of the meetings are monitored by certain members of the group.

Types of meetings
- formal
- informal
- organizational
- informational
- problem solving

Some specialized types of meetings
- panel discussions
- buzz sessions

Robert's Rules of Order contain the most commonly used procedures for the smooth running of a meeting.

The responsibilities of the leader
- draw up an agenda
- arrange the meeting place
- act as leader and encourage positive group roles

The responsibilities of the recorder
- take minutes
- note who will take action on decisions made

The responsibilities of participants
- be prepared
- play positive group roles
- communicate well

Important elements that make a meeting a success
- an appropriate meeting place
- a well-prepared agenda

MAKING IT WORK

1. (a) Divide into small groups and plan a class field trip to observe different kinds of meetings. Include opportunities to attend council meetings, individual business, or club association meetings and specific task-oriented meetings.
   (b) Describe the arrangements made for the meeting, the meeting place and environment selected, the rules or procedures followed in running the meeting, and the effect of each on the success or failure of the meeting.

2. Use one of the following business topics to prepare and present a symposium.
   (a) In what ways has the concept of teamwork changed the way business is presently conducted?
   (b) How can consumers, as citizens, influence government policy?
   (c) In what ways do economic security programs conflict with the goals of economic freedom?

3. The shop foreman is meeting with the union steward and the plant manager. They are discussing the fact that one of their workers has let personal problems interfere with his performance on the job. He is away a great deal of the time and when he is on the job, he produces only half the volume he used to. The union steward is asking that the company give this employee time and provide professional help to resolve his problems. The shop foreman has applied for a promotion and wants to impress the plant manager with his ability to make management decisions. The plant manager does not know the employee in question very well and is torn between the shop foreman and the union steward.

   Assign the roles of shop foreman, union steward, and plant manager to three different members of the class and ask them to role-play the meeting.

   In small groups discuss
   (a) why the three participants said what they did;
   (b) how each member of the group perceived one another; and
   (c) how the problem could be resolved.

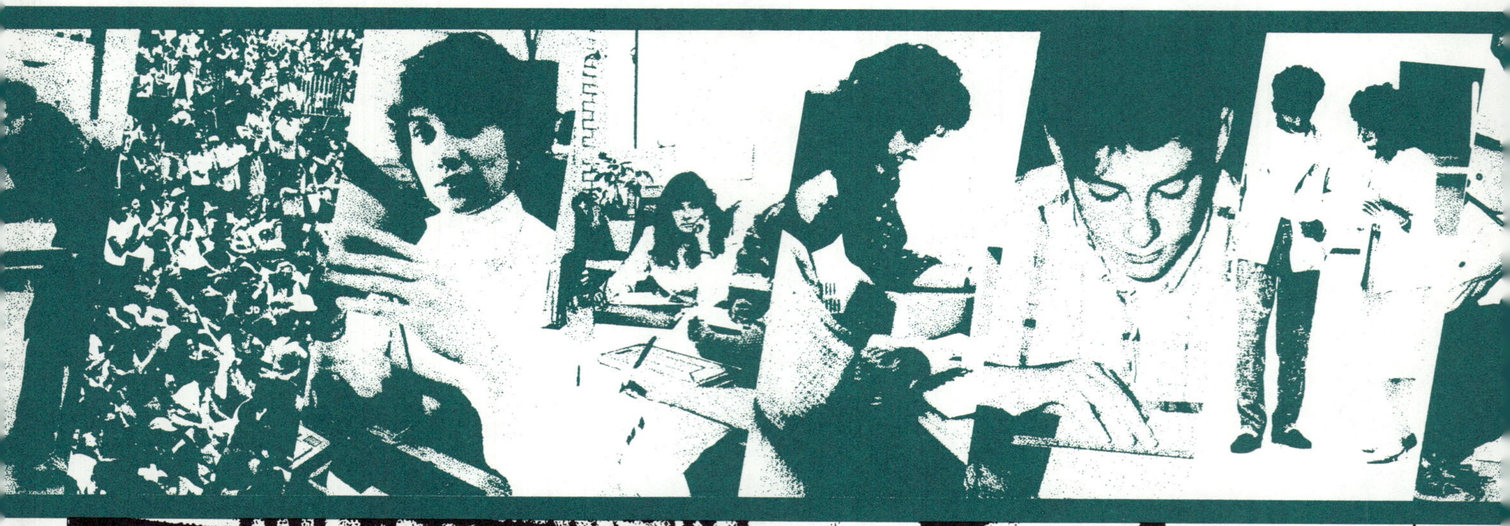

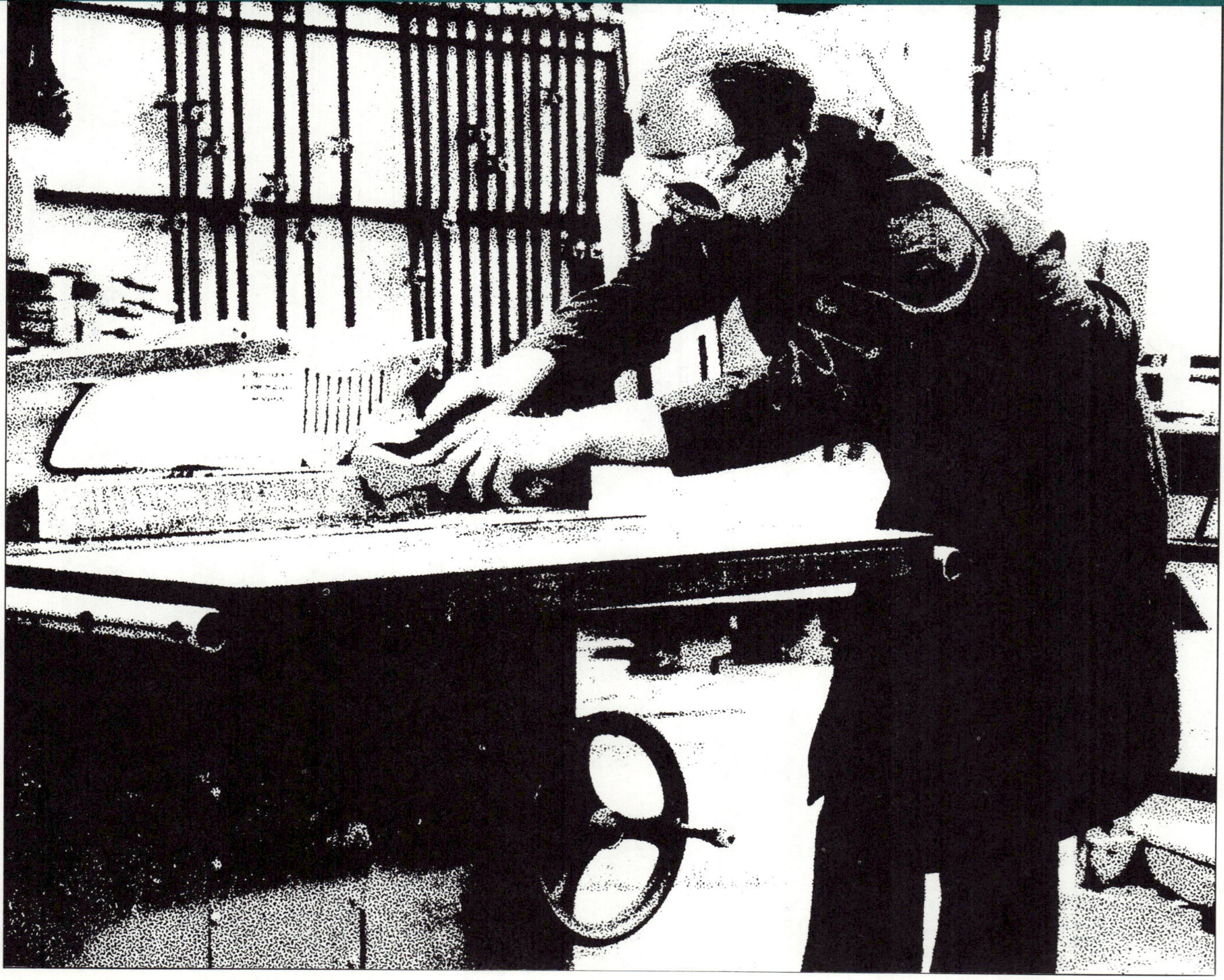

CHAPTER 15

Job Search

GOALS

At the end of this chapter you should be able to

1. analyze your years of schooling in terms of your school career;
2. plan your work career in terms of your interests, aptitudes, and skills;
3. carry out a job search;
4. write a résumé and a letter of application;
5. prepare for and take part in a job interview; and
6. demonstrate good communication skills after starting work.

VOCABULARY BUILDING

career
interests
aptitudes
skills
chronological résumé
functional résumé
job description

VIEWPOINTS

Sometimes it seems as if endings are really beginnings. It is the last day of school for all the students you have met in this section of your textbook, and they are all looking toward the future. Jorg, whom you met in Chapter 1, is going to college; Sol and Kyle, whom you will remember from Chapter 5, are going to Europe for the summer. Mai, from Chapter 4, will be working full time as a bookkeeper for her uncle. Dominic has been hired full time by Eastern Publishing. The garage where Sandy (whom you met in Chapter 2) works has taken her on as an apprentice. Let us listen to Mai, Sol, and Lionel as they leave school for the last time.

MAI: Bye, Sol! Don't forget to send us a postcard from Greece. Lionel, you're very quiet. You haven't talked at all about what you're going to do. Do you know?

LIONEL: I guess I'll be looking for a job.

MAI: You seem rather glum about job hunting.

LIONEL: I'll miss school. I'm used to this old place. And every time I open a newspaper, I read about how hard it is to find work these days.

MAI: What do you want to do?

LIONEL: Well, that's the problem. I'm not sure.

MAI: What are you interested in? I know you love playing around with computers.

LIONEL: Yes, and I think I'm really good with figures.

MAI: You also get good marks and get along well with everyone. Have you thought about programming or some kind of data processing?

LIONEL: The guidance counsellor suggested that, but, you know, I don't think I would find sitting at a desk all day very fulfilling. I like being active and I like talking to people. You can't have an interesting conversation with a computer.

MAI: Hey, I know. What about computer sales? My uncle says there are lots of job openings there.

LIONEL: You mean selling computers to companies? That could be interesting.

MAI: I think my uncle has some contacts in the computer business. I'll ask him tonight. Now cheer up! It's the last day of school!

QUESTIONS

1. Knowing your skills and interests can help you decide on a career. List in three columns Lionel's abilities, the skills he has learned, and his interests.
2. Using the problem-solving model you learned about in Chapter 8 and the information in the dialogue, analyze Lionel's problem. Remember to follow the six problem-solving steps. Is your solution different from Mai's?
3. Leaving school and looking for work are difficult because they involve leaving a familiar world for an unfamiliar one. What things concern you most about being out of school and looking for a job?

Figure 15-1
Starting your first job means leaving a familiar world for an unfamiliar one.

INTRODUCTION

Just as Mai, Lionel, Sol, and Kyle are ending one part of their life and starting another, you are ending this course of study and probably thinking of new beginnings that will face you in the future. You may have been asked "What direction do you think your career will take?" Perhaps, like Lionel in Figure 15-1, you will react to this question with some uncertainty. In some ways, the choices of possible careers are limitless; in others, because of job competition, your choices may seem very limited indeed.

The word **career** means the work you are doing now, and will do throughout your life. It does not necessarily mean one particular job, but it does imply that you will choose a particular path to follow through the years you work. At the moment, you have a career as a student. In the future, you will build on the skills you have learned as a student when you enter the world of employment.

This chapter will help you to put the skills you have learned and the experiences you have had as a student, particularly a student of Business English, to work for you as you shape your future career.

Take a moment now to consider your past experiences in terms of your school career. The questions below will probably help you form your ideas and communicate them to others.

A career is a chosen path through life in study or employment.

APPLICATIONS

1. In small groups prepare answers to the following questions:
   (a) What are your long-term school plans?
   (b) At what point in these plans are you now?
   (c) What decisions have you made along the way?
   (d) What alternatives have you had?
   (e) What outside interests influenced your career as a student?
   (f) Do you now feel that you may have made any inappropriate choices?
   (g) What can you do about these?

2. Using the answers developed to the questions listed in Question 1, outline the school careers of two or three members of your group. Identify the points in each career where there were choices to be made. What reasons do you think were used in making those decisions?

You will see from Lionel's uncertainty and from the activities that you have just completed that it is not always easy to identify at the beginning of your school career where your choices will take you in the future. To the best of your abilities, however, at each point in time, a decision has to be made, based on your goals and choices.

In the same way, it is impossible to predict with any certainty exactly where you will be, what job you will have, or how many successful experiences you will have five or ten years from now. Your working career will be much like your school career — full of alternatives that require decisions. Each decision will be influenced by a variety of factors including your work-related goals at that particular point in time.

Assuming that you are nearing the end of your school career, like most of us you will now be looking out into the world of work to determine what work you would like to do and where you will have to go to get that kind of job. The career choice you make now should reflect your **interests**, or things you enjoy doing, **aptitudes**, or activities you are good at, and **skills**, or things you have learned to do well. Look now at these three areas to plan what kind of job you want. It is important to know where you are going before you set off.

Your career choices are influenced by
1. your interests
2. your aptitudes
3. your skills.

APPLICATIONS

3. Using sheets of blank paper, prepare a set of charts as illustrated in Figure 15-2. Identify your likes, dislikes, successes, and failures. Summarize the information by determining your interests, aptitudes, and abilities in the summary section at the bottom of each chart. Ask for help from your school counsellor or a job placement officer and, using the information contained in your summaries, prepare school-related and work-related goals.

4. With the help of your school guidance counsellor or another adviser, list a number of jobs that interest you and where you feel you could use your special skills.

5. When you have identified employment possibilities for the future, find out through your school guidance centre about education or special programs that would help you achieve your goals. With the help of your teacher or a guidance counsellor, plan a possible course to follow through your school or work career.

JOB SEARCH

Perhaps you are ready to step into the world of work right now, or perhaps you are considering possible summer jobs that will be of use to you in the future. In either case, make up your mind that you will actively search out every possible job opportunity. Be determined, optimistic, and flexible. Your determination will mean that you will be prepared to do everything possible to get what you want. Your optimism will mean that you will be confident that you will find a job that suits your talents. Your flexibility will mean that you will be able to accept compromises when necessary.

Above all, be assertive and active in your job search. Rather than sit back and wait for a lucky break, seek out as many opportunities as you can and explore every possibility. The most exciting part of job hunting is not knowing from where your opportunities will come.

Figure 15-2
Draw up charts like these to help you analyze your interests, aptitudes, and skills.

Tick the relevant columns

INTEREST/HOBBY ACTIVITIES	LIKES	DISLIKES	SUCCESSES	FAILURES

SUMMARY STATEMENT		
INTERESTS	APTITUDES	SKILLS

Tick the relevant columns

WORK RELATED ACTIVITIES	LIKES	DISLIKES	SUCCESSES	FAILURES

SUMMARY STATEMENT		
INTERESTS	APTITUDES	SKILLS

Tick the relevant columns

SCHOOL SUBJECTS	LIKES	DISLIKES	SUCCESSES	FAILURES

SUMMARY STATEMENT		
INTERESTS	APTITUDES	SKILLS

Tick the relevant columns

SCHOOL ACTIVITIES (extra-curricular)	LIKES	DISLIKES	SUCCESSES	FAILURES

SUMMARY STATEMENT		
INTERESTS	APTITUDES	SKILLS

SUMMARY SHEET			
	INTERESTS	APTITUDES	SKILLS
SCHOOL SUBJECTS			
SCHOOL ACTIVITIES			
INTEREST/HOBBIES			
WORK RELATED ACTIVITIES			

WORK/CAREER PLANS	SCHOOL/EXPERIENCE PLANS

Figure 15-3
What do you think are some of the interests, aptitudes, and skills of the young salesperson in this photograph?

It is important not to take rejection to heart. Believe in yourself. Keep your spirits high. Be persistent. Write letters and ask for interviews even when you think your chances will be very slim. Although there may be no openings at the time, people will remember your perseverance and your positive attitude when a job does become available. Even if you are not immediately successful, you will have the satisfaction of knowing that you are doing everything possible to get a job.

Before you are able to work in Canada, you must have a social insurance card. If you do not have one already, your local Canada Employment Centre will be able to help you. Take your birth certificate (in Quebec, a baptismal certificate will do) along with a second piece of identification such as a driver's licence, a library card, or a club membership card. If you were born outside Canada, you will need your Canadian Citizenship card, Immigration 1000 form, or a passport with your Landed Immigrant stamp.

The steps you take in your job search will probably take the following form.

1. Based on your knowledge of your skills, aptitudes, and interests, visit local employment agencies and placement offices to examine opportunities that they have listed. Your guidance counsellor or local placement officer will also be able to give you pointers on the best way to find the job you seek.
2. Call your previous employers. Ask if they have any openings. If they have none, ask for suggestions about where you might look for employment.

3. Read the newspapers, checking the want ads every day. Only a small proportion of people find work through Help Wanted ads, but reading the advertisements can give you an overview of the sort of jobs that suit your background. Do not be put off by advertisements that ask for experienced help. You have nothing to lose and everything to gain by applying for everything you think you might be able to do. Find something in your past experience that relates to the skills identified in the advertisement and apply for the job. You will at least gain experience in writing letters of application and you may make some contacts in the process.
4. Check with your family, friends, and acquaintances, especially those who are working or who have family members in the work force. Do not be shy about telling everyone that you are looking for work. They may be able to tell you about a job that has not been advertised yet. Ask permission to mention their names and follow their leads.
5. Write letters of application and send résumés. If you know the kind of work you want to do, find out what companies employ people to do that kind of work and then write to each one of them. Outline your qualifications, list any work experience you may have, and indicate your willingness to learn.
6. Each time you make a job contact, set up a file card listing the information you have gained. (Figure 15-4 is an example of such a file card.) By storing these cards in alphabetical order, you will have an accurate record of your job search. This record can provide you with valuable information in the future if you decide to change jobs.

Job resources are
1. *guidance and employment centres*
2. *previous employers*
3. *help wanted ads*
4. *family and friends.*

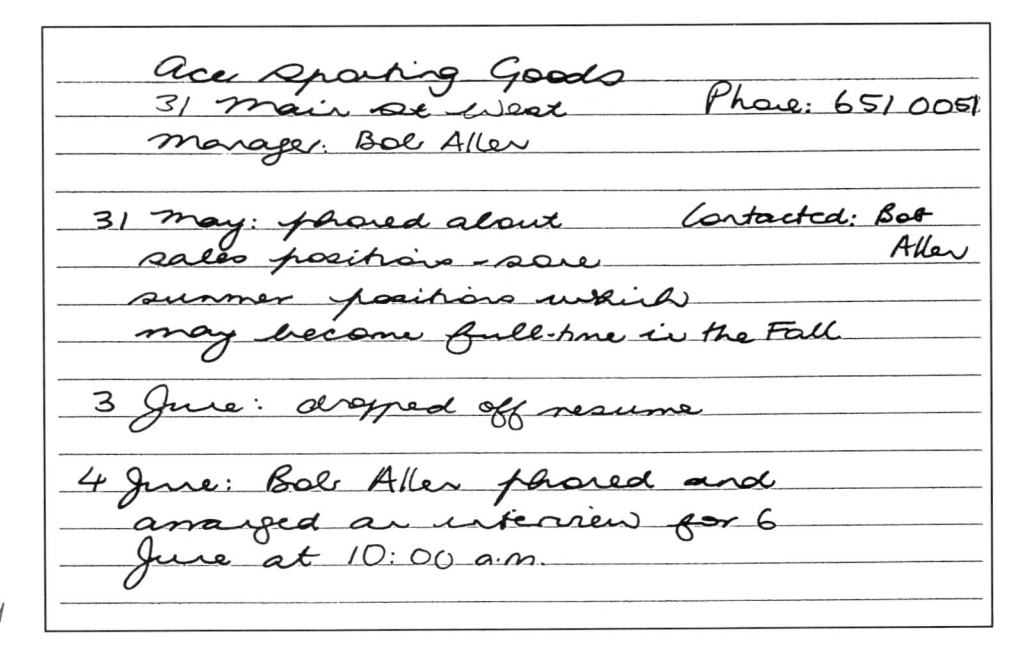

Figure 15-4
A job search record card

APPLICATIONS

6. Using two of the resources listed, find the names of two companies or organizations that you would be interested in working for either full time or part time.
7. Call these companies, finding out if they hire people with your background.
8. Keep Job Contact Record Cards for each contact you make.

YOUR RÉSUMÉ

In following your initial contact, or, if you write to a potential employer, in the initial contact itself, you will be expected to have your résumé on hand. A résumé is a brief history or description of who you are. Most employers will use your résumé to

- gain an overview of your background;
- identify your ability to perform what they might expect of you; and
- ascertain that you can communicate well in writing.

Your résumé will be used primarily to give prospective employers an indication of how well you might fit into their organizations. Employers will want to read about your education, your skills, and your achievements. If a résumé indicates that the applicant will best meet the company's needs, an interview will be arranged.

It is important to have an up-to-date résumé always on file. Such résumés can take different forms, depending on the way the information is organized. The two most common forms, the **chronological résumé** and the **functional résumé**, are shown in Figures 15-5 and 15-6. The chronological résumé lists information under the headings *Education* and *Work Experience* with the most recent information first. The functional résumé, so-called because it lists information according to the function it serves, lists this employment history under different skills. Again, in these sub-headings, the most recent information is placed first.

If you already have a résumé, follow the instructions below to bring it up to date. If you do not have one, follow these instructions to help you write one.

1. Keep your résumé short and to the point. Most people will not bother to read through several pages. In general, résumés should not be longer than two pages.
2. Use action words that emphasize your strong points. (See Figure 15-5 for examples of action words.) Remember that your résumé is often your only way of getting an interview. Sell yourself and your abilities in a positive and interesting manner.
3. Include your name, address, telephone number, education, work experience, and references. You may also want to include your special interests and goals. If you feel that it will help to sell your skills, include your date of birth; however, if you already feel at a disadvantage because of your age, you need not draw attention to it.

4. Under "education," list all the schools you have attended, giving the dates. Mention your grades if they are above average. List any scholarships or awards you have won and any sports, teams, bands, or school activities in which you have been involved.

5. Under "work experience," you can follow the example given in Figure 15-5, and list all the jobs you have held starting with the most recent one, giving the dates of employment, the company you worked for, and the nature of your responsibilities.

   If you choose to write a functional résumé, carefully select three or four skills that you feel are most important in the field of work in which you are interested. Under these headings, list examples of their application in your employment history.

   If you have never held a job before, list any work that you have done for others, including volunteer work, help given at a particular school or school function.

6. If you choose to list your interests, try not to mention activities that show your religious or political affiliations. Such information is personal. You will probably want to list any clubs or organizations to which you belong, and note hobbies and spare-time interests. This information will help a prospective employer determine what sort of person you are.

7. If you feel you have a good chance of getting a specific job, you will want to supply a potential employer with the names and addresses of people who will speak highly of your past performance at work or of your special qualities. Supply a minimum of two and a maximum of three names. The people you select to serve as a reference for you should be from a cross-section of your background. Never give the name of a relative as a reference. Potential employers are looking for people who will give an objective evaluation of your abilities and qualities. It is best to identify someone who will attest to your educational background, someone else who will be able to speak about your work habits or your commitment to a particular undertaking, and perhaps a friend or work associate who knows what kind of person you are — honest, conscientious, etc. Never list people as references without first receiving their permission to do so.

   If you are mailing many copies of your résumé, it is probably best to simply state that references will be supplied on request. If you do make this statement, you need to be prepared to supply a neatly typed list of the names, addresses, and telephone numbers of two or three people who have agreed to serve as references for you.

8. Keep your résumé visually attractive. It should be neatly and accurately typed on 21.5 cm x 28 cm (8 1/2" x 11") bond paper, and set up attractively on the page.

9. Purchase white 23 cm x 30 cm (9" x 12") envelopes so that you will not have to fold your résumé.

Include in your résumé
1. *name, address, telephone number*
2. *education*
3. *work experience*
4. *references if appropriate*
5. *date of birth, interests, and goals if you wish.*

Figure 15-5
An example of a chronological résumé

Résumé

M A R I E   L U B O W I T Z

13 Rose Avenue
Nepean, Ontario
K2G 2K2
(613) 663-0031

EDUCATION

1987	Diploma Medical Secretary	HUMBER COLLEGE 205 Humber College Blvd. Rexdale, Ontario M9W 5L7
	Given direct entry into second year of the program.	Typing 50 wpm. Shorthand 130 wpm. Word-processing (IBM) Senior First Aid Certificate (St. John's Ambulance)
1986	Graduated from Grade 12 of a combined four-year Arts & Science and Business Program.	BELL HIGH SCHOOL 40 Cedarview Road Nepean, Ontario K2G 2K2

EXPERIENCE

Feb. 1987	During Field Placement during College training, I - typed medical and technical material for doctors - organized filing system - handled reception of a busy medical practice.	EASTERN MEDICAL CENTRE 71 East Street Toronto, Ontario M4R 2P5
1986	As a part-time Switchboard Operator, I - took calls for doctors two nights per week, and Saturdays, during the school year - handled emergency calls from patients.	LAKESIDE MEDICAL CENTRE 511 Lakeshore Blvd. Toronto, Ontario M6R 2X3

...continued...

...page two...
Marie Lubowitz

1985	As a summer Filing Clerk, I	KLEIN'S HARDWARE CO. LTD. 130 Ross Street Nepean, Ontario K2R 3P3

- filed customers' orders and bills
- mailed out statements of outstanding balances
- dealt with customers in the store.

1984	As a Factory Worker, I	WRIGHT PHARMACEUTICAL COMPANY 111 South Street Ottawa, Ontario K2P 3X3

- packaged and stamped boxes of medications
- worked as junior shipper in the warehouse.

SPORTS

Swimming, tennis, and basketball.

HOBBIES

Knitting and crochet.

REFERENCES

Can be supplied on request. Letters of recommendation can also be shown at an interview.

Figure 15-6
An example of a functional résumé

Résumé

M A R I E   L U B O W I T Z

13 Rose Avenue
Nepean, Ontario
K2G 2K2
(613) 663-0031

CAREER OBJECTIVE

To work as a medical secretary for a family-oriented medical practice.

SECRETARIAL SKILLS

I have
- typed medical and technical material for doctors during field placement
- handled the paperwork for Klein's Hardware Co. Ltd.

INTERPERSONAL SKILLS

I have
- handled reception for a medical practice
- answered calls for doctors, including emergency calls, as a switchboard operator
- dealt with customers' at Klein's Hardware Co. Ltd.

ORGANIZATIONAL SKILLS

I have
- organized the filing system for a busy medical practice
- filed customers' bills as a filing clerk for Klein's Hardware Co. Ltd.

EDUCATION

1987	Diploma Medical Secretary	HUMBER COLLEGE 205 Humber College Blvd. Rexdale, Ontario M9W 5L7
1986	Graduated from Grade 12 of a combined four-year Arts & Science and Business Program.	BELL HIGH SCHOOL 40 Cedarview Road Nepean, Ontario K2G 2K2

...continued...

...page two...
Marie Lubowitz

WORK EXPERIENCE

Feb. 1987	<u>Field Placement during College</u> training	<u>EASTERN MEDICAL CENTRE</u> 71 East Street Toronto, Ontario M4R 2P5
1986	Part-time <u>Switchboard Operator</u>	<u>LAKESIDE MEDICAL CENTRE</u> 511 Lakeshore Blvd. Toronto, Ontario M6R 2X3
1985	Summer <u>Filing Clerk</u>	<u>KLEIN'S HARDWARE CO. LTD.</u> 130 Ross Street Nepean, Ontario K2R 3P3
1984	<u>Factory Worker</u>	<u>WRIGHT PHARMACEUTICAL COMPANY</u> 111 South Street Ottawa, Ontario K2P 3X3

SPORTS

Swimming, tennis, and basketball.

HOBBIES

Knitting and crochet.

REFERENCES

Can be supplied on request. Letters of recommendation can also be shown at an interview.

APPLICATIONS

9. In Chapter 6 you learned that it is important to identify your audience before you begin to write. It is equally important to know your audience when you prepare your résumé. Put yourself in the place of the person who will read your résumé and prepare it in draft form. Remember that you are trying to sell yourself to a potential employer. There is no room for modesty.

10. In groups of two or three, exchange your résumé with another person in your group. When you read your partner's résumés, pretend that you are a potential employer and prepare a written comment on what each presents. Use the following questions to guide your comments.
    (a) What impression does it convey?
    (b) Does it identify accomplishments as well as job responsibilities?
    (c) What mental picture do you have while you read this résumé?
    (d) Would you interview the applicant or not? Why?

11. Return each résumé to its originator. Discuss each reviewer's comments and rewrite your résumé until both you and your reviewers are pleased with the way it reads.

12. Type or print out your résumé, then use the following checklist to evaluate it.
    - Is it neatly and accurately typed?
    - Is it attractively set up and on good quality paper?
    - Is it well organized?
    - Is it complete and informative?
    - Have you listed your name, address, and telephone number at the top of the first page?
    - Have you included your education and work experience?
    - Have you mentioned your interests, hobbies, and goals?
    - Have you included any awards or recognition for achievement in either your school or your work experience?
    - Have you used an appropriate writing style?
    - Are the grammar and punctuation correct?
    - Do most of the statements use action verbs?

LETTERS OF APPLICATION

A letter of application, written either when applying for an advertised position, or as a letter of enquiry to a firm or organization that interests you, serves as your introduction to a potential employer. It creates the employer's first impression of you. You would not go to an interview without looking clean, alert, and properly dressed. For the same reason, your letter of application should not be poorly typed or set up in an unattractive way.

Letters of application should be short and interesting. They should highlight only your most important qualifications. All other details should be included in your résumé. You might mention how you learned about the job opening, tell the reader why you feel you could handle the job, and invite the reader to contact you for an interview.

If you are writing a general letter to a company that has not advertised for help, follow the same letter format and state the kind of work that you are looking for. By phoning the company first, you can find out the name of the person to whom the letter should be addressed. Get the proper spelling and the correct title. Mention any of your qualifications that you feel might be valuable to the company. Enclose a copy of your résumé when you send off the finished letter. Although it is acceptable to send a photocopy of your résumé, each letter of application should be an original. Figure 15-7 is an example of a letter of application.

Letters of application should
1. *be clean and neat*
2. *be an original*
3. *state important qualifications*
4. *sell your abilities*
5. *invite an interview.*

```
April 30, 19__


Mr. A.P. Horowitz
Director of Sales & Marketing
Trilow Computer Services
31 Bloor Street West
Toronto, Ontario
M8X 909

Dear Mr. Horowitz:

Could Trilow Computer Services make use of my wide knowledge
of computers, combined with my strong background in business
and accounting?

I am particularly interested in working in computer sales, as
I would like to combine my ability in computer studies with my
accounting and marketing skills.  In addition, I have solid
interpersonal abilities.  I believe that a position as sales
representative for an aggressive and innovative company such
as yours would be an ideal combination of these qualities.

If there is no position open for which I might be considered
at this time, I would appreciate it if you would keep my
application on file.

I look forward to discussing my potential employment with your
company in the near future.

Yours sincerely,



Lionel Symons
```

Figure 15-7
A letter of application

APPLICATIONS

13. As a class, using the classified section of your local newspaper, select an advertisement for a job opening. Apply the writing techniques identified in Chapter 12 and write a letter of application in response to the advertisement.
14. When your letters are ready, display them and prepare a list of interesting opening and closing paragraphs. Identify the statements that describe an applicant's skills and abilities in an interesting way.

THE INTERVIEW

Preparation

Each year, thousands of well-qualified applicants fail to get the jobs they want because they cannot communicate their qualifications effectively in a job interview. Their letters and résumés may have won them interview appointments. Their references may have checked out extremely well. But they do not make a sufficiently good impression to be hired.

Think of your job interview in the same way as an athlete thinks of an important race or game. Like the athlete, you are out to win, and to do this, you must be adequately prepared.

Much of what has been already covered in this book applies to good interview techniques. Take a few minutes to review the important skills of listening, speaking, thinking, and decision making. Identify some of the important points in the use of body language. Take another look at the interview simulation in Chapter 9. A successful job interview will depend on how well you have learned to communicate, how effectively you display appropriate attitudes in both what you say and how you use body language, and the knowledge and skills you have acquired. Remember that you want to make a better impression than anyone else being interviewed. Prepare for your interview just as you prepared for the letter of application you wrote. Think about the kind of person who will interview you. In an interview situation, the interviewer is your audience. What will this person be looking for?

How you see yourself will affect how others see you. If you are confident, others will have confidence in you. A character in one of Kurt Vonnegut's novels says "We are what we pretend to be, so be careful who you pretend to be." In other words, think confidently: your image will reflect your confident thoughts.

You can prepare for an interview ahead of time by using the research skills outlined in Chapter 11 to find out more about the company or organization to which you are applying. Use your library or make enquiries among family or professional contacts to gain background knowledge. This knowledge will help you to ask informed questions during the interview itself.

Remember in the *Viewpoints* section of Chapter 1 how Jorg's older sister Erica helped him to give notice to his employer by role-playing the situation? Role-playing the interview with a friend or family member can also be of help.

Preparing an imaginary **job description** — a list of specific tasks that an employee will be expected to perform — for the job you are applying for can help you clarify the skills that would make you a suitable employee.

Before the interview, list a number of questions that you might be asked and prepare answers to them. Here are some sample questions to get you started.

- Why do you think you want to work for this company?
- What are your responsibilities at your present job?
- What are your strengths and weaknesses relative to the job you are applying for?
- What was your greatest accomplishment at your last job?
- What are your hobbies and interests?
- How did you find out about this job opening?
- What have you done to prepare yourself for this interview (or for this kind of work)?
- Why did you leave your last position?
- How did you spend your spare time at school?
- How do you feel your education has prepared you for this job?
- What motivates you to do a job well?
- How would you define a successful career?
- What words would you choose to describe yourself?
- What major problems have you had in your work experience and how have you dealt with them?
- Describe a bad decision you made this year and elaborate on how you handled it.
- What did you learn from that situation?
- Why does this particular position appeal to you?
- Why is it suitable for you?
- What is the most important question I could ask you about your ability to perform the duties of this job?

You will also be asked "Are there any questions you would like to ask me?" Have some questions ready. You should want to know something more about what the company does, how successful it is in its field or industry, and how your work would fit into the overall picture.

The Interview Itself

Figure 15-8 shows some of the stages of applying for a job and going to an interview. Be on time arriving for your interview, and be polite and courteous to everyone you meet. Even the impression you make on the receptionists could influence your chances of being hired.

◀ **Figure 15-8(a)**
Lionel begins his search for a job as salesperson in the computer industry by using all the resources of his local Canada Manpower Centre and of his school guidance centre. He checks the newspaper for help-wanted ads. There are no jobs advertised that he would be qualified for, but he does see that Trilow Computer Services is advertising for other positions, and decides to send a résumé to the sales and marketing manager since Trilow Computer Services seems to be an expanding company.

▶ **Figure 15-8(b)**
Lionel prepares his résumé. He knows that this is his first introduction to a potential employer, so he uses a school computer to ensure that it is neat and well-designed. He takes time to plan it so that it really sells his abilities and skills.

◀ **Figure 15-8(c)**
Lionel writes a letter of application to the sales and marketing manager of Trilow Computer Services. After he has done a draft of the letter, he has someone else look it over through the eyes of a potential employer. He wants to be sure his letter grabs the reader's attention, and lists his strongest qualifications for working for Trilow. Figure 15-7 shows the letter of application that he writes. Can you think of any ways to improve it?

▶ **Figure 15-8(d)**
Lionel is lucky, and Alan Horowitz, the sales and marketing manager for Trilow Computer Services, calls Lionel to tell him there will be an opening in his department in a couple of weeks. Lionel does some careful research into the computer industry and finds out some information about the company which is interviewing him. He writes a list of questions which he would like to ask Mr. Horowitz, and questions which Mr. Horowitz may ask him. Then he takes the time to role-play an interview with a friend, basing the interview on these questions.

◀ **Figure 15-8(e)**
Lionel decides ahead of time what he will wear for the interview. He dresses conservatively and neatly, in clothes in which he feels comfortable. Just for luck, he wears the tie-pin that his brother gave him for being an usher at his wedding. It reminds him that his family are thinking of him and that gives him confidence.

◀ **Figure 15-8(f)**
Lionel arrives at the interview a few minutes early, having worked out ahead of time how long it will take to get there. He approaches the receptionist and remembers to treat her with courtesy and respect.

▶ **Figure 15-8(g)**
After he has filled in a company application form, Lionel still has a few minutes to wait until Mr. Horowitz is ready to see him. He knows he is on show as he waits, so he tries to feel calm and confident.

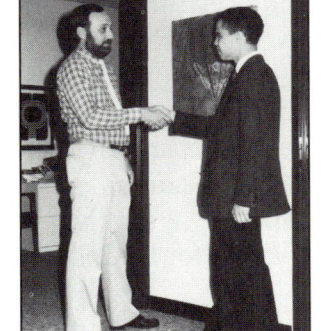

◀ **Figure 15-8(h)**
Mr. Horowitz is ready to speak with Lionel. Lionel is careful to look him fully in the eye, address him by name, and speak clearly. He shakes Mr. Horowitz by the hand firmly, knowing that this shows confidence.

▶ **Figure 15-8(i)**
During the interview, Lionel tells Mr. Horowitz why he would like to work for Trilow Computer Services. He responds to Mr. Horowitz's questions with interest and shows his interviewer that he is familiar with the work the company does. He tries not to be shy in talking about himself, and his body language shows openness, confidence, and respect.

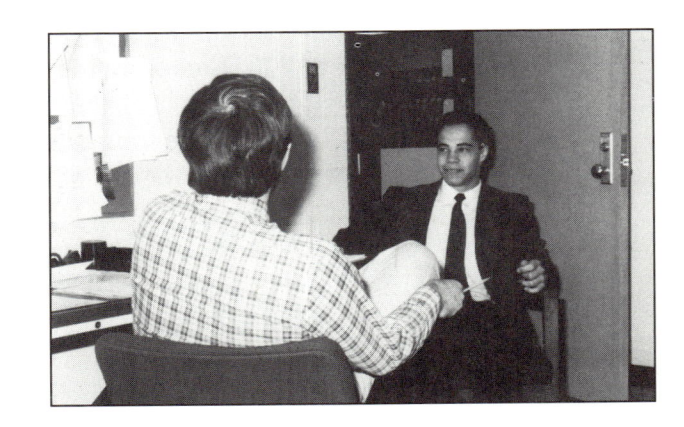

◀ **Figure 15-8(j)**
The next day, Mr. Horowitz calls Lionel to tell him he has got the job. Lionel is thrilled, and tells Mr. Horowitz how eager he is to work for Trilow. But he is careful to be business-like as well, and confirms during the telephone conversation such details as the day he starts working, the hours he will work, and the salary he will get.

JOB SEARCH

Be prepared to complete a company application form when you arrive. Carry a card in your wallet on which you have listed your social insurance number, health insurance number, and postal code. If you carry a spare copy of your résumé and a list of references, you should be able to provide all the information, such as dates and addresses, required in the application form.

Address the person who will be interviewing you by name, for example "Thank you for seeing me (interviewer's name)." Be prepared to shake hands but let the interviewer make the gesture first. A firm handshake will communicate self-confidence to the interviewer. Maintain eye contact throughout the interview. Show that you are sincere and interested.

Be prepared to talk about yourself. The employer might not come right out and ask why you should be hired, but instead, might say "Tell me about yourself." You will have to show that you are eager and enthusiastic, and have exactly the kind of attributes that are needed by the organization.

Dress comfortably and appropriately for the interview. Loud colours or flashy jewellery will not make a good impression. In Chapter 2 you read that you are not likely to listen as attentively if you are self-conscious about your appearance, so look your best and feel good about how you look. Dress in neat, clean, and conservative clothing that is not too casual. Remember, your appearance can make as much of an impression as your résumé. Rightly or wrongly, employers may make up their minds about your suitability for the job within the first couple of minutes of the interview.

To make sure that you arrive on time for the interview, find out ahead of time how long it will take you and allow a bit of time for poor traffic conditions.

Avoid the following pitfalls.
- Do not rush through filling out the application form. It will be read with an eye for neatness and clarity of expression.
- Do not talk in a derogatory fashion about a past or present employer. It is disloyal and unprofessional.
- Try not to be drawn into an argument. People who work together will often have different opinions and it is important for them to be able to come to terms with their different ideas.
- Salary negotiations should not be attempted until you have sold yourself as a strong candidate.

Bear in mind that, according to the Canadian Human Rights Act (1978), an employer cannot refuse to hire a candidate for a job because of the candidate's race, national or ethnic origin, colour, religion, age, sex, marital status, physical handicap, or conviction for which a pardon has been granted.

Before the interview
1. *research the company*
2. *role-play the interview or prepare a job description*
3. *list the questions you might be asked and prepare answers to them.*

At the interview
1. *be polite to everyone you meet*
2. *fill out application forms neatly and accurately*
3. *carry information you may need and a copy of your résumé.*

After the interview
1. *write a thank you note*
2. *fill out your job search record.*

After the Interview

It is courteous to send a written thank you note to the interviewer for taking the time to speak to you. It also creates a good impression to thank formally any contacts who have helped you research job opportunities. Compose your thank you note as soon as you get home, but keep it brief. Say thank you for the opportunity of the interview and summarize your qualifications. Close by saying that you hope you will hear from the interviewer soon. Then mail the note immediately.

After every interview, take out the file card you started for that company and make detailed notes about what you learned. This information will be useful to refer to when you need to know who interviewed you, the kinds of questions you were asked, and how you answered them.

Figure 15-9(a)
Dressing appropriately is important when you are being interviewed for a job, but the clothes you wear for an interview may depend on the job itself. What do you think these people would have worn to their job interviews?

Figure 15-9(b)

JOB SEARCH

335

APPLICATIONS

15. List different components of a person's appearance, for example, hair, clothing, accessories, hygiene, or eye contact, and identify what characteristics could cause negative or positive distractions.

16. Choose a partner whom you do not know very well. Take turns introducing yourself and talking about your friends, family, and interests. In three or four minutes, change roles and repeat the activity. When you are the listener, ask questions about topics as they are introduced.

STARTING OUT AT YOUR JOB

Congratulations! You have been hired for the job you wanted. You will probably feel a little uncertain, as well as excited, about the path your career has taken. Many adjustments will be made to your life as you move out of a school environment into a full-time job. Now, more than ever, you are responsible for the way you communicate with those around you. To fulfil this responsibility, remember these points.

1. Learn what your employer wants you to do. Ask questions to make sure you understand each objective in your job description.
2. Be pleasant and be punctual. Make sure you arrive on time and stay as long as you should. Continued absence is a sign that you are either not very interested in your job, or not capable of handling it. Try to schedule personal appointments outside of your working hours.
3. Get enough rest so that you have the energy you need to get through the day.
4. Keep personal telephone calls to a minimum.
5. Dress properly. Appropriate dress will vary from job to job. Make sure you project an image that reflects a positive, efficient, and interested person.
6. Be part of the team. Examine the teamwork skills identified in Chapters 3 and 14 and keep in mind that your success will depend on the efforts of every member of your team.
7. Take an active interest in your work. Show initiative. Once you are sure you can handle your job assignments, look for ways to improve what you are doing. Discuss your ideas with your supervisor.

JOB PERFORMANCE EVALUATION

If you take your job seriously, you will be continually evaluating your performance yourself. In addition, more formal evaluations take place. Chapter 9 introduced job evaluation interviews and the techniques that can help make them a valuable part of the evaluation process.

New employees can expect to have their performance evaluated after a three-month probationary period, or trial period, is completed. (If this is not customary in the organization where you work, you may want to ask your supervisor for an informal evaluation session at this time. Such sessions provide you with the feedback you need to do your job well.)

Whether performance reviews are formal or informal, they usually contain a component of self-assessment, whereby you are asked to evaluate your own performance; an assessment of your work made by your supervisor (this can be formal, or it may be based on observations your supervisor has made of your work); and an interview between you and your supervisor. Performance reviews usually result in statements, whether oral or written, that describe the employee's strengths, accomplishments, and areas for recognition or for improvement.

CHANGING JOBS

When the time comes to leave your place of employment, show your employer courtesy and consideration.

- Leave properly. No matter what your reason for leaving, give your employer two weeks to one month's notice.
- Finish as much of your work as possible and leave a description of what still needs to be done.
- If a new employee is hired to fill your position and you are asked to train that person, do your best to teach the new person your job and do not discuss any grievances you may have.
- Leave a forwarding address and telephone number.
- Ask your employer for a letter of reference. It might come in handy in any future job searches.

For successful employment opportunities
1. *remember your communication skills*
2. *be polite, courteous, and considerate to those around you*
3. *continually evaluate yourself as a way of doing your job well.*

APPLICATIONS

17. Write an imaginary job description for Lionel's job as computer salesperson (see the *Viewpoints* section of this chapter). His duties include selling computers to small businesses, keeping accurate records of sales calls, attending large trade fairs, and attending in-company sales meetings. Your teacher will help you establish a format to use for the job description.

18. In pairs, role-play a performance interview for Lionel. (Remember that such interviews should include assessment by employer and employee, an outline of the employee's strengths and accomplishments, and recommendations for recognition or improvement.) Refer to Chapter 9 to help you conduct the interview.

19. From the Help Wanted columns of the newspaper, find a job you would be interested in. Write a letter of application for the job.

JOB SEARCH

20. In pairs, role-play the interview for the job you have applied for in Question 19.

21. Using the resources of your library, guidance centre, or friends, find the name of a company you would be interested in. Write a letter of enquiry to the person in charge of hiring for that company.

22. In pairs, pretend to be the company official receiving your partner's letter of application. Make suggestions to your partner on ways to improve the letter.

CHAPTER SUMMARY

Your career is the professional path you have chosen to follow through study or employment. Plan your future career by examining your interests, aptitudes, and skills.

Preparing for a job search
- have a winning attitude
- obtain a social insurance card

The steps of a job search plan
- visit employment agencies or your guidance counsellor
- call previous employers
- check the help wanted ads
- tell family, friends, and acquaintances that you are looking for work
- write letters of application and send out résumés
- keep a job search record on file cards

Chronological or functional résumés
- short
- contain action verbs
- contain your name, address, telephone number, education, and work experience (also have your birth date, interests, and goals)
- visually attractive
- mail in a large white envelope

Letters of application
- clean and neat
- short and interesting
- contain your qualifications for the job
- addressed to an individual
- should be an original copy
- should be sent with a résumé

Preparing for an interview
- think positive and confident thoughts
- research the company or organization
- role-play the interview

- prepare an imaginary job description
- list possible questions and answers

During the interview
- be polite to everyone you meet
- have information with you to help fill out an application form
- have a copy of your résumé and a list of references
- address your interviewer by name
- be prepared to talk about yourself
- dress comfortably and conservatively
- be on time

After the interview
- write a thank you note
- fill out your job search record

After starting work
- learn your job
- be punctual
- get enough rest
- keep personal telephone calls and appointments to a minimum
- dress appropriately
- be part of a team
- be interested

Leaving an employment
- give adequate notice
- finish as much work as you can and leave a description of what still has to be done
- leave a forwarding address and telephone number
- ask your employer for a letter of reference

MAKING IT WORK

1. (a) If you are already working, obtain a blank copy of a job evaluation form from your company. If your company does not have evaluation forms or if you are not working, ask a family member or friend to obtain one for you.
   (b) Write in point form what you consider to be the most important features of the job evaluation form you have obtained. Be prepared to give a short presentation in class on the features of the job evaluation form.
   (c) After members of the class have given their presentations, decide as a class what seems to be the main features that the job evaluation forms have in common.
2. Read the following case, then answer the questions that follow.

    Bill Lee is getting ready for a job interview with Mary Polanski, the owner of a stationery shop. Bill has worked really hard to prepare for this interview. He has gathered the following information:

- Mary started the store herself more than 30 years ago and managed it alone for all these years.
- She employs three part-time and two full-time people. Each one of her employees has been with her for more than seven years.
- The store is open from 10 a.m. to 10 p.m. six days a week.
- Mary works an average of twelve to fifteen hours every day.
- Mary is opposed to labour unions and social benefits.
- She is a strong supporter of the women's movement.
- A new shopping centre has just opened a few kilometres down the road.

Brett, Bill's best friend, calls him the day before his appointment with Mary to make sure that Bill is all set for his interview. Bill shares what he has found out about Mary and her stationery store with Brett and tells him that he feels very good about the preparation he has made. Brett suggests that Bill should make up a list of questions that Mary might ask him and, based on what he has learned about the business, that he should be prepared with answers so that he would not be caught off guard at the interview.

(a) Is Brett correct, or does Bill know enough about the business to be able to handle anything Mary might ask at the interview?
(b) If Bill should decide to take Brett's advice, what questions would Mary be likely to ask and what kind of answers should Bill prepare?
(c) Relate the preparation of questions and answers to what you know about the communication process.

3. Read the following case, then answer the questions that follow.

Mr. Inouye came home from work, dropped into his comfortable armchair, and said to his wife, "I've just about had it at work.

"That young kid who joined our cleaning staff will drive me out of my mind. You'd think he could see that I'm a lot older than he is, and just working part-time to add a few dollars to our little pension.

"Well, he races through his job and gets back to the lounge way before I can. When he sees that it takes me longer to get my work done he chuckles, and tosses his equipment into the cupboard.

"What really gets me though, is that I know I'm doing a good job. My supervisor has always given me a good performance appraisal. But when this kid finishes his work and says to me, "Oh, you're not finished yet?" I'm ready to let him have it. Today, after he finished cleaning, he sat down, put his feet up on the counter, and began to tell me how I could get my job done faster if I did it this way or that way. I'm going to go in tomorrow and put this kid in his place."

(a) What are the barriers that are getting in the way of effective communication in this situation?
(b) Assume that both Mr. Inouye and the young man want to get along with each other on the job. What would you do if you were the young man? What would you do if you were Mr. Inouye?

4. Read the following case, then answer the questions that follow.

You have just been hired as the manager of a 20-person advertising and public relations department in a large corporation. During your first week on the job you discover that the staff in your department do not seem to be too thrilled working for you. They have heard that your background is in accounting and not marketing, and they do not feel you have the expertise needed to be an effective leader. Whenever you stop to talk to them, they answer politely, but coldly, and then go on with their work. You have also just learned that almost half of them applied for the position for which you were just appointed.

(a) You plan to hold a department meeting to "clear the air." What will you say?

(b) How will you go about building a better working team spirit?

APPENDIX A

English Usage

In the communication process, the sender encodes the message and the receiver decodes the message. If the sender and receiver are not using the same code, the message will not be understood. An essential part of the code is grammar, and therefore the usage of correct grammar is vital to the understanding of the message.

This appendix is intended as a reference section to be used for clarification of grammatical points, punctuation, and style. The content has been arranged in alphabetical order for quick and easy reference.

For further help we recommend that you consult a reliable dictionary such as *The Concise Oxford Dictionary of Current English* (Oxford: Clarendon Press) or *The Gage Canadian Dictionary* (Toronto: Gage Publishing Ltd., 1983). In addition, both *The Canadian Style: A Guide to Writing and Editing* from the Department of the Secretary of State (Toronto: Dundurn Press, 1985) or *The Little English Handbook for Canadians* by James B. Bell and Edward P. J. Corbett (Toronto: John Wiley & Sons, 1982) are handy references.

	Examples
a, an Use "an" before words that begin with a silent "h" or a vowel. Use "a" before all others.	an example, an hour a guarantee, a dog
ABBREVIATIONS As much as possible avoid abbreviations in business writing, unless their use is widely accepted and understood, as in the following examples:	
• abbreviate titles before and after a person's name	Mr., Mrs., Ms., Dr., Jr., Sr., B.A., Ph.D.

- abbreviate words such as Company, Corporation, and Manufacturing in a firm's name only if the firm uses the abbreviation. When in doubt, check the letterhead of the firm.

- never abbreviate cities and provinces in the body of material. Provinces may be abbreviated in the inside address of letters or in tabulations.

   Alta., B.C., Man., N.B., Nfld., N.W.T., N.S., Ont., P.E.I., P.Q. or Que., Sask., Y.T. or Yuk.

- never abbreviate Fort, Port, Point, or Mount in place names. As Saint varies, check an atlas before writing.

   Fort Erie, Port Alberni, Point Claire, Mount Forest, Saint John, N.B.; St. John's, Nfld.

- do not abbreviate points of the compass.

   The firm is located at 56 Main Street South. The firm is located on the south-east corner.

- never abbreviate days of the week or months of the year unless they are in a tabulation.

   May, June, and July cannot be abbreviated.

- a.m. and p.m. should be in lower case accompanied by a figure. With noon and midnight, a.m. and p.m. are not used.

   We arrived at 8 p.m. We arrived at eight o'clock. We arrived at 12 noon.

- write the following abbreviations without periods: acronyms (see definition below), names of well-known organizations, radio and television stations, names of well-known government agencies

   COBOL = Common Business Oriented Language, IBM, CNIB, CHUM, CFRB, CTV, CBC, UN, NATO

- use No. before figures and Number when it is the first word in a sentence.

   His insurance policy is No. 458602. Number 2154 has been cancelled.

"&" can be written to mean "and" in company names, but not as a short form of "and".

James Gregory & Sons

above
"Above" can be used as an adverb or a preposition. It should not be used as an adjective or a noun.

Do not say "See the above." or "...the above-noted material."

accept, except
"accept" means "to take"

We accept your explanation.

"except" means "with the exclusion of"

All except John went home.

ACRONYM
An acronym is a pronounceable word formed with the first letter or letters of each of a series of words.

radar, from radio detecting and ranging

adapt, adept, adopt
These three words are often confused.
"adapt" means "to change to suit"

They will adapt the new program to their needs.

"adept" means "particularly good at something"

She is very adept at giving presentations.

"adopt" means "take as one's own"

They will adopt our program.

adept - see adapt, adopt

ADJECTIVES
An adjective modifies a noun or a pronoun. Forms of adjective comparisons: quick, quicker, quickest.
A compound adjective is one in which two independent adjectives are joined by a hyphen to modify a single noun, e.g., first-quality.

adopt - see adapt, adept

adverse, averse
Note the difference in the meaning of these words.
"adverse" means "unfavourable"

The adverse reaction to the product caused sales to drop.

"averse" means "opposed"

I am averse to public speaking.

advice, advise
"advice" is a noun
"advise" is a verb

The advice was free.
They will advise us soon.

ADVERBS
An adverb describes, explains, or limits a verb, adjective, or another adverb. An adverb usually answers one of the following questions:
what, why, when, how, how much, how little, where, to what extent.
Conjunctive adverbs connect two independent clauses in one sentence and act as regular adverbs in the second clause. Examples are accordingly, however, nevertheless, therefore, consequently, likewise, otherwise, thus, furthermore, moreover, then, yet.

affect, effect
These words are often confused because they are frequently pronounced the same way.
"affect" is a verb meaning "to influence"
"effect" is a noun meaning "a result"

The cold affects us adversely.

The effect was startling.

"effect" is used infrequently as a verb meaning "to bring about"

Better working conditions effected a change in the workers' sense of well-being.

allowed, aloud
"allowed" means "permitted"

They are allowed to go there.

"aloud" means "using voice"

They read aloud to us.

ENGLISH USAGE

all ready, already
Note the difference in meaning.
"all ready" means "prepared"

"already" means "before this time"

The boardroom is all ready for our use.
The boardroom was already packed.

all together, altogether
"all together" means "in one group"

"altogether" means "entirely"

The animals are all together.
It was altogether wrong.

already - see all ready

altogether - see all together

among, between
Use "among" when there are more than two people or things involved.

Use "between" when there are two people or things involved.

Mai, Gerry, and Dominic will share the work among themselves.
Mai and Gerry will divide the work between themselves.

APOSTROPHE
An apostrophe is used
- in place of omitted letters or numbers

It's too late to walk and there aren't any buses.
In '93 the school will hold its tenth anniversary reunion.

- to indicate the possessive by adding 's to a singular or plural noun that does not end in "s" or adding ' to a plural noun that ends in "s"
Note:
Apostrophies are used only with nouns to show possession. Pronouns do not use an apostrophe to show possession.

girl's, boy's, cat's
children's, men's
girls', ladies',
boys', teachers'

their coats, her car, its cover
The coat is hers.

appraise, apprise
"appraise" means "to estimate the value of"

"apprise" means "to inform"

They will have the painting appraised before insuring it.

They have been apprised of the value of the painting.

as if - see if

as, like
"like" usually means "similar to" or, as a verb, "to enjoy"

This page is like the one before.
I like reading.

346 APPENDIX A

"as" is a conjunction introducing a clause

I'm sure you will enjoy the book as I did.

as though - see if

between - see among

can, may, could, might
"can" means "able to"
"may" expresses permission
"might" and "could" express doubt or imply a possibility

I can sit up.
May I sit up?
We might be able to sit up if we could use our hands.

CAPITALIZATION
Capitalize
- the first word of a sentence, a direct quotation, a complimentary closing, and each item in a listing

Anna said, "Our new assistant works well."
Yours sincerely
a. Application form
b. Résumé

- titles of books and magazines; prepositions of four or fewer letters are not capitalized

The Language of Business Communication
Environmental News

- people's titles written after their names on envelopes and in inside addresses

Mr. F. Lawry, Manager
Chrata Investments

- people's titles before their names

Prime Minister Baker

- capitalize titles after names only when they refer to a high-ranking government official

A. Sorensen, Premier of Saskatchewan, was at the meeting.
Ms. Henshaw, the chairperson of the school board, called.

- the names of places

Ireland, Main Street
Stanley Park
The East Coast is a beautiful area to visit.
Caledon East

Compass points are capitalized if they designate a specific region or are part of a proper noun.

- "city" when it follows the name of the city

Quebec City, city of Ottawa

- the names of companies, organizations, schools, political parties, etc.

John Wiley & Sons, Big Brothers, Chamber of Commerce, Sheridan College, Liberal Party, Methodist Church

- brand names

Which facial tissue would you like, Kleenex or Facelle?

- days of the week, months, and holidays

  Monday, January, Thanksgiving, Christmas, Yom Kippur

- proper adjectives (adjectives derived from proper nouns)

  Spanish, British, Russian, Inuit

- specific course titles

  I enrolled in Auditing I, Advanced Accounting, and one science course.

choose, chose
"choose" is the present tense of the verb meaning "to pick out"

They choose their work carefully.

"chose" is the past tense

They chose to dress quickly.

cite, sight, site
"cite" is a verb meaning "quote or commend"

She was cited in the newspaper article.

"sight" is a noun meaning "vision"

They lost sight of John.

"site" is also a noun meaning "place"

They will move to a new site.

COLON
A colon is used
- before a list

  These are the most important factors to consider: the size of the audience, the location of the meeting, and the time we have been allocated.

- to separate hours and minutes

  The train leaves at 5:30 p.m.

COMMA
A comma is used
- before the conjunction (and, but, or, nor) joining two clauses

  The size of the audience is important, but we should also consider other factors.

- to separate three or more items listed in a series

  Listening, speaking, and reading are useful skills.

- after an introductory word, phrase, or clause

  Fortunately, I took the car to be serviced by Sandy before the problem became serious.

- before a non-restrictive phrase or clause. Non-restrictive means it is not essential to the meaning of the sentence.

  Send your insurance claim to E. Jong, who is our representative in your area.

- to set off a parenthetical expression. Parenthetical expressions are words or phrases that may be removed from a sentence without affecting the meaning.

  I am not pleased with my report, to be honest.

- to set off an appositive. An appositive is a word or group of words used to explain or to give additional information about the first expression.

  Please arrange an interview with Mrs. Knuttell, our office co-ordinator.

- to set off titles or degrees following a person's name

  Further research by M. Damiani, M.D., will help those suffering from spinal injury.

- to set off Inc. or Ltd. in a company name

  Debouche, Inc., is a new company specializing in urban planning.

- to set off the year when the month is given

  On May 14, 1990 there will be a retirement party for him.

- to set off the province when a city is given

  I moved from Stratford, Ontario to Aylmer, Quebec.

- to separate two figures that follow each other

  In 1987, 350 employees were hired.

compare to, compare with
"compare to" is used when comparing different things

His walk was compared to the flight of a bird.

"compare with" is used when comparing similar classes of things

They compared his walk with hers.

complement, compliment
"complement" means "something that completes"

They will move when their full complement of helpers arrive.

"compliment" means "praise"

They sent their compliments to us for your work in this field.

confidant, confident
"confidant" means "a trusted friend"

She is my confidant.

"confident" means "being sure of oneself"

I am confident that we will win.

CONJUNCTIONS
Conjunctions are words used to connect words, phrases, or clauses.
Co-ordinating conjunctions: and, but, or, nor
Correlative conjunctions are used in pairs to connect like grammatical elements: both ... and, not only ... but also, either ... or, neither ... nor, whether ... or
Subordinate conjunctions join subordinate clauses to other clauses:

| after | before | provided that |
| when | although | even if |

ENGLISH USAGE

since	whenever	as
for	so that	where
as if	how	than
wherever	as soon as	if
that	whether	as though
in case that	unless	while
because	in order that	until
why		

continual, continuous
Subtle differences in meaning exist between these adjectives.

"continual" means "happening often"	Their continual calls for new clerks gave us some concern.
"continuous" means "happening without interruption"	The continuous hum of equipment was distracting.

council, counsel
Council is a noun; counsel is a verb.

"council" means "a group of people"	The council will meet tomorrow.
"counsel" means "to give advice"	Counsel your friends to start working.

DASH
A dash is used

- for emphasis

  The first job I applied for — I got.

- for summarizing

  Safety boots, a hard hat, and safety glasses — these must be worn at all times.

- for repetition

  Right now — at this very moment — our operators are awaiting our calls.

DOUBLE NEGATIVES
A double negative in a sentence cancels the negative intent, for example,
   We can't hardly hear it. (incorrect)
   We can hardly hear it. (correct)
Negative words that do not need an additional negative: scarcely, only, hardly, but, never

effect - see affect

eligible, illegible
These words are frequently confused.

"eligible" means "suitable or qualified"	She is an eligible candidate.
"illegible" means "unreadable"	His handwriting is illegible.

emigrate, immigrate
These words have opposite meanings although they sound similar.

"emigrate" means "move out of a country" — They will emigrate to New Zealand.

"immigrate" means "to move into a country" — They have immigrated here.

eminent, imminent
"eminent" means "noteworthy" — An eminent lawyer is in town.

"imminent" means "about to happen" — The bell is imminent.

except - see accept

EXCLAMATION MARK
An exclamation mark is used to express strong feelings. It may be used after
- a word — Congratulations!
- a phrase — Such a shame!
- a sentence — You are so lucky!

Exclamation marks should be used sparingly, if at all, in business writing.

farther, further
"farther" shows physical distance — They could see farther up the road than we could.

"further" means "additional" — They will take further action.

foreword, forward
"foreword" is a noun meaning "preface" — Read the foreword to the book.

"forward" is an adverb meaning "onward or ahead" — Go forward into the forest.

formally, formerly
"formally" means "in a formal way" — They were formally introduced.

"formerly" means "before" — He came from Dawson City formerly.

forward - see foreword

further - see farther

good, well
"good" is an adjective and modifies nouns — They earned good grades.

"well" is an adverb and follows verbs — They did their work well.

hear, here
"hear" means "to listen to" — Can you hear the birds call?

"here" denotes a place — Bring the book here.

ENGLISH USAGE

if, as if, as though, wish
after any of these words use "were" instead of "was"

You would find it amusing if you were here.

illegible - see eligible

immigrate - see emigrate

imminent - see eminent

lay, lie
Note the difference in meaning between these verbs.

"lay" means "put down"

Lay your papers on the table.

"lie" means "recline or to tell a falsehood"

Lie in the sun tomorrow.
She didn't intend to lie about her actions.

lead, led
"lead" has two meanings; as a noun it means "a metal"; as a verb it is the present tense of the verb "to lead"

It is made of lead.
You lead the way now.

"led" is the past tense of the verb "to lead"

You led the way last time; now it's my turn.

lie - see lay

like - see as

loose, lose
"loose" means "not tight"

Her clothing was loose.

"lose" means "mislay or miss"

Don't lose your place.

may - see can

MODIFIERS
Modifiers are words or phrases that go with another word to make the meaning clear. Misplaced modifiers not only make the meaning difficult to discern but also result in unintentional humour.
e.g., Walking down the street, we saw a cemetery.
    We saw a cemetery walking down the street.

NOUNS
Nouns are words that refer to something that can be seen, heard, or talked about. Proper nouns are names of people or places. They are always capitalized.

NUMBERS
In business correspondence, numbers are more often written in figures than in words.
- write numbers one through ten in words and use figures for numbers over ten

There are three records on sale.
Over 15 garage sales were held today.

• be consistent when numbers are used in a series	The following texts must be ordered: 7 Math, 25 History, and 37 English.
• if a number begins a sentence, spell it out	Fourteen people won prizes in the lottery.
• when one number immediately follows another number, spell the smaller of the two numbers	A course requirement is two 10-page essays.
• use figures with a.m. and p.m. When using the 24-hour clock, time is expressed in two figures followed by a colon and the last two figures.	The plane arrives at 2 p.m. The plane arrives at 09:00.
• use figures for amounts of money	The book cost $5.95.
• use a "$" rather than dollars	The company is valued at $2 million.
• use figures with "cents" unless the dollar sign is used elsewhere in the sentence	The toy cost 89 cents. The stapler cost $7.95; the tape dispenser, $14.98; and the pen, $0.59.
• use cardinal numbers (1, 2) when the day follows the month	July 7
• use ordinal numbers (1st, 2nd) when the day precedes the month	7th of July
• use figures with "percent" in isolated cases	Our company owns 50 percent of the farm.
• use figures with "%" when percent is used frequently	We offer discounts of 2%, 5%, and 7% depending on the size of the order.
• use figures with metric units Metric units are not followed by a period unless they end the sentence; neither are they pluralized.	This pattern required 4 m of fabric. The recipe calls for 1 kg of chicken wings. Buy a 100 ml tube of toothpaste.

PARAGRAPHS
A paragraph is a group of related sentences. The main topic of a paragraph can be summarized in one sentence and is usually the introductory sentence. Paragraphs in business writing are normally about three to five sentences long.

PARENTHESES
Parentheses are used

• to enclose words that give additional or explanatory information	The terms are 2/10, n/30 (our standard rate) for your order.
• to emphasize additional information, use commas or dashes; to de-emphasize additional information, use parentheses	Parentheses (brackets) are used to enclose additional information.

ENGLISH USAGE

- to set off references and directions

  The minutes state that the sum is $2500 (see Appendix A).

- to enclose numbers or letters used in enumerated material

  We need the following information: (1) your SIN, (2) your health insurance number, (3) your passport number.

PERIOD
A period is used at the end of
- sentences

  I applied for the job.

- most abbreviations

  etc., Ltd., Inc.

personal, personnel
"personal" implies belonging to a particular person

I have my personal beliefs.

"personnel" means "employees"

Our personnel records are confidential.

PLURAL NOUNS
The most common nouns form their plural by adding 's' to the singular form.

tree - trees
boy - boys
girl - girls

Common nouns ending in s, sh, ch, x, and z form their plurals by adding "es" to the singular form.

lens - lenses
brush - brushes
branch - branches
tax - taxes
topaz - topazes

Plurals of compound nouns are formed on the most important word.

maid of honour - maids of honour
major-general - major-generals

Plurals of nouns ending in "y": if the "y" is preceded by a consonant, the plural is formed by changing the "y" to "i" and adding "es";

supply - supplies

when the "y" is preceded by a vowel, the plural is formed by adding "s".
This rule does not apply to proper nouns.

valley - valleys

Some nouns change the vowel when made plural.

man - men, goose - geese, foot - feet
mouse - mice,

Some plural nouns end in "en" or "ren".

child - children
ox - oxen

Some plurals of nouns ending in "f" or "fe" change the "f" or "fe" to a "v" and add "es".

shelf - shelves
life - lives

Others simply add "s".

chief - chiefs
safe - safes

Some nouns are the same singular or plural.

deer, Chinese, cod, sheep, politics, corps, statistics, scissors, etc.

precede, proceed
"precede" means "to go before" — An announcement will precede the concert.

"proceed" means "to go forward or carry on" — She proceeds with her work, allowing no interruptions.

principal, principle
"principal" as an adjective means "most important" — The principal word in the sentence was omitted.

"principal" as a noun means "head" — The principal of the school saw the accident.

"principle" means "law, rule, or truth" — The principle here is honesty.

proceed - see precede

PREPOSITIONS
A preposition is a connecting word that shows the relationship between a noun or a pronoun and some other word in the sentence.
- commonly used prepositions — about, above, after, among, at, before, below, beside, between, off, until

PRONOUNS
A pronoun is a word used to replace a noun. — I, you, him, they it, she, me, who

PUNCTUATION
Punctuation helps the writer achieve clarity. As you are inserting punctuation in your writing, ask yourself whether the punctuation will help the reader to understand your message. Too much or too little punctuation can cause ambiguity. When in doubt about the rules of punctuation, consult an English usage text that covers the subject.

raise, rise
These two verbs have different meanings.
"raise" means "to lift up" — They raised their hands.

"rise" means "to get up" — The sun will rise tomorrow.

right, write
"right" as an adjective means "correct" and the noun means "in accordance with what is good, proper, and just" — The answer was right. He has a right to a fair trial.

"write" means "communication by writing" — Write your answers here.

rise - see raise

ENGLISH USAGE

SEMICOLONS

A semicolon indicates to the reader a partial stop and is used mainly in compound sentences

- to join two independent clauses when the conjunction has been omitted

The sender encodes message; the receiver decodes it.

SENTENCES

A sentence is a group of words that represents a complete thought. It contains a subject and a verb.

Subject - What the sentence is about. It can be a single word or a group of words.

Verb - A word that asserts or assumes action, condition, or state of others.

Below are some common sentence problems.

Fragment - A group of words without a verb is an incomplete thought or a sentence fragment. It leaves the reader wondering what the statement is about.
> e.g., If the account is correct. (fragment)
> If the account is correct, I will pay it. (complete)

A comma splice - Two complete sentences joined by a comma when they should have a period between them.
> e.g., I was amazed to receive such a big lunch bill, I found the food bland and the service poor.
> I was amazed to receive such a big lunch bill. I found the food bland and the service poor. (correct)

Run-on sentence - Is a sentence that due to its length loses its initial meaning.
> e.g., Some of the best duck-shooting in the world may be enjoyed along the northern shores of the great lakes, and the marshes which in places are formed along the low coasts of Ontario and Erie are among the favourite feeding-grounds of the ducks when they halt for a few days' rest during their migration to the south.

Misplaced words in a sentence - Sometimes a sentence is ambiguous or difficult to understand because a word or phrase that explains another word is not placed next to it.
> e.g., He saw the place where the Battle of Hastings was fought last year. (misplaced modifier)
> Last year he saw the place where the Battle of Hastings was fought. (clear)

stationary, stationery

Note the difference in the meaning of these two words. One is an adjective; the other a noun.

"stationary" means "not moving"

The train is now stationary.

"stationery" is a noun meaning "writing materials"

They used the hotel stationery to write home.

that, which

"that" begins a clause that defines (sometimes called a restrictive clause), that is, the clause makes the noun it modifies more specific

The meeting that we attended was boring.
The book that I lent him was returned.

"which" begins a clause that is non-defining, that is, the clause does not limit or define the noun it modifies. Instead the clause gives a reason or additional information. Non-defining clauses are set off by commas.

My book, which he said he enjoyed, was returned.
The meeting, which was well attended, was boring.

APPENDIX A

their, there, they're
Note the differences in meaning.

"their" is a pronoun — Their books are here.

"there" refers to a place — Their books are over there.

"they're" is the abbreviation of "they are" — They're looking for their books.

there - see their, they're

they're - see their, there

to, too, two

"to" is a preposition — I went to school.

"too" means "also" — He went there too.

"two" is a number — I bought two of them.

UNDERSCORE
Underscore, or underline, titles of books, magazines, and newspapers.

VERBS
A verb is a word that asserts or assumes action, condition, or state of being, for example, do, act, think.

well - see good

who, whom, whose, who's
These pronouns are frequently confused.

"who" is a pronoun used as the subject in a sentence — Who will send it?

"whom" is a pronoun used as the object in a sentence — To whom shall I send it?

"whose" is a possessive pronoun — Whose books are these?

"who's" is the abbreviation of "who is" — Who's coming for dinner?

your, you're

"your" is a possessive pronoun — Your books are here.

"you're" is the abbreviation of "you are" — You're here now.

ENGLISH USAGE

APPENDIX B

Letter and Memorandum Formats

Generally accepted formats for letters and memorandums are provided in this appendix. However, most companies have their own preferred formats for employees to follow. When you begin a new job, ask your supervisor for guidance, or ask to see samples of the various documents you will be writing, so that you can follow the established format. Large companies may have a section of formatting guidelines in their company manuals.

1. Parts of a Letter

The various parts of a business letter are illustrated in Figure B-1. Three different formats are illustrated in Figures B-2, B-3, and B-4.

Letterhead - Most companies have preprinted letterhead paper for their correspondence. Included on the letterhead is the company name and address, and often a logo or slogan and the telephone number. Other information that might appear on the letterhead is a list of regional or branch offices, officers or partners of the company, and products offered for sale.

In order to make a good impression on customers, companies want their letterhead to be attractive. Letterhead paper is usually of high quality, sometimes tinted, and the printed portion may be embossed and/or produced in colour. Some organizations, particularly community or charity groups with small budgets, may have the secretary keyboard the letterhead on plain paper to avoid the expense of printed stationery.

Return Address - If the return address is not included in the letterhead, then it appears directly before the date, as shown in Figure B-3. The standard format for addresses is to have the street address on one line and the town or city and province on another line. The postal code can either follow the province if there is sufficient room, or appear on a new line. Unless abbreviations are used, there is no need for punctuation at the end of the lines.

Figure B-1
Parts of a letter

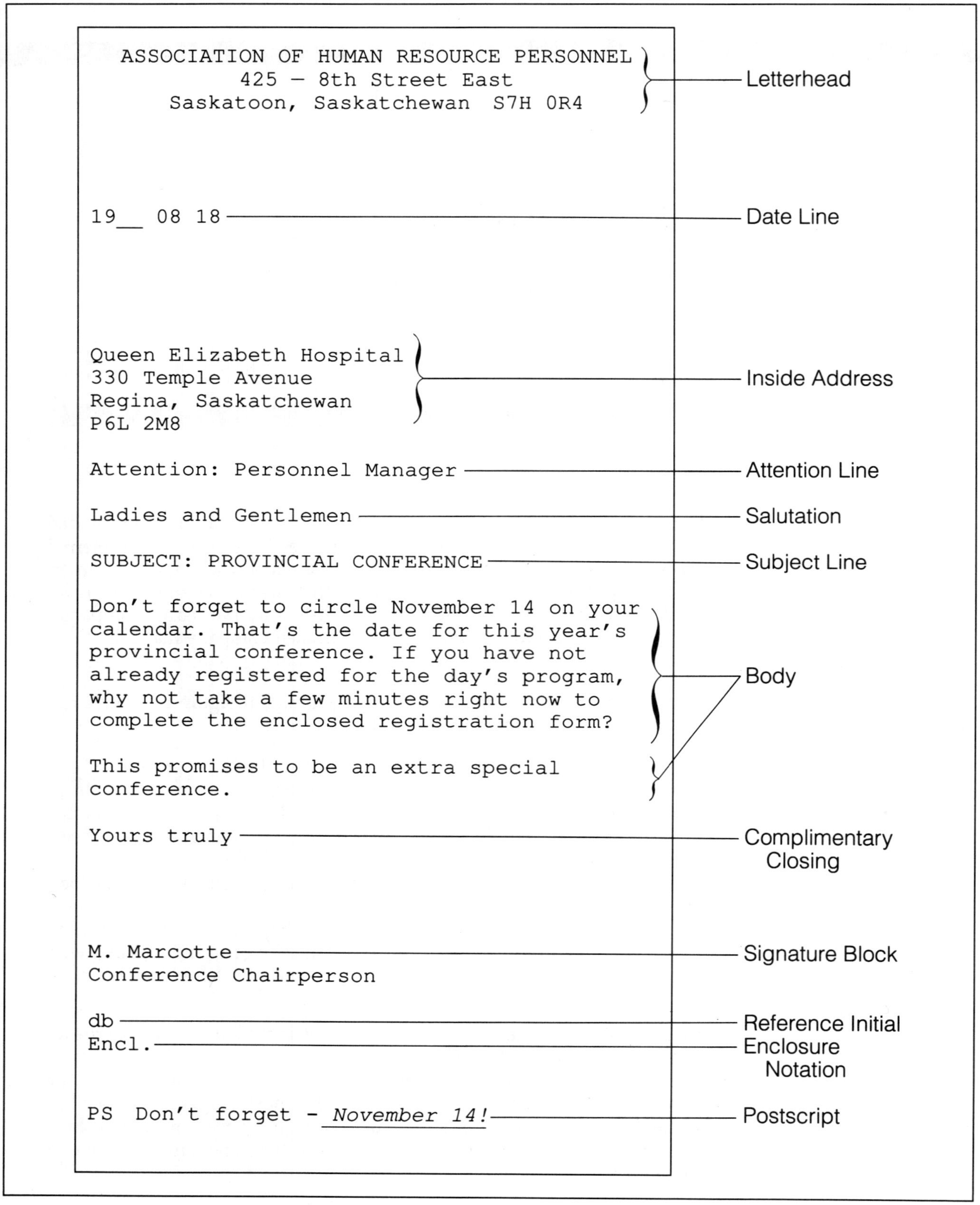

```
        ASSOCIATION OF HUMAN RESOURCE PERSONNEL  ⎫
               425 — 8th Street East             ⎬──── Letterhead
          Saskatoon, Saskatchewan  S7H 0R4       ⎭


   19__ 08 18 ──────────────────────────────────────── Date Line



   Queen Elizabeth Hospital  ⎫
   330 Temple Avenue         ⎬──────────────────────── Inside Address
   Regina, Saskatchewan      ⎪
   P6L 2M8                   ⎭

   Attention: Personnel Manager ────────────────────── Attention Line

   Ladies and Gentlemen ────────────────────────────── Salutation

   SUBJECT: PROVINCIAL CONFERENCE ──────────────────── Subject Line

   Don't forget to circle November 14 on your  ⎫
   calendar. That's the date for this year's   ⎪
   provincial conference. If you have not      ⎪
   already registered for the day's program,   ⎬──── Body
   why not take a few minutes right now to     ⎪
   complete the enclosed registration form?    ⎭

   This promises to be an extra special
   conference.

   Yours truly ─────────────────────────────────────── Complimentary
                                                       Closing



   M. Marcotte ─────────────────────────────────────── Signature Block
   Conference Chairperson

   db ──────────────────────────────────────────────── Reference Initial
   Encl. ───────────────────────────────────────────── Enclosure
                                                       Notation

   PS  Don't forget - *November 14!* ───────────────── Postscript
```

360 APPENDIX B

Figure B-2
Full block style, no-point punctuation

```
                    FARAJ IMPORTING/EXPORTING
                         447 Shuster Street
                    Montreal, Quebec   P4R 7S9



19__ 10 03



Mr. D. McDonald
Southwest Printing Limited
18 Kennedy Road South
Brampton, Ontario
L6V 3N2

Dear Mr. McDonald

SUBJECT: LETTER FORMAT

Full block style has become very popular because it is fast and
easy to format. Notice that all parts of the letter begin at
the left margin. No-point punctuation is usually used with this
style. This means that there is no punctuation after the
salutation, after the complimentary closing or other addressing
or closing lines.

A subject line may be used to inform the reader of the content
of the letter. "Re" or "Subject" may or may not be included at
the beginning. The line may be keyboarded in block capitals or
initial capitals only.

If the company name appears after the closing, it is keyboarded
in block capitals and is aligned with the closing.

Yours truly

FARAJ IMPORTING/EXPORTING



L. Britten
Manager

db
```

LETTER AND MEMORANDUM FORMATS

Figure B-3
Semi-block style, open punctuation

                                              14 Wellington Street
                                              Winnipeg, Manitoba
                                              T3W 6L8
                                              March 3, 19__

Mr. D. McDonald
Accounts Payable
Southwest Printing Limited
18 Kennedy Road South
Brampton, Ontario
L6V 3N2

Dear Mr. McDonald

     Semi-block style is the same as block style except that the paragraphs are indented five spaces. Although not used that frequently by businesses any more, it is still common in personal handwritten letters.

     If you are using paper which does not have preprinted letterhead, then the return address is written above the date line as illustrated in this example. Notice that the name of the person or organization is not included in the return address as this appears in the closing of the letter.

     The reference initials, db, which appear in Fig. 10/3 and 10/5 are the initials of the person who keyboarded the letter. If changes are required after proofreading the letter or if there is a later query about the letter, the author knows which secretary to approach. In a handwritten letter, reference initials are not required. Notations such as Encl., c (copy), P.S. are placed below the reference initials.

                                                      Yours very truly

                                                      Arthur Hubbard

P.S. If information is added at the end of the letter, a postscript is used.

Figure B-4
Block style, two-point punctuation

```
                    FARAJ IMPORTING/EXPORTING
                         447 Shuster Street
                     Montreal, Quebec  P4R 7S9


                                        March 3, 19__

REGISTERED



Southwest Printing Limited
18 Kennedy Road South
Brampton, Ontario
L6V 3N2

Attention: Publicity Manager

Ladies and Gentlemen:

If you use block style, the date and closing begin at centre.
As this letter illustrates two-point punctuation, there is a
colon after the salutation and a comma after the closing.

If a letter is short, increase the number of lines between the
date and inside address and/or in the signature space to give a
more balanced placement. Sometimes a letter of less than 10
lines is double spaced to improve its appearance on the paper.

Notations such as REGISTERED, CONFIDENTIAL, and PERSONAL are
keyboarded on the envelope as well as on the letter.

An alternate way of addressing a letter to an individual in a
company is by using an attention line. An attention line begins
at the left margin and may be underscored. The salutation is
Gentlemen, Ladies or Ladies and Gentlemen, whichever is
appropriate for the company.

If the author of the letter is male, the title Mr. is not
keyboarded with his name. Miss, Mrs. or Ms may be keyboarded if
the author is female.

                                        Sincerely yours,


                                        Mrs. R. Higgins
                                        Manager

db
```

Letters are approximately centered on the page. Consequently, the length of the letter will determine how far from the top edge of the page the first line of the return address will appear. However, a margin of at least 4 cm should be left at the top and bottom of a page.

Dateline - The date used is the date the letter is keyboarded rather than the date the letter is drafted. The month is written out in full. No punctuation is used after the year, and the day of the week is not included as part of the date. Some companies use a metric format in which the date is represented by numbers ordered as follows: year, month, day. Figure B-2 shows a dateline in metric format. Note that no punctuation is used in a metric dateline.

Inside Address - The inside address identifies the party to whom the letter is being sent. When directing your letter to a specific person, use either a courtesy title (Miss, Mrs., Ms., or Mr.), or a professional title (Dr., Professor, Reverend), but do not use both. Ms. should be used if you do not know a woman's marital status, or if the woman prefers that title. If you are unable to determine the sex of the person, state the name in the inside address as you know it, for example, J. Mills. The salutation in this case would have to be Dear J. Mills.

If the position of the person is to be included, it can appear either on the same line as the name, or on the next line.

The complete name and address of the business or organization should follow the name of the person. Abbreviate only those words in the company name that the company itself abbreviates. If you are unsure of the correct spelling or the exact address, there may be past correspondence from the company with the information you need, or possibly you can find it in the telephone directory.

Lines in the inside address should not extend beyond the mid point of the page, unless it is unavoidable. Do not use punctuation at the end of a line unless the last word is abbreviated. For letters sent outside Canada, the name of the country appears as the last line of the inside address.

Two examples of inside addresses follow.

Mr. P. Lorenzo	Dr. S. Ng, Director
Vice-President	Medical Research, Inc.
Litho Print Company	407 Third Avenue
66 York Road, Unit 8	Red Deer, Alberta
Buffalo, N.Y. 93218	T4N 4L7
U.S.A.	

Attention Line - The attention line is gradually dropping out of use, as it is more formal than including the individual's name with the inside address. One way in which an attention line is useful, however, is to solve the difficulty of knowing the position but not the name of an individual, as shown in Figure B-4.

Salutation - The salutation is a greeting to the party named in the first line of the inside address. If this is a specific person, then use the person's name in the salutation. The degree of formality in the salutation depends on how well you know the addressee. If you know someone well and are on a first name basis, you could say, for example, Dear Keith. Otherwise you would use a courtesy title and surname — Dear Mr. Stoness.

If the letter is addressed to a company in general, any one of the following salutations is acceptable: Gentlemen, Ladies, Dear Sir, Dear Sir or Madam, Dear Ladies and Gentlemen. If you are unsure of the proper salutation to use in a special case, consult a secretarial reference book for the correct form.

Subject Line - The subject line is used to draw the reader's attention to the main topic of the letter. Very often "Re:", meaning "with regard to" is used instead of "Subject." The use of block capitals, underscoring, or boldface is a matter of personal preference or company practice. No punctuation appears at the end of the subject line.

Body - The body can be formatted in one of two styles — block or semi-block style. In block style, the paragraphs are not indented; they begin flush with the left hand margin. In semi-block style, paragraphs are indented, usually five spaces. When a word processor is used, there is also the choice of a ragged right margin or a justified right margin (the words at the ends of lines are flush with the right hand margin). Companies, or individuals within companies, may have a style preference. If not, it is simply a matter of personal preference which style you adopt.

Business letters should be divided into three or more short paragraphs that reflect the content. In that way they will be more appealing visually and more readable. When writing a composition, you try to attract the reader's interest right at the beginning. Similarly, for business letters it is important to catch the reader's interest in the first paragraph by incorporating an idea that relates to the reader — a "you" message.

Paragraphs should be separated by a blank line, with the rest of the lines single spaced.

Complimentary Closing - Conventional closings for business letters include: Yours truly, Very truly yours, Sincerely, Yours sincerely, and Sincerely yours. Note that only the first word of the closing begins with a capital.

Company Name - Whether or not the company name appears below the complimentary closing depends on company policy. If the company name appears, it may indicate that the company is legally responsible for the letter rather than the employee sending it. Once again, there is no punctuation at the end of the company name unless it ends in an abbreviation. Figure B-2 shows the placement of the company name.

Signature Block - The signature block consists of the writer's signature; the writer's name in full, keyboarded; and the position or title of the writer, keyboarded. Sometimes a department also appears. There is no punctuation at the end of the lines in the signature block.

Reference Initials - The uppercase initials of the writer may appear below the signature block, followed by the lowercase initials of the person who keyboarded the letter, for example, BSN/hw or BSN:hw. Most common today is to have the lowercase initials of the person who does the keyboarding. If the writer does the keyboarding, no initials will appear.

Copy Notation - If a copy of the letter is being sent to someone other than the addressee, a copy notation appears below the reference initials, for instance, c A Conti.

Enclosure Notation - An enclosure notation, abbreviated as "Encl." should appear if there are enclosures sent with the letter. A number may follow the enclosure notation if there are several enclosures. In this way, the secretary assembling the enclosures and the person receiving the letter can easily check to make sure the enclosures are complete.

Postscript - A postscript (PS or P.S.) follows the same paragraph format as that used in the letter, that is, either block or semi-block style. Originally used to add extra information to a letter, it is now often used to emphasize material in the body of the letter.

Figure B-5
Second page of a letter

```
Southwest Printing Limited
Page 2
19__ 10 03


If the letter in Fig. 10/3 had been longer and necessitated
going to a second page, the second page would have looked like
this. The second and successive pages are keyboarded on plain
paper. The heading is keyboarded 2.5 cm from the top edge of
the paper and includes the first line from the inside address,
the page number, and the date. The arrangement shown is fast
and easy to format. However, if preferred when using block or
semi-block styles, the heading can be formatted as follows:

Southwest Printing Limited   2                      March 3, 19__

This is a slower method as the page number is at the centre
point and the date is pivoted.

When you must continue material onto another page, leave a
margin of 3 cm at the bottom of the first page. This is for
appearance so that your material does not seem to be falling
off the bottom of the page. To aid the reader, there should be
at least two lines of a paragraph on both pages, and the last
word on the page should not be hyphenated.

                                     Sincerely yours,



                                     Mrs. R. Higgins
                                     Manager


db
```

Second Page - If the letter runs to a second page, the addressee, page number, and date usually appear. Two examples of second page formatting are shown in Figure B-5.

2. The Envelope

Most businesses and organizations use envelopes with a preprinted name and return address, including postal code. Often the company logo appears on the envelope as well, and it may be in colour. If you are using a plain, unprinted envelope, the return address should be keyboarded or handwritten in the upper left corner.

The addressee's name and address will be exactly the same as the inside address. If an attention line has been used in the letter, it is placed on the line after the company name on the envelope. Figure B-6 shows the format of a typical envelope.

```
A. Hubbard
14 Wellington St.
Winnipeg, Manitoba
T3W 6L8




                    Mr. D. McDonald
                    Accounts Payable
                    Southwest Printing Limited
                    18 Kennedy Road South
                    BRAMPTON, Ontario
                    L6V 3N2
```

Figure B-6
Return address and main address on envelope

LETTER AND MEMORANDUM FORMATS

In order for Canada Post equipment to read the postal code on the envelope, the following steps must be observed.
- The postal code should be keyboarded in block capitals with one space between the two parts of the code.
- No punctuation or other marks may appear anywhere in the code.
- The code must be the only item on the last line of the address.
- No writing may appear on the envelope below the postal code.

3. The Interoffice Memorandum

The interoffice memorandum (memo) is used for written communication among employees of the same company. They are often written quickly and concisely, and tend to be more personal than letters. The salutation and complimentary closing are omitted. An example of memo formatting is given in Figure 12-5.

In many companies, memo forms with preprinted headings are used to speed up memo writing. Sometimes preprinted memo forms with several attached parts are used. The sender writes the message on the top copy and the message is copied automatically on the attached parts. One part is retained by the sender, the other parts are circulated, and a reply comes back to the sender on another part.

APPENDIX C

Business Forms

Businesses often design forms to make it easier for the person who is transmitting information, and for the person who is receiving this information. You have already encountered some of these forms in this book. Preprinted memo forms and preprinted telephone forms (see Figure 9-5) ensure that messages are clear and unambiguous. Preprinted invoices (Figure 11-5) are designed so that the required information can be quickly filled in and easily identified.

In addition, forms are sometimes designed so that they can be easily filled in on a typewriter or a computer. They often have two or three carbon copies attached, one or two copies remaining on file with the sender and one or two sent to the receiver.

Some common types of forms used in business to keep track of financial transactions are purchase orders, invoices, statements of account, and cheque requisitions.

Purchase Order - When a company wants to buy goods from a supplier, a purchase order is completed and sent to the supplier. In Chapter 12, we discussed how to write a letter to purchase goods if preprinted purchase order forms were not available. Look at the purchase order form in Figure C-1. You can see that it is easier to send such a form than to write a letter requesting goods. Note that a purchase order has space for a company official's approving signature, special terms that outline the conditions under which the order is made, and the date by which the shipment is required.

Invoice - When a supplier fills the customer's order, an invoice (or bill) is sent to the customer. Look again at the example of the invoice in Figure 11-5. Compare this invoice with the purchase order above. What information is the same? What is different?

Figure C-1
A purchase order

JOHN WILEY & SONS CANADA LIMITED Nº 011628
22 WORCESTER ROAD, REXDALE, ONTARIO M9W 1L1 (416) 675-3580

TO

SHIP TO

THIS ORDER IS CANCELLED IF NOT RECEIVED WITHIN 6 MONTHS	DATE REQUIRED

DATE	TERMS	ACCOUNT NO.	VIA	F.O.B.	PPD	COLL	

ITEM	QUANTITY	DESCRIPTION	UNIT PRICE	AMOUNT
		PLEASE SUPPLY THE FOLLOWING, SUBJECT TO THE CONDITIONS STATED.		

TERMS:
1. ACKNOWLEDGE RECEIPT OF THIS ORDER CONFIRMING PRICES AND DELIVERY DATE
2. NO SUBSTITUTIONS OR CHANGES WILL BE ACCEPTED UNLESS AUTHORIZED BY US
3. WE RESERVE THE RIGHT TO CANCEL THIS ORDER IF SHIPMENT IS NOT MADE IN QUANTITIES AND AT PRICES AND DELIVERY DATE SHOWN
4. SALES TAX LICENCE NUMBERS ARE APPLICABLE WHEN SHOWN

DIVISION MANAGER DEPT. MANAGER	COMPANY OFFICER

PURCHASE ORDER
COPY 1 - WHITE—VENDOR / COPY 2 - YELLOW— ACCOUNTING DEPT. / COPY 3 - PINK—ORIGINATOR

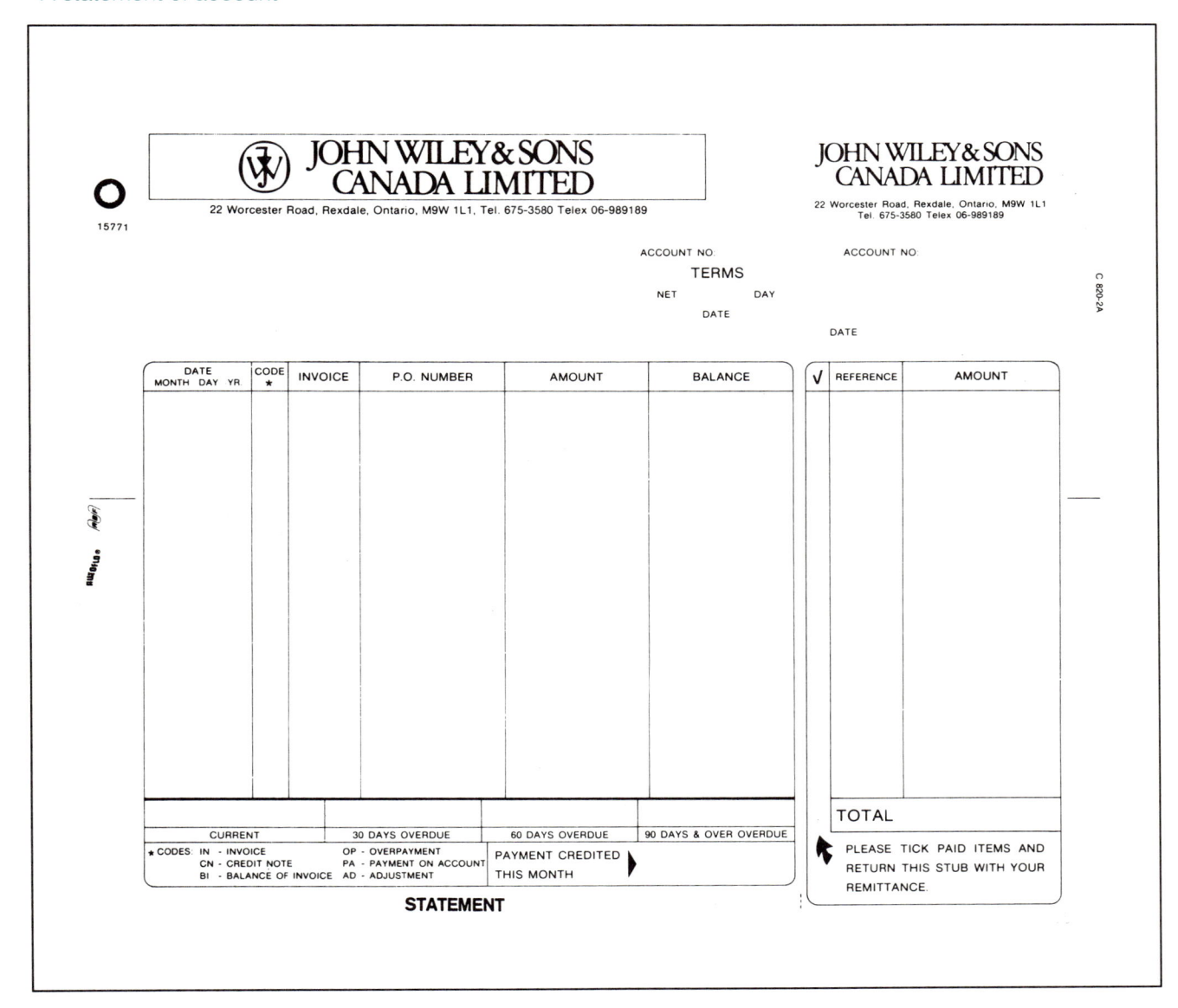

Figure C-2
A statement of account

BUSINESS FORMS

Figure C-3
A cheque requisition

ACCT. USE ONLY		
DUE DATE		
MO.	DAY	YR.
VENDOR NO.		NEW A/C

JOHN WILEY & SONS CANADA LIMITED

CHEQUE REQUISITION

DATE		
MO.	DAY	YR.
INVOICE NUMBER		

PAYEE NAME & ADDRESS

DETAILS OF PAYMENT	AMOUNT	

ACCOUNT	DEBIT		CREDIT	
	Dollars	Cents	Dollars	Cents
– –				
– –				
– –				
– –				
– –				
– –				
– –				
– –				
– –				
– –				
– –				
– –				
– –				

REQUESTED BY	
APPROVED BY	

Statement of Account - Each month, the supplier prepares a statement of account for each customer (Figure C-2). The statement indicates the balance due from the previous month and lists in chronological order any payments or purchases made during the month. The top copy is sent to the customer and the supplier keeps a copy. You will see that a statement lists invoices with their purchase order numbers, and shows a running balance of the amount owed. It also breaks this amount down, so that the customer can tell how much money is owed from invoices sent one, two, and three months ago.

Cheque Requisition - A large company has an accounting department, and even a small business has someone who performs the accounting functions. Rather than have employees verbally request cheques, a form called a cheque requisition is used (Figure C-3). Companies usually design this form to meet their individual requirements. Sometimes a cheque requisition is attached to an invoice when payment is requested.

APPENDIX D

Glossary

ad hoc	set up for a specific purpose
aesthetic	having a sense or love of beauty
agenda	an outline of the issues that will be covered in a meeting
ambiguity	possibility of being understood in more than one way; lack of clarity
anecdotes	short narratives of interesting events
appendices	plural form of appendix; material added at the end of a book or report
aptitude	natural talent or ability
aspiration	strong desire, longing, ambition
assertive	making aggressive claims or statements; putting oneself forward insistently; positive
automatic headers and footers	information printed at the top or bottom of each page
axis	in graphs, the straight line forming one arm of a pair of intersecting arms
bias	a predisposed point of view; prejudice
brainstorming	act of generating all possible ideas on a subject in a non-critical, non-evaluating atmosphere
brash	recklessly hasty, impudent, or tactless
brevity	shortness of expression; conciseness
camaraderie	good comradeship; friendliness among comrades
career	a profession or occupation; course and progress of a person's life
carriage	the manner of holding the head and body
categorize	to put in categories or classes within a system

chain of command	the power structure within a company with regard to authority and communication
chairperson	a person who presides over a meeting; the leader of a discussion
chronological résumé	a résumé organizing information into education and work experience sections
communication	the act of sending a message that is received and processed by a receiver
communication environment	the physical space or conditions through which a message is sent
concurrently	occurring at the same time
conformity	following established rules and procedures; action in accordance with rules and customs
connotation	an associated meaning or overtone that a word can take on besides its dictionary meaning
consensus	general agreement
constitute	to make up; form
copy (advertisement)	the text of an advertisement
cost-efficient	well done for least cost
counter-productive	having a result opposite to that intended
crosshatching	shading done with a series of intersecting parallel lines
cross-reference	reference from one part of a book, index, catalogue, etc. to another; a code written on related pieces of material which will be kept in different places to allow retrieval
decode	the process of interpreting a message in order to understand its meaning
deductive reasoning	the process of reasoning from the general to the specific
demeanour	outward behaviour
denotation	specific meaning of a word; dictionary meaning
designate	specify; indicate; point out
dialect	form of speech characteristic of a district or a particular group of people
discriminating	selective; distinguishing accurately; making a distinction in favour or against someone or something
dispel	drive away; disperse
dissension	strong disagreement
editing	reviewing and making necessary changes to a manuscript
empathy	ability to understand and share another person's feelings
encode	the process of arranging and transforming thoughts into words
essential	necessary and important
evaluate	judge the worth or value of someone or something
expend	use up
extemporaneous	delivered in a conversational style using brief notes only
facet	a single part or aspect
feedback	the reaction on the part of a receiver to a sender's message; it may indicate understanding or lack of understanding of the message
footers	information printed automatically at the bottom of each page of text

functional résumé	a résumé organizing information according to the function it serves, e.g., employment history is listed under different skills
gauge	judge, estimate
go off on tangents	change suddenly from one thought to another
grapevine	a person-to-person method of relaying information, gossip, or rumour
group dynamics	the interaction among members of a group
hard copy	printed output from a computer
headers	information printed automatically at the top of each page of text
headline (advertisement)	that part of an advertisement written in larger type and designed to attract attention
homonyms	words having the same sound but different meanings
hyperbole	exaggeration not intended to deceive
idiom	phrasing peculiar to a language or dialect; an expression whose meaning cannot be derived from its constituent parts, e.g., run for office, make the most of, turn a deaf ear, bite the bullet
impaired	diminished; lessened; reduced
incorporate	blend; include; combine with something already formed
inductive reasoning	the process of reasoning from the specific to the general
inference	a conclusion reached from evidence and reasoning
inflection	change in the tone of voice
intact	entire; without change
interest	something that arouses one's concern or curiosity; pleasurable preoccupation that holds one's attention
internal	communication that occurs when one thinks; one is both sender and receiver of the message
interpersonal	communication that occurs between two or more people
job description	a list of the duties and responsibilities an employee is expected to perform in a particular position
keying	inputting data into a computer, by means of a keyboard
leaders	a row of periods used to connect left-hand information to right-hand information, as in a table of contents
malapropism	ridiculous misuse of a word through confusion with one of similar sound
maxim	an established principle
mediated	communication requiring an inanimate medium to pass along the message
medium	the instrument, form, technique or means by which communication is carried out
message	the set of words, symbols, or art form selected by the sender to represent an idea, thought, or information
modem	MOdulator/DEModulator, a device that converts computer signals to telephone signals and vice versa, making possible communication between computers over telephone lines
moderator	presiding officer at an assembly
monotone	a single unvaried tone lacking inflection

norms	rules that govern the behaviour of a particular group. These norms can be common dress, habits, customs, and behaviour
nuances	subtle distinctions or variations; shades of meaning
off on a tangent	changing suddenly from one course of action or thought to another
onerous	burdensome; laborious
parameters	determining factors or characteristics
passive	submissive; without resistance
pompous	characterized by excessive self-importance
preliminary	leading up to the main part; introductory or preparatory
probationary period	trial period after an employee has been hired (usually three months)
procedures manuals	booklets describing the way personnel in a company carry out certain tasks
random	lacking a definite plan or pattern
rapport	harmonious or sympathetic relationship
receiver	the person who receives a communication from a sender
rectify	correct; to put or set right
redundancy	unnecessary repetition in expressing ideas
respectively	relating to each of several in the order given
right justification	lines of text having an even right margin
roles	patterns of behaviour that are expected from individuals who interact with others
salient	most obvious
sender	the person who begins the process of communication
sequential	arranged in a progression, logically ordered
simulate	copy; imitate; give the appearance of
skill	the ability to do something well
software packages	computer programs or sets of programs designed for a specific application
stereotype	a conventional or standardized image or impression of an individual or group, often inaccurate and sometimes damaging
stilted	stiffly formal
synonyms	words having the same meaning but different connotations
unabashed	unembarrassed or unashamed
verbal communication	the sending and receiving of ideas, thoughts, or information by means of spoken or written words
warrant	justify, to give justification for
word processing	computer software that allows a person to input ideas in no particular order, then rearrange, alter, or add to them using quick, simple commands

Index

Abstracts *see* Summaries
Active voice, in sentences 134, 144
Ad hoc groups 300
Advertisements 164; Help Wanted 321, 332; parts of 102
Advertising 54, 100-3, 162; AIDA formula in 102; audience for 102; emotional appeal of 203; purpose of 101-2
Agendas 55, 57, 62, 303, 306, 308-9
AIDA formula 101
Appendices, of reports 284
Application forms 333, 334
Applied Science and Technology Index 208
Appreciative listening 40
Attention, in listening process 30-1, 35
Audience 166; in writing 116-17; of presentations 202, 205; of reports 265
Audio-visual aids 213-15; *see also* Visual Aids
Authoritarian leaders 57-8

Bias, as barrier to effective listening 34-5, 37
Bibliographies 272, 283
Body language 20, 31, 68, 71, 100; as feedback 37-8, 178; in interviews 176-8, 330, 333; in speaking 81-2; with customers 187
Brainstorming 156, 304

Business Periodicals Index 208
Buzz sessions 305

Canada Employment Centres 320, 332
Canadian Human Rights Act (1978) 334
Canadian Periodical Index 209
Careful listening 182
Careful reading 93, 98, 107, 230
Carriage *see* Body language
Chairpersons 302-3, 304, 306, 308-9; *See also* Leaders
Charts 19; flow 277; organizational 158, 276-7; *See also* Graphs
Cheque requisitions 374, 375
Communication: barriers to 22, 23, 165-6, 168; definition of 5, 6; formal 158-9, 168; in business 154-67; informal 159, 168; in groups 51-4; kinds of 19-21, 168; levels of 52-4, 62, 160-2; lines of 158-9, 168; *See also* Listening, Mass communication, Mediated communication; Non-verbal communication, Speaking, Verbal communication, Viewing, Writing
Communication process 6-10, 24
Complimentary closing, of letters 360, 365
Comprehensive listening 41, 178, 182
Computer conferencing 309

383

Computer searches *see* Data banks
Conclusions, in reports 270-1, 283
Connectives, between paragraphs 139, 144; in sentences 137, 144
Connotations, of words 12-13, 103, 128-9
Conversations 71-2, 84
Copy, in advertisements 103
Copy notation, of letters 365
Critical listening 41, 178

Data banks, use of in research 208
Dateline, of letters 360, 364
Decoding, of messages 9, 10, 11, 13, 24-5
Deductive reasoning 203-4
Democratic leaders 58
Denotations, of words 12-13, 128-9
Directions *see* Instructions
Discriminative listening 40-1
Documents, in business 240-60; *See also* Forms, Letters, Memorandums, Reports
Drafting, in writing process 120, 121, 141-2

Editing: of report 271; of summary 106; of writing project 125-42, 144; standardized marks for 141
Electronic meetings 309
Emotions, appeal of advertising to 203; in communication process 16, 25
Empathy, in communication process 17, 25; in listening 37
Employment searches *see* Jobs, searching for
Enclosure notation, of letters 365
Encoding, of messages 8, 10, 11, 24-5
Enunciation, in speech 80, 84
Environmental interference 6-7, 8, 9, 16-17, 24-5, 166
Evaluation, in communication process 9, 23, 25; in effective reading 98, 228; in listening process 30, 41; in problem solving 154, 155, 157; of communication process 9, 23, 25; of performance 187-9, 194, 336-7

Facial expressions *see* Body language
Feedback 7, 9, 10, 23-5, 31-2, 37, 42, 166-7; in business communication 166-7; in effective listening 37-8, 42; in interpersonal communication 54, 178, 180, 182; in mass communication 162; on job performance 337
Flow charts 277
Fluency, of speech 80, 84

Form letters 250-1
Forms 231-2, 250-1, 271-5, 371

Grammar 343; *See also* Sentences, Words
Graphics *see* Visual aids
Graphs 19; bar 275, line 274; pie or circle 275-6
Group interaction 49; 52-5; patterns of 55; *See also* Participants, in groups
Groups 56-61, 166; advantages of 293-4; disadvantages of 294; participation in 191-2, 195-6; roles of members in 56-8, 59-62; *See also* Group interaction; Participants, in groups

Headlines, in advertisements 102
Hearing, compared with listening 29
Homonyms 131, 144

Illustrations, in advertisements 102-3
Inductive reasoning 203-4
Instructions, giving of 73-4, 84, 182, 194; pictorial 103
Interests, in career choice 318-19
Interference, in communication process 6-9, 16-17
Internal communication 52, 62, 160, 168
Interpersonal communication 52-4, 62, 160, 168, 176-95; among peers 191-2; between supervisors and employees 192-3; between supervisors and management 193-4
Interpretation, in listening process 30
Interviews: for employment 176-80, 194; in performance evaluations 187-9, 194; in research 207
Introductions 66-70, 181; of speakers 76-7, 84; rules for 67-9, 84, 186
Invoices 231-2, 371

Job descriptions 188-9
Jobs, changing 337; searching for 318-35

Language 128; *See also* Grammar, Paragraphs, Sentences, Words
Leaders, in groups 57-8, 62; kinds of 57-8
Letterhead 359, 360
Letters: favourable 252-3, 262; form 250-1; of application for jobs 321, 328-9, 332; of information 247-51, 262; of reference 337; of transmittal 248, 272-8, 279; parts of 359-60, 364-5, 367-8; persuasive 256-7, 262; styles of 361-3, 365, 366, 367; unfavourable 254-5, 262

Libraries, research in 207-9, 224
Listening 29, 72; barriers to 32-5, 44, 179; improvement of 36, 44; levels of 40-3, 44; process of 30-2, 44

Magazines: indexes to 208-9; kinds of 224-5
Malapropisms 131, 144
Mannerisms *see* Body language
Mass communication 162, 168
Mediated communication 54, 62, 160, 168, 309
Medium 6, 7, 8, 24, 25, 54, 62, 166
Meetings 301, 306-9; kinds of 302-5, 309; *See also* Groups
Memorandums 368; favourable 252-3, 262; of information 247, 262, of transmittal 272, 278, 279; persuasive 256-7, 262; printed forms for 368, 371; unfavourable 254-5, 262
Messages 6, 10, 24, 30, 31; mixed 11; visual 19
Minutes, of a meeting 306-7, 309

Newspapers, indexes to 208-9; in research 208
News releases 258-60, 262
Non-verbal communication 19-21, 31, 37, 72; in business 165, 166, 168, 176, 180, 182; *See also* Body language
Norms, in group interaction 55, 62
Notes: as summaries 105-6; card files of 208, 210, 269-70, 321, 335; in prewriting 117; taking of 39, 44, 208, 210, 228

Observing, in listening process 31
Organization, in writing 118; *See also* Organizational patterns
Organizational patterns in spoken and written communication 39, 118-19, 201, 212, 270, 282
Outlines, in business writing 245; of presentations 210-11; of writing projects 118
Overhead transparencies 214-15

Pacing, in speaking and writing 113-14
Panel discussions 304
Paragraphs 139-40, 144, 353; connectives between 140; length of 139; structure of 139
Parallelism, in sentence structure 137-8, 144
Participants, in groups 56-7, 62, 191-2, 195-6, 294; *See also* Group interaction
Passive voice, in sentences 134, 144
Performance evaluations 187-9, 194, 336-7
Periodicals, indexes to 208-9

Permissive leaders 58
Personal spacing 20, 165
Person-to-group communication 161, 168; *See also* Presentations, Speaking, Viewing, Writing
Pitch, of voice 79, 84
Posture *see* Body language
Presentations: at symposia 304-5; kinds of 201-4; model of 215-16; outline of 210-11; planning of 205-6; research for 206-10
Prewriting 116-19
Primary sources, in research 207, 269, 282, 283; *See also* Bibliographies, References
Probationary period 187-8, 337
Problem solving, steps in 154-7, 168
Procedure manuals 231
Pronunciation 80, 85
Proofreading 93; standardized marks and symbols in 141
Publication: of reports 271-2; of writing projects 142, 144
Punctuation 343, 355
Purchase orders 371, 372

Rapid reading 94, 96, 107
Rate of speed, in reading 92; in speaking 79, 84
Reader's Guide to Periodical Literature 208
Reading 91-100, 107-8; effective, steps to 97-8, 108; in business 223-32; of drafts of written projects 127-8; rate of 91-2; styles of 93-6, 107-8
Receiver, of messages 6, 8, 9, 10, 24-5, 165-6
Recommendations, in reports 270-1, 283
Recorders, role of in groups 57, 62, 306, 309
Redundancy, of words, 132, 144
Reference initials, in letters 360, 365
References: in research 208-10; in reports, listed 283; in résumés 323; letters of 337
Reports 266-85; parts of 278-85; steps in writing of 265-72; styles of 267; types of 267
Research: for presentations 207-10; for reports 269; in prewriting 116-17; into a business 223-8, 330, 332
Response, in listening process 30
Résumés 321, 322-7, 328-9, 332; chronological 322, 324-5; functional 322, 323, 326-7
Rewriting 114, 141-2
Robert's Rules of Order 305
Role perception, in communication process 17, 25
Role playing 331, 332

Salutation, in letters 360, 364
Scanning, as reading style 95, 108, 226-8
Secondary sources, in research 207-9, 269, 282, 283; *See also* Bibliographies, References
Secretaries 306; *See also* Recorders
Self-assessment, in performance evaluations 337
Self-perception, in communication process 17, 25
Sender, of messages 6, 7-9, 24-5, 165-6
Sentences 133-9, 144, 356; connectives in 137; length of 136; parallelism in 137-8; structure of 134-6, 137-8; word order in 137-8
Signature, of advertisements 103
Signature block, of letters 360, 365
Skills, in career choice 318-19
Skimming, as reading style 94-5, 98, 107, 226-8, 230
Social insurance cards 320
Speakers: introduction of 76-7; thanking of 77
Speaking: characteristics of 79-82; in business 161-4; in person-to-group communication 161; types of delivery in 74-6; *See also* Speech, Speeches
Speech, characteristics of 80-1, 84-5, 186; *See also* Speaking, Voice
Speeches 216; after-dinner 204; extemporaneous 75, 84; impromptu 75-6, 84; read from a script 75-6, 84
Statements of account 373, 375
Summaries, how to make 105-6, 108; of reports 280, 282
Symposia 304-5
Synonyms 131, 144

Tables 19, 273-4; of contents 272, 284
Teams *see* Groups
Telecommunications 190, 309
Telephone skills 182-8, 194; placing calls 186-7, 194; providing verbal feedback 183; receiving calls 184, 194; taking messages 184-6; telemarketing 187; voice, role of 183
Therapeutic listening 42
Thesauruses 131
Title page, of reports 272, 278, 279-80
Tone, of voice 80, 84

Value systems, in communication process 16, 25
Verbal communication 19, 37-8, 72; in business 163-4, 168, 180, 182; *See also* Listening, Speaking
Video conferencing 309
Viewing 91, 100-5, 223-32; effective, steps to 104-5, 106-7

Visual aids 201-2, 213-15, 273, 282; charts 276-7; graphs 274-6; tables 19, 272, 273-4
Visual communication 74, 100-5, 201, 203; *See also* Body language, Non-verbal communication, Visual aids
Voice (active or passive, in sentences) 134, 144
Voice (in speech) 31, 79-80, 84, 166, 183, 187
Volume, of voice in speaking 79, 84

Word processing 114-15, 121
Words 12-13, 128-33, 144; changes in 129-30; choice of 81, 85, 103; connectives 137; connotative and denotative 12-13, 103, 128-9; general and specific 129; levels of usage 132; order of, in sentences 127; *See also* Grammar
Writing 111-21, 125-42, 240-62; editing of 125-42, 144, 246, 271; features of 113-14, 121; process of 116-20, 245; publication of 142, 144, 271-2; purpose of 116; stages of 116-20, 121, 271; *See also* Editing, Letters, Memorandums, News releases, Paragraphs, Reports, Rewriting, Sentences, Words

Acknowledgements

For permission to reprint copyrighted and trademarked material grateful acknowledgement is made to the following. W. Ivor Castle/DND/Public Archives of Canada, Figure 1-5; Universal Press Syndicate NY, Figure 1-6; Camerique/Miller Services, Figure 1-9; Mark Antman/Stock, Boston, Figure 1-10; Imperial Oil, Figures 2-2, 10-1, 14-1, 14-7, 14-8, 14-9; Tribune Company Syndicate, Figure 2-3; The Toronto Star Syndicate, Figures 2-7, 2-8, 2-9, 5-6(a), 5-6(b); Roberts/Miller Services, Figures 3-5, 8-1; Carol McMurray, Figure 4-9; Alan J. Hirsch, *Physics For A Modern World* (Toronto: John Wiley & Sons Canada Limited, 1986); Barouk Eaton (Canada) Ltd., Figure 5-7; Lorraine O'Byrne, *What Is It? A Gallery Of Historic Phrases* (Cheltenham, Ontario: The Boston Mills Press, 1977), Figures 7-3(a), 7-3(b); Don Harron, *Charlie Farquharson's histry Of Canada* (Markham: PaperJacks Ltd., 1972), Figure 7-4; Lois Tarnai, *The Canadian Office Today* (Toronto: John Wiley & Sons Limited, 1982), Figures 7-7, 14-10; The Citizen, Ottawa, Figure 7-8; Optimist International, Figure 7-9; Bata Footwear, a division of Bata Industries, Figure 8-6; John Deyell Company, Figures 9-5, 11-5; InfoGlobe, a division of The Globe and Mail, Figure 10-4; Dow Chemical Canada Inc., Figure 10-5; Alberta Environment, Figure 11-3; Cambrian Parsons, Figure 11-4(b); Information Services, Sheridan College of Applied Arts and Technology, Figure 12-6; Industrial Accident Prevention Ontario, Figure 13-11; Wright Communications, Figure 15-2; Lenore Wilson, all photos not otherwise credited.